Life as Insinuation

SUNY series in American Philosophy and Cultural Thought
―――――
Randall E. Auxier and John R. Shook, editors

Life as Insinuation

*George Santayana's Hermeneutics of
Finite Life and Human Self*

KATARZYNA KREMPLEWSKA

Cover image courtesy of dreamstime.com

Published by State University of New York Press, Albany

© 2019 State University of New York

All rights reserved

No part of this book may be used or reproduced in any manner whatsoever without written permission. No part of this book may be stored in a retrieval system or transmitted in any form or by any means including electronic, electrostatic, magnetic tape, mechanical, photocopying, recording, or otherwise without the prior permission in writing of the publisher.

For information, contact State University of New York Press, Albany, NY
www.sunypress.edu

Library of Congress Cataloging-in-Publication Data

Names: Kremplewska, Katarzyna, 1973– author.
Title: Life as insinuation : George Santayana's hermeneutics of finite life and human self / Katarzyna Kremplewska.
Description: Albany : State University of New York Press, [2019] | Series: SUNY series in American philosophy and cultural thought | Includes bibliographical references and index.
Identifiers: LCCN 2018021843 | ISBN 9781438473932 (hardcover : alk. paper) | ISBN 9781438473949 (pbk. : alk. paper) | ISBN 9781438473956 (ebook)
Subjects: LCSH: Santayana, George, 1863–1952. | Self (Philosophy)
Classification: LCC B945.S24 K74 2019 | DDC 126—dc23
LC record available at https://lccn.loc.gov/2018021843

10 9 8 7 6 5 4 3 2 1

Contents

Abbreviations	vii
Acknowledgments	ix
Introduction	xi
Chapter 1. Guises of the *Self*	1
Chapter 2. The Conception of the *Self* and Some Basic Concepts of Santayana's Philosophy	29
Chapter 3. The Hermeneutics of Human *Self*	59
Chapter 4. Life as Insinuation	97
Chapter 5. Coping with Finitude: Santayana Reading Heidegger	113
Chapter 6. The Tragic Aspect of Existence	149
Chapter 7. Beyond the *Self* (into the Political Realm): The Essential Negativity of Human Being and Rational (Self-)Government	195
Notes	211
Bibliography	251
Index	261

Abbreviations

Works by George Santayana

APS	*Apologia pro Mente Sua*
DL	*Dialogues in Limbo*
DP	*Dominations and Powers*
HA	*"Hamlet"* in: *Selected Critical Writings of George Santayana*
IPR	*Interpretations of Poetry and Religion*
LR	*The Life of Reason: Or, The Phases of Human Progress*
OS	*Obiter Scripta: Lectures, Essays and Reviews*
POML	*Physical Order and Moral Liberty: Previously Unpublished Essays of George Santayana*
RB	*Realms of Being*, one-volume edition
SAF	*Scepticism and Animal Faith: Introduction to a System of Philosophy*
SiELS	*Soliloquies in England and Later Soliloquies*
STTMP	*Some Turns of Thought in Modern Philosophy: Five Essays*

Works by Other Authors

BCAP	*Basic Concepts of Aristotelian Philosophy* (M. Heidegger)
BPP	*Basic Problems of Phenomenology* (M. Heidegger)
BT	*Being and Time* (M. Heidegger)
CPR	*Critique of Pure Reason* (I. Kant)
MM	*Matter and Memory* (H. Bergson)

OAA   *Oneself as Another* (P. Ricoeur)
RSTV   "Reflections on Santayana and Tragic Value" (C. Padron)
SSIFPP *Subjectivity and Selfhood: Investigating the First-Person Perspective* (D. Zahavi)
SSMMI   *The Sources of the Self: The Making of the Modern Identity* (Ch. Taylor)
SZ   *Sein und Zeit* (M. Heidegger, the copy with Santayana's marginal notes)

Acknowledgments

This book originates, partially, from my PhD dissertation devoted to George Santayana's conception of *aporetic self* (*Mask and Thought: The Conception of the Aporetic Self in George Santayana's Philosophy*) written and defended in 2015 under the supervision of professor Agata Bielik-Robson (Institute of Philosophy and Sociology, Polish Academy of Sciences), whom I wish to thank for an ongoing philosophical inspiration.

During the years of my scholarship leading to the emergence of this book I was supported by the members of Santayana Society in many ways and I would like to express my sincere gratitude for that. In particular I would like to thank John Lachs and Charles Padron. My acquaintance with John Lachs's work and conversations with the author have been invaluable for my scholarship. Charles Padron provided me with editorial and linguistic support when preparing the article: "Coping with Finitude: Santayana Reading Heidegger," which was published in *Transactions of the Charles S. Peirce Society* in 2015. An enlarged and revised version of this article appears, with the consent by Indiana University Press, as chapter 5 in this book. I have also had an opportunity to confront my own reflections on the idea of the tragic in Santayana with those of Charles Padron as contained in his dissertation on Santayana and the tragic value.

Moreover, as a participant of international conferences (SAAP, New Jersey 2013; APA, Philadelphia 2014; 5th Conference on George Santayana, Berlin 2016) and during my research stay in the United States in 2013 (sponsored by Kościuszko Foundation, New York) I had an opportunity to talk to a number of outstanding international scholars of Santayana, among them Michael Brodrick, Martin Coleman, who was also my guide at Santayana Edition (IUPUI), Edward Lovely, Daniel Moreno, Richard Rubin, Herman Saatkamp, Krzysztof Skowroński, and Glenn Tiller. Furthermore, I would like to emphasize that the possibility of publishing the fragments of my ongoing work in *Overheard in Seville: Bulletin of the Santayana Society* has been a rewarding and encouraging experience. Two subchapters of this book—3.3 "Narrative and dramatic strategies of sustaining self-integrity" and 6.3 "Between spiritual dissolution and the invention of the human"—are revised versions of the texts that appeared earlier in the *Bulletin* in 2015 and 2017, respectively.

The results of my research have also been published in Polish journals such as *Przegląd Religioznawczy*, *Analiza i Egzystencja*, and *Diametros*. Chapter 4 "Life as Insinuation" is a translation of a revised version of my article in Polish that appeared in *Diametros* in 2017.

I would like to thank National Science Center in Poland (Narodowe Centrum Nauki), which finances my current research on Santayana's philosophy of politics and culture: project no. 2016/23/D/HS1/02274. The seventh and final chapter of this book entitled "Beyond the *Self* (into the Political Realm): The Essential Negativity of Human Being and Rational (Self-)Government" has been written as part of this research project.

Finally, I thank my family and friends for their priceless presence in my life.

Introduction

In this book I am undertaking the challenge of reconstructing George Santayana's conception of human *self* as embedded in a larger project of philosophy of life. Meanwhile, I am tracing the connections in-between different areas of Santayana's philosophical engagement—from his ontology through literary criticism to his critique of culture—while striving to bring to light its hermeneutic coherence, corresponding to the idea of hermeneutic unity of life, which I find constitutive of an overarching project inherent in Santayana's philosophical endeavor. I choose the metaphor of life as insinuation—borrowing it from Henri Bergson—to emphasize the dramatic, theatrical style of the hermeneia in question. By setting the thinker from Avila in dialogue with selected twentieth-century representatives of the so-called continental philosophy, I hope to enrich the interpretive potential developed in the course of Santayana studies so far and stimulate further discussion of his legacy.[1]

The delayed reception of Santayana's work and his status of a philosophical outcast in early twentieth-century America was related to the fact that both his idea of philosophy and his philosophical method were at odds with the trends reigning at the American intellectual scene, where actors oscillated in-between Darwinism, radical empiricism of William James, social constructivism of John Dewey, Charles S. Peirce's commitment to panpsychism, and the idealism of Josiah Royce. When his contemporaries started to reduce the role of philosophy to the philosophy of science or "a procedure of linguistic sanitation," Santayana was devoted to creating a "synoptic vision" of *conditio humana*[2] and a corresponding *philosophy of self-procured salvation*, as I call it in reference to the ancient, therapeutic meaning of philosophy. In other words, a few different but convergent and intertwining streams in Santayana's eclectic thought—from his idiosyncratic, nonreductive naturalism through a sort of *ancient* and to an extent *sapiential* style of philosophical engagement to astute criticism of culture—stood in stark contrast to the increasing professionalization of philosophy at that time.

Among the alienating factors there were also Santayana's intellectual sympathies and cultural identifications like the advocacy of a cosmopolitan, Epicurean individualism, which was viewed by his contemporaries as verging on a decadent nihilism. "To subordinate the soul fundamentally to society or the individual to the state is sheer barbarism,"[3] Santayana would declare in the age when this sort of personal autonomy was rather unpopular in America. Particularly harsh critique came from the side of pragmatists on account of the alleged "uselessness" of Santayana's "anti-social" doctrine for any constructivist project.[4] This misreading of the idea of *disinterestedness* implicit in Santayana's vision of spiritual life is an example of some common misunderstandings of his thought.[5] "I care very little whether, at any moment, academic tendencies favour one unnecessary opinion or another"[6] wrote the thinker many years after he moved to Europe, giving an explicit expression of his detachment from the mainstream academic culture, which in time became deliberate and cultivated.

A serious overlooking in the early reception of his *oeuvre*, as noted one of the scholars in the 1980s, rested in the underestimation of "the special signature of his genius"—a synthesis of materialism with a peculiar kind of transcendentalism.[7] Meanwhile, Santayana's engagement in developing the ontology of realms within the frame of his idiosyncratic naturalism, viewed by some early critics as an attempt to revive scholastic metaphysics, had a counterpart in the so-called ontological turn in continental philosophy, as represented by thinkers like Henri Bergson or Martin Heidegger. Interpreting and understanding a philosopher's work involves, among others, placing it in a broader comparative context of other thinkers. Even though the two final decades of the twentieth century brought a remarkable revival of interest in Santayana's heritage, little attention has been devoted to the possible relations between the thinker from Avila and contemporary continental philosophy. Bridging this gap, as I suggest, may enhance our interpretive potential in relation to Santayana's thought even to the point of rethinking his entire *oeuvre*.

Today a variety of interpretations is available. Some focus on his materialism and nonreductive naturalism as rendering his thought valid and inspiring for the contemporary continuation of these traditions. Scholars like Timothy Sprigge, John Lachs, and Angus Kerr Lawson undertook the task of an in-depth analysis of Santayana's ontology as well as discussed his writings from the perspective of philosophy of mind and action. Others read Santayana as a critic of American culture or looked at his work via the lens of literary interpretative categories.[8] The scope of comparative contexts in Santayana scholarship ranges from Democritus, Plato and Aristotle, through Spinoza and Schopenhauer to his contemporaries, the pragmatists.[9] Santayana also came to be viewed "as anticipating a major theme in existentialism."[10] Michael Hodges and John Lachs uncovered the (post-)modern face of Santayana's "ironic ontology" by juxtaposing it with the late Wittgenstein's thought. Thus, they confirmed Whitehead's and Putnam's opinions about Santayana being ahead of his time and misunderstood in some respects.[11] Santayana has also been viewed as a philosopher of religion and a phenomenologist.[12] Most recently, Daniel Moreno proposed a reinterpretation of Santayana's thought focusing on the ontology of realms of being and the idea of philosophy as a form of life that Santayana himself is said to embody.[13] While Santayana scholarship is becoming international, an increased interest in his philosophy of culture and politics may be noted.

Still, as already mentioned, surprisingly little has been written with respect to Santayana and European thinkers of the twentieth century, even though it is occasionally mentioned that during the last thirty years of his life, which he spent in Rome, the thinker, removed from the philosophical currents of the day, "struggled" with his reading of the seminal works in phenomenology and existentialism.[14] The "late" Santayana for a long time has been viewed as a thinker encaged in a glass house of his own philosophical idiosyncrasies, radicalized by a growing mystical bent.

Meanwhile, Santayana's correspondence and the recently published marginalia seem to disavow this stereotype. In the 1930s and 1940s the thinker, while completing his opus magnum *Realms of Being*, followed by his last book *Dominations and Powers*, was engaged in an intense dialogue with existentialist and phenomenological texts of the day. Perhaps no other thinker of the era was the recipient of such a long-lasting appreciation on the part of Santayana as Heidegger was. "I think my separate army corps are all alive and advancing slowly towards the appointed positions. Heidegger, whose book has splendid broad margins, which I cover with notes, is a great stimulus" Santayana wrote to his secretary, Daniel Cory, in February 1936.[15] It is also certain that Santayana read Husserl and Bergson, the latter being perhaps his last major intellectual fascination.[16]

One of the aims of this book is to set the thinker from Avila in a broader dialogical context with a number of contemporary (in a broad sense of this term) philosophers—from Nietzsche, through Bergson and Heidegger, to Paul Ricoeur. As for Heidegger, I am discussing possible similarities between his thought and that of Santayana with the support of

Santayana's marginal notes in his copy of *Sein und Zeit*, which have never been subject to research thus far. Establishing this kind of hermeneutic dynamics between both thinkers contributes to the task of reconstructing Santayana's philosophy of life as a modern philosophical project which I propose to call *contemplative vitalism*.

As mentioned at the beginning, the thematic axis around which a large part of this dialogic and comparative book oscillates is the issue of human *self*. What made Santayana's perspective to an extent exceptional was his reliance on the classical pairs of concepts, like matter-spirit, existence-essence, or *vita activa-vita contemplativa*. This, in the eyes of his colleagues the pragmatists, revived some old, unwelcome dualisms. There seems to appear a problem of connection, or rather, a danger of disconnection, between psyche and spirit, followed by a disquieting suggestion of a double *self*: a psychic agent and a spiritual, *oneiric self*. Moreover, Santayana, by means of the recognition of the ideal realms of essences and spirit, declares consciousness irreducible to material processes and at the same time deprives it of causal efficacy by announcing spirit *impotent*. As I argue in this book, this sort of nonreductive ontology, this trace of idealism in Santayana's architecture of being is of incomparable benefit from the point of view of philosophy of life and culture. While inquiring into the intricacies of Santayana's enigmatic and *aporetic* conception of human *self*, I explore the potential of his ontology as making the reality of human life irreducible to the relations of power.

The scarcity of research in respect to the issue of human *self* is not particularly surprising given that Santayana's anthropology and his treatment of the questions concerning the subject and *self* seem haphazard and fragmentary. What is more, the thinker quite explicitly claimed that "subjectivity is a normal madness in living animals. It should be discounted, not idolized, in the philosophy of the West."[17] He thus secured for himself an opinion of a staunch opponent of philosophy of subjectivity (as exemplified by German idealism in particular). Having said this, I find the above quoted words of Santayana—particularly in the light of his well-known critique of egotism in philosophy—*tellingly misleading* and forming an inspiring couple with those of Heidegger, selected as a motto for one of the chapters of this book, namely: "Philosophy must perhaps start from 'subject' and return to the 'subject' in its ultimate question, and yet for all that it *may not* pose its questions in a one-sidedly subjectivist manner."[18]

What I mean is that despite the fact that one may search in vain for an exhaustive treatment of the issue in question in Santayana's body of work, a reader of Santayana's philosophical and literary works may be under an impression that, paradoxically, *this* question, more than any other, is the unuttered "wager," the main but silent preoccupation of his philosophical effort—the *unsayable* of Derrida. This of course must remain only an arbitrary impression, but whether one agrees with it or rejects it, Santayana's conception of selfhood calls for an inquiry. By way of digression, at least one thinker—Kenneth Burke—regarded the question of selfhood as central for Santayana's thought. However, it is not Fichte's idealistic, absolute and pure Ego that one finds there but rather the *self* who is both a conscious agent, the center of a dramatic world, and a subject of spiritual life, of *vita contemplativa*, where essences, as appearances, enjoy the dignity of becoming ends in themselves. In this latter case, claims Burke, we are dealing, in a sense, with a "contemplation of death," which makes us realize that "the realm of essence is ultimately a *thanatopsis*" (!).[19] Whether such a treatment of consciousness does indeed make, as Burke suggests, for a "philosophy of retirement" and brings a prospect of a "long life of euthanasia"[20] will be left for the reader of this book to judge.

Furthermore, once we become sensitive to this issue and start asking ourselves what kind of the *self*, and possibly what conception of human being, is implied by the basic philosophical categories like *psyche, animal faith*, or *impotent spirit*, we are likely to have at once an intuition that the question abides no unequivocal answer, that the *self* emerging from this philosophy is problematic, or, as I propose to call it—*aporetic*. This is evident when comparing the available scholarly opinions. Daniel Moreno argues that a dissolution of the *self* occurs in the context of Santayana's atheism, his critique of egotism, and his objectivist ontology of material flux set against the eternity of essences and truth.[21] One may think of it in the context of post-modern subject, which—after Nietzschean deconstruction of the *self*, backed up by the logical investigations of Russell and Wittgenstein—may at best be a logical or a useful construct, if not an epiphenomenon of larger, objective processes. The question is whether Santayana's non-egological perspective is enough to speak of a dissolution of the *self*. Besides, there is in his philosophy a powerful idea of psyche linked to that of an individual life and its interests, which promises a stronger and more affirmative vision of selfhood rooted in the plane of action. This reading, confirmed by many passages in Santayana,[22] has been persuasively presented by John Lachs.[23] Yet another perspective comes from Irving Singer, who sees the different conceptions of the *self* held by Santayana and by pragmatists to be the key to "all their mutual distrust, mistaken criticism, and inability to appreciate one another."[24] Santayana, claims Singer, opts rather for a "kernel" model, i.e., one assuming an external or "separate," presumably immutable center, surrounded by concentric circles of experience. Pragmatist thinkers, in turn, view the *self* in terms of an experiential circle or a spiral devoid of any "real" center. Signer's brief discussion inspires a number of questions, for example, what kind of "kernel" is meant—a Cartesian, a transcendental one, or maybe a Lockean center of control? These concerns will be addressed later in this study. For now the juxtaposition of the three dissimilar interpretations of Santayana's conception of the *self* illustrates the complexity and ambiguity of the issue, which resonates in the idea of "aporetic *self*."

I have drawn the reader's attention to two research problems, namely, Santayana's possible affinities with continental philosophy of the twentieth century and his conception of human *self* as part of his overall project of philosophy of life. I have also signaled that the main aim of this study is an inquiry into the latter in the context of the former. At this point let me introduce another issue to be tackled in this book, namely, the idea of the tragic.[25] As I will try to show, there is an interesting connection between Santayana's conception of the *self* and his understanding of the tragic. Putting this relation into scrutiny allows for shifting the whole discussion into the context of Santayana's critical philosophy of culture and politics. Finally, in reference to the analysis of the tragic, I am going to employ the idea of (tragic) necessity, *ananke*, as one of the interpretive keys—next to the ideas of governing the living and rationality—helpful in a preliminary and sketchy attempt at "unlocking" and rethinking Santayana's philosophy of politics. This final part will allow us to go beyond the individual perspective into the common world and, thus, complete the task of unveiling Santayana's philosophy of life.

The structure of the book, its division into sections, is thematic and problem-centered. Each section addresses a specific question, some provide an overview or merely a digression supporting a thesis or illuminating some additional aspects of the issue. The first and the sixth chapters stand out in that they are largely devoted to tracing the history of an idea and offer critical, selective overviews meant to articulate and develop key philosophical questions relevant for the discussion that follows. The method of my inquiry is predominantly hermeneutic, at some points enriched with phenomenological and speculative elements. In more technical parts of the book, I reconstruct and/or reinterpret parts of Santayana's thought on the basis of the analysis of his texts with respect to the basic philosophical concepts in their mutual relations as well as in comparative contexts with other thinkers and in reference to the existing secondary literature. Hermeneutic approach seems especially helpful in comparative sections, in particular whenever two non-analytical thinkers, coming from different cultural backgrounds and using a different set of philosophical concepts each, are compared. In line with the hermeneutic tradition, possible shifts, tensions, and ambiguities within meanings of particularly problematic concepts are treated—within reasonable boundaries—as an evidence of the vividness of philosophical language. When tracing Santayana's conception of human *self*, so vaguely and fragmentarily treated by the thinker himself, I was initially inspired by Derrida's method of inquiry into the *unsayable* and his investigations into the "missing" concepts in other philosophers' work, as exemplified by his well-known book *Of Spirit*.[26]

For the sake of clarity and due to the large thematic scope of the book, let me summarize the above introductory remarks in points. After providing a brief, selective overview of the history of the idea of the *self* in the first chapter (1), in the second (2) and the third one (3) I analyze the basic concepts of Santayana's philosophy and trace the passage from naturalistic philosophy of action toward mature ontology with particular attention given to the impact this ontological turn must have had on his conception of the *self*. I argue that the setting of Santayana's ontology makes his conception of the *self* inescapably *aporetic*. Placing the categories of Santayana's nonreductive materialism in a phenomenological and existential-hermeneutic context allows me to uncover and elucidate a number of *aporias*, which I later address with reference to, among others, the Aristotelian distinctions *zoe-bios* (as reinterpreted by some contemporary thinkers) and *process-activity*. This interpretive strategy promises a possible solution to the controversy around psyche-spirit connection and allows to see a creative potential resting in the *aporias*, particularly if set within the holistic framework of Santayana's philosophy of life, which I call *contemplative vitalism*. What emerges out of this interpretive endeavor is a multidimensional (triadic), non-egological conception of the *self*, which combines a naturalistic anchoring with an idealistic/transcendental bent.

In the third chapter I also address the problem of the integrity and freedom of human beings within the framework of hermeneutic unity of life. With references to Paul Ricoeur's idea of *authorship of life*, as well as some conceptions coming from contemporary philosophy of mind, I hope to offer a novel perspective of looking at the controversial problem of freedom and free will in Santayana's thought. The analysis of the recurrent motives of *masks* and *theatre* as well as the concept of *authenticity* helps to illuminate Santayana's peculiar, dramatic *hermeneia* of life. Finally, in this section I suggest yet another interpretive venue for the idea of a hermeneutic *self*. Guided by hints provided by Santayana, I translate the triadic structure of the *self* into the categories of the Holy Trinity, with reference to Paul Ricoeur's interpretation of the biblical concept of *kerygma*.

In the fourth chapter (4), entitled "Life as Insinuation," I analyze certain aspects of Henri Bergson's philosophy of life, with particular attention given to the metaphysical make up of his dramatist vision of human life and freedom. I point to interesting affinities within these two—Santayana's and Bergson's—apparently utterly dissimilar philosophies.

In chapter five (5), on the basis of archival materials, namely Santayana's marginalia in his private copy of Heidegger's *Sein und Zeit*, with the support of other primary sources, including Santayana's letters, I raise the question of possible similarities between both thinkers. The discussion is centered around (although not limited to) the core matter of Santayana's "negotiations" with Heidegger's text and the guiding problem of this book—the issue of the *self* and the way it is embedded in a philosophy of life. My thesis is that one may speak here of a number of similarities, some of which stem from a common source of inspiration being Aristotle. The return to ancient sources and the choice of ontological language within a major endeavor *to reconcile finitude with freedom* emerge as the main strategic affinities between both thinkers. The wager of the very preoccupation with the *self* in the case of both thinkers is, as I suggest, a "worldly salvation," or—in other words—working out such a strategy of entering into the relation with one's own finitude, where this *finitude becomes voluntary*. It is possible to say that both thinkers' anti-subjectivist sympathies do not serve to dissolve the *self*, but rather to strengthen it by redefining and exorcising the demons of an isolated "ego." The redefinition of selfhood inescapably involves winning back time, the world, and finitude for the *self*—a task which arises as one of the main issues in the subsequent discussion of the tragic.

In the sixth chapter (6), I focus on the idea of the tragic, which, besides being a problem on its own, may serve as a heuristic tool which: a) allows to shed a different light on the *aporetic* nature of the *self* and b) allows for a meaningful passage from the technical analysis of concepts and the "structure" of the *self* into the context of Santayana's critique of culture, which—as I argue—is of high relevance for the whole discussion. An overview of a broad spectrum of other philosophical conceptions of the tragic—from Aristotle, through Hegel, to Nietzsche, provides a background for the articulation of the specificity of Santayana's approach. Next, I discuss Santayana's critique of Nietzsche, which I interpret in terms of a polemic on the possibility and the necessity of spirituality. Yet another comparative perspective—Harold Bloom's and Santayana's interpretations of Hamlet—

illuminates the fact that understanding Santayana's conception of the *self* is incomplete without regard to his critique of culture (in particular his critique of egotism and instrumentality in thinking). References are made to the well-known idea of instrumental reason developed by the members of Frankfurt School, which I connect to the temporal perspective called by me "immobilizing fallacy" and elucidate with the support of Northrop Frye's analysis of tragedy and his idea of fatalistic reduction.

The final, seventh chapter (7), being the shortest one, goes beyond the individual perspective to the common world, while keeping in mind and developing the findings and theses of the previous sections. It offers a preliminary, synthetic look at Santayana's philosophy of politics and a very brief reconstruction of its conceptual apparatus by employing the idea of *managing necessity* as the main interpretive key.

What follows is a highly selective overview of the evolution of the idea of selfhood and subjectivity. I largely rely on the work of those thinkers who have already accomplished this task—Charles Taylor and Dan Zahavi in particular. Martin Heidegger's critique of Cartesian and transcendental models is also of help. My aim is to select, articulate, and associate certain ideas so as to prepare a mental setting that will subsequently serve as a source of concepts, ideas, and criteria helpful in reconstructing Santayana's conception of the *self*. Throughout the review I also gradually formulate a side thesis, or a major digression, namely that certain philosophical strategies of weakening the "ego" may be viewed as serving the strengthening of the *self* rather than its dissolution.

1

Guises of the *Self*

1.1 An Antidote to the *Self*

The anticipation of the Cartesian *Cogito* can be traced back to the work of Augustine, where self-examination is synchronous with the desire to meet God.

> A: Oh God, ever the same. May I know myself, may I know Thee, that is my prayer.
>
> R: Do you, who wish to know yourself, know that you exist?
>
> A: I know it.
>
> R: How do you know it?
>
> A: I do not know.[1]

Augustine, with his emphasis on interiority was the forerunner of the future "career" of subjectivity. The certainty as to the existence of ourselves, derived spontaneously from the belief in the reality of our conscious experience, delineates the boundary of rational inquiry. This configuration will find its continuation in Cartesian *Meditations*. Furthermore, the epistemic situation reflected in the final "I do not know" resonates in what is referred to in contemporary philosophy as basic, tacit beliefs. While it is difficult to overestimate the impact of Augustinian principle of interiority on modern thought, it is crucial to note that the preoccupation with subjectivity would leave the fideistic scope of interest (self-appreciation in the light of the divine) in favor of an epistemological one, and ultimately—an instrumental one.

From Charles Taylor's perspective of the history of the internalization of the sources of the *self*, the idea of subjective unity enjoying a privileged status begins with Plato, whose ideal of self-mastery was based on the assumption of a soul, which—under a certain spiritual discipline—could become a seat of intellectual harmony attuned to the ideal cosmos. The "salvation" of the soul, to anticipate the Christian idea, required a center responsible for the integration of blind vital forces, so that ultimately they could be sublimated under the aegis of an uninhibited *theoria*. This ideal of "self-collected awareness"[2] along with human freedom, which began to be associated with it, then, depended on the receptive faculty to synchronize with "the beyonds" or an *external* order. One of the most insightful contemporary theoreticians of selfhood writes,

> The soul is *de iure*, in principle, one; it is a single locus. The experience of it as comprising a plurality of loci is an experience of errors and imperfection. The unity of locus, and hence the new notion of the soul as this single site of all thought and feeling—as against the 'psyche' as life-principle—is an essential concomitant of the morality of rational hegemony. The soul must be one if we are to reach our highest in the self-collected understanding of reason, which brings about the harmony and concord of the whole person.[3]

The search for a unifying principle anticipates the modern exaltation of reason as liberating from the oppression of finitude and necessity, which reached its peak in eighteenth- and nineteenth-century philosophy. One may look at it via the lens of the dilemma *inside-beyond*, which was resolved differently in each of its guises. This is nothing other than, as contemporary theoreticians of selfhood from phenomenological and hermeneutic perspective might have remarked, an unceasing attempt to accommodate theoretically the ever-changing phenomenon of *transcendence*, which is essential to human *self*.

The illumination, sought by Plato outside the cave, according to Augustine was attainable via introspection. The turn of attention toward the inner man along with trinitarian inspiration result in a vision of a complex, reflective *self*, the moral integrity of which relies on its capacity to turn toward God. Most importantly, the sense of interiority involves a discovery of dependence and otherness within. It is the case, we may say, of enlightening (self-) transcendence mediated by inwardness. Now, unlike the ancient masters, the thinker from Hippo articulates the autonomy of human will, the "perversity" of which is no more caused by ignorance. As it is brilliantly exposed by Taylor, unless the whole attitude of inwardness aims at uncovering the illuminating dependence within, the aforementioned "perversity" appears. It is "a drive to make ourselves the center of the world, to dominate and possess . . . This is both a cause and consequence of a kind of slavery . . . *Evil is when this reflexivity is closed upon itself.* Healing comes when it is broken open."[4]

This ancient "discovery" is one of the pillars supporting Taylor's main point—namely that human *self*, always embedded in a culture and involved in a dialectical relation with it, calls for some "external," objective sources of qualitative differentiation and articulation of the realm of lived experience—a requirement neglected by modernity. Leaving aside the fact that Santayana would probably be skeptical as to the objectivity and universality of the values we live by, Taylor's analysis is highly relevant for understanding the rationale of critical, anti-subjectivist and anti-egotist strands in the twentieth-century thought, of which Santayana—as I emphasize in this study—is a prominent representative. In particular, with his book *Egotism in German Philosophy* and his essays on American culture, Santayana became an important (even if, for different reasons, not sufficiently audible) voice in this debate, one able to switch between different perspectives within the so-called Western culture. Some of his intuitions and concerns either anticipated or paralleled those of major critics of culture.

I will formulate one of the main problems emerging from this selective overview as follows: the very father of the odyssey into the inner man—Augustine—meant it *to contain an antidote for itself*. The most influential threads of modern thought, losing from view this subtle but crucial principle of selfhood, embarked upon an uncompromising subjectivist and egotist path, conducive to the development of instrumental, procedural reason.

Another example of the ancient wisdom which promoted selfhood equipped with "an antidote" or "a cure" for itself can be traced in an early vision of a unified subject proposed by Seneca and explored recently by Michel Foucault. Based upon the Socratic idea of *epimeleia heautou* (care about oneself) and *gnothi eauton* (know thyself), Seneca draws an image of a "withdrawing subject," one which reaches "the highest peak," a *locus* from which it can see the ways of this world and its own place in it, winning thereby a subjective freedom from the worst kind of servitude—"*sibi servire*" (servitude to oneself).[5] One finds here an echo of the Platonic juxtaposition of the soul and the body, but—free from Platonic otherworldliness. Seneca's subject is neither fully withdrawn nor disengaged; it remains in a close connection with the world. To set Foucault's consideration into the logic of our discussion—in the withdrawal into the proper place the subject finds the aforementioned *antidote* to its own worldly egotism and gives it an expression in practicing partial rejection of worldly goods, known as *askesis*. What is at stake here is not a dissolution of the *self* but—to the contrary—"a conversion to oneself" (!).[6]

A relational and action-focused conception of human *self*, one which may be regarded as an alternative to the aforementioned Platonic, Augustinian, and Stoic models of simple, integrated centers of control, emerges from the work of Aristotle. A psychic and rational being is given a chance of achieving integrity in the process of mastering a plurality of aim-oriented activities, while shaping a life which is good—namely one, through which the potential of human *being* is realized and fruition or perfection is achieved. The articulation of choice, action, and performance shifts subjective prerogatives to the area of skills, attitudes, and conduct vital for *zoon politikon*. Aristotelian *self* achieves unity in the process of a worldly and active life while becoming a subject of virtues and, above all, of *phronesis*, practical wisdom.[7] This is conducive to a happy life, the autonomy of which rests not in a forced self-integrity but in its being *autotelic*. Heidegger interprets *praxis* in Aristotle as arising out of care and plurality of concerns, each having certain *telos*. Thus, human worldly life is determined by "the agathon" (the good). In Heidegger's reading *the good* is treated as *eschaton*, that which individuates, completes, and thus delineates the shape of finite existence.[8] To restate the point—if we may speak of an autonomy of human *self* in Aristotle, it is to be worked out of the plurality of practices which present the sole opportunity for mastering the art of deliberation conducive to a good and happy life. However, the picture is incomplete without a note on contemplation, *theoria*, in which a truly good and dignified human life commences. To make no mistake about the nature of the relation between good life and contemplation, it is not that contemplation is "a good because it figures in the good life. It is much more that this life is good, because . . . it includes contemplation."[9] *Vita contemplativa* crowns a happy life attesting to its unity. It is a reward and a sign of human *self* released from the burden of *sibi servire*, a higher level of vitality. As we shall later see, this and other aspects of Aristotle's thought had a considerable impact on Santayana's conception of psychic and spiritual life.

1.2 The Modern *Self*: Between Reflection and Power

Of the aforementioned ways of arriving at subjective integrity it is predominantly the Augustinian path that echoes in the Cartesian *Cogito*. Within a dualist framework a subject of control and objective inquiry is set vis-à-vis a mechanistic universe. Rational hegemony over the objectified world is recognized as the source of human dignity. Its *locus* is an isolated subject, a thinking substance defined in the opposition to the material world, of which one's own body is a part. The soulless body—although sensitive and perceptive—is not properly conscious and the only knowledge *res cogitans* may have of its existence is mediated by ideas. Thus, one's own body comes to be approached in a scientific manner.[10] Human subject is epistemologically tested against the correctness and the certainty with which it inquires into the nature of the universe. At this point, claims Taylor, rationality turns from substantive into a procedural one. Human subjectivity is faced in this vision with something deeply "inferior," something calling for domination. What is out there is not a source of knowledge, but merely something calling for the application of reason. Taylor, sensitive to the sociocultural underpinning of philosophical doctrines, remarks on the favorable background of Protestant spirituality with its—defined earlier by Max Weber— "inner-worldly asceticism" leading to the " 'innerwordly liberation' of the soul"[11] Even though the ideal of the hegemony of reason and self-control has been inherited from Plato and the Stoics, unlike in their case, modern self-mastery recommends shaping our lives by the principles constructed by "our reasoning capacity . . . according to the appropriate standards."[12] An inwardness which used to be responsive to the divine is replaced by "an inwardness of self-sufficiency," self-transparence and "fullness of self-presence." As a result, *"what I now meet is myself"* (!).[13]

Heidegger was critical of *Cogito* as alienated both from God and from the world of existence to the effect that scientific knowledge became its only access to the phenomenon of the world. Thus, Descartes's ontology reduced being to a being present objectively.[14] Self-conscious *self*, correspondingly, was something self-contained and self-standing. With the subject's status quo being the seat of the required certainty *what is left for the world is to generate error and deception*.[15] Thus, *Cogito* is set on an isolated position, separated even from the body which it habitually calls "its own" and which remains on the side of Augustine's "unredeemed" nature. The relation between subject and the world is informed by scientific rigidity and distrust toward any means of accessing the latter that do not comply to the standards of certain, objective knowledge. The Cartesian model of subjectivity and reflexivity seems to have had an enormous and long-lasting impact on the future ideas of selfhood. The very idea of the gap has been decisive in respect to modern culture, affecting even apparently alternative approaches to subjectivity, where it received simply a different location and articulation. The Cartesian "alienating factor" resonates even in the *Cogito* of *fin de siècle*, namely—one informed by the uncanny "unconscious," as most notably manifest in the nineteenth- and twentiety-century psychoanalytical theories.[16]

Part of the heritage of this mental experiment in liberation from contingency and necessity was an increasingly problematic relation of man with the world and with his own finite singularity. Nevertheless, the self-mastery of John Locke's "punctual self" marked an enormous cultural change—the emergence of a human *self* who is "able to remake himself by methodical and disciplined action."[17] Santayana, skeptical both about Cartesian and Lockean vision, comments on the latter as follows,

> The limits of his personality were those of his memory, and his experience included everything that his living mind could appropriate and re-live. In a word, he was his idea of himself: and this insight opens a new chapter not only in his philosophy but in the history of human self-estimation. . . . Each man was a romantic personage or literary character: he was simply what he thought to be, and might become anything.[18]

This aspiration to self-modeling requires that the *self distances itself not only from the world but also from its own experience*. The price for the atomization of experience is "a new, unprecedentedly radical form of self-objectification . . . [and] far reaching reformation." Even the meaning of the notion of "habit," notes Taylor, changed from the Aristotelian, where "our '*hexeis*' are formed against the background of a nature with a certain bent," to an instrumental one.[19]

What is important for our discussion, the humanistic dignity of the whole idea of self-mastery implies a problematic distancing of oneself from all particular features. *The punctual self thus loses singularity in favor of an impersonal center of power.* Taylor's remark touches upon a crucial distinction between the types of "individualisms," which too are easily and indistinctively blended in contemporary discussion under one abstract label of "individualism." Individualism may lead either to the recovery of singularity (Montaigne) or to its neutralization (Locke). While the Canadian thinker stresses the difference resting in the method of individuation and the type of reflexivity, I think that the difference in question rests also in the stakes. More specifically: *in the latter singularity is at stake, in the former it is power*. Locke's *self* is an efficient agent, who—like *any* agent—can be recognized as responsible for his actions and subject of law.[20] Hence it is a *self* of great practical importance for modern societies and no wonder this vision of selfhood has proved more influential. The freedom aspired to by this model is an apparent freedom from any essentialist dogma—apparent, because like any doctrine, it carries its own dogmas inexplicitly. Notwithstanding the fact of all the gains this vision of selfhood secures for the members of modern societies, Santayana may have a point in concluding that "morally this system thus came to sanction a human servitude to material things."[21] The disengagement from one's particular nature, tending to produce an ungrounded *self*, preceded radical questioning of the very reality of the *self* by David Hume, whose empirical inquiry led to the conclusion that there can be no corresponding impression to the commonly held idea of a constant self-identity. The basic object of experience is "the mind's moment," a perception, and a successive "bundle or collection of different perceptions" is what the so-called "self" is reducible to.[22] Yet, man exhibits a peculiar propensity to feign—justified biologically and socially—and the idea of "self" is one of such fictions fueled by memory and habits of the mind. One may be tempted to think of Hume's achievement as an illustration of the self-annihilating logic of enlightened subjectivism. Not a mainstream representative of the era, Hume exerted a powerful influence on much later thinkers, such as American pragmatists, or Gilles Deleuze, a critic of transcendental and phenomenological theories of selfhood and a proponent of a philosophy of difference and multiple subject.[23]

Deleuze rereads Hume, articulating processual and functional nature of subjectivity, which is a manifestation of human nature, the essence of which is going beyond the mind and the given via *believing* and *inventing*.[24] Human nature may also be defined in terms of imagination which has become subject to the principles of association and passions, which resonate in the empirical subject. Concrete circumstances along with the principles individuate the subject. The subject is time-binding: drawing upon habits (repetition) and anticipation, it claims more than it can know, it judges, and invents. Its experience organizes the past, habit—the present, imagination and anticipation—the future.[25] This temporal synthesis is the seat of its creativity; this is where something new may arise and "reorganize" subjective time.

Unlike in the case of a transcendental subject, here subjectivity is an "impression of reflection."[26] Purposive in its integrity, Humean subject becomes aim-oriented under the rule of utility, and mind becomes a system. But the system could never have worked unless human beings enjoyed the deepest conviction that they are free agents in a substantial world. This is the "going beyond" typical of human nature and the subject may be considered in terms of "mediation and transcendence."[27] The "I" of self-reference is fictive and habitual, just like culture and the human world are.[28] The *selves* are practical phantasms or useful illusions essential for the moral sphere. In other words, as *selves* we arise out of memories, fantasies, and beliefs. Partaking in a culture and a society, we do not satisfy our immediate desires but rather their reflections resonating in imagination. Hence the distinction between nature and culture is merely conventional.[29]

Kant followed the Humean path of the desubstantialization of subjectivity but at the same time introduced another sort of subjective reality—different than merely empirical, namely—the transcendental "I think." For the sake of further discussion of Santayana's conception of the *self*, let us look at Kantian subject in some more detail. In his representational theory of cognition, Kant assumes that representations have both an *a priori* grounding in self-consciousness, which is the source of the principle of unity, and an object. In fact, Kant derives "a constant and enduring I" from the fact (of the unity) of representations.[30] Conscious experience is conditioned by the dialectic of original spontaneity, the so-called pure apperception of "I think," and empirical, reproductive passivity, "without relation to the identity of the subject."[31]

However, the status of the transcendental subject cannot be understood without taking into account Kant's dichotomy between appearances as objects of our consciousness and things in themselves as objects of appearances. As a result, the object gets "doubled" and the latter type of object, inaccessible for consciousness, is called "the nonempirical object, i.e., the transcendental object = x (. . .) which object is actually always the same, = x, in all our cognitions."[32] The pure concept of this unknown, transcendental object is what conditions our reference to any object at all and allows for the constitution of objective reality in general. An analogous situation occurs on the side of the transcendental subject: the *I think*, as a source of unity, conditions my self-reference, my conscious self-identity.[33] Self-consciousness, then, makes possible an object as such and, most interestingly, *the transcendental subject seems to be a (non-intuitable) correlate of the object x.*

Furthermore, for Kant appearances are conscious insofar as they are subject to apperception—the source of the categories of intellect. Intellect/thinking, in turn, is blind unless applied to sense. The function of imaginative synthesis is to bring the two—sense and apperception—together. As Kant famously states, "pure imagination" is "a basic power of the human soul which underlies a priori all cognition."[34] While its productive synthesis makes up for pure understanding, passive or reproductive synthesis relies on experience.[35] Imaginary operation on perceptions is called apprehension.[36]

The most obvious bearing these dichotomies of the Kantian model of conscious experience have on the subject and human *self* is the distinction between pure and empirical subject, and the problematic nature of the connection between the two. Kant finds no satisfactory answer to the question, which he immediately labels as "paradoxical": *how does the I/ego cognize itself?* The "I think" exists as an intelligence, which is limited by time relations, which are "obscure" and beyond understanding.[37] In experience we are dealing only with appearances, but since empirical consciousness has no reference to the subject as such, we "reconstruct" the subjective identity of ourselves by synthesizing the representations of ourselves.[38] We are presented to our own *selves* psychologically, we intuit ourselves via inner sense "only as we are inwardly affected *by ourselves*."[39] The mysterious "I," then, can be known to itself only either as a phenomenon or reflectively, *via* its thinking (i.e., a thought *that* it exists). The paradox is that "we thus stand in a passive relation to ourselves,"[40] because "I" is never recognized "in terms of what it is in itself." The transcendental "I" becomes a *post-factum* "I." In other words, self-consciousness is an inadequate form of cognition of oneself.[41] The quoted passages attest to the fact that we are dealing here with a sort of *schismatic self*. In his reading of these *aporias*, Heidegger speaks of three aspects of Kant's subject—*personalitas transcendentalis* (pure I), *personalitas psychologica* (empirical subject) and *personalitas moralis*.[42] The first one, the core of self-consciousness, is exclusively subjective and cannot be experienced or objectified since it is already assumed as the basis for every experience. The second may be referred to as "the soul" and it is always found "already there"—hence the previously quoted Kant's remark about our "passive relation" to ourselves. The paradox mentioned by Kant rests in that we meet ourselves always empirically. In the sentence "I am thinking about myself" both *personalitas* resonate, but "I" is inevitably always overshadowed by "myself."

As for *personalitas moralis*, indispensable in the case of Kantian human subject, it involves a "moral feeling," which expresses our respect for the moral law of which we are the source and which guides our will, revealing thereby the ontological structure of a human person/*Dasein*.[43] It seems that it is predominantly the moral aspect that accounts for the integrity of the subject. Here we are crossing the borderline between the technical makeup of Kant's project and its cultural significance. The Kantian subject owes its unity and freedom, notes Polish thinker, a contemporary of Santayana, Marian Zdziechowski, to man's moral autonomy. Thus, this subject has fully internalized its moral sources along the lines of the Augustinian idea of the transformation of the will. It is often noticed that this status involves "suspending" natural necessity or, at least, limiting its influence on human realm. Yet, it is equally often overlooked that the "suspension" means that the conjunction freedom—duty overshadows the inconvenient opposition necessity—freedom. Freedom no more consists in a capricious choice, but is predetermined by obligation, which—in a sense—*seems to bracket and imitate necessity*. We may call this strategy "necessity by proxy with a moral face." Nevertheless, the absolute and universal nature of moral law made Kant's vision of freedom at the level of community—risky, and at the level of an individual—excessively demanding, a "narrow gate," as Zdziechowski called it, and Santayana would agree.[44] Interestingly, the transcendental condition of freedom, to which Kant had given the form of human capacity to establish "relatively new beginnings" in the chain of events, had the potential of grounding freedom symbolically and would inspire future narrative conceptions of selfhood and of freedom (the so-called authorship of life), based on subtle, narrative techniques of disrupting and "manipulating" time.

From the viewpoint of philosophy of culture, we are witnessing here another stage in suppressing singularity and finitude in favor of the liberating power of universal reason. This trend in modern philosophy "rebels against nature as what is merely given . . . and insists on an autonomous generation of the forms we live by. The aspiration is ultimately to a total liberation."[45] On the reverse of this aspiration, there is an *overlooking* of the found, the unique, and the accidental. Aware of the sweeping generalization involved, Santayana is still right to notice that subjective autonomy, understood in this way, was made absolute by Hegel *by the price of shrinking the significance of finite singularity* to that of a momentary flashlight under the sun.[46] From Descartes to Kant, Fichte, and Hegel, comments Heidegger, the subject is understood in the horizon of cognition, self-consciousness, and self-knowledge. This kind of "ungenuine subjectivism" neglects the fact that the subject "has not brought itself to existence by its own power."[47] Kant was unable to account for the unity of the three *personalitas* or, in other words, of a human person proper, concludes Heidegger; and German idealism proved "unable to solve the problem of the existence of Dasein because the question is not at all asked."[48]

This position of Heidegger articulates a major turn in philosophical approach to the issue of subjectivity, one which had been anticipated by Schopenhauer and Kierkegaard, if not by Pascal. Kierkegaard, in an act of rebellion against the "arrogance" of Hegel's vision, and aware of the fact that an overgrown modern subjectivity needs an antidote for itself, followed a subjectivist path accompanied by an unceasing existential concern. This concern led the Danish thinker to the ultimate confrontation with an irrational abyss which abides no other transactions than a leap of faith. In

Schopenhauer's vista, the fusion of the aforementioned opposition between finitude and freedom with the dichotomy thing in itself—appearance, reached its peak. The thinker from Gdańsk ridiculed the freedom of a single, concrete and self-conscious individual by counting it as an illusion, but nevertheless cared to reach for human suffering as one of his major themes. Suffering, reminding humans of their imperfect being, was but the last prerogative of the fading reality of subjective experience.

This is where Nietzsche enters the stage, and—inspired initially by the tragic dualism of his master—embarks upon the path of restoring the dignity of reality and the sense of significance to a concrete, bodily human being. Nietzsche wanted to divorce the ideal of uninhibited self-creation not only from the ghost of epistemological, objectifying theoretical *self*, but also from the tyranny of any ontic order. The result was an uncanny hybrid of natural vitality with the heroism of self-creation united agonistically in a super-human *self* willing to overcome itself. Much as Nietzsche's rebellion was a reaction against the Christian way of identity-shaping, it opposed the "mentality" of German idealism, leaving aside the fact that it was informed with elements of both. The radicalism of his alternative Evangelical targeted indiscriminately most of the prerogatives of subjective freedom which had previously been achieved. Leaving aside his critical genius, the question whether Nietzsche managed to propose a worthy alternative to what he had deconstructed remains open. Santayana believed—for reasons we shall discuss later—it did not. For now, let us say briefly that Santayana believed—as some other early critics of Nietzsche did, Karl Jaspers for example—that in the light of Nietzsche's early dualist metaphysics self-creation can be but a desperate and, in a sense, futile effort. Moreover, by dissolving the truth of this world, the thinker left us with serious doubts why anything would matter at all, or how anything would make any difference whatsoever. Behind the subjective well-being of the human animal, there lurks a disquieting abyss, which makes dubitable any sources and criteria for a meaningful integrity. One possible answer to that, a line of defense perhaps, seems to be that Nietzsche in fact reintroduces a sort of Cartesian *fiat* but on the basis of pure willing and against the horizon of nothingness. But this was a strategy Santayana was skeptical about.

1.3 A Shift of Metaphors: From a Unitary *Self* to a Stream

Nietzschean efforts in deconstructing Western models of subjectivity were still heavily informed with the shade of a unitary *self*—hence the ideas of "will to power" and eternal return could come to the fore. Nietzsche's vision was paralleled by other, more moderate trends which, instead of a total critique, offered new vistas from within philosophical tradition. A breakthrough in thinking about subjectivity was the idea of stream of consciousness. It was developed—on both sides of the Atlantic and in a very different vein—by William James, Edmund Husserl, and Henri Bergson.

What is constant in an ongoing flow of thoughts and what provides for the sense of continuity of "myself" is precisely *the stream*, claimed James in his naturalizing theory. A majority of scholars interpret James's vision as *ego-less*, in a clear contrast to both substantial and transcendental subject, although they suggest we may perhaps speak of a "minimal," experiential *self*. The proper—empirical and narrative—*self* develops along with the stream. There is no need, says James, to postulate a "metaphysical entity like the Soul, or a principle like a pure Ego, viewed as out of time" as long we recognize that the "Me" is an empirical aggregate of things objectively known" centered around its nucleus—"the bodily existence felt to be present at the time." The knowing "I" itself is a *Thought*.[49] Owen Flanagan, whose theory of conscious *self* draws on James's ideas, summarizes Jamesian *self* as follows: "The *self* emerges as experience accrues, and it is constructed as the organism actively engages the external world. . . . In this sense the ego is an after-the-fact construction," not a transcendental postulate.[50]

A vital message of James's legacy is that "we can be egoless without vaporizing. Some egoless beings are embodied persons. Personal selves abound. We are examples."[51] What is important, James distinguishes between ego, subject, and *self*. Flanagan frames the ego-less *self* within a broader context of self-concern and care, based on memory and "anticipatory models," which account for the unity of thoughts, which themselves are "thinkers." Framed by care, the *self* develops as thoughts accrue. We are given a clear-cut answer to the fundamental question: "Who does the seeing? Who is the seer?"—namely—"the whole organism."[52] This naturalistic and empirical account can be made philosophically more interesting by being combined with phenomenological descriptions of the first-person experience, as well as—due to its emphasis on history, memory, and change as constitutive of selfhood—with a narrative theory.

Since James, ego-less or center-less visions of human *self* may be said to dominate in philosophy. Having said this, one can still agree with Manfred Frank as to the fact that post-analytical philosophy is characterized by a return to the problem of subjectivity.[53] This is partly possible due to thinkers like James, in whose work, as already mentioned, one comes across a very useful (although still inexplicit) distinction between the notions "subject," "ego," and "self." James's importance rests, in my view, in his showing that ego-less vision does not necessarily equal the dissolution of selfhood. Naturalistic and empirical *self*, due to its accumulative and appropriative nature and the principle of self-concern, may become its own condition of possibility. Thus, James contributed to the shift from a somewhat mythical idea of the ego/I as a transcendent observer and a controlling agent, to a more modest one, of a conscious, caring being, still acting but caught in a net of dependencies. Flanagan's eclectic, ego-less theory of conscious *self* may be recognized as an example of contemporary appropriations of James's legacy.

Let us now take a glance at Edmund Husserl's analysis of human *self*. Given the development of Husserl's theory and its increasing complexity, the author could not avoid some technical details. The reader is free to treat this part as a longer digression and leave it out if she/he wishes. Husserl undertakes the idea of the stream of consciousness as a primordial mode of self-presentation.[54] A phenomenal world is constituted via intentional acts of a transcendental Ego, whose immanent temporality can be retrieved on the basis of the stream of "lived temporality" and bodily self-experience. Husserl speaks of three dimensions of consciousness: pre-reflective self-awareness, intentional (objectifying) acts, and reflective self-awareness. The recognition of the first one and its anchoring in inner time consciousness is emblematic of the phenomenological take on subjectivity. Conscious experience is based on a tacit, nonrelational, non-objectifying, minimal self-awareness. The "minimal self" idea is Husserl's answer to the key question about the first-person-givenness: itself objectless, it precedes any intentional and objectifying act. A prior "self-luminosity" of states and acts is the intrinsic feature of any conscious experience.[55] Mature Husserl's inquiry into the nature of subjectivity shows that the subject perceives temporal objects within a temporal field—"the width of presence" of triadic structure. This modality of givenness explains how conscious acts can occur within the flow and how we experience change. The cornerstone of Husserl's solution rests in the idea that the "now-moment" may become appearance of an object only if accompanied by a future orientation and the retention of the bygone phase.

Husserl's model reveals a major *aporia* bothering modern theoreticians of selfhood—namely that of lateness, emptiness, a gap, or a blank point within conscious experience.[56] The impossibility of the proper self-cognition of the "I think"—the same that bothered Kant—is a manifestation of it. As for Husserl in Derrida's interpretation, "consciousness . . . presents itself to itself across the difference between now and not-now."[57] Consequently, self-awareness is "characterized by . . . a historical heritage. . . . Presence is differentiation; it *exists* only in its intertwining with absence."[58] Husserl explicitly remarks that the pure Ego reaches self-transparency only via reflection, while only when nonreflecting on itself can it be "straightforwardly given." "Self-perceived actual presence" seems "temporally enduring"[59] but the "immanent temporality of the identical ego . . . [contains] no real moment."[60] Elsewhere we read that "self-remembrance obviously includes the fact that the pure Ego . . . is conscious of itself as bygone."[61] Finally, also in its empirical aspect the conscious subject is based on "retrospective remembering."[62]

Sartre detected an apparently similar "blank point," or a fissure resting in the difference between *self* (in Sartre's vocabulary: a basic, experiential component of consciousness) and an ego (an object of self-awareness, mediated by the other). The temporal alienation of Husserl's *bygone self* seems more fundamental than Sartre's contention that self-reflection is self-alienating. In Merleau-Ponty's explicit comment, "temporality contains an internal fracture that permits us to return to our past experiences . . . [yet, it] prevents us from fully coinciding with ourselves. There will always remain a difference between the lived and the understood."[63]

Mature Husserl's analysis of human *self* gets increasingly complicated—it combines transcendental and Cartesian elements with a phenomenology of embodiment and Aristotelian inspirations. There is a trace of a classical Cartesian dualism in Husserl's pair: spirit (pure Ego, constitutive of the stream of consciousness and being part of it)–body. Yet, this simplicity is undermined by two more distinctions: between transcendental subject (Pure Ego) and empirical one ("I as a man" in a spatiotemporal world), and between animated body as an agent [*Leib*] and body as an object [*Körper*]. In the phenomenological analysis of embodiment the animated body, called "real incarnation of subjectivity," enjoys priority.[64]

Psychic, empirical and bodily subject of properties is "related to the lived experience of consciousness in such a way that it has them, lives them, and lives in them."[65] An analogy is said to occur between observable, physical behavior and "psychic properties in corresponding lived experiences." Psyche represents *fixed* properties which seem to—along with external circumstances—codetermine the experiential flux. Yet, the specificity of the psyche is that it at once determines/precedes and emerges out of experience. This is explained by the fact of psychophysical unity: the psyche is intimately interwoven with the body and they exhibit "lasting psychic properties, which are expressions for certain regulated dependencies *of the psychic on the Bodily.*"[66] The psychophysical unity stands behind what

Husserl calls the "formal idea" of "unity of lasting properties in relation to pertinent circumstances."[67]

With the unity there emerges the problem of the tension between subjectivity and factuality, which Husserl labels as the paradox of the external and the inner. It is manifest in the incongruity between psychic life and history-less material reality. Psychic reality "as a matter of principle *cannot* return to the same total state."[68] In this case, the formulation about fixed properties related to external circumstances as well as the full analogy between psychic life and material manifestation become problematic. Without getting into all the details of this analysis, the solution provided by Husserl seems to rest in the multidimensional reality of human being—next to *the natural* (the material body), and the so-called *supernatural* (the soul) there is *the psychic*, which is internally complex and involves two aspects—the natural and the *idiopsychic*. The latter is a radically non-objectifiable reality implicit in human subjectivity. If I understand Husserl correctly, this translates itself into nothing other than unpredictability and uniqueness of each (stream of) experience. Under the same external circumstances the flux of experience pertaining to the same soul is "lived" differently than it would have been lived had it occurred at a different time, for "the psychic unfolding of states could not be the same."[69] *The idiopsychic is a peculiar synthesis of change and continuity and the very result of subjective individuation.*

The quintessence of Husserl's considerations seems to be contained in the following words:

> Psychic reality is constituted as reality only through psychophysical dependencies. . . . The unity of the soul is a real unity in that, as unity of psychic life, it is joined with the Body as unity of the Bodily stream of being . . . The result of the consideration: . . . *what we have to oppose to material nature as a second kind of reality is not the "soul" but the concrete unity of Body and soul, the human (or animal) subject*.[70]

To summarize the above considerations, the human subject and the human person are irreducible to scientific and naturalistic terms because of the condition and experience of incarnation. Individual personality is shaped in a net of dependencies and "man is what he is as a being who maintains himself in his commerce with the . . . surrounding world and who, in doing so, maintains his individuality throughout."[71] These words testify to Dan Zahavi's remark about the mutual dependence, a co-shaping occurring between the subject and the world, being a basic mark of phenomenological viewpoint. Interestingly for our discussion, Husserl's dualism, finally, is at a remove from Cartesianism; it is rather an untypical sort of phenomenological transcendentalism, one which both respects and aspires to transform what I will further refer to as *the human sphere of helplessness*.[72]

Husserl's ideas influenced and inspired his critics and followers, whose diverse phenomenological standpoints share a few basic assumptions concerning subjectivity and selfhood. Dan Zahavi mentions the following: (1) the assumption of a pre-linguistic, pre-reflective, non-objectifying, experiential dimension of subjectivity (minimal *self*), which implies an immediate access to one's own mental states and makes intentionality possible;[73] (2) primary mutual dependence between the *self* and the world, and; (3) intersubjectivity, instead of being an "existing structure," is derived from and sustained only "in relation between world-related subjects (. . .) The subject must be seen as a worldly incarnate existence, and the world must be seen as a common field of experience."[74]

Heidegger's existential-hermeneutic *Dasein*, which will be discussed in more detail in the fifth chapter, marks an altogether new approach toward selfhood. *Dasein* always finds itself affected and co-disclosed along with the world. Still, as against some readings, according to which *Dasein* is constituted *post-factum*, Zahavi claims that we are presented rather with a "form of self-acquaintance that precedes reflection."[75] Merely reflective or passive self-interpretation is for Heidegger a fallen modality of self-givenness. *Dasein* belongs to a larger project of philosophy understood as a form of "*counterruinant movement*,"[76] i.e., one providing such a model of subjectivity, which facilitates the *self* to regain the postulated composure or temporal integrity called "authenticity," while avoiding the trap of both solipsism and objectification. As for his method, Heidegger's modified phenomenology may be recognized as a sort of living self-reflection, which "rather than adding new distorting components and structures to the experience reflected upon . . . [is] accentuating structures already inherent in the lived experience."[77] Intentionality is still central in this approach but it is a modified sort of intentionality—spontaneous "being-with" or "being-in." As Crowell summarized Heidegger's effort, it is "explicitly cognitive-illuminative self-recollection," a kind of "intuitive self-having."[78]

There is a tendency, mistaken in my view, to read Heidegger in terms of the deconstruction of the subject and dissolution of the *self*, while his non-egological standpoint may as well be interpreted as strengthening the selfhood, by replacing the isolated, ghostly ego-pole with an existential, dynamic being, which aspires to self-authorship. This has not escaped

Charles Taylor's attention, who distinguishes carefully between the aforementioned thinkers of the "escape from the self" and Heidegger's striving to legitimize and "reconnect the *self* with some larger reality, to overcome the slide towards subjectivism in modern culture," yet without imposing any explicit "hypergood."[79]

The analysis of selfhood in terms of the hermeneutics of time and the possibilities of being places Heidegger in the circle of hermeneutic conceptions of the *self*, which have been influential in contemporary philosophy since Schleiermacher. Both hermeneutics and personalism, the latter largely neglected in recent decades, have attempted to restore the significance of both singularity and "personality" in the discussion of selfhood.[80] Max Scheler's example exhibits a rare and peculiar combination of a modern, phenomenological, nonsubstantial, relational, and dynamic vision of *self* with elements of idealistic realism. The intertwining dimensions of the finite and the infinite (the ideal sphere of values) result in a vision of an irreducible person—a subject who is essentially always engaged in acts and unceasingly self-transcending. The person experiences herself and others through acts and her identity is therein exhausted. The acts at once individualize and personalize.[81] In her unique and singular "style," or "how," the person escapes any attempt at objectification and reduction. Hence being a person abides only a "who" and not a "what" question.

One of the most influential conceptions in the twentieth century is that of the hermeneia of the *self*, where the *self* is emerging from the process of interpretative self- and world-disclosing. Typically of hermeneutics, the *self* can be defined "only in a semantically innovative way, i.e., by interpreting it as a source of modifications which are being grafted upon linguistic structures which disclose the world of interpretative acts."[82]

Heidegger's vision may be recognized as its most radical form and his notion of *being* as providing for an ontological-hermeneutic environment more fundamental than that of culture, language, or ethics. Time constitutes the ultimate subject matter for interpretation, which is a mode of being proper to the beings which are constantly projecting a meaningful horizon. Meanwhile, time disintegrates any unity, hence hermeneutic visions carry an implicit deconstructive potential. Hermeneutic *self*, due to its reflective and projecting dynamics, is never present, never simultaneous with itself, or, to use Heidegger's phrase, *never at home*. Hermeneutics is an alternative not only to the ideas of a universal subject, but also to those visions, in which the *self* is secondary to anonymous systems and structures, as well as to some analytical approaches, which tend to isolate and focus on narrow issues such as identity, sameness, or persistence in time. Flexible and eclectic as they are, hermeneutic conceptions are capable of providing reconciliatory solutions to the *aporias* and polarities within contemporary approaches to the *self*, which often oscillate between *egological* and *non-egological* extremes, between unequivocal existence of the subject and its negation, between autonomy and sheer heteronomy, or between attributing the subject with causal efficacy and declaring free will as a mere illusion. It is symptomatic, by the way, that it is the latter alternative that is more commonly accepted in the time of post-Nietzschean, or—to use Taylor's phrase—post-Schopenhauerian subject. Hermeneutic conceptions "organically" distrust such clear-cut and radical alternatives insofar as these are based on certain narrow conceptual commitments.[83] Instead, they offer more nuanced solutions, while admitting of *detours* or *circuits*, drawing on metaphors, subtle conceptual distinctions, and eclectic philosophical framework. The most emblematic example is that of Paul Ricoeur, whose inherently relational but still *autonomous self* attests to the fact that non-egological approach does not necessarily imply the dissolution of selfhood, although it may do so as is the case with some post-modern visions, (which also often adopt the idea of a narrative *self* but set it in an altogether different, heteronymous context)—as a subject of colonization, a battlefield of parasitic powers, or an epiphenomenon of structural differentiation.

The recognition of the multidimensionality of the *self*, anticipated by the Husserlian analysis of incarnation and the introduction of the *idiopsychic* which resonates in Ricoeur's *ipse/idem* distinction, reveals the tension between finitude and freedom, and prompts searching for different ways of *coping with finitude*. Heidegger, for instance, expelled finitude into the horizon of death so that he could rightly say that "*Dasein never perishes.*"[84] Ricoeur translated finitude into the net of ethical commitments, which generate a multidimensional sphere of the recognition of the *self* and the other. This was possible due to the deeper, temporal-narrative dynamics of selfhood, masterfully anchored by the French thinker in an ontology inspired by Aristotle. One of the most original, temporal interpretations of finitude was provided—as I would like to suggest in this book—by Henri Bergson, whom I will discuss in one of the subsequent chapters in more detail. Some other thinkers, committed to a post-modern version of narrative selfhood, like Richard Rorty, situated the self-interpreting animal in the fluid environment of temporary "vocabularies" and identities.[85]

Contemporary philosophy questioned universality, which was the postulate of German idealism, and engaged in regaining singularity and replacing the idea of universality with that of intersubjectivity.[86] It has also become rather difficult, after Merleau-Ponty, to deny that "unless self-experience is embodied and embedded, intersubjectivity will be neither possible nor comprehensible."[87] Naturalistic perspectives of a nonreductive type, and other theories committed mainly to the basic, experiential dimension of selfhood, combine well with narrative conceptions as long as "it takes a *self* to experience one's life as a story."[88] For instance, in Owen Flanagan's vision, which I will refer to in the next section, both an experiential and a narrative component are embedded in a naturalistic context, and a subject/a *self* is conceptualized in a threefold way, namely as a (1) living organism, which (2) exhibits a phenomenological/experiential dimension, and (3) becomes a subject and a conscious agent via a sort of narrative unity.[89] These eclectic visions have on one hand largely replaced isolated pure egos, and on another, compete with those reducing consciousness to material processes and selfhood to an illusion. The latter, by the way, may also draw on the idea of a narrative *self*, as exemplified by an influential contemporary naturalist thinker Daniel Dennett. Dennett considers the *self*, in Darwinian terms, to be a useful, adaptive and entirely fictional construct, reducible to biological processes, and he famously calls it "a center of narrative gravity."[90]

An example of yet another voice in the contemporary debate is Dennett's staunch opponent, Manfred Frank, who posits a minimal, a priori *self* of experience, meant to continue the German transcendental tradition while disclaiming its excessive aspiration. With the support of a number of theoreticians, from Johann G. Fichte through Franz Brentano to Sydney Shoemaker and Héctor-Neri Castañeda, Frank holds that reflexive and perceptual models of self-consciousness are unacceptable. By the same token he addresses the famous "bundle theory" by David Hume, who denied the existence of an "I" on the ground of its being non-perceptible. But why assume that "I" is an object of perception in the first place?—asks Frank.[91] Frank assumes that there is no "doubling," no subject-object relation in the very basic, pre-reflective self-awareness. A *"de se"* (*Selbstwissen*) must be given prior to any *"de re"* and *"de dicto"* identifications.[92] In Frank's theory, a non-reductive *"de se"* which he calls "I"/*Ichkeit* exhibits three aspects: (1) phenomenological self-consciousness (what-is-it-likeness, self-acquaintance or self-intimation); (2) a sort of self-awareness of the "I," which borders on self-knowledge and is more cognitively demanding *(Selbst-erkentniss)*; and (3) a direct self-consciousness *(Vertrauheit)*, which constitutes an anonymous field and generates the experience of "me-ness."[93]

Models like Frank's "I" merit by the recognition and inclusion of embodiment, so emphatically insisted upon by phenomenologists. Zahavi in his inquiry into contemporary discussions of selfhood argues that phenomenology is *the* approach that brings the subject back from timeless isolation into the relational, spontaneous, embodied being in the world, without dissolving it altogether. Hence his articulation of an *experiential invariant of the first-person givenness*[94]—a nonreflective, minimal *self*, which constitutes the implicit self-reference of all experience, and contains already in itself a differentiation and dynamics of sort, be it obscure and impenetrable. This invariant, called by Husserl *transcendence in immanence*, is synthetic in relation to time consciousness, and allows for establishing a narrative unity. This position seems to be in-between Manfred Frank's decisive defense of an a priori "I" and Flanagan's idea of an empirical, narrative, and natural "I," which is real enough but rather a *post-factum* construct.

1.4 A Digression on Freedom

The desubstantialization of the subject, the recognition of its complexity, the differentiation between subject, ego, and *self*, as well as controversies around the very reality of *self*, paralleled the emergence of more nuanced approaches to subjective freedom. The paradigm of ego's *fiat* was questioned along with its Cartesian premises. In transcendental philosophy the invariant pure ego and rationality were the seat of human freedom, but Kant divorced natural causality from the one we ascribe to ourselves in the realm of phenomena and shifted the meaning of freedom into the moral realm. Husserl spoke of the net of dependencies out of which the "I" of a human being emerges, yet at the same time he pointed to the sphere of freedom delineated by the constitutive and synthetic activity of pure Ego. Despite the strong presence of some Cartesian elements in his thinking, his version of the dualism transcendental-empirical marks a new quality in thinking about subjective freedom. *Man may be at once dependent and free.* Nevertheless, it is a weak conception of freedom, one restricted to an epistemic and imaginative dimension.

The opposition determined-undetermined is hardly the only alternative available or even hardly the right one in this respect. Determinism, to which many philosophers today ascribe, is no more synonymous with a total deconstruction of the idea of subjective freedom. The so-called compatibilism seeks to reconcile some forms of causal determinism with subjective freedom defined anew. Some philosophers of mind note that even deflating theories of consciousness and *self*, such as epiphenomenalism, are not necessarily mutually exclusive with some conceptions of freedom.[95] One possibility of negotiating the margin of subjective freedom in the light of the growing awareness as to the actual degree of dependence is Harry Frankfurt's idea of free will, where "second-order desires must correspond harmoniously with the deeper *self* for the sense of self-determination to be preserved."[96] Another formula of freedom comes from Paul Ricoeur and his idea of *the authorship of life*, founded on his theory of agency and narrative unity. An example of an eclectic, egoless vision of the *self*, where both consciousness and freedom are at least partly saved from reduction, is the already mentioned constructive naturalistic theory by Owen Flanagan. An "actual full identity," which is constantly emerging, aspires to the status of "the most enlightened version of the story of the self." Flanagan defends some notion of the truth about the *self*, i.e., there is at each time a status quo concerning this *self*, about which one can be more or less mistaken, further or closer to the "most enlightened" interpretation. Even though the story is said to be "multiply authored," "once our characters are well formed and we have a good grasp of them, our powers of self-authorship increase dramatically"[97] and we gain freedom to become subjects to "radical self-transformation."[98] Thus, Flanagan refers back to the ancient motto *know thyself*. This is not merely to say that the *self* is relatively free in its narrative (reflective) dimension: "the causal efficacy of self-representation is fairly obvious when we are actively engaged in representing ourselves."[99] Flanagan, like Husserl and James, assumes that there are two dimensions of consciousness, and the thinking *self* synthesizes the two, as long as it "exists as a complex dispositional structure."[100]

Discussing the positions of philosophy of mind and cognitive science in this respect goes beyond the scope of this study. Let me just mention that some philosophers of mind explain freedom in relation to contingency. Material causality (brain processes) as determining every state of consciousness is a fact, claims John Searle, but the state of neurobiological processes in a given moment is not enough to determine completely the next moment's state. There are gaps, so the process is not deterministic, human actions are not determined causally and the freedom in question is related to contingency.[101] What is important for our discussion is that Searle represents a nonreductionist standpoint on consciousness, which obviously influences one's perspective as to the reality of the *self*. Nonreductionism has been sometimes adopted by phenomenological and hermeneutic visions of the *self* because it offers greater potential for defining freedom than reductionism does. Moreover, granting some sort of reality to qualitative, experiential dimension of first-person experience supports preserving the very "self" from being dismissed as an illusion. A number of contemporary philosophers like John Searle, Ned Block, David Chalmers, and Pascal

Engel, insisted upon the recognition of "what it is like" factor. Respectively, Searle has voiced a crucial, in my view, intuition that *it is a decision and not a scientific discovery to recognize the reality of mental events.*[102] It is a fact, claims Searle, for some life processes to be qualitative, subjective and first-personal. As I said, it is impossible and unnecessary here to get into the details of contemporary philosophy of mind; my intention is rather to point to a certain tradition of nonreductive materialism and/or naturalism of which Santayana was an early representative. The choice of John Searle is not accidental because—not unlike Santayana himself—Searle was committed to causal reductionism but *not to ontological one*. What is more, some sort of nonreductionism, especially when we differentiate between different aspects or dimensions of consciousness, may combine well even with some forms of epiphenomenalism, to which—arguably, as some critics claim—Santayana might have been attracted at least at some points of his intellectual biography. "At worst" we may speak of an "authorship emotion," a *quale* of a conscious, free will. It should be stressed here that the freedom of will in question does not have to be treated as a mere illusion unless we are obsessed with the Cartesian *fiat*.[103]

Obviously, the stakes in assuming nonreductive viewpoints go far beyond this technical discussion. The recognition of the objective status of the qualitative dimension inherent in conscious experience is part of the case against the instrumental mind and a merely functional *self*. The topic has been explored and persuasively exposed by Charles Taylor, whose inquiry into the history of the idea of selfhood has hardly a match in contemporary philosophy. What follows is the last section of this chapter—a brief summary of Taylor's theory of the so-called expressivist turn and its echoes in modern and post-modern culture.

1.5 Regaining the *Self*: The Expressivist Turn and Beyond

Taylor's main assumption is that *praxis* is articulated through ideas and that there is an equivocal dialectical relation between cultural trends and philosophical formulae.[104] Hence, Taylor, tracing the history of the internalization of the sources of the *self*, is cautious of its sociocultural underpinnings. To simplify part of the detailed inquiry of his *opus magnum*, the so-called ethics of ordinary life preceded and paved way to Deism, which—with its assumption of the universe of Providential order and the idea that religious belief should be transparent to a rational mind—prepared a favorable ground for Enlightenment. The decline of belief in God and religious practice known as secularization involved the discovery of new sources of the *self*, which did not require divine legitimacy. The change in the way one positioned oneself toward God and the novel plurality of *the loci* of moral sources may be interpreted in terms of an epistemic shift, which inevitably involved changes in the ways of self-modeling and the available patterns of identity. Besides traditional theism, one might choose among atheism known as secular humanism, the ordered universe of Deism, and finally, the idea of the order of nature internalized by humans and calling for expression, which anticipated Romanticism. The dignity of rationality in Kant and Locke might still be of divine origin, yet the logic of Deism—insofar as we ourselves, as part of Providential order, have full access to it through our faculties—led to the formation of a disengaged subject standing "in a place already hollowed out for God; he takes a stance to the world which befits an image of the Deity."[105]

All in all, one may speak of two models of the *self* related to two forms of unbelief: the punctual, powerful, and controlling *self*, exemplified by the Lockean model, and the *self* expressive of a particular hidden nature, which is at once a moral source and manifests itself via some medium and with the support of the transmuting power of imagination.[106] The latter form, symptomatic of what Taylor calls "the expressivist turn," fed on the less typical areas of the complex intellectual landscape of Enlightenment, which were alternative to the core experience of Enlightenment being disenchantment of the mind and its rational fortification. Pascal and Montaigne, each in a different vein, opposed the enlightened anthropological optimism and advocated a "denial of self-transparency."[107] Needless to say, the skepticism of David Hume, who belonged to the line of the disillusioned ancient thinkers like Lucretius and Epicurus, questioned any idea of Providential order and the very existence of a unitary *self*. These alternative strains of thought conspired to the birth of a proto-romantic trend called by Taylor a *hybrid of naturalism with expressivism*, associated also with modern paganism. According to Goethe's audible voice "the ideal of expressive integrity fitted better with the "pagan" outlook of the ancients than with the transcendent aspirations of Christianity."[108]

The Canadian thinker points to certain nuances of the counter-Enlightenment movement to present it as part of the emancipatory effort yet representing a different "style." We read that the aim of the atheism of Epicurean-Lucretian type (as represented by Montaigne), was not—unlike radical Enlightenment—a far-reaching self-transformation but rather emancipation from the oppressive spiritual aspirations of Christianity. Behind the liberation in question stood the acknowledgment of the dignity of finitude, a kind of "*home-coming . . . a graceful acceptance of limited space . . . within which something can flower.*"[109] The poetics of the passages I deliberately choose to quote rather than to paraphrase renders the spirit of the disillusioned Enlightenment, dear also to later thinkers such as Wittgenstein and—at least partly—Santayana.

Leaving for now aside the variations of enlightened attitudes, eighteenth- and nineteenth-century mainstream culture brought about a profound change in the perception of one's own lifetime to the effect of the birth of a new, *self*-authored, disengaged *self*. Particular situations and real-life events filled the canvas of one's life story. The co-presence of a disengaged *self*/a witness/a narrator provided integrity to the narrative and the linear model of identity manifest in the rise of new literary forms such as the novel and autobiography. The model, by the way, from Rousseau and Goethe, through Dickens and Santayana, who was the author of a novel *Last Puritan* and a canonical autobiography *Persons and Places*, survived successfully up until today, only slightly influenced by modernist and post-modern genera. Phenomena like the rise of individualism, protection of privacy, articulation of feelings, and "craving for identity" conspired to replace older, more dependent models of selfhood.[110]

In the nineteenth century the idea of cosmic logos is overshadowed by that of nature resonating in us via our own lives and art, and accompanied by the growing attention to interiority and depth. This change is recognized by Taylor as a powerful countermovement against the mechanistic universe and the epistemological *self* of Enlightenment. Expressivism gives rise to yet another idea, one that will become the common denominator of both romantic and post-romantic (modern and post-modern) cultural patterns—namely that of *epiphany*. It involves an assumption that *human life and activity constitute a unique epiphanic dimension for otherwise intractable undercurrents of life and sense*. The idea reappears explicitly or tacitly in forms so diverse and even opposed to one another as modern subjectivism and *anti*-modernist movement, manifest in the well-known debate between the classics and the moderns in the United States. In expressivist terms, humans articulate their inner nature; in counter-expressivist ones, external energies resonate through humans. Even though some representatives of the latter trend such as E. Pound, T. S. Eliot, or (arguably) R. M. Rilke have declared anti-romantic, anti-subjectivist and apparently counter-epiphanic, they were deeply embedded in (if not defined by) what they opposed.

The proliferation of studies on interpretation and theories of symbol goes hand in hand with the spectacular career of the idea of creative imagination, the medium, the form. Thus, the link between the *self* and the world is reestablished on the basis of "new languages of personal resonance."[111] It is at once a response and an alternative to the instrumentalist self-alienation—a paradoxical situation typical of enlightened disengagement, where human *self* is disconnected from any thinkable natural endowment and gains an "ungrounded extra-worldly status of the objectifying subject."[112] The ghost of an isolated, unitary subject/ego is so powerful that it would haunt even late twentieth-century theories targeted against the existence of an ego (like that by Thomas Metzinger.)[113] A radical reaction against the isolated *self* emerges in the form of "post-Schopenhauerian" model, in which selves are overwhelmed by an uncontrollable, hostile dynamics or structure. We are following the footsteps of Nietzsche and his "rebellion against the standard form of modern anthropocentrism, along 'the tragic axis.'"[114] Nietzsche "had already explored this dizzying thought, that *self* might not enjoy a guaranteed, a priori unity."[115] Santayana believed that the *radical rejection of both Cartesian and Hegelian hegemonic visions unaccompanied by the rejection of their logic*, must have resulted in their paradoxical *reversal*, as exemplified by philosophies of will to power. He was not the only one to have similar intuitions. Adorno and Horkheimer thought in terms of the logic of vengeance when explaining how myth took its toll on the *self* of Enlightenment by reducing it to an empty place in a system. Since then a variety of reductive, depersonalizing, and dehumanizing tendencies—often at odds with one another—seem to have been infiltrating Western culture. What links contemporary thinkers like Foucault, Derrida, or Deleuze is their reluctance to the idea of the inner sources of the *self*. They present the *self* as an epiphenomenon of hidden and alien processes. However, while it is rather commonly agreed upon that the dominant post-Nietzschean trend in the theory of human *self* may be labeled as deconstructing the myth of interiority, Taylor uncovers that something is overlooked in this simplified view.

Even the so-called "dissolved" subjects do rely on some conception of expression, epiphany, or at least reflexivity. The modern subject, argues Taylor using a large spectrum of examples from twenetieth-century culture, is either the expressivist or post-expressivist subject, having some "depth," "correlative of the power of expressive self-articulation."[116] This is evident in the already mentioned debate between the moderns and the classics in America, where both sides were influenced by expressivist understanding of selfhood, the difference resting in the nature of the epiphany they recognized. One of the problems with modern subjectivism, as diagnosed by a number of cultural critics, involving Santayana and his critique of egotism, was severing the bonds with the world, resulting in, among others, an extreme objectification of subjectivity and the marginalization of lived experience. Taylor views the "subjectivist self-celebration"[117] in the work of Richard Rorty as attesting to the concerns of anti-subjectivists about the spiritual impoverishment of human life. The urge to recover the contact with the world and ourselves came from the awareness about the spiritual condition of "instrumentalist society" and the egotistic or *schismatic* heroes it generated, ones "*cut off from the world and hence grace.*"[118] Paradoxically as it may seem, the anti-subjectivist trend (the classics) is located within the epiphanic, post-romantic paradigm and can be viewed in terms of the Augustinian idea of the transfiguration of the *self*, which I interpreted as finding "an antidote" to the *self*, now enriched with "the modern sense of the place and power of creative imagination."[119] This, coming back to Goethe's remark about paganism being more conducive to expressivist spirit, is not at all irrelevant to the Christian idea of gifts, grace, and vocation.

Realists, naturalists, neo-classicists, imagists, and other intellectual and artistic circles associated with the so-called anti-subjectivist movement are often drawing on some form of the idea of the transforming power of imagination and epiphany. "Naturalist epiphany is also an epiphany transforming the real."[120] A nonreductive, subtle form of naturalism, particularly if inspired by Aristotle—and this happens to be Santayana's case—offers perhaps a more "fundamental" vision of epiphany than romantic visions do. So does Bergson's philosophy of life, Heidegger's peculiar phenomenology, or the hermeneutics of Ricoeur—all these forms of philosophical reflection try to restore the validity of subjective experience, yet they proceed in such a way that the connection with the world is at once reestablished. In order to achieve this goal they usually acknowledge some reality in itself, be it of ontological, hermeneutic, or ethical nature. Only on the basis of such an equilibrium can one hope to

> counter the imperial claims of an all-embracing mechanism, strengthened by the march of an advancing technology . . . [and] the instrumental world which offered to reduce even our sensations and feelings to its exceptionless laws. The obvious recourse against this all-pervasive leveling was *interiority*: that lived world, the world as experienced, known and transmuted in sensibility and consciousness, couldn't be assimilated to the supposedly all-encompassing machine. Bergson with his doctrine of the irreducibility of experience to external explanation, of *durèe* to the spatialized time of physical explanation, was the great source of liberation . . . And

the banner under which Husserl sailed, 'phenomenology,' has been appropriated for the distinct but parallel enterprises of Heidegger and Merleau-Ponty, while in quite different terms, similar revolutions in thought and sensibility have been inspired by the late writings of Wittgenstein, or have been attempted by Michael Polanyi.[121]

What justifies my ample references to Taylor's analysis is the fact that it sets the whole previously sketched problematic of selfhood in a cultural context and provides an incomparable thematic framework for any further discussion of Santayana's eclectic heritage. Interestingly, Santayana "as a phenomenon" seems to confirm Taylor's thesis. Santayana's anti-subjectivist declarations and his siding with the classics in the aforementioned debate should not overshadow his share in the modernist intellectual milieu and the expressivist and epiphanic strands in his thought. His idea of essences influenced poets and scholars, to mention only Wallace Stevens, who found in Santayana's work a life-long theoretic support for his conception of poetry as a way of life. The philosopher emerges out of some of the poet's writings and lectures "as the single illustration illuminating a whole complex of ideas essential to the understanding of Stevens himself."[122] Santayana's theories might have been inspiring for a number of the so-called objectivist visions of art. Early twentieth-century imagists, who allegedly formed a counter-epiphanic movement, were

> part of the refusal of the overlay of inauthentic meaning of the accretions of the instrumental society and the inauthentic . . . feelings it generated. To cleanse these and allow reality its full force, to retrieve genuine experience, it was necessary to return to *the surface of things*.[123]

Santayana's realm of essence with its liberating aspect provides an adequate conceptual back-up, even though it may seem—as David Dilworth recently claimed—to represent a "dangerous" form of nihilism.[124] Nietzsche, perhaps inspired by Winckelmann's studies on Greek art, once remarked—very much in the "spirit" of Santayana—"Oh, those Greeks! They knew how to live. What is required is to stop courageously at the surface" of things.[125] Taylor also evokes these words in reference to imagism, when he comments on "the Greeks who were deep enough to stay at the surface of things."[126] Still, this apparent rejection of too literal a sense of interiority may suggest a more subtle, *metaphorical detour towards interiority via objectivity*.

Anti-subjectivism, then, marks a specific style of reflexivity. From this perspective, the *decentering* of the subject, and even its dissolution, fits into the logic of self-annihilating subjectivism, but at the same time marks the first step toward regaining an objectively existing reality. This may not be an explicit conclusion of Taylor, but this is the way I interpret his (dialectical) interpretation of the modern guises of the *self*. As for Santayana, not only was he a life-long advocate of the idea of creative imagination as the prerogative of human dignity and the means of worldly salvation, but he also can be interpreted as synthesizing in his *oeuvre* the opposing tendencies of his era, while confirming Taylor's thesis about the dominant, post-romantic, reflexive thread uniting the apparently agonistic parties.

To sum up the discussion and bring together its parts, one may say that the power of anti-subjectivist ideas had its share in the emergence of the crucial distinctions between "ego"/"I," the subject, and the *self*. Also the idea of human freedom, previously narrowly understood, became broader and more nuanced. It makes sense to say that saving the notion of an integrated selfhood happens at the price of diminishing the aspirations of "ego" and subjectivity. Or—to put it more succinctly—*that regaining selfhood benefits from the suppression of egotism*. After Heidegger, selfhood may be conceived of in relational terms of care, as "a being who exists in a space of concerns,"[127] and Taylor may say that we are "are selves only in that certain issues matter to us."[128] Ricoeur says, for that matter, that "the *self* of autonomy can and must be preserved from contamination by any sort of egological thesis," with autonomy thinkable only in the context of heteronomy.[129] The *self* is hardly exhausted by first-person consciousness, linguistic self-reference, lasting identity, or memory. No matter which aspect we decide to articulate when discussing selfhood, in the background we are dealing with a temporal, dynamic, relational being, which—let us risk a suggestion—inexplicitly exhibits some "nature," the *locus* of which—let us risk further—is some reality *an sich*. Still, the *self*, "occurring" as part of the world, where it is balancing between autonomy and heteronomy, is irreducible to this reality. It entails becoming, acting and suffering, assuming identities and continuous self-positioning toward others and the world. Bergson's and Heidegger's efforts at winning back time for the subject made it plausible to place the *self* in the horizon of *a quest* in which "the future [is] to "redeem" the past."[130] It is the time of existence and hermeneia that individuate the *self* and not an extra-worldly position, which is not to say that a transcendental element is altogether excluded. It simply and decisively ceases to play the main part.

2

The Conception of the *Self* and Some Basic Concepts of Santayana's Philosophy[1]

> Wisdom lies in voluntary finitude.
>
> —Santayana, Realms of Being, 55

2.1 Psyche as "The Deeper Self"

Knowledge as a Wager

Let me start by establishing the meanings of the notions "psyche" and "spirit" as the point of departure. "Psyche" is a "mythical" term for a living organism in its aspect of an organizing principle of a single material life. As part of existential flux, psyche is material and dynamic, being a seat of "specific potentialities existing at specific places and times."[2] Psyche displays a relatively flexible pattern of change, a trope, or a blueprint, which provides boundaries for a single life to happen. "Spirit" is a more ambiguous term. In the context of hermeneutics of life, I assume it to denote the conscious *aspect* of life. Sometimes Santayana speaks of spirit in a broader sense of a naturally grounded, conscious *form* of life; elsewhere he simply equates spirit with consciousness or the first-person perspective.[3]

Any consideration of selfhood in Santayana must take into account the fact that a naturalistic and quasi-pragmatic philosophy of action precedes and—to some extent—determines the shape of his mature ontology. Consciousness is proper *only* to an embodied mind or a living body moving within a uniform field of action, being the field of existence. To be conscious is to be *out there*, "to-be-in-the-world," in a state of "wakefulness or attention . . . aroused . . . by the stress of life."[4] Consciousness begins with an immediate awareness, "wakefulness," psychic means of orientation in an environment and intelligent action. This is the predominant view in Santayana's major philosophical work—being also the exposition of his criticism targeted at skepticism and solipsistic idealism—*Skepticism and Animal Faith* (1923), where psyche, by means of spirit, becomes an effective agent in the field of action.

Along with the discernment of psyche and spirit, which I interpret as *two aspects of a dynamic, conscious life*, yet another conceptual distinction—that between *existence* and *essence*—is introduced and pronounced in Santayana's philosophy. This reformulation of the classical, metaphysical dualism allows for an ontological description of existence—otherwise defined as a spatiotemporal net of external relations—in terms of material embodiment/instantiation of essences. This formula supports Santayana's effort to save the very idea of consciousness from empirical and materialist reduction, which became common in his time. Despite the priority of the field of action perspective, one can still speak—particularly in the context of contemplation—of *pure* consciousness/spirit or *pure* intuition having as its object only an abstract *essence*. Technically speaking, exclusively essences—infinite in number, "timeless . . . self-identical forms of every degree of determination,"[5] may be direct objects of consciousness. Nevertheless, in the context of existence—and this is the context that interests us at this point—consciousness provides lived experience with an irreducible intrinsic *quality*. Material tensions and impulses are transmuted into intuitions, and, under the influence of psychic intent, elevated to the imaginative level, where they become symbolic of material reality, i.e., the flux of existence. Psyche's material transactions with the world are developed in the light of consciousness into the actual and immediately projected back onto existence, like a negative film is processed and developed into a positive photograph. The result of the synthesis is the projection of a phenomenal world, which carries hints regulating action.

In this context, the basic aim of knowledge, says Santayana, is "simply to recognize in a judgment the actual relation in which our living bodies stand to their environment."[6] Santayana generally tended to naturalize and later ontologize epistemology, even though—unlike pragmatists—he cared to save the idea of an absolute, objective truth. Nevertheless, Cartesian standards of knowledge seem here artificial and unnecessarily high, if not idolatrous. Knowledge of existence, an "urgent and perilous adventure,"[7] cannot and need not be literal. It is symbolic of the world and *transitive*, meant to be relevant to action and to inform about situations and relative facts. Objects of perception are known for their existential status in relation to ourselves, symbols merely mediate what "we know . . . by intent, based on bodily reaction."[8] While we gain orientation in the dynamic world, material events as such remain to some extent obscure.

> In the knowledge of fact there is instinctive conviction and expectation, animal faith, as well as intuition of essences; and this faith (which is readiness to use some intuitive category) while it plunges us into a sea of presumption, conjecture, error, and doubt, at the same time sets up an ideal of knowledge, transitive and realistic, in comparison with which intuition of essence, for all its infallibility, is a mockery. *We might almost say that sure knowledge, being immediate and intransitive, is not real knowledge, while real knowledge, being transitive and adventurous, is never sure.*[9]

Marked by error and mediated by symbols, "cognition" at a very basic level stands for a sort of uncertain acquaintance, a Pascalian wager laid by conscious existence. It is fueled by what Santayana calls *intent* and experientially verified *animal faith*—a condition *sine qua non* of sanity, a realistic belief that I encounter, register and recognize autonomous things in the world.[10] Both intent and animal faith cherish primacy in relation to *intuitions*, which are treated mainly instrumentally, serving as "clues to the physical world."[11] John Lachs summarizes it as follows: "the animal whose psyche gives rise to a series of conscious acts does not accept the essences intuited at face value, but habitually deputizes them to stand for and report the movement of ambient forces."[12] Conscious existence, then, reminds a fishing escapade into dark, dangerous waters.

At this point we may start assuming that a "minimal *self*" of a human being is a bodily, self-oriented in its environment, and self-projecting onto the field of action "*deeper self*, which is a living part of that world, existing only in contact with the rest, . . . immersed in the current of automatic events."[13] To borrow a helpful category from contemporary theories of selfhood, we may further risk saying, after Thomas Metzinger, that this still hardly reflective, closely interconnected with the environment *self*, involves *a sustained projection of a virtual model of its own dynamic, interactive being.*[14] By means of this "model," which transcends organic life onto a conscious and imaginative level, psyche may exercise its "retentive, imitative and inventive power" in action.[15] This naturalistic conception of a *deeper self* related to animal faith might be combined with a phenomenological version of an objectless, tacit, minimal self-awareness, which assures the sense of "me-ness" to every conscious experience.

The Skeptic's Revelation

The idea to naturalize and later to ontologize cognition and discuss it in terms of spontaneous hypothesis and risk-taking is related to the experiment with radical skepticism. To recapitulate it briefly, the so-called *solipsism of the present moment*, sometimes abbreviated as SOPM—this acronym will reappear in the study—is related to the Humean sort of test to which Santayana puts an honest epistemological skeptic. The Cartesian *Cogito* is not, according to the thinker, the ultimate claim of someone who "doubted whatever is not in principle beyond doubt."[16] A consistent questioning and dismissing of any belief which cannot be backed up by a rational proof must lead to the dismissal of all existential assumptions, including those about the existence and continuity of the world and of my own mind along with an "I." Thus, Santayana arrives at a sort of radical *epochè*—an ultimate skeptical position, which is limited to a bare "something now," reminiscent of Humean perceptive kernel. The conclusion is not only, as Sprigge notes, that a perfectly rational being cannot be but a *solipsist of the present moment*, but also that anyone who is *not* a solipsist—"and that includes all who speak to persuade"—"believes some things for which he can offer no properly rational ground."[17] We all rely, then, "on some irrational persuasion or prompting of life."[18]

In his next step, Santayana dismisses radical skepticism on pragmatic grounds and restores the "natural," moderately realistic attitude, which is one of *faith* as a mode of being making room for knowledge.[19] As long as we assume that knowledge is not literal, we may admit that "faith is Gnostic."[20] However, the honesty of radical skepticism, and the bare "something now" resulting out of the experiment, never ceased to "haunt" Santayana's thought and, as I believe, influenced the thinker's conception of human *self*, making it to some degree akin to the late Wittgenstein's agnosticism.[21] This sort of reliance on our most fundamental, habitual convictions, is, as Bielik-Robson notes, a trademark of an anti-Cartesian turn in modern reflection on subjectivity, from Hume, through Wittgenstein and Heidegger, to Foucault. Two typical notions appear in this kind of discourse—that of an (existential) "flux" and that of "trust/faith," which replaces "certainty."[22]

The irony of ignorance being fundamentally inscribed into knowledge, the inescapable agnosticism revealed by the experiment implies that conscious life is a wager sustained by the principle of psychic intent and faith, or, differently put, our mode of being exhibits "a fideistic basis on which all our transactions with the world are conducted."[23] In the same work, *Sketpicism and Animal Faith*, Santayana announces his quite famous "negative revelation"—namely—that "nothing given exists," whereby he puts a sort of *caesura* between the realm of appearance and that of material reality. While the object of consciousness is always an essence, the object of knowledge (and usually of perception)—is existence. This sort of "inverted" and naturalized Platonism resonates also in his mature ontology, which articulates the *otherness* of matter in relation to spirit, as well as in his thinking about subjective temporality—the so-called *sentimental time*—to the effect that he would, almost imperceptibly, switch in-between two ways of developing the acronym SOPM: "the solipsism of the *present* moment" and "the solipsism of the *past* moment."[24] Husserlian difference between the "now" of conscious acts and the temporality of "generation and perishing,"[25] mentioned in the first chapter, echoes here. *Thus, Santayana, having bracketed the classical Cartesian body-mind dualism, introduces a different kind of an ontological split or a difference into the heart of conscious life.* It has to do with temporality, and specifically, the share of eternity and ideality introduced by the idea of essences being the only immediate objects of spirit. The subtle change of "present" into "past" suggests that conscious life acquired for Santayana a certain shade of detachment—if not "otherworldliness." Technically, the principle governing the relation between material and mental events, between the latter and their subjective, synthetic, intuitive rendering, as well as the relation between intuition and knowledge, seem enigmatic. The idealistic tendency, quite unusual for a naturalist thinker, results later in the distinction of four autonomous realms of reality in his life's work—*Realms of Being*.

All this must have a bearing on the conception of the *self*. Taking seriously into account the declared by Santayana continuity inherent in his *oeuvre*, we may assume that the psychic agent, the *deeper self* implicit in his philosophy of action, turns into a more complex *self*, one which is "crossed" by autonomous, ontological planes of reality. Guided by a hermeneutic sort of intuition, I would suggest that the difference of registers turns out central for the *self*. An expectation is imposed upon the *self* that it somehow accounts for a *life-giving bridge, a passage* between the dynamics of existence and the continuity of conscious experience. The unifying function played by *animal faith* in respect to intent and intuition provides a pragmatic explanation in terms of an observable attitude and a principle of action, but perhaps it is not enough to account for the ontological and existential "structure" of selfhood, of which it is rather an expression, a manifestation, or a modality. The peculiarity of the experience of time, perhaps modestly influenced by Santayana's reading of Husserl and Heidegger, reveals the *aporias* of selfhood, as evident in fragmentary phenomenological descriptions of conscious experience contained in the unpublished essays and *Realms of Being*.

2.2 The First-Person Perspective: Traveling Now, Sentimental Time, and Migrating Ego

Here-and-Now

After exposing the naturalistic and quasi-pragmatic premises for the discussion of selfhood in Santayana, I pointed to the competing idealistic tendencies in his philosophy. Spiritual endowment in its intuitive and imaginative function constitutes a sort of transcendental unity of apperception—the Kantian idea adapted in a limited and naturalized form by Santayana to his own doctrine.[26] Intentional acts of the caring psyche are realized as intuitions due to the *epiphanic* aspect of consciousness, inherent in Santayana's conception of impotent spirit, which opens up a "space" where the world is disclosed. This aspect reminds us of the previously discussed Husserl's "self-luminosity" of conscious acts and the "width of presence." The "world" here, in contrast to the *flux* of existence mentioned previously, is understood as a phenomenal manifestation of adaptation, an ongoing attempt to interpret what is constantly delivered by the "encountering" activity of the psyche to the light of spirit.

Behind this world of subjective experience there is material reality, the intrinsic dynamics of which is recondite to pure consciousness but through human body and its environment constantly shapes, modifies, and affects the landscape of conscious experience. Care and expectation are principal psychic modalities. Psyche, anchored in the *flux*, is constantly open for "something" and fearful of "nothing." As poetically phrased by the thinker,

> a vague world is posited as existing; for in expectation and intent, as in memory and the sense of movement, there is a tacit expectation of things removed, threatening, as yet unknown. There is accordingly nothing pure in this sense of existence. . . . Care fills its heart as it does our dreams.[27]

As one may conclude from the fragmentary phenomenological descriptions of the first-person experience inscribed into a broader temporal landscape, moments of intuitive recognition, occurring in confrontation with memories and projections, are gathered around an "I" of a particular consciousness, and only through this "I" may become assimilated by what Santayana calls the psychic *deeper self*, as its own temporality. Once adopted, they serve as spatiotemporal reference points for the *self*, which from now on can articulate itself by "soon," "too late," "not yet," "long ago."[28] Both intuitions pointing adequately enough to a certain reality "beyond," and those being mere play of fantasy constitute the continuity of the imaginative texture of consciousness.

"Wherever it is, it is here; whenever it is, it is now,"[29] Santayana tells us about the specific temporal actuality of the spiritual vantage point. From the perspective of the spirit (which is exclusively and irreducibly the first-person perspective), with its Cartesian illusion of autonomy and transparence, it may even seem that the plurality of *here-and-nows*, or, in other words, a succession of intuitions, is enough to sustain the "I."[30] The *here-and-now* is indicated by Santayana as the very basic "mark" of the world- and self-referentiality of conscious experience. With memory and the intent of an enduring psyche in the background, the spirit, guided by attention, consists in identifications of the specificity of an intuition, putting a stamp on each moment as belonging to the time of subjective experience. Only on this condition of subjective temporality fed by memory and imagination can the relative world be established. A momentary recognition of a quality, a vision, a sensation, an idea, becomes a "revelation of a moment"[31] or "a possibility of being . . . of a moment."[32] But can one say that a succession of moments engenders an "I"?

Upon closer inspection, any *here-and-now* appears on the background of a different "now," one prolonged up to infinity, one which "leans rather towards the future . . . [and] forms a sort of wider now, the temporal landscape open to intuition,"[33] a field of attention called the *specious present*. The "I" "feels" itself a center of continuity within a beam of *traveling now*. The stretching "now" of *specious present* corresponds to psychic retentiveness and expectation, which is itself "keener than perception" and "engages the centre of the man."[34] To conceive of "I" as a flow of "moments" would be to picture it as a disembodied spirit, a *self* uprooted from its own existence. The idea of *here-and-now* serves rather to establish a sort of transcendental "setting" for intuitions. It accounts for the subjective unity of apperception, sustained by psychic intent, which is manifest in attention. Moreover, the *here-and-now* is central for conscious experience, which is always "my own." It introduces an aspect of *repetition*—a "familiar" framework, in which something new may appear. A reference point and a catalyst for the experience of time as past and future, it is a sign of the subjective *anchoring* in the world and of the fact of *embodiment*. The "now" becomes a requisite and reference point for a contextual and—as Santayana calls it—dramatic mode of being proper to humans. It serves as a *locus* meant to anchor the living *self* in time and in action. The initial *here-and-now* assertion, its "first cry," gains power of an immobilizing projection over nature, and grows into the "sublime *always* and the tragic *never*"[35]—signs of a "mature" *sentimental* temporality.

Sentimental Time

The field of attention described as "now" that is leaning toward the future, along with the sensation of the passage of time, hang on memory and intent, which in Santayana's vocabulary are psychic faculties. A spontaneously held linear idea of time reflects the movement of emerging and passing away, which describes the mode of being proper to the psyche, which is "retentive, full of survivals and preparations," and "full of potential."[36] The temporal landscape centered around an "I" or—perhaps—radiating *as* a subjective perspective of lived experience is what Santayana calls *sentimental time*. In other words, psyche via spirit synthesizes existential *flux* into a dimension of *sentimental time* and *pictorial space*, obeying the principle of distinction between past and future—the only way of representing the *flux* of which *she* is a part. The term *sentimental* conveys not only the sensation of pastness, but also the fact that this subjective temporality is inevitably saturated with emotions, as long as it belongs to an "I" of a certain caring psyche, in the context of which hardly anything is utterly meaningless and morally neutral.

The previously mentioned ontological split at the bottom of conscious experience manifests itself in the experience of time and may be counted as one of the *aporias* of the *self*. An illusionary spiritual "witness"—always present, actual, attentive, arising out of the imaginative field and apparently having no visible boundaries—is crossed by an irresistible awareness of time flowing, of all experience immediately becoming irrevocably past, and all projects being "not yet." The similarity between *sentimental time* and *ressentiment* may be accidental but it is still telling. Whatever "has been," or—as Nietzsche phrased it—"*t'was*," is more or less explicitly qualified and evaluated in a certain context and along the lines of psychic preferences, building up a specific experiential burden upon the reflective "I." The *crossing* of the two temporal modes—that of actuality and that of the future passing into non-being and leaving a residuum in memory—seems to rest at the core of the experience of the *self*.

The crossing beneath *here-and-now* reveals, on one hand, the transcendental dimension of the spiritual function of actualization and, on another hand, its natural grounding and empirical function of meeting the demands of locality and contextuality. In other words, the universal is confronted with or crossed by the singular and the concrete, timelessness of essences meets the material *flux*. Every intuition is already contaminated existentially. A sense of self-orientation and "having a world" conditions the ability to act, think, and express oneself in speaking. Santayana points to the function of the so-called "shifters," such as "here," "now," "this," "there," "I," as basic marks of finding oneself located within the *sentimental-pictorial* framework. Paul Ricoeur discusses the indicator "I" and the deictic terms "here" and "now" as fundamental in the "anchoring" of a speaking, acting and suffering subject.[37] In his polemic with analytical philosophy, the depsychologizing and linguistic context of which poses a paradox of the substitutionality of the "I" (while the very phenomenon of anchoring is to secure to the "I" a unique singularity), the thinker calls for "the utterers in flesh and blood, *their* experience of the world, *their* irreplaceable perspective."[38] The point is that, via *hic and nunc*, a "migrating" "I" should become an anchored "I," an "ego" assignable with a proper name of one's birth certificate. Then, the deictic "now" becomes "*dated now*," and "zero point here" becomes "*localized here*."[39]

In Santayana's account, the constant, dynamic undercurrent of psychic reality is present in the light of spirit as a "poetic version of the march of existence."[40] *Traveling now*, the first-person equivalent of *migrating ego*,[41] in each case marks its own conscious, actualizing "irruption" into existence through "now!," in which the actuality of the moment is revealed and immediately inscribed into the *sentimental perspective* circumscribing the field of action. Santayana describes the "now" as "the least sentimental term," which "marks the junction of fancy with action,"[42] the concept of "junction"—like that of "crossing"—being crucial for understanding the nature of the *self* in Santayana and the way it is "anchored."

Anchoring, claims Ricoeur, requires a sort of more fundamental reality, like that provided by "the absolutely irreducible signification of one's own body."[43] The body is of twofold nature—it counts at once as a fact/an object and as the organ of the "I," in accordance with the Husserlian distinction *Körper/Leib*. Consequently, we may distinguish in the condition of incarnation the (Husserlian) "sphere of ownness" and what I call in this book "the sphere of helplessness."

The requirement of a more fundamental reality, solving at once the problems of the formal emptiness of an "I" of designation, the relativity of "here-and-now," and the uprootedness of the Cartesian *Cogito*, is met within the framework of Santayana's naturalism and, more specifically, his conception of psyche, which provides a firm footing for the emergence of selfhood. To use the distinction proposed by Ricoeur, in Santayana's conception both terms of the dialectic *ipse* (sameness) and *idem* (selfhood) involve psyche in some of its aspects. To put it into Aristotelian categories, one may link the former to the first psychic *entelechy* and the latter to the second. Still, there remains the paradox of the body as a fact and as a subject, which is deepened by Santayana's materialism, which shares with any ontology using the notion of impersonal events, "in the sense of incidental occurrences," the tendency to dissociate action from an agent and the question "who?" from "what?" and "why?"[44] I will return to the issue of this dissociation later.

Coming back to the main topic of this section, the *sentimental* landscape on the whole is vague, obscure, day-dreaming, immersed in memories and fantastic projections. It tends to fall easy prey to habits of the mind, illusions, deception, fantastic projections of psyche's desires. To anticipate the comparison with Heidegger, it is worth noting that the specificity of *sentimental time* may evoke associations with the ecstatic mode of being of *Dasein* and the *vulgar/ordinary* conception of time based on *kairological* moments, whereby *Dasein* "makes present" the world and the *self* to itself in the so-called inauthentic mode. Heidegger says:

> The being there [*Da-sein*] which is being encountered has its own temporality, and this is something we are concerned about and attend to . . . : *as not yet, as to be . . . for the first time, as already, as approaching, as until now, as for the time being, as finally.* These may be designated as *kairological moments* of being-there [*Da-sein*]. It is only on the basis of this temporality that all the basic moments of time can be understood.[45]

The problem of inauthenticity involved in "making present" may be compared to the lateness and distortion typical of the state of spiritual distraction and the impact it has on *sentimental* time, which—leaving aside the fact that it is always "late" anyway—may be literally "dragging behind" existence, gathering an enormous amount of "spam," which distracts the spirit, jeopardizes sanity, and predetermines the nature of future by debilitating in some measure the ability to attune oneself intelligently to the demands and opportunities of time and place. This parallel is important insofar as it sheds light on the existential challenges involved in Santayana's conception of impotent spirit as the space where the world is subjectively revealed.

I will return to the question of possible parallels with Heidegger and Ricoeur, especially in the light of Aristotelian inspirations, later in this study. Now, with some support of John Lachs's canonical analysis, let us have a glance at Santayana's mature ontology and see what kind of conceptual setting it provides for the discussion of the nature of selfhood that has been developed up until this point.

2.3 Realms of Being and the *Aporias* of Selfhood

Ontology and the Self

Existence belongs, in Santayana's system, to the *realm of matter*—the dynamic *flux* of events with their primordial temporality. The realm of matter is the only plane of reality to which Santayana attributes power in the sense of causality. But it is not the only reality. "The blind thrust of matter embodies, 'existentializes' set after set of essence."[46] The *realm of essence* correlates with the *realm of spirit*, which replaced the "realm of consciousness" of Santayana's early works. In the light of spirit essences are actualized as intuitions and—on the ground of *psychic care* and *animal faith*—the reality of experience and action becomes crystallized into an intelligible, contextual, and organized world of things and situations.

The idea of existence as instantiation of essences justifies the emergence of spirit in nature. Otherwise reality would not exhibit any intelligible or observable aspect whatsoever and would not generate conscious beings. I agree with scholarly emphasis on the capital status of essence-existence distinction in Santayana's philosophy. Yet, I'm inclined to a view that the opposition between the two allows for a dynamic interplay or a dialectic under the condition that a third element—that of a conscious life/a psycho-spiritual unity—is introduced. Perhaps another conceptual pair—that of essence and matter—is more fundamental ontologically, yet both pairs are conceptual derivatives from the idea of dynamic existence understood as actualization of some possibilities.[47] Such a conception of existence legitimizes the three remaining, ideal realms—essences, spirit, and truth—but by no means implies that essences are some sort of "entities" building material reality. Neither are they Platonic ideas or forms in an Aristotelian sense, but rather, a source of all difference and necessary terms of determination or discernment applicable to reality. In temporal terms, Santayana sometimes speaks of *natural moments*[48] representing some determinate stages in the ever-changing material flux, the synthetic correlates of which he calls *moments of spirit*. One might speculate that from the viewpoint of Santayana's general strategy of justifying the very reality of consciousness, it makes even more sense to think of the fourth realm—the realm of truth—as the one which forms an opposition to and a counterpart at once with the realm of existence, in the sense that the latter refers to reality as dynamic and the former as eternal.

Those essences that are the immediate objects of our intuition are in fact "products" of the mind, triggered by psychic processes, not *the* essences actually instantiated in a "portion" of flux we are confronted with and intending at. Not only are the essences intuited merely indexes to those embodied in the flux, but, as if paradoxically, the ultimate object of knowledge and ordinary perception is existence, not essence. Epistemologically, this situation provokes a question about the possibility of knowledge, but this is not where Santayana's inquiry is directed. To use Heidegger's example, a conscious being in this vision *exists* in such a way that it always already *understands* the world of which it is part in a degree sufficient for intelligent action. Strictly speaking, the very notion of "object" applies exclusively to that of "pure spirit," while what Santayana calls "knowledge" has no proper "object," being rather a state of awareness and a mode of being. Finally, it is this being aware of the world of existence that furnishes the preponderance of our experience and not a stream of individual intuitions. John Lachs calls the thinker a "realist in the extreme" in that he nearly dissociates this "mediated object" of everyday consciousness (i.e., awareness) from mental acts as such.[49]

Leaving any in-depth inquiry into the nature of cognitive processes to neurobiology and other sciences,[50] and distrusting analytical philosophy in its fixation on language, Santayana is concerned rather with a general situation of a conscious being in the world, its sanity, the way it finds and experiences itself and the world, and its possible wellbeing. While a number of scholars—such as Timothy Sprigge, John Lachs, Angus Kerr-Lawson, and others—have addressed Santayana's ontology and philosophy of mind in a comprehensive way, my intention is to assume a new, hermeneutically oriented take on Santayana's general strategy with respect to its bearings on his conception of selfhood and philosophy of life. What seems most interesting and intriguing in Santayana's ontology from this perspective is that conscious being in the world involves a dialectic of absence and presence, of transcendence and immanence, for—as John Lachs notes—"intent deputizes an essence to stand for an existent," there is an "urge *to use what is present and presented for the representation of the absent . . . , and the changeless . . .—to yield knowledge of change.*"[51]

As for the general strategy, the introduction of an intelligible plane into the reality of conscious experience is typical of hermeneutically oriented philosophies, ones which draw a picture of human being as an interpreter of reality and of himself, if not—to phrase it more radically and probably more adequately in reference to Santayana, who (at least declaratively) avoided anthropocentrism—as *a "piece" of self-interpreting reality.* To conceive of essences as embodied or exemplified in existence is to *believe* that material reality exhibits an intelligible, qualitative dimension, which addresses conscious existence and which requires philosophical articulation, and, furthermore, it is to believe that there is an ultimate veridical standard—the truth—corresponding to this ideal dimension of reality.

All in all, Santayana's ontological distinctions allowed him to (1) endow reality with a dimension of intelligibility, (2) legitimize this ideal dimension with reference to objective truth as an ultimate standard and reference point for thinking and acting; (3) establish a margin of human freedom by delineating a sphere of spiritual life, where one may speak of the primacy of possibility in relation to fact and essence in relation to existence;[52] (4) transcend pragmatic orientation and enter another level of conscious functioning, where imagination for its own sake and disinterestedness are not only thinkable but valued; and—most importantly from the hermeneutic viewpoint—(5) inasmuch as essences in themselves do not "mean" anything, being pure realm of definiteness or difference, their share in reality represents a *cathartic, emancipatory and deconstructive potential, which may serve to "blast all . . . superstitions" and "ideolatry."*[53]

The distinction of the four ontological realms, then, makes Santayana's vision of conscious life legible for hermeneutic interpretation. At the same time, his nonreductive materialism, which grants to the realm of spirit an autonomy and reality in no way inferior to that of matter,[54] suggests inescapably an *aporetic* vision of selfhood. The first major *aporia*—the intrinsic temporal difference of registers—reflected in the phenomenology of time experience and the partial dissociation of pure consciousness from the dynamics of existence—has already been pointed out. The second one is the Cartesian illusion of spiritual independence reinforced by the ontological prerogatives of the spirit. To some extent it is a spontaneous and life-saving illusion, a default human conviction sustained by animal faith. But Santayana strips off its egotistic potential by the controversial idea of the impotence of spirit. Thus, on one hand the thinker emerges as a declared opponent of the Cartesian *egology*, and on another hand—a critic of the other extreme, the Nietzschean attack on the idea of consciousness as such. As a result, we seem to be left with a somewhat disquieting idea of an *autonomous yet impotent spirit*—conscious and "suffering" but powerless. This results, according to John Lachs, in a duality of self-experience—as "agent and [as] spectator."[55] Needless to say, the suggestion of this somewhat disturbing discontinuity appears in the previously discussed *solipsism of the present moment*. We have come across similar issues when discussing the lack of integrity within Kantian subject, Husserl's twofold structure of the body, and Ricoeur's double dimension of incarnation. Two questions, which will be addressed directly and indirectly throughout the following sections of this book, arise here: *To what extent and how can these* aporias *be explained?* And: *What do they tell about selfhood?*

Materialism as a Liberating Viewpoint: Toward a Hermeneutic Self

I have mentioned Paul Ricoeur's reservation toward any ontology of event as responsible for some disturbing dissociations undermining the idea of subjective agency. I noted that this problem perhaps might arise also in Santayana's philosophy, one which recognizes objectivist realm of material events and grants it generative primacy and causal exclusiveness. It might be reinforced by the doctrine of impotent spirit—one which costs Santayana perhaps more criticism than any other aspect of his thought.

In my reading the presence of an impersonal materialistic perspective belongs to Santayana's strategy—a strategy not uncommon since the beginning of the twentieth century—of weakening the egotistic, solipsistic, and too radically anthropocentric patterns of thinking about reality.[56] Its price is a split and a tension between a series of events, in terms of which any particular human being might be described, and a subject of experience, endowed with a unique sentimental landscape and able to narrate its own life story. *What we call "a person," exhibiting a certain character and entering into relations with others, "occurs" on the crossing of these two perspectives, and so—as I would suggest—does the self.* The twofoldness in question, evident also in Husserl's analysis of *self*, reappears under different guises throughout Santayana's philosophy and generates *aporias* like the tension between subjectivity and factuality, and—related to it—between the body as mine and as one of the bodies objectively existing. This involves recognition of an aspect of passivity within conscious experience, tractable already in Hume and Kant, and prominent in Husserl and Heidegger. The discovery of passivity and "lateness" inherent in human existence brings us directly to the existential requirement of the recognition of one's own finitude—perhaps the most vital question for Santayana. Let us also note that the *self*—in view of these discontinuities and gaps—emerges as increasingly enigmatic and earns the name of "the oddest one."[57] As mentioned previously, the distinction of the realm of spirit may be recognized as a means of avoiding the reduction of conscious life and, consequently, of human being, to objectively observable processes. Some scholars note that the fact that causality remains wedded to the realm of matter provokes doubts about human agency and free will. While an analytical approach—partly due to Santayana's loose vocabulary and his attachment to poetical, metaphorical language—may tend to radicalize these *aporias*, a hermeneutic perspective with some support of Aristotelian ontology—which I have employed in this study—helps to uncover the *self* as an integral agent.[58]

The *aporias* mentioned up to this point do not exhaust the problematic reality of selfhood in terms of its structure or experience, but reveal something about the relation of the *self* to the world. That there is a material reality, existing objectively and reflected in the realm of truth is a basic, realist assumption made by Santayana and admitted to be a tacit object of *faith*. Neither material reality as such nor the eternal, divine viewpoint of the realm of truth is indirectly accessible to subjective consciousness, which is constantly put to the test of "veracity" in the sense of successful interpretation of symbols, on which any individual life—also quite literally, in terms of life and death—depends. Such ontology discloses a finite and conscious being, finding itself *twice, as it were, in-between two abysses: that of existence and truth and that of matter and essence.*

This condition of blindness of a sort is conducive to what Santayana calls a perpetual spiritual distraction from the required "sane" equilibrium between letting the world be revealed in a possibly "true," free from distraction way, and the outgrown protective mechanism of "disfiguring" reality for the sake of "ego" and its phantasms. Moreover, when the "ego's" aspirations of ordering the world around it grow excessive, it becomes manipulative, distorts the reality, which it thinks to be at its service, and dominates selfhood, reducing otherness, which is implied in the intrinsically relational and inclusive idea of the *self*. This is an egotist subject, of whom Santayana, as a pluralist intending to prevent thinking from becoming subjectivist and totalitarian, is critical. Thinking aspires to wisdom, which requires constant education through experience, reflection, and confrontation with otherness in a variety of contexts. The aim is to acquire "the ability to detect arbitrariness in dogma and to appreciate perfection in alien contexts."[59]

There is a kind of humility in Santayana's philosophy attending to the idea of the recognition of human finitude as a condition for preserving sanity and living a good life. The quality and opaqueness of an individual *sentimental* landscape influences one's personal narrative and life's chances of arriving at fruition. Hence Santayana's emphasis on what he metaphorically calls "cleaning the windows of one's soul"—a spiritual catharsis, meant to relieve a "perpetually bothered self," to use Matthew C. Flamm's phrase, from the burden of parasitic influences and self-made phantasms.[60] *A thinkable equilibrium between the two extremes, a sort of a golden rule, would be to restrain the ego, which has been an explicit postulate of Santayana's philosophy, for the sake of a "broader," more "inclusive" self, the self which cannot escape representing psychic self-interest, but does so with respect to finitude and worldly reality (in Santayana's language—respect for "the authority of facts") on one hand, and the aptitude for disinterestedness and imaginative life on the other.*

Where, then, is the liberating potential suggested by the title? The specificity of Santayana's nonreductive materialism rests in that it "by no means implies that nothing "exists" save matter . . . [but rather that] matter is the only substance, power, or agency . . . not the only reality."[61] In his declaration of materialism one finds an absolutely crucial remark, namely that the material plane of reality is the only one dominated by the relations of power. From the fact that there are other, equally *real* ontological planes follows that not all the reality is determined by the relations of power. In other words—*reality is not exhausted by power*. Even if we agree there is something "ironic" about Santayana's ontology, it does not cease to imply at least that *conscious life is occurring partly on a plane which is potentially free from the domination of force, fact, necessity, and contingency alike* (!). Not only is a space of freedom grafted upon the contingent, material reality, but this space has its medium: essences. What is achieved thereby is the (imaginative) possibility of stripping each conscious experience down to self-identical essences of equal status—meaning a potential for novelty in thinking relying on the power of imagination. *This deconstruction having its obvious limits, essences do introduce a sort of a "fresh breeze" into the life of a caring human, a promise of an unending possibility of negotiation between the texture of one's own life and the world, of an unending novelty of experience, in other words—of constant revelation.* Santayana comments on it as follows: from the viewpoint of the "indispensable" faculty of imagination, which is "a principle a-priori"[62] of reason, and "the true realm of man's infinity . . . , behind the discovered there is the discoverable, beyond the actual, the possible."[63] Essences break open the factual context in which the *self* always finds itself immersed. As an ontological "decision," the distinction of essences may be interpreted also as serving the purpose of establishing a hermeneutic vision of a dynamic, relational *self*, which by means of imagination, on the one hand, expresses its own idiosyncrasy and, on the other, breaks with its individualistic seclusion and translates this idiosyncrasy into an intelligible, "universal self, the common and contagious element in all individuals," making communication possible.[64] The virtual infinity of the spiritual plane, being a psychic perfection, at once allows to exercise rationality in the service of life and fosters free play of spiritual life, be it in its artistic, religious, humanistic, or purely contemplative/mystical dimension. The recognition of this liberating spiritual autonomy was "forced" upon Santayana precisely by his materialism, as he declares in *Apologia pro Mente Sua*.

Still, not to go too far risking a naïve optimism and not to present Santayana in an alien light, the plane of spirit and that of truth never cease to be, each in a different sense, indebted to the generative power of matter. The focal point of interest from the viewpoint of our discussion of the *self* is the fact that psyche becomes self-conscious. The ideas of *psyche* and *entelechy*, inspired by Aristotle, seem decisive in our understanding of selfhood plausible within Santayana's thought. What I mean by this determination is that the *self* is best understood in the context of the transmutation of material processes into conscious activities, the translation of material impulses first—into the intelligible medium of essences, and second—into a knowledge symbolic of the world, which is both a field of action and an imaginative source of inspiration for spiritual life. This amounts to saying that the natural context for the *self* is one of a broadly understood hermeneia of life, which may be conceived of, for example, as a naturalist version of Charles Taylor's *expressivist model* described in the first chapter.

As we have suggested earlier, whatever kind of hermeneutic circularity may be deduced from Santayana's ontology and his symbolic idea of knowledge,[65] the emergence of the spirit may be first understood in the light of a caring psyche, who is the agent proper. Becoming one involves on her part establishing herself—by means of a hypostatic "I"—as a subject. *Thus, the "I"/"ego" appears to be psyche's proxy in the world of phenomena*. Via an "ego" the caring psyche may assume identities and have a sustained image and memory of herself. The *self* proper, as I propose, stands for a *triadic, temporal structure* of psyche-spirit-"I," or, alternatively, body-psyche-spirit.

In other words, one may speak of a psycho-spiritual unity with an irreducible first-person perspective. If so, any further determination of the nature of the *self* requires taking a closer look at Santayana's conception of psyche. Prior to doing that, it remains for us to conclude that while Santayana—arguably—may be interpreted as coming close to contemporary non-egological conceptions,[66] he decisively defends the reality of *self* as rooted in a caring, conscious life.

Psyche in Action

At the outset of this study we described Santayanan psyche as: a "mythical" term for a living organism in its aspect of an organizing rule for a single material life. Ontologically, as a part of existential flux, psyche involves materiality, but is not a substance. It may rather be described as a "mode of substance," "a set of embodied tropes" being "a relatively stable vortex in the universal flux."[67] From the definition of existence as a "passage from potentiality to act"[68] follows that psyche, as a part of the flux, is a seat of "specific potentialities existing at specific places and times."[69] Inspired by the analogous Aristotelian concept, psyche displays a relatively flexible pattern of change, a trope which provides boundaries for a single life to happen. From the viewpoint of the realm of truth, in turn, psyche may be described as a "system of vital events."[70]

Within the boundaries delineated by tropes, life is potentially free to possibilities, which may be realized as its approximations.[71] *The initial "blueprint" is so abstract from a human point of view, that it is right to say that its actualization in a concrete life is undetermined.*[72] Having in mind Timothy Sprigge's idea of a blueprint, I think it benefits from an additional perspective. The existential freedom a human being enjoys rests in the "how" of arriving at *the self* and concerns the process of the sublimation of impulses via realm of spirit, which, again, may be viewed through the lens of Aristotle's distinctions process-activity, and possibly *zoe-bios*. The latter, by way of digression, would prove inspiring in the late twentieth century and was made popular by Hannah Arendt, Michel Foucault, and later by Giorgio Agamben with his conception of *bare life*. Throughout this book I am referring to these contemporary reinterpretations of the Greek concepts. Following Santayana's reasoning, one may understand the relation of psyche to a natural living body as its first entelechy, and that of spirit to this body—as the second entelechy or "the psyche in act."[73] John Lachs, then, proposes that the relation of spirit to psyche is one of the actual to the potential. In this light, he notes, consciousness should be considered in terms of "flowering of human organic process . . . both an end product without further issue and an end in itself, and as such intrinsically valuable."[74] Thus, following Aristotle's reasoning, "psyche exists for the sake of spirit."[75] I think this interpretation is valid in Santayana but only to an extent. First, it may be said to represent the impersonal perspective of nature expressed in ontological terms, and second, spirituality indeed stands for a vital achievement, life's intrinsic value in no need of further justification. This is expressed in Santayana's inclination to speak of life in aesthetic terms, and pronounce the idea of cherishing essences, of stopping "at the surface of things." This, leaving aside the fact that one should be cautious of drawing sharp distinctions between the aesthetic and the moral in Santayana, by no means exhausts the perspective of selfhood. The issues of freedom and agency were for Santayana of equal concern. Having in mind the fact that in the context of Santayana's realms causality, literally understood, remains within the boundaries of material processes, a question arises: *What about agency and selfhood in the light of the crucial Aristotelian distinctions process-activity and zoe-bios?* Let us tackle these issues in the following section.

Narrative and Dramatic Strategies of Sustaining Self-Integrity

Let us consider yet another interpretive venue for the discussion of the problem of agency and freedom in Santayana scholarship, with the question of self-integrity in view.[76] We have looked at human *self* as having its origins in the psyche and transcending—by means of spirit—the boundary of a blind process to become a self-caring and self-referring life. The shift in-between two vital registers accounts for the emergence of intelligent action, which may be interpreted as life's overall strategy of sustaining self-integrity. Let me remind us that Santayana's intention is not "to discredit in thought what we rely on in practice" and despite all *aporias*, he holds a very "primordial" sense of action as a "physical but adaptive and sometimes intelligent interplay of the individual with his or her environment."[77] Agency, then, is ascribed not to a disembodied "ego" but to a psychic life, which is the center of potentialities and power, and which "has" a body continuous with the field of action. At the basic level of self-interpretation "I impute a nature to myself . . . no less definite than those belonging to the things I face." I believe in my power to act because of the continuity of my *self* with the existent reality and the access I have, through animal faith, to an objective world. Most importantly—it is "one's nature [that is] a permanent source of what one does."[78]

In its processual, mechanical dimension, *zoe* is no more than a series of material events following some natural pattern or a system of habits. Yet, in Santayana's scheme, we cannot speak of a human psyche prior to the emergence of activity, which is always conscious. It is so because the very notion of "psyche," as he explicitly claims, is "mythical." It concerns the aforementioned habits of matter not in their most fundamental sense of a blind thrust but in a dimension of some larger, intelligible "units," describable—to use Santayana's example—in terms of observable behavior or other regularities studied by psychology. As we already know, the spirit appears *only* on behalf of a life and it is only by means of spiritual mediation that the passage from material processes, described in terms of causality and contingence, to conscious activities, of which we may speak in teleological manner as having some motive and some aim, may take place. If one considers spirit in isolation, as "pure," then its activity is indeed an end in itself, while *mere* states of consciousness, as *pure* qualities, are powerless. How could a collection of intuitions be powerful? But the perspective of selfhood requires some idea of intelligent agency and it is met by the fact that ultimately Santayana locates the *self*, or, as he sometimes calls it, the *deeper self*, in the psyche, *making its actions consistent and continuous with its nature*.[79] Timothy Sprigge says:

> the psyches of human beings are their very *selves* . . . I am my psyche, and though I may in the last resort be a partly mythical entity, I can hardly therefore give up speaking of myself . . . The consciousness which arises from the state of my organism at any moment understands by the terms "I" and "You" . . . something deeper than any act or series of acts of consciousness, and something more recondite than the organism, in whose activities it manifests itself . . . The *self* is a thing of indefinite hidden potentialities.[80]

Agency, then, may be explained with reference to the adopted by Santayana Aristotelian idea of psyche as a seat of potentialities and existence as a passage from potentiality to act. As a living, distinguished part of existence, one *guided by its own principle*, including an element of self-preservation, human psyche—we should say—*not only acts but is involved in material causality*. As long as human action is said to be intelligent, human *self* acts in an intentional way and is—to some extent—aware of its actions. Mind you that a similar explanation of human *self* being the principle of own actions—as a psyche (physical aspect of a change) and as a *self* (its teleological aspect)—is what Paul Ricoeur postulated for a satisfactory idea of agency.[81] We will return to Ricoeur in a moment.

At this point we are close to Santayana's idea of personal freedom as closely related to self-integrity. As noted by Matthew C. Flamm, Santayana's conception of "vital liberty" was an alternative to the ideas of "vacant freedom" and the "liberty of indifference."[82] The former, according to Santayana, is "the moral illusion of free action without a definite impulse in an existing world,"[83] the latter stands for "human ability to choose this rather than that for no reason or motive."[84] Santayana would be also dissatisfied both with the abyssal freedom and imposed responsibility of Sartre with its sense of "a scary power to create the world on behalf of all humanity,"[85] and the pragmatic association of free will with morality, responsible for producing "a perpetually bothered self forced to conform . . . to contingent and practically relevant standards mistaken as ultimate ends."[86] All in all, Santayana defined his standpoint in opposition to what Flamm calls a "misattribution" turning "the mind into a magical instrument of profound creation."[87]

Reluctant toward the obscure knot of philosophical concepts and cultural dogmas inherent in these models, Santayana offered a "disillusioned" view, which entailed a weaker conception of freedom and a more humble understanding of agency. Will is psychic, it has material locus and belongs to the side of limitations. Now, by contrasting the burden of will with spirit's "affinity to the eternal," Flamm associates Santayana's conception of freedom mainly with a life that is thoroughly spiritual.[88] It is true that individual spirit is a *drop* or a *capsule* of freedom in nature, a spark of transcendence within immanence, which opens the way to *vita contemplativa*. Much as I agree with the scholarly emphasis on Santayana's advocacy of spiritual life, I am cautious of thinking that spiritual freedom exhausts the meaning of freedom implicit in Santayana's thought. As the reader has noted, I am attempting a more holistic interpretation within the framework of hermeneutics of life.

Having mentioned that the main strategy of sustaining self-integrity consists in intelligent action, action being a manifestation of thinking, I assume that it is thinking as such that delineates the sphere of freedom.[89] Mature Santayana found himself misunderstood in that his critics ascribed to him a view that thinking is impotent. He responded that "sensation, passion and thought are . . . efficacious materially in so far [sic] as they are material [!]"[90] It is true, according to Santayana, that a pure essence or a mere appearance "cannot determine existence."[91] Yet, the continuity and dialectic in discourse he called "physical,"[92] language and syntax-tropes "grafted upon wholly different, biological tropes,"[93] attention and logical reasoning—fundamentally material processes, rationality—a higher-order impulse aspiring to harmony. Thinking, then, in a basic sense, is an existential (and conscious) expression of a changing psychic status quo and the direction of psychic movement. All the underlying material tropes, finding their expression in thinking, are not irrelevant but represent the nature and interests of *this particular life*. Despite their plasticity, they are autonomous rather than heteronymous, one's own rather than foreign, even though autonomy definitely requires much more than just to be born and alive. Still, "to be free," says Santayana, "you must first be born and have some will in particular."[94] A chain of intuitions might be a sign of or an index to a change, in which a thinking animal, through its psychic agency, has its share, which entitles it to claim the status of an agent. The *self* spontaneously believes in the possibility of action because the source of action is its current psychic dynamics. Should we say, perhaps, metaphorically, that the *self insinuates* that it is free just as it tends to *insinuate* that things in the world are thus-and-so?

Decisions and choices enjoy a limited range of freedom, because they are expressive of psychic principle of selection, represented by will. It is typical of Santayana to believe that the narrower the range of choice faced, the freer the agent, for he has gained self-possession and self-knowledge. The *deeper self* or the psyche of a human being is not only the principle of change but also the principle of action. Obviously, spiritual perspective, with reflection and the free play of imagination, plays a vital corrective function in relation to any vital interest and principle, and it often prevails over a mere performance of this or that principle, establishing in fact a new principle. Thus, intelligent action, along with the degree of satisfaction it brings to the subject, may be recognized as a manifestation of self-integrity in the sense of self-mastery.

Coming back to Ricoeur, he speaks, in a similar vein, of "a principle [of action] that is a self, a self that is a principle."[95] This brings to the fore the issue of self-identification—what makes me identify as an agent in the first place is my *psychic self* as a carrier of potentialities, which call for realization on different levels of sophistication and sublimation.[96] The possible range of my self-identification is limited physically/spatiotemporally by my body, logically by my capacity to reason, historically by my past narrative, and socially by the narratives or scenarios that are available for me to share. Above all—it is limited by the scope and the synthetic power of my imagination and my vocabulary.

Ricoeur, in his extensive search for a unifying philosophical support for his idea of selfhood as inclusive of subjective agency, which is constantly undermined by analytical philosophy of action, refers to a number of standpoints, starting with Kant's third conflict of transcendental ideas. Natural causality, according to Kant, is not the only one; another sort of causality is observable in the realm of phenomena, where we act exercising our freedom. Another possible way of speaking about agency is to borrow Wittgenstein's idea that we should distinguish between two pairs, which belong to two separate *language games*: motivation-action and cause-event.[97] Yet, this dissociation of cause and action is too radical for Ricoeur, who cares about restoring some coherence here. Finally Aristotle's philosophy is recognized as most appropriate an answer to Ricoeur's question: *What ontology in view?* Not getting involved into the details of the study, I mean to highlight that by using the Aristotelian basic concepts of *energeia*, act, potentiality and *entelechy* as the bedrock of his theory, the thinker accounts for the self's freedom of will and its power to act in narrative terms. "By narrating a life of which I am not the author as to existence," says Ricoeur,

> I make myself its coauthor as to its meaning. Moreover, it is neither by chance nor by error that, in the opposite sense, so many Stoic philosophers interpreted life itself, life lived, as playing a role in a play we have not written and whose author, as a result, retreats outside of the role. These exchanges between the multiple sense of the term "author" and "authorship" contribute to the wealth of meaning of the very notion of agency.[98]

Coming back to Santayana, by trespassing the threshold between *zoe* and *bios* we are entering into a hermeneutic and dramatic realm or simply—the realm of plots.[99] Greek *bios*, from which stem words such as "biography" and "autobiography," in our context stands for a life that gives rise to a personal narrative and a drama—the main means of sustaining self-integrity. In Charles Taylor's poetic language—to evoke it once again in this book—the *self* here finds itself in the horizon of a "quest" in which "the future [is] to 'redeem' the past."[100] The idea of personal narrative conveys a specific kind of freedom closely connected to human mimetic and metaphorical capacity.

Unless we are committed to the Cartesian *fiat*, we may consent that psyche, being a principle of action, does convey a certain meaning of freedom—namely the freedom to be oneself, or the freedom of the *self* to exercise its deeper nature, corrected by Santayana's advocacy of self-limitation, his belief in the possibility of learning by experience, and the decisive influence self-knowledge and reflection may have on the experience and the course of one's life. Santayana seems to have been committed to a controversial equation of the idea of free will with the freedom of acting according to one's own nature. He calls it an

> intelligent freedom, such as appears in actions expressive of the ingrained bent of living creatures, actions adapted to the circumstances, and prophetic of the result which, if fortunate, they are likely to have. Such moral power of self-expression is possible only because that previous fatality . . . in the sense of absolutely groundless action [in matter], has already established particular psyches and initiated in them an effort towards specific kinds of perfection.[101]

This *positive formula of freedom*, by the way, resonates with the idea of *ars vivendi*, which I refer to in another part of this book.

As stated previously, freedom is possible only on the ground of a finite life and limitations. For Santayana, as I read him, freedom starts with external limitations and commences in voluntary ones. The burden of material constraints and will generates a situation of choice-making. The initial, psychic, and

> partial predetermination of life—which in man is especially imperfect, and dependent on the chances of education and experience—is the source of the generic; the general, absent from the realm of essence, is omnipresent in intent and action. Every living creature aims at and needs something generic, not anything in particular.[102]

While experience accrues and self-knowledge matures, needs and demands become specific. In this process of education, the disparity between capacities and demands leaves the psyche always partly unsatisfied.

> *Not this, not all this, not merely this*, says the psyche at every turn. Experience at the same time clarifies the instincts which it disappoints; and it is in terms of actual perceptions, expurgated or transformed, that secret ideals can first come to expression.[103]

Selfhood emerges out of these dialectical transactions of the psyche and the world, and finds fruition in the actual. The whole psychic history imprinted in her ways shapes her action. Psyche is intrinsically temporal and whatever she brings into experience, including the whole burden of the past, defines her and "the momentum and direction of her life at the [given] moment." In spirit the experience of the *self* in the world is revealed and qualified. The revelation, backed up by reflection, makes the whole difference in that it yields "unprecedented character to the sum of existence."[104]

At this point the function of the dramatic hermeneutics and the specificity of freedom it grants to a human *self* begin to be manifest. The specific, vital articulation of the actual, which crowns the material, reflects the enormous, complex effort of the psyche to find herself and assert herself in the world. Hermeneutics constitutes—in a sense—the "substance" of the dynamic *self*, which constructs, reflects upon, and reexamines meanings by a constant juxtaposition of the whole with its parts. Mind you that Santayana speaks of "*the sum of existence*," its synthetic vision. "Memory lights up perspectives which in nature can subsist only as dead relation between dead facts; and expectation, contradiction, doubt and surprise vivify" the whole.[105] An element of creativity is there and "[we] should never become poets in the end had we not been essentially poets from the beginning."[106] New experiences enforce the constant reconfiguration of the vistas of life—past and future—an activity supported by the strategies of attachment and detachment, from intelligent planning, through self-reflection, to the contemplation of pure essences. Santayana at the outset of his *magnum opus* declares himself an advocate of "the free life of mind."[107] He means the freedom from instrumentality and servility to power which give birth to spiritual misery. Salvation and rebirth start with a humble recognition of partial dependence, the recognition of actual possibilities and self-limitation, which—paradoxically—may result in "overcoming the world without doing it violence."[108] This strategy of sustaining self-integrity assumes the renunciation of power for the sake of gaining a different "power"—power of self-knowledge and self-possession. Free life of the mind requires mastering the art of pausing, waiting, using attention selectively, concentrating on the moment, switching in-between larger vistas, and—to use Michael Brodrick's words—"transcending means and ends."[109] All this is to avoid "idle escape from one error into another."[110] In a way similar to the ancient masters of the therapy of the soul, Santayana is interested in the quality of the life of the mind with an overall good life in view.

Attending to the quality of the life of the mind is an exercise in self-integrity and freedom. Despite the idea of disinterestedness inherent in this vision, it is far from being impractical or useless, as it brings about a far-reaching transformation of life. It is demanding and perhaps not attainable without knowledge of the *self*. How is this knowledge possible if, to quote Santayana, "the psyche remains a mystery in her intrinsic operations"?[111] Santayana advocates a practice which he calls "auscultation"—a medical term which I propose to translate into *everyday phenomenology of the psyche*—a careful, reflective tracing of psychic patterns as expressed in "verbal and dramatic conventions."[112]

> Not knowing what we are, we can at least discourse abundantly about our books, our words, and our social actions; and these manifestations of the psyche, though peripheral, are faithful enough witnesses to her nature.[113]

The results of *everyday phenomenology* are subject to correction and modification. This stage of criticism is described as follows,

> All the errors ever made about other things, if we understand their cause, enlighten us about ourselves; for the psyche is at once the spring of curiosity and the ground of refraction, selection, and distortion in our ideas. Summary reaction, symbolization, infection with relativity and subjective coloring begins in the senses and is continued in the passions; and if we succeed in removing, by criticism, this personal equation from our science of other things, the part withdrawn, which remains on our hands, is our indirect knowledge of the psyche.[114]

The twofold strategy of the *phenomenology and criticism of the psyche*, leading to self-knowledge, reminds of a task of deciphering a foreign language of material existence. Interestingly, in the passage quoted above, Santayana advocates applying the method of *hermeneutic phenomenology* upon *psychic hermeneutics*. We have a peculiar doubling here. Having performed a hermeneutic work on our very own psychic hermeneutic activity (which entails "summary reaction, symbolization, infection with relativity and subjective coloring"), we proceed to employ a phenomenological *epochè*, by detaching ourselves to a greatest possible degree from our own spontaneous experience of the world, to assess, from a distance, its specific subjective bent. The subject matter of our inquiry is nothing else than the form of our own finitude reflected in the specificity of the hermeneutic and mimetic activity of the psyche. Psychic trope, mutable but to some extent repetitive and predictable, is imprinted in the sum total of our reaction to the world and our appropriation of it. Santayana might have simply said—study your character—but his strategy is more subtle because he wants us to focus on ourselves not directly but indirectly—by way of a *detour*, via the world. He speaks of, to quote it again, "removing a personal equation from our science of things." *Equation* is a "statement of equality between two expressions consisting of variables and/or numbers. In essence, equations are questions."[115] We are looking for an invariable which defines our subjective bent and is the question mark symbolizing our finitude. This liberating hermeneia of life attests to the therapeutic benefit that an ontology like Santayana's—one which builds an "impossible" liaison between pragmatic orientation and elements from metaphysical tradition—bestows on human self-understanding. To understand for Santayana is

> pre-eminently to live, moving not by stimulation and external compulsion, but by inner direction and control. . . . Ideals . . . are possible forms of being . . . and he who . . . is able to embody them at least in part and for a season, has to that extent transfigured life, turning it from a fatal process into a liberal art.[116]

We strive to understand the pattern of our existence and probe its peripheries and boundaries for their plasticity, with the possibility of self-transformation in view. The intrinsic language of existence being unknown, the dramatic language of human world is under scrutiny. A narrative is nothing else than a meaningful rendering of a master trope of existence.

> The path of existence, will elude us if we are content to express it lyrically, by eliciting the intrinsic essences of its single moments; but it may be partly described dramatically, in epic tropes, in terms, which are formulae or types of sequence.[117]

To refer to Paul Ricoeur's categories, we discern the scenarios, the plots available for us to join. We recognize other patterns and configurations, involving other human selves, into which our *selves*, as certain configurations, may become involved. This is a hermeneutic and at once a dramatic strategy called by Ricoeur *emplotment*. Borrowed originally from Aristotle's *Poetics*, and set in the context of existence, emplotment involves reconfiguration within our own dramatic plot, a movement prompted by the reflection on the whole in juxtaposition to its episodes and in the light of new events. Assessing one's possible position in the configuration of stories allows for establishing what Ricoeur—in reference to Kant's idea—calls the "relatively first beginning with respect to the entire course of the world."[118] In other words, the beginning of our action "takes its place in a constellation of beginnings."[119] A human *self* is conceived of here as a piece of self-interpreting reality. This *self* presents a recognizable character, defined as "the self under the appearances of sameness."[120] It "has a history, which it has contracted [yet] what sedimentation has contracted, narration can redeploy."[121] Both literary and existential fictions "remain imaginative variations on an invariant, our corporeal condition experienced as the existential mediation between the self and the world."[122] The substance of this mediation is composed of narrative events, which have a peculiar effect of changing necessity into chance and chance into fate. A narrative creates a synthetic meaning by the price of annulling the natural contingency of events. Emplotment, inspired by Aristotelian categories of *mimesis* and *mythos*, is possible due to a crucial faculty of human imagination and language—namely—the faculty of *semantic innovation*, manifest in the ability to invent metaphors. Both metaphorical reference and mimetic function of emplotment, reminds Ricoeur, make sense in reference to the temporal realm of living and acting humans, as Aristotle explicitly noted in *Poetics*.[123]

How is emplotment thinkable on the ground of Santayana's ontology? Precisely by way of psychic phenomenology and criticism, by tracing and reflecting upon the regularities expressive of tropes meant to enhance our understanding of the share we, as *selves*, can afford within the observable dynamics. "The fundamental contingency of existence," asserts Santayana, coexists with "intelligent freedom, such as appears in actions expressive of the ingrained bent." Then, "at whatever point we call a halt in our backward survey of history, we find extant some arbitrary state of things, determining the forms which intelligent action shall then assume."[124] This clearly seems to correspond to Ricoeur's "relatively first beginnings."

Looking at the dynamics of selfhood which one may elicit from Santayana's *oeuvre*, one may also speculate—somewhat in the vein of poststructural reflection—that this *self* may exercise its integrity and intelligence by means of the principle of infinite qualitative difference, ensured by the realm of essences and the phenomenon of repetition occurring in nature, including psyche. The mind is where both are synthesized by means of images, symbols, and concepts:

> [H]abits and passions of each creature . . . are the principles of reiteration; they involve repetitions in action, and they find and use repetition in nature, answering to their own precision in form. Organisms are instruments of repetition; and they rely in their existence and prosperity, on the repetition of opportunities for the repetition of their acts. Were this reliance not justified, or this mechanism unstable, there could be no life, no experience, or act in the world.[125]

To conclude this part of our reflection, let me say that the synthetic and deconstructive capacity of the spirit along with the synoptic capacity of the psyche, which maintain the realm of sentimental time and pictorial space, collaborate, by means of different metaphorical and mimetic strategies, to sustain vital self-integrity. They collaborate under the aegis of the hermeneutic principle pars pro toto. Santayana, with his lifelong emphasis on creative imagination, metaphor, and poetry, was keenly aware of their importance as dramaturgical and narrative tactics belonging to the strategy of sustaining self-integrity.

Becoming oneself inescapably involves bearing witness to "my [own] fatal character—or my fatal acts, making irruption from moment to moment into my character."[126] The point is to overcome the viewpoint of fatality. In line with Ricoeur, Santayana claims that only by understanding life can we become its authors. The sort freedom is hermeneutic in nature and dramatic in style. Santayana's realms add a sense of ontological profoundness to this hermeneia of life. The vertical temporality of the spirit breaks into the horizon of daily existence offering a chance for every moment to become a new beginning. Thus, existence can be redeemed from the mechanical repetition of *zoe*. This earthly redemption relies on the undetermined relation between the flux of events and their interpretation, and draws on a partial irrelevance and redundancy of the human trope as seen from the perspective of nature.

> Life at our level has adopted a vehicle which—like all natural vehicles—has a form and a story of its own, apart from the inherited movement which it serves to propagate. The individual . . . has become a redundant trope, surrounding that other with epicycles and arabesques and prolongations useless to the march of transmissible life, yet enriching it at its several stations.[127]

3

The Hermeneutics of Human *Self*

3.1 Endurance and Narrative: A Twofold Individuation

Let us consider for a moment the following question: *What counts as principio individuationis in respect to the human self in this vision?* The hermeneutic context employed by us so far allows us to notice a certain twofoldness of individuation, emerging in the light of Santayana's non-reductive materialism and his conception of psyche. The *hermeneia* of life—interpretation and self-narration—which involves assuming identities, seems to be crossed at its core by an ongoing passage from potentiality to act, which maps the psychic *blueprint* and is manifest in a vortex of objective occurrences in time and space, which, in turn, may be said to form a *trope* unique for a concrete human being.

To evoke Ricoeur's helpful concepts once again, the latter may be linked to *ipse* (sameness), and the former to *idem* (selfhood), both being terms of the dialectical dynamics of the *self*. Psychic temporal endurance manifests itself in the presence of *my body* and at once in *my character*, a set of more or less persistent dispositions and traits recognizable for others as this or that *person*. The (horizontal) time of individuated endurance is intertwined with or centrally crossed by my (vertical) sentimental, narrative projection, where I experience and think of myself as *self* and as another at once. In this dimension I am the co-author of myself, constantly in the making, interacting with others and striving to coin my *body* into a *flesh*, to diminish my *sphere of helplessness*, accordingly to what Santayana says of the "flesh as a power that liberates us from the flesh as obsession [body]."[1]

We might stop at noticing this twofoldness of the individuation of human *self*—it seems satisfactory for our purpose. Yet, Santayana's ontology provokes us to probe deeper. Let us risk, then, an intellectual exercise and see what else we can deduce about human *self* from the four realms of being, without promising any definite answer. "Pure" matter as potentiality, the genesis of all change and hence of life, is unfathomable and cannot be given. Merely "an object of belief,"[2] it is exempt even from the realm of truth, which reflects events in their individuality, not their "material other."[3] The occurrence of life ontologically means a manifestation of a trope/system of tropes via a psyche in her mode of being named by Aristotle *enetelechia*. Psyche herself, as a principle, is not the best candidate for an exclusive individuating factor. It is rather the concrete, singular trope that is of interest. The obscure "thisness"—to employ loosely a handy medieval term here—rests in the occurrence of the trope not in the trope itself, or, in other words, in "that it occurred" in the first place and not merely "what occurred." The trope does indeed carry within itself the reminder of the fact *that* it occurred, that it has a certain *there-and-then*, which is its trace of potentiality and a residuum of sort. It did not escape the attention of Aristotle who cared to conceptualize it as *upokeimeno eschaton*. Perhaps Santayana gives us some more hints saying that "definition whether sensual or verbal does not individuate: that which individuates is a contingent position of a neutral entity in a chain of material events. . . . In beginning to exist it ceases to be neutral."[4] What individuates a human being in the most fundamental sense, then, is the occurrence of a psychic trope in all its complexity and with all its mutations. The evidence of this individuation is the first psychic *entelechia*—a living human body. But this is not where individuation ends, for Santayana speaks also of spiritual individuation which "from being passive and imputed here becomes positive and self-assured."[5] In other words, subjective consciousness adds a new dimension to individuation, one which involves freedom of interpretation and allows for communicating the other plane of individuation in meaningful and self-asserting terms of acting and suffering (suffering as symptomatic of the element of passivity, an indispensable part of selfhood).

Now, if we look at human life as a whole, individuation may seem to fall short of existence. Nathan A. Scott, Jr., for instance, thinks of *haecceitas* in Santayana's rendering as ascribable mainly to an essence, as determining "that radical particularity" in respect to "the given *Gestalt*," the "indelible impression . . . that a particular chunk of reality, scores upon the mind."[6] What Scott has in mind, however, is the way the world is being individuated for us spiritually. He grasps the particular aspect of Santayana's philosophy that made it inspiring for at least a couple of major American poets.

What about existence, then? The trace of it is contained in the trope. An event is a sequence of natural moments and a realization of a trope, which is a pattern of change. Human life may be said to constitute such a complex event being the realization of a complex trope *mythically* referred to as "psyche." "The chain of events," from Santayana's definition, involves existence and truth. In the case of human life, the unique "thisness" of its occurrence might be pointed at *post-mortem*, by evoking one's name accompanied by the dates of birth and death. From the point of view of existence this particular birth and death are unrepeatable and as events most radically *individualize* the life of a human being by bracketing the *history of individuation*, which involved the hermeneutic movement of the *self* conveyable for example by an autobiography. Ideally, the same essential individuality might be repeated in a course of other lifetimes, but factually, *this* material life and *the* lived experience of *this* life occurs *irrevocably and only once*.

The two-dimensional individuation of a human *self*, taking into account human finitude and assuming the autonomy of spirit, makes sense in the context of life. It respects both *zoe* and *bios*, leaving room for the freedom involved in the hermeneutic movement of sustaining selfhood. Both dimensions of the actualization of a given psychic trope structure the proper dynamics of the *self*, *this* human *self*, which—by way of a *detour*—seems to be binding the two planes together within one life. One may speak of a dialectic of sorts, which contains three moments of selfhood: event, identity, and life.

Furthermore, this account of individuation makes for such a complexity within a singularity, that there is a sphere where the generative priority of matter does not translate into the priority of existence over essence. Hermeneutic individualization allows for the reversal of this relation, although not in a straightforward or definite manner. The force of event never ceases to impose itself upon consciousness, but imagination may be a decisive factor in the determination of the essence-existence relation. It is true that the *self* is always confronted with *some* facts but it has some freedom in the way it appropriates them into its history. This is the right moment to evoke again the liberating impact of materialism mentioned by Santayana. His realist recognition of objective and in themselves meaningless (but potentially intelligible) events independent of any mind, opens a spectrum of hermeneutic freedom for the *self*. *The ability to isolate, name, and then to reconfigure and rename the patterns of existence, which furnish the scenario of the drama of life, means freedom to weave the cloth of one's biography on the psychic warp.* This freedom, quite obviously has its limits, but "absolute freedom" for Santayana was clearly an oxymoron. Let me quote a parable which throws light on the existence-essence interplay. They are two registers, which are never continuous, but

> may be simultaneous dimensions of the same world. . . . The eternal self-identity of every essence is therefore a condition for the possibility of change; and complete as the realm of essence is in its ideal infinity, and unaffected there by the evolution of things, yet it is intimately interwoven, by its very eternity, with this perpetual mutation. Allowing matter a dynamic priority (matter and not essence being the seat and principle of genesis) we might describe in a myth the temporal discovery of eternity. Becoming, we might say, in the fierce struggle to generate he knew not what, begat Difference; and Difference, once born, astonished its parent by growing into a great swarm of Differences, until it exhibited all possible differences . . . [-] the whole realm of essence. . . . Becoming, who was a brisk bold lusty Daemon, . . . painful as it was for him to see any truth whatever, . . . couldn't help suspecting that he lived and moved only through ignorance, not being able to maintain the limitations of any moment nor to escape the limitations of the next, like a dancing Dervish that must lift one foot and then the other from the burning coals. It is by its very ideality, non-existence, and eternity, then, that essence is inwardly linked with existence, not by being an extension or a portion of that which exists.[7]

The essence-existence interplay, involving time and timelessness, rests at the heart of conscious life and, hence, of the dynamic *self*. Coming back to the *solipsism of the present moment*, in the context of our discussion, we may interpret it as a sort of revelation of the existential void in consciousness. This void, reached by means of a radical *epochè*, reveals also that there is an aspect of selfhood that transcends physical time—a blessing and a curse at once—one might be tempted to say. This recognition of human "blindness" to one's own existential core speaks volumes about Santayana's conception of *the self* and his granting to *animal faith* the role of a pillar of human life.

The question of human individuation in the light of the tensions existence-essence and matter-spirit is a very complex one and hardly yields itself to a definite interpretation. By inviting the reader into this quasi-scholastic discussion, I hoped modestly to bring to the light *an unspoken aspect of human life*, which seems to be, in a sense, decisive. To refer to the previously quoted parable, what I mean is that human being is a being, who—as a result of his blindness to his own becoming (the impenetrability of existence)—thrives on Differences begat by this becoming. Let me conclude by saying that *Santayana's anthropology involves the idea that human being is a being that does not remember his own beginning and won't be able to experience his own death, because at birth and at the moment of death he becomes equal with the event and hence—unconscious.*[8] *To be born is to be cut off from the material event, to live is to constantly transcend the event, and to die is to become equal with it. Hence, life for Santayana involves—if not stands metaphorically for—transcendence*, and the prominence of spiritual life, which is intrinsically transcendent in the sense of partaking in the timeless realm, is promoted to the capital "L" Life. There is one single birth and one unique death neither of which can be said to be "experienced" but both "irrupt" into existence and frame a horizon for an unsubstantial, self-interpreting *self* that is constantly transcending existence, which, in turn, each and every time reminds the spirit of its finite genesis.

The conception of life containing an element of impenetrability or resistance to consciousness brings to the fore the whole issue of finitude, which I consider key in Santayana's philosophy and which I will discuss in one of the following chapters. The emphasis on finitude goes hand in hand with Santayana's naturalistic, pluralistic individualism, variegated with an idealistic build-up.

There is yet another element of interest emerging from our analysis. It belongs to Santayana's Gnostic sympathies, which he sometimes declared. I mean the aforementioned impenetrability of matter and its foreign, radically alien status in relation to conscious life. This aspect of Santayana's thought provokes a comparison with another thinker of the time, namely—Henri Bergson. We shall attempt such a comparison in the following, fourth chapter. For now let us continue for a while our reflection on selfhood.

3.2 Hermeneutic *Self* as a Unifying Concept

Psyche as the Principle of Selection and the (In)efficacy of Thinking

Psychic *deeper self* triggers its proxy "ego" and in the spiritual space, via the medium of essences, receives, due to the faculty of imagination, the picture of itself in the phenomenal world, symbolically representing material reality. Thus, psyche is endowed with an "ego" "acting" on its behalf in the world of phenomena, which "uncover" the stage of action. The "I," then, a self-referential core of this interpretative context, forms an object of animal faith and as such is part of the knowledge of the world. It may think of itself as an existing entity but it is rather a hypostatic nucleus of the hermeneutic activity having its ground in the psyche. Within a synthetic vision of a temporal stretch, a current situation is assessed in juxtaposition with memory and prediction, allowing for the projections of the future. Preferences are shaped in response to the principle of selection resting in the psyche, in confrontation with the world, which offers a shared, symbolic field, providing occasions and criteria for evaluation of things and situations. Choices and decisions are manifestations of the confrontation of the undercurrent process of life with the world. Psychic needs, at the outset generic, in the course of lived experience become specific and sophisticated. The broader and more diversified the symbolic field at the *self's* disposal, and the more vivid the work of imagination, the greater the spectra of choice and vistas of self-realization, and the greater the demand for self-knowledge. While the latter increases, the dependence on one's impulses and habits, or—to use Mari Ruti's phrase—on one's "affective trajectory," is diminished.[9] *Thus, the fatality of mechanical repetition is increasingly neutralized.*

Psychic selectivity is realized via thinking, which basically refers to the capacity of the psychic *deeper self* to relate, adapt to and interact with the world be means of constant negotiations between what it finds already "in itself" and "out there." Pragmatically, the key hermeneutical concept of *understanding* begins with finding oneself as contextual, and "what a process of understanding reveals to us . . . is not an accomplished fact, but a possibility, a dramatic figment," meaning a situation, an occasion to act.[10] Reflection and self-knowledge would be utterly irrelevant if it weren't for the principle of selectivity which, in Santayana's vocabulary, here influenced by Aristotle, is attributed to the psyche. The interpretative activity is taking place in the horizon of the constantly receding unfamiliarity of the world. Language, memory, knowledge, and habit provide for the so-called pre-understanding, so the quality of a new experience always depends, on one hand, on the previous potential for understanding, and on the other the potential semantic innovation.

According to my reading, Santayana's point of departure is always a dynamic unity and whatever is said to lack efficacy, like "impotent spirit," acquires a function in the context of this whole. Thus, the triadic existential dynamics involving psyche, "I," and spirit, which I elsewhere identified as event, identity, and life, or—alternatively—body, psyche, and spirit, constitutes the *self*, and may also be described as the movement of life itself, which is self-representing with the support of spiritual realm, against the horizon of which it obtains its self-image, the "I," incorporated into the image of the world. As for the debate in Santayana studies concerning the controversial impotence of spirit, having assumed the unity I propose here, we see no contradiction between the impotence of spirit, which is its modality of being, and its *activating* role in the process of life, as long as we notice that spirit is an inseparable aspect of this life.

Thinking, as part of life, is no less material than spiritual. I am repeatedly articulating the efficacy of thinking, partly against Santayana himself, who—quite misleadingly—occasionally spoke of its inefficacy, while having in mind an isolated idea of mind *as* pure consciousness.[11] However, in an attempt to disambiguate his idea of impotent spirit, misread by those who translated it into a sort of "impotence of thinking," late Santayana replies—as mentioned previously—that thinking is potent insofar it is material. This confirms the validity of our holistic approach inspired by the concepts of life and interpretation, where spirit is an aspect, an enriching/perfecting dimension of a *single* process, and where the idea of spiritual impotence serves to emphasize the fact that human life is not reducible to a single dimension—the dimension of power.[12]

By way of digression, to borrow from the language of contemporary philosophy of mind—which seems relevant in the case of Santayana's nonreductive naturalism—we may refer to the widely accepted distinction between phenomenal and access consciousness, first proposed by Ned Block. Phenomenal consciousness (p-consciousness) denotes subjective, experiential dimension, or "what-it-is-like" aspect, and access consciousness (a-consciousness) is functionally definable, usually in terms of the flow of information needed for reasoning, acting, and reporting. Only the former type of consciousness has to do with *qualia*.[13] There are different interpretive possibilities concerning this distinction, one of them being—as Owen Flanagan shows—that it supports some sort of epiphenomenal view by ascribing lack of causality (although not uselessness) to p-consciousness. An experiment with blindsighted persons[14] is believed to prove that

> consciousness-p module feeds the executive system responsible for issuing high-quality reports and sensibly guiding actions . . . According to this model, it is *not* the absence of consciousness p that *directly* causes poor performance or its presence that *directly* causes good performance. Good performance depends on whether or not information gets into the executive system, and it gets into the executive system only if it goes through the consciousness-p module. The absence of

> consciousness p is an indication that the executive is not able to play its . . . role, and the presence of consciousness p is an indication that it is able to play" it.[15]

This is the interpretation favored by the author of the distinction between consciousness "a" and "p." When speaking of impotent spirit as consciousness, Santayana probably means what is meant by phenomenal consciousness, namely the quality of subjective experience. One finds no "access consciousness" in his dictionary, but his naturalist conception of thinking extends far beyond spirit to organic/neural processes. What is called "access consciousness" in Santayana's account (although not in his vocabulary) seems to belong to psychic life and be manifest in behavior, which may be subject to empirical study. This is in accordance with some contemporary epiphenomenal interpretations of a-consciousness. Most interestingly for this study, there appears the so-called "authorship sensation/emotion"—the "illusion" of a free, conscious will.[16]

Returning to p-consciousness, one might compare Santayana's "essences" to *qualia*. Jessica Wahman's research goes in this direction. Thinking process is basically an organic one and the conscious awareness "gives us no direct access to the powers that generate it."[17] Reductive materialism relies fully on highly mediated results of scientific observation, the overwhelming spell of which denies ontological reality to subjective qualities of experience, while their language is too flat to grant them another sort of reality. In contrast to this position, Santayana's subtle semantic differentiation of the verb "is" allows for preventing the reduction of consciousness to brain processes, without giving up the materialist premises of his naturalistic position.

> To describe or explain a fact is to situate it within a specific disciplinary context according to a given mode of discourse. We may accept that there is one natural event—as do both the materialist and the non-reductive naturalist—but deny that one form of discourse can fully capture the issues involved with the mind-body problem.[18]

Some current scholarly disagreements might benefit from Santayana's vocabulary insofar as their points of disagreement are rooted in different understanding of identity (and the verb "is"), most notably their confusing of what Santayana described as "is" of *derivation* with "is" of *identity*. Materialists, for instance, tend to understand the claim that "consciousness is not a brain state" as synonymous with ascribing to it a supernatural status. "They confuse the denial that consciousness is *identical* to brain activity with the denial that consciousness *is derived from* brain activity."[19]

Once we have brought into focus the question of the role of language in some reductionist confusion, let me refer to yet another contemporary figure whose standpoint has some relevance to our discussion and to Santayana's position—namely John Searle. Actually, a number of thinkers of some sort of materialist orientation such as David Chalmers, Thomas Nagel, and Peter Engel stress the need to distinguish carefully between causal and ontological reduction and to avoid the latter. This—to stress it again—not only requires a refined vocabulary but implies a decision of sorts. To quote Searle once again, when speaking about recognizing mental events, "we are looking for a *decision*, not for a discovery."[20] In this light, Santayana's emphasis on spirit's specific autonomy is precisely such a decision of serious implications for his anthropology and the vision of the *self*.

I am leaving this digression inconclusive. As previously mentioned, Santayana's language is not disciplined and technical enough to be the ground for any decisive commitment as to his allegiance to any particular school of contemporary philosophy of mind, yet his participation in the naturalistic tradition of nonreductive sort makes the discussion relevant. To return now to the main context of our analysis, thinking for Santayana is existential as long as it is based on tacit assumptions of *animal faith*, which are instinctive, and "in which active impulse is redirected by reflection and judgment."[21] Movement of attention and logic involves transition and suggests that "an existential and moving factor is at work, namely attention, and whatever may be [its] basis or organ."[22] This "organ" is psyche, whose mode of being is intent defined by Santayana as "a sort of projection through faith, positing a relation of which only one term is given . . . [plus] a sense of direction indicating what and where the other term ought to be."[23] Thinking is a psycho-spiritual, interpretive way of exercising psychic power and expressing its nature. "The application of its [psychic] powers itself is selective, designed to protect and promote its interests. The psyche is a directed charge of energy."[24] The ability to isolate, identify, and recognize existing material regularities is the main function of thinking and the hermeneutics of the *self* is to some degree material.

Material events behind the phenomenal world may remain unaffected by mere essences, but they are affected by one another, which must be reflected in consciousness, provided that man is attentive and has mastered intelligent action, which is attested to by the ability to predict future events. "Every mental development," we read, "has some material significance, since it cannot help being an index to its material ground."²⁵ The word "some" is telling, for there is no single, predetermined way of translation. Translation depends on the sociocultural context, the vocabulary and imagery one possesses, and the way one uses one's attention. These factors, decisive for the possibility of a good life, seem to be among the stakes of Santayana's dramatic hermeneutics and his *contemplative vitalism*—an alternative term I propose for naming his nonreductive naturalism.

Contemplative Vitalism and the Diversification of Lifetime

As I have repeatedly stressed in a variety of contexts, the *self* emerging from Santayana's *oeuvre* draws on the distinctions between psyche and spirit, and between daily existence and spiritual life, insofar as these suggest a need for a unifying translation in-between different dimensions of reality and planes of experience. The scope of the *self* extends beyond the imaginative life of the mind and reaches its hidden genesis—a radically idiosyncratic life, which, "willing" to be released from mechanical repetitiveness, plunges into the infinite sea of definiteness.

At this point let me address John Lachs's pragmatic concern. "It is not clear whether Santayana considered the spiritual life as *livable*. It must be livable to some extent and at any rate, if it is not to be a wholly delusive ideal."²⁶ The hermeneutic reading of the *self* allows for viewing the problematic distinctions psyche—spirit, and *vita activa*—*vita contemplativa* in terms of a dynamic interplay rather than simple dichotomies. The unifying hermeneia of life would be expressive of an overall characteristic of Santayana's thought, being "always in pursuit of synthesis. . . . The blending of divisive energies, the fusion of oppositional tensions; these were challenges which appealed to him."²⁷

Looking at the attempted marriage between animal-in-man and man's somewhat "otherworldly" spirituality, the spirit, except for its function of securing a greater efficacy and independence to a life, changes dramatically the mundane vital automatism into something altogether different. It hosts vision and interpretation and thereby constitutes the space for the hermeneutics of the *self* and the world, by means of which human life occurs in part on an imaginative and symbolic plane. The *symbolic self* remains a living, meaningful, and constantly evolving whole. I recognize the idea of spirit's *activating* or *inspiring passivity* as central to Santayana's *contemplative vitalism*, where life potentially involves—as I for the time being, beyond any political context, presume—three types of freedom: (1) freedom of intelligent action, (2) freedom to become oneself—the so-called "vital liberty," and (3) the free life of the mind.[28] These are relevant to the idea of a good and fulfilled life, the possibility of which seems indeed better secured when life involves a margin of independence from the material realm. This margin from the viewpoint of nature may seem to be a "redundancy" achieved by life. Yet, a redundant human trope means *a possible passage from a life to Life*. As for the capital "L" Life, standing for spiritual life, it entails the controversial idea of pure contemplation of qualities as an activity being an end in itself. Michael Brodrick identifies contemplation as transcendence of the existential time of "the not given" proper to the anxiety-ridden, psychic sense of temporality.[29] Life in its sublimated and contemplative form enjoys the actual and plays with it. The distinction grants the possibility of shifting in-between two different perspectives. Santayana was not a faithful follower of Aristotle, and spiritual life need not be viewed exclusively as commencing in contemplation of essences. I would suggest it was rather a *part of a wider spiritual discipline leading out of the straightjacket of instrumental reason by transferring part of a lifetime into the dimension of disinterestedness, which means—out of the relations of power and the constraints of linear temporality*. Let us note that, according to the classical definition formulated by the Frankfurt School, the inability to conceive of the idea of *autotelela*, namely that something may exist and flourish for its own sake, belongs to the nature of instrumental reason.

Contemplation is an intrinsically disinterested practice, but, as such, does not cease to belong to a wider dynamics of an individual life. It is true that "for Santayana, one of the most satisfying ends is transcending means and ends"[30]—and yet, ironically, it is still an "end." Within his ontological framework, which involves an aspect of eternity, Santayana may defend a position that *vita activa* neither excludes nor opposes contemplative practice as long as we hold a broad understanding of activity. Wasn't for Aristotle *vita contemplativa* the crowning of human activity?

Even Santayana's idea of impotent spirit by no means excludes the possibility that the share of spiritual dimension in living one's life may bring about radical changes and add a new quality to it.[31] First of all, spirit is but an offspring of material psyche, acting on behalf of the life that gave rise to it; whatever occurs in the realm of spirit makes a difference in the overall vital dynamics. Second, if this intelligent life, in the process of recognition of its own potential and interests, has learned by experience the liberating impact of its own spiritual practice on the quality of lived experience and, consequently, on the level of its happiness, it may seek to increase the share of spirituality among the planes of self-actualization that are at its disposal. The latter is a self-imposing contention in the light of

Santayana's life-long advocacy of the virtues of learning by experience, self-knowledge, self-possession, and self-limitation. Moreover, the perspective of liberation in question, which concerns certain elusive aspects of life such as the quality of experience, self-knowledge, or happiness, represents a "register" potentially autonomous in relation to the so-called material efficacy. The issue of agency in the narrow sense of material causality—denied by Santayana to pure spirit—is not the focal point here. Let me remind the reader that we are assuming a holistic perspective of a hermeneutics of life. Finally, the very idea of disinterestedness may be viewed as a challenge to all sorts of utility-oriented worldviews.

Leaving for now aside the issue of contemplative attitude, which is an option of an added value, spirit—as consciousness and as a condition of possibility of imagination—is "transcendental to all feeling and thought" and in this single respect Santayana declares affinity to the German tradition. Heideggerian *Dasein*, as an explicit example of a hermeneutic *self*, or—for a faithful reading of *Sein und Zeit*—the condition of possibility of a hermeneutic *self*, offers a promising and—as I would suggest—intriguing comparative context for Santayana's model of selfhood. I will attempt such a comparison in one of the following chapters. For now let me quote Heidegger's ontological definition of "understanding" as "disclosing": "the existential being of the ownmost potentiality of being of *Da-sein* in such a way that this being discloses in itself what its very being is about."[32] As a concrete existence, *Da-sein* is the manifestation of the actualization of its own possibilities of being. In other words—*it is true in its project of itself*. As factical, it inevitably becomes historical, which for Heidegger means that its inherently relational being (being-in-the-world) is intelligently *disclosed* as contextual. Relationality, then, when temporalized, becomes contextuality. Contextuality at once implies meaningfulness—indeed, *Dasein's* interpretative mode of being (self-interpretation via the world) is synonymous with the emergence of meaning. If we may use a slightly more traditional philosophical language, we may ask: *What is the transcendental condition of this dynamics?* It is possible due to *Da-sein's* ontological constitution, which is one of a temporal "stretching," uncovers an empty "space," a "clearing" of sorts (*Lichtung*), which calls for meaning. *Da-sein*, then, is never "present" here and now. Consequently, it can never be objectified and properly defined; it is always self-projecting and on its way to itself.

As for the specificity of Santayana's *self*, as it emerges from our analysis, it rests in that the *self* is expressive of the realization of psychic potentialities and it is "founded" on the ontological difference between existence and essence. Interestingly, not unlike in the case of Heidegger, the dynamic of the *self* involves a sort of "cognitive" precariousness, which I discussed earlier in connection with the "emptiness" aspect, the blank point, which must be unceasingly overcome within the existential-hermeneutic process of life. Needless to say, this "gap" is a result of the ontological discontinuity between existence and essence.[33]

By way of digression, let us note that the early Santayana, prior to announcing his doctrine of realms of being, distinguished between sensual, psychic intelligence, being a kind of intelligent interaction with the environment, and abstract "thought intelligence," the distinctive criterion being the immediacy of the presence of the object.[34] The reflective and projecting "thought intelligence" is worth attention insofar it is said to refer "to what is . . . absent."[35] The ability to deal with absent objects is just an "ordinary" manifestation of spiritual transcendence as the ground for imagination. One may think of spirit, then, as a transcendental condition of being a human. Moreover, spiritual realm, as mentioned previously, is a dimension, where the priority of the order of existence may be waived or—to phrase it differently—the life of spirit is subject to different principles, even though for Santayana it never ceases to be part of nature.

According to my reading of Santayana, *human life, dependent on its spiritual aspect, is contained within the boundaries of nature but—not those of immanence. Santayana rejects the supernatural but not the transcendent* (!). Spiritual realm breaks the horizon of immanence by introducing a vertical dimension into nature. The concept of life is embedded within that of nature, human life—within that of nature as the interplay of existence and spirit, or, in other words, as the epiphany of nature. With every spiritual actualization of an essence and every epiphany of the world, a ray of eternity irrupts into both physical time of nature and the sentimental time of daily life. *Santayana with his ontology achieves an effect of the temporal diversification of life.* We may speak about the time of action, the time of contemplation, and the overarching, hermeneutic time which binds the two remaining. Thus, the dynamics of the *self* draws on horizontality and verticality crossing one another. Perhaps, rather than arguing about Santayana's alleged *epiphenomenalism*, we should focus more on the significance of the *epiphanic* aspect of spirit in respect to nature. Now, let me invite the reader to take a look at the ways interpretation, as a kind of transcendence, targets the aforementioned "emptiness" aspect.

The Empty "Now" and Selfhood

The previously mentioned "absence" of the object draws our attention back to the section "Ontology and the *Self*," where I discussed the temporal difference between the two registers (existence-essence) resulting in the strategy of using "*what is present and presented for the representation of the absent.*"³⁶ Reformulating it slightly, this strategy is an example of transcendence engendered by the ontological difference essential to the *self*. Technically speaking, the only immediate and direct objects of intuition are essences. An intuition appears in a certain *here-and-now* field under the label of the present moment, while the psychic continuity and endurance place it in a *sentimental* perspective of past and future, organizing subjective time of existence. Unless we are engaged in a deliberate fantasizing or solving mathematical problems, the intent of caring psyche is directed toward the oncoming "now," the nearest future, toward something that just in a moment may occur or be encountered. In other words, intent is directed at *the time of existence*, i.e., the relations called by Santayana "external," which in fact are *missed by conscious acts*. Consequently, with perception being "originally true as a signal, but false as description,"³⁷ *hypothesis* becomes the basic strategy of conscious life.

By way of this symbolic, discreet hermeneutic detour, we register existent beings but we are neither confronted with the real *flux* nor do we take a pure essence for what it is. It seems that because intuition is always "late" in relation to the *flux*, the intent of psyche is either unfulfilled or at least "deceived" in its temporal aspiration. The current configuration being the target of intent is literally missed and has to be satisfied with an intuition, while understanding and the success of thoughtful action hangs on the ability to "transcend" the data by placing them back, as symbols, into the existential context. We are presented here with a *movement of reiteration*. Intent triggers an intuition that transcends the *flux* in an act of spiritual actualization of essences, which must be rendered—by the price of hypothesis, insecurity and ontological anxiety—existentially meaningful. Only then is the standard of understanding met, if, to quote Santayana, understanding is meant to reveal "a possibility, a dramatic figment."³⁸

Santayana addresses this question in different contexts. Sometimes he talks about the impossibility of any conscious grasp of material change. Matter as change remains recondite. Elsewhere, in passages reminding of Derrida's interpretation of the present moment in Husserl, we read that in terms of temporality, mind can be but "the voice of the passing moment." Its own existence seems to the *self* as constantly passing into non-being. The *here-and-now* claimed by the "I" turns out to be in-between "events in one direction faded and in the other uncertain," facts becoming "present in their absence." Ultimately, in sentimental perspective, both past and future turn into "the one a ghost, the other nonentity."³⁹ But while we still may have a memory of the past and a fantasy about future, the "now" of existence we partake in or are carried by, seems to be largely overlooked by conscious experience. And if it is somehow "revealed" with a force greater than usual, it tends to happen in a surprising, or strangely "embarrassing," or even alienating way—via affects, uncontrolled reactions, often hardly communicable and explicable only *post-factum*. In this sense, the dynamic core of one's own existence tends to remain beyond the lucidity of consciousness. A question arises—*What impact has this temporal "failure" of consciousness resulting from Santayana's ontology on the self?* Or maybe—*What does it tell us about the self?*

The problem of the "failed" "now" leaves us, in a sense, with an "empty" object of intent, or a "false" replacement. As evidenced by the experiment in radical skepticism, existential claims must rely on *faith as compensating for this peculiar human blindness. By believing we insinuate that we know* (!). The gap on the ontic level is covered by the presumed familiarity with the world, secured by animal faith and, consequently, it disappears from pragmatically oriented considerations. *But the premonition of discontinuity and insinuation never disappeared from Santayana's work and informs, in a more prominent way, his mature thought.*

It is in this light that one may appreciate the hermeneutic significance of transcendence. Despite the constant "lateness" of intuition in its relation to the flux of existence, the intent of the living *self* unceasingly "engages . . . all faculties, in readiness to meet the unknown at a moment not predictable."[40] A spiritual being "must at once feel and endeavor to transcend the mutation of things and its own mortality."[41] The transcending effort is so central to conscious life that even memory of the past is "a sort of inverted expectation,"[42] and an act of introspection exemplifies inward-inverted transcendence. The necessity of transcendence, which results out of the tension emerging on the intersection of material flux and consciousness, is of vital-hermeneutic nature. *Interpretation—as if triggered by and constantly "revolving around" the emptiness of "now"—is a strategy of coping with finitude by means of inscribing the potential infinity of spirit into the texture of existence.* Hermeneutic requirement in Santayana's vision is multi-leveled and concerns (1) the discreet process of the actualization of essences in intuition, followed by (2) the inscription of intuitions into the symbolic, phenomenal world, and (3) the ongoing activity of composing and re-composing the narrative or the dramatic structure of life. Metaphorically speaking, *the necessity to interpret is the homage paid by the psychic self for the privilege of its own actuality, and interpretation—in relation to existence—seems to be a kind of "insinuation."* By "insinuation" I mean—in reference to the ancient roots of the term—presenting what is *false as true or what is absent as present, in order to achieve a hidden aim.* The idea of insinuation is further developed in the chapter on Bergson.

When talking about the empty "now" as a "moment" triggering the interpretive movement, I am referring to, by means of hermeneutic tools, John Lachs's remark that the discussed inadequacy or lack of continuity between perception and material reality may be the key to the sustaining of subjective autonomy in Santayana's vision.[43] When Santayana speaks about spirit in terms of transcendental apperception which allows for the world to be revealed, he seems to mean it is "a space," "a clearing" (to refer to Heidegger again), or—if we think about *the self* in dynamic terms—"a moment" within the psycho-spiritual *self*. *While its core "I" is hypostatical, the self itself escapes definition and denotes or rather—stands for—something that neither rightfully "is" (ideally) nor "exists" (substantially), and yet—calls for a name and an identity. The dynamics of the self involves self-interpretation of a single life.*

The *self* is occurring at the crossing of the existential flux and essences—"the infinite background of everything."[44] The "material other" of existence defined as "a perpetual genesis of the unwarrantable out of the contingent, mediated by a material continuity,"[45] enforces itself onto consciousness of the incarnated *self* in the guise of affects and "brute facts."[46] This twofold trace of nothingness (the "nothing" of matter and the hermeneutic "nothing" of pure essence) correlates with the "nothingness" (openness to something) inherent in the spiritual aspect of the *self*, which— via the already mentioned reiterating movement of interpretation—at once overcomes and asserts its finitude. Only at the spiritual intersection of the realms of matter and essences "something" may appear to an intentional, conscious life. This appearing actualizes the spirit and justifies its function, while the spirit sustains the "phenomenality" of the world.[47] Having said this, however, from a certain deconstructive perspective (or a perspective of suspicion), Santayana—in line with Heidegger—may well be suggesting that human way of existing "is a way in which the world [potentially] discloses itself as nothingness."[48] It seems to me that the Gnostic aesthetics of Santayana's doctrine of spirit tends to articulate this effect. I am leaving the issue of the negative revelation of the world open, hoping to provoke the readers to contemplate it on their own.

To sum up, the author of *Realms of Being* designs an ontology in the light of which the structure of conscious life contains an ontological fissure, of which the *self* is either a manifestation or a closing. Searching for the *self* we have arrived at a dynamically structured hermeneutics of life that is bridging the aforementioned blank point. Not unlike for Heidegger, the transcending movement of interpretation in question concerns not as much the subject as *subjectivity*, but rather "the subject as a *being*, since it denotes an ontological and not an epistemological relation."[49]

The concept of the *self* appears randomly in Santayana's texts. Almost by principle, its meaning is vague, problematic, if not perplexing for the thinker himself, who speaks of "that odd creature which I call man, or that odder one which I call myself."[50] The disquieting, abyssal genesis of selfhood makes the human being in Santayana's eyes an "odd creature" like the *uncanny* man of Sophocles, evoked by Ricoeur,[51] or the *eccentric* man of Helmuth Plessner. In more poetic parts of *Realm of Spirit*, Santayana's man seems to be hovering around hesitatingly in-between animal and spirit incarnate.

Still, while making the parallels with contemporary hermeneutics and phenomenology, one should keep in mind Santayana's materialism, which adds to it a peculiar sense of ontological profoundness. Selfhood, on one hand, is expressive of a deeper process, which on some ultimate plane simply *occurs*, and on the other hand, it both constitutes and is constituted by the phenomenal reality, in which it somehow "subsists." The "I"/ "ego," in turn, which is but an aspect of the *self*, is sometimes called by Santayana and by scholars a "hypostatic effect." This corresponds to Santayana's critique of egotism and solipsism, which—in my reading—preserves selfhood as representing psyche and as an ontological support for his unwavering advocacy of individualism. In the following sections we will reconsider the theme of interpretation in the context of the dramatic hermeneutics favored by Santayana.

3.3 Dramatic Hermeneutics

> Masks afford us the pleasing excitement of revising our so accidental birth-certificate.
>
> —*SiELS*, 128

Masks as Traces of Interpretation

The meanings of "masks" in Santayana's writings converge in a general metaphor for the interpretative way of being of the "odd creature," for whom "knowledge of nature is a great allegory, of which action is the interpreter."[52] The choice of theatrical vocabulary is not unrelated to Santayana's materialism.⁵³ The dramatic hermeneutics describes—in expressivist terms—the passage from the recondite flux into the imaginative, worldly plot, where man figures thrice: as a participant—in a double sense of an *actor* and a *person* in the play—and an *observer* at once.

> Whatever desperate efforts empiricism may make to deny it, . . . [E]very figure crossing the stage of apprehension is a symbol or may become a symbol; they all have some occasion and arise out of some deeper commotion in the material world. . . . To its invisible substance the spectacle owes not only its existence but its meaning since our interest in the scene is rooted in a hidden life within us. . . . Fair *masks*, like flowers, like sunsets, like melodies wrung out of troubled brains and strung wire, cover for us appropriately the anatomical face of nature; and words and dogmas are other *masks*, behind which we too, can venture upon the stage; for it is life to give expression to life, transmuting diffused movements into clear images.⁵⁴

A few meanings of "masks" may be distinguished here. First, masks are all the meaningful units that simultaneously cover and uncover the world for us. Regrettably, Santayana never developed a "theory" of images or symbols, so the reader has to be content with a general idea. Masks originate in the realm of essences—idiosyncratic universals of constructive and deconstructive potential—being the source of all possible definiteness and identity. The transcendental status of an essence then, makes it *an anticipation of a mask*.

In a larger scale, masks are forms of *expression* of a given *life*, meaningful paraphernalia of identity-assuming. Psyche, to become phenomenally representative of herself, develops an imaginative life, in which she obtains her own reflection—an "ego"—and assumes masks. Here Santayana fits into Taylor's expressivist paradigm, particularly in its indebtedness to Aristotle's idea of the potentiality of nature. My expressivist self-experience rests in that "in realizing my nature, I have to define it in the sense of giving it some formulation . . . I am realizing this formulation and thus giving my life a definite shape."⁵⁵ The activity of expressive articulation of one's inner nature is "closely tied to the [very] idea of a self."⁵⁶ Partaking in a culture and in a society, both of which for Santayana are also "masks," and interacting with other *selves*, the "ego" puts on masks of convention, profession, social roles, and may be approached as *a person*—a synthetic mask, behind which there is a certain character, a personality recognized by others.

Masks are requisites that belong to the stage where the play of life is being acted out. Let me quote a longer passage illustrating Santayana's dramatic hermeneutics:

> Nature, like a theatre, offers a double object to the mind. There is in the first place the play presented, the overt spectacle, which is something specious and ideal; and then there is something material and profound lying behind and only symbolically revealed, namely, the stage, the actors, and the author. The playful spectacular sort of reality we can pretty well dominate and exhaust, if we are attentive; indeed the prospect, in its sensuous and poetic essence, is plastic to attention, and alters its character according to the spectator's station and faculty; a poetic theme develops as interest in it is aroused, and offers different beauties and different morals to every new critic. The instrumentalities, on the contrary, which bring this spectacle before us, whether they be material or personal, are unfathomable. . . . In the beginning, as for a child at his first pantomime, *the play's the thing*; and a human audience can never quite outgrow this initial illusion, since this world is a theatre nobody can visit twice.[57]

Daniel Moreno compares Santayana's dramatic vision with "the inverted echo of Paul Claudel's positions."[58] Claudel believed that "we are converted essentially into actors in a drama" by "an infinitely wise and benevolent author." In Santayana's vision, there is no author and "we are condemned to live dramatically in a world that is not dramatic." Moreno articulates the negative, deconstructive power of this vision, attributing to the thinker a specific sort of nihilism, which he calls "ironic nihilism," "aristocratic nihilism," and, after Anthony Woodward, "courteously conservative nihilism."[59] While I find Moreno's metaphors inspiring, I am trying to illuminate the liberating and creative power of this deconstructive aspect in Santayana's thought.

In reference to the threefold position of man in the drama of life, mentioned at the beginning of this section, it can be transposed onto the threefold structure of human *self*. There is a deeper, psychic *self* being an *actor*, a *person* (the role acted out), represented in each moment by a masked *ego*, and, finally, the spirit as a self-reflective *spectator* or a witness.

One may consider masks also in the context of our previous discussion of the blank point within *self*. Whatever is subject to understanding is approached *as* something. The *self*, involving self-reference, is no exception from this rule. The early Heidegger considers *Dasein's* "fallen" mode of being as constantly positing itself in front of the question "*as what?*" This activity, called *making present*, amounts to a sort of *hermeneutics of having-been*, or of matter-of-factness. The failed "now" of Santayana has a similar existential effect—masks, making up for this failure, may be compared to Heideggerian "*as what?*"

By means of masks psyche anticipates herself as an *ego* of *here-and-now*. But the unfortunate anticipation, which is looking forward, has only a mask—something definite, fixed, "late," and "past" already at the outset. And indeed, Santayana compares masks to the traces of interpretation, conventional language, patterns of sedimentation. "Presence," just like for Heidegger, in some contexts comes to mean "pastness" or "deadness." There is no possible literal answer to the existential question *who am I?* Emptiness, or merely a mask is uncovered instead. It is so for reasons discussed in the section on individuation—insofar as the *self* is constantly evolving, it is indeterminate until framed by death.

The experiment in radical skepticism—an errand to the boundaries of human rationality and the fragile pillars of sanity—may also be viewed as a revelatory contemplation on the temporal abyss between consciousness and real time, between appearance and existence. The realm of pure essences offers a *vista* of infinite specificity but it may appear to a conscious life as nothingness. Therefore there is a suspended suspicion that underneath any mask there is nothingness, that a mask—just like the world of phenomena posited by animal faith—is merely a hypothesis. Let me quote Heidegger once again: *Da-sein* "speaks about itself and sees itself in such and such a manner, and yet this is only a mask which it holds up before itself in order not to be frightened by itself. . . . Such visibility is the mask in which it comes forth and appears before itself as though it literally "were"—in this masquerade."[60]

Moreover, any meaningful continuity of conscious existence is made possible for the *self* on the ground of the *repetitiveness* (the transcendental *here-and-now*) of the interpretation of reality, which puts predictable masks[61] on the face of new events and situations, while allowing the world each time to come to light in a meaningful, *new-but-familiar* way. But besides the formal repetitiveness of interpretation, there is repetition also in nature.

Psyche, as a trope, exhibits certain predictable patterns of entering into external relations, or in other words, temporal patterns.

Human psyche imposes limitations on the virtual infinity of spiritual field and culminates in a personal drama. Meanwhile, masks are formed whenever there appears a recognizable pattern. Repetitions in nature, including psychic *deeper self*, are appropriated by the formal *here-and-now*, and receive specific identities through the essential realm of qualitative difference. This is part of the already discussed mimetic strategy of *emplotment* as a means of sustaining self-integrity.

Finally, the imagery of masks throws some light on Santayana's declared appreciation for Heidegger's exposition of the notion of nothingness. The *self* is threatened by the meaninglessness of the world, a situation when things may be encountered "in just such a way that they are of no relevance at all, but can show themselves in a barren mercilessness. . . . This means that our heedful awaiting finds nothing in terms of which it could understand itself, it grasps at the nothingness of the world."[62] Likewise, Santayana speaks of "the horrid sense of something alien and undiscoverable."[63] To "encounter" means to come across and recognize/find intelligible, so the reason for psychic anxiety is the possibility of missing something or maybe—of *missing everything*. The fear of the nothing equals the fear of the impossibility of a meaningful self-identification, which on the plane of action means the impossibility of an adequate finding oneself in situation. Man, besides being "odd," is inevitably a "creature of circumstance"[64] and finds himself always in a situation. This existential concern is for Santayana a major factor in the constitution of sentimental time as an imaginative, retentive, and projecting rendering of the continuity of man's finding himself thus-and-so, where everything appears under a certain mask. Correspondingly, Heidegger used the notion of *vulgar/ordinary temporality* for a commonsensical conception of time arising out of the fear of encountering oneself without mask.

Let us sum up these considerations by asking: *What is being masked and what is being unmasked by masks?* Masks cover "nature" in the sense of material reality; it is a life-saving mediation, since for the spirit a literal exposure to nature "would be deadly."[65] Masks uncover "nature" as a symbolic, phenomenal reality, relative to a concrete life. Another way of addressing this question is to look at the mechanism of interpretation and the "structure" of the *self* within the setting of realms of being. One might say, then, that what masks *mask* is the blind spot within the *self*, and what they *unmask* is the result of interpretation—a specific pattern of a given life as revealed in the actual, a "poetic variation" on a deeper process. Thus, masks stand for both the actual and the nothing.

The Authorship of Life: Authenticity and Freedom

By maintaining the conceptual distinctions between matter and spirit, and psyche and spirit—which became rather untypical in his times—Santayana gave voice to a certain duality inherent in human experience and persistently reflected in philosophical and religious traditions belonging, according to the classification from *Life of Reason*, to all the three imaginative phases of human experience—pre-rational, rational, and post-rational. We may assume further that the endurance of this ancient distinction points to some universal trait of what is customarily referred to as the human condition and/or nature. As I have been trying to show, the hermeneutics of the *self*, which equals the hermeneutics of conscious life, challenges this dualistic topology by means of a dynamic unity, which is unceasingly giving birth to an individual, dramatic plot. Masks are traces left by the unending and always incomplete synthetic activity of understanding, which accompanies the spontaneity of the evolving and unrehearsed play of life, and overcomes the rigidity of the past and the stillness of each momentary vacuum. To understand, according to Hans G. Gadamer, means to overcome certain recalcitrance, to "escape from something that . . . held us captive."[66] Understanding relieves from the captivity of finitude experienced as resistance by transmuting it into inspiration. That is why Santayana relates understanding to freedom.

Santayana once wrote that "those who deny a medium of knowledge, if they have any speculative competence at all, have to introduce a medium of ignorance instead."[67] Essences and masks fulfill this hermeneutic requirement of a medium of understanding. A philosopher, like Hermes, is: he "who unravels, who relieves . . . He interprets us to the gods and they accept us."[68] Not only philosophy, but also history, arts, science, and other communicable paths of interpreting the reality of human experience are but masks. What is referred to as culture and tradition is an enduring community of sharing and developing a technique or a craft of mask-making. This technique, as Santayana believed, puts a stamp on the way selves are shaped and identities assumed.

While a vivid and self-reflexive tradition supports understanding, dogmatic masks of ideologies and tight conventional identities paralyze consciousness, lead to double standards, and to what Santayana referred to as pathological madness—a situation when phantasms of parasitic symbolic orders overwhelm thinking and dislocate reason, turning its mechanism against life. Likewise, the direction of an individual psychic intent may enter a permanent intro- and retro-spective mode. This possibility of a "backward" sentimental time, of lived experience which closes upon itself evokes associations with the Nietzschean idea of ressentiment and Bergson's closed society.

Masks may also petrify individuality in the course of a lifetime, when they assume a too definite tragic, comic, or ironic character. Comic personages perceive themselves as partaking in a *peripeteia* governed by accident, which levels actors, masks and events, and abandons the completion of any human effort to circumstances, whereby failure no less than success seems equally welcome as long as the first repeats the comic effect of the inadequacy of human ideals with chance, and the latter confirms the general rule by a humorous exception. An ironic distance, as if in a premonition of an almost certain disillusionment, suspends or limits one's vital and moral engagement in the pursuit of ideals. *Personas* wearing tragic masks, in turn, express the graveness of facing and accepting one's lot. Santayana names also mundane masks of routine and masks of will to power, which tend to immobilize and fossilize life.

Thus, certain masks pose a threat to life and spirituality, and count among the factors of spiritual distraction conducive to the crisis of reason or—simply—the crisis of humanity, as rendered by the thinker in terms of the Pauline metaphors of the world, the flesh, and the devil. The whole vision, saturated with an air of Gnostic poetics, easily provokes associations with Heideggerian description of *ruinance*, where understanding is feigned and masks are means of satisfying vain curiosity or conforming to convention and popular opinion rather than facing issues of fundamental existential concern.[69]

The metaphor of masks is part of Santayana's reflection on vital liberty and individual autonomy. It is particularly meaningful in the context of the hermeneutic-existential fact, discussed here amply, that the feedback received by human intent in the form of intuition is such that intent—in a temporal sense—remains unfulfilled and the process is unending. Intuition is "temporally homeless" and knowledge "is always about the not given."[70] Thus, "the odd creature" is fragile, incomplete, threatened in its autonomy by alien "orders of signification," susceptible to distraction and madness. The Gestalt of *animal rationale* emerging in the background is preceded by a hermeneutic ghost—a question mark. Meaning appears only in response to a question. Questions may be asked only by a finite and caring life. The ephemeral, ineffable *self* is *aporetic* in a double sense: by being problematic and probably not definable in any final and fully satisfactory way, and by the nature of its own questioning attitude. In the course of this questioning, the passage from the indefinite to the actual, and from the actual to the meaningful occurs. This passage, this translation constitutes the "how" of the *self* emerging right out of this questioning. It is determined both by psychic and spiritual endowment and by the influences that are impressed on it in the course of existence, influences constantly probing the unclear demarcation lines of psyche.

Masks in Santayana's account are *differentia specifica* of humanity, which involves interpretation, projection, and idealization, and therefore carries an inherent semblance aspect, or a mimetic aspect. Human experience lacks in absolute immediacy hence, "*to experience*" *for a human being always means* "*to bear true witness to oneself,*" as brilliantly phrased in the essay "The Tragic Mask."[71] We should start, perhaps, with a contention that this "doubling" is inevitable since

> literalness is impossible in any utterance of spirit, and if it were possible it would be deadly. Why should we quarrel with human nature, with metaphor, with myth, with impersonation?[72]

The whole phenomenal reality of the world, then, is a mask of nature. Things and facts are revealed to us under the guise of symbols, our *selves*—through the masks of *personas* we enact in private and publicly. Concealing what is "unfathomable," masks are at once the only chance to *reveal* something. Their formality is a means of providing definiteness for what otherwise would remain hidden. Were it not for masks, no experience of beauty and love, and no creation would be possible. Something that might have remained a blind impulse, in the light of imaginative life turns into a recognized object of interest, influencing the direction of the play's action and reconfiguring the meaning of the screenplay.

The masks and costumes man clothes his reality with are expressive of his psychic endowment, but also are subject to endless variation. In other words, the way psychic trajectory is translated into the language of the drama is partially subject to negotiations. Co-writing the screenplay implies negotiating autonomy within participation. This is the margin of the *freedom of authorship*, which makes all the difference in human life, both individual and collective. To repeat, "the playful spectacular sort of reality we can pretty well dominate and exhaust, if we are attentive."[73]

Elements of spiritual practice support the enactment of this kind of freedom on an individual level. They involve the suspension of all masks—the most radical form of transcendence available to the *self*, in which it is focused on its moment of spiritual, receptive opening. The obligation to understand one's situation, crucial in the pragmatic layer of

Santayana's thought, here gives way to unrestrained "seeing," the herald of which is touching the Pure Being. Once freed from the constraints of animal faith and commonsensical interpretation, essences become *empty masks*, in which the object merges with the medium, facilitating a total integrity of attention.

This is an exercise in freedom by means of loosening the "oppressiveness" of facts and the overwhelming power exerted on consciousness by whatever has been crystallized into the so-called "past." Sentimental entanglement in time along with all its fixations, dependence on ready-made interpretations and worldviews, which tend *to dominate the main part in the play and put on the mask of fate*, becoming self-fulfilling prophecies, are suspended if not crushed. This releasing of attention for a pure play of imagination may become a discipline and an art capable of transmuting the whole performance of life. From this perspective, spiritual discipline—save for the fact that it may define a specific form of life[74]—endows the interplay between essence and existence with an ancient, therapeutic sense.

The *self*, as it emerges from my attempt to clarify its meaning, is constantly receding into the enigma of the ineffable *passage* from the automatism of material life to a character in a play. A hermeneutic reading, with the support of Taylor's expressivist model, helps to understand the *self* as being in each case *a particular enactment of the principle* underlying the passage, illuminated by self-knowledge, which "like any art or science, renders its subject-matter in a new medium, the medium of ideas, in which it loses its old dimensions and its old pace."[75] This self-interpreting rendering completes a single "circle" of selfhood and reveals a person. What is important,

> our *deliberate* character is more truly ourselves than is the flux of our involuntary dreams. The portrait we paint in this way and exhibit as our true person may well be in the grand manner . . . but if this style is native to us and our art is vital, the more it transmutes its model the deeper and the truer art it will be.[76]

Among the types of freedom discernible in Santayana's thought I placed freedom to become oneself, more or less synonymous with what Santayana called "vital liberty," which is manifest in "assurance and peace in being what one is, and becoming what one must become."[77] This inescapably leads us to a controversial category of authenticity.[78] Becoming oneself involves bearing witness to "my [own] fatal character—or my fatal acts, making irruption from moment to moment into my character."[79] On an everyday level, the *self* that does not act compulsively and does not resign in the face of fate, is not doomed to mechanical reproduction of a routine mask but rather presents a vivid mask, and when this mask turns into a face, life is lived *authentically* and with *grace*. "You must pull off the mask to see clearly and to breathe freely . . . and relapse into your honest *self* . . . there is no face like one's own, for comfort to the wearer."[80]

Authenticity is a *quality* of expression that suggests self-integrity. It is not a permanent state or something which can be taken for granted, but a fragile equilibrium, which depends on a sustained engagement in life.[81] As I try to articulate in this book, a new dimension of the priority of essence over existence is possible on the ground of Santayana's ontology. No matter what epistemological obstacle be the price for an ontology like this, for the issue of the *self* it is an environment of added value. It allows for—theoretically—a new beginning at each moment. The liberating impact of the spiritual mode of being rests in that it literally disrupts the "dead-end" of the matter-of-factness aspect of existence to the effect that *finitude becomes voluntary* (!).[82] It does so *neither by way of a futile denial of facts, since these are very clearly irrevocable for Santayana, nor through an amor fati attitude, but by the denial of the reduction of human life to the dimension of fact*, and by articulating the freedom for perspective, freedom for thinking, and freedom to fancy. Metaphorical variations and emplotment, in the face of new events, not only may but must modify somehow the past from the point of view of a biographical unity man constantly and ultimately approaches. If life necessarily contains a hereditary, material, self-reproducing nucleus, the principle of which is a caring psyche, the same life, as spiritual, contains the grain of liberation toward Life by means of self-transcendence. In the light of Santayana's *contemplative vitalism*—let us repeat—"it is the flesh as a power that liberates us from the flesh as obsession [body]. That which is liberated is still love."[83] So under favorable circumstances, a living mask may become a source of an aesthetic phenomenon and an alternative to the *tragic sublime*, namely—of *grace*.

Grace

The modern idea of authenticity has its roots in the romantic, expressivist paradigm. In contemporary philosophy it was made popular by existentialist thinkers, who assumed individualistic perspective on human life. Heidegger famously contrasted authenticity to the fallen mode of being. In Santayana's reflections, authenticity is devoid of the specific, "forceful" style implied by Heidegger's rhetoric of "mobilization," decisionism, withstanding the question, or "holding out in the asking of a question," responding to a calling, etc.[84] On the contrary—the authenticity valued by Santayana is of a graceful kind, even though it does not cease to involve a degree of challenge, of "winning" oneself out and against contingency and necessity at once. The two perspectives—graceful and challenging—share in associating authenticity with the idea of freedom to become oneself, which originates, at least partly, in the Aristotelian sense of *autotelic* life.

In Santayana's "scenic" vocabulary, authentic human existence wears a vivid mask. It involves both self-integrity and openness for what is out there, for other forms of perfection. Authenticity is desirable in the light of the idea that every life is intrinsically justified to strive for its own fruition. This acquires a deeper meaning when accompanied by Santayana's idealistic contention that it is better if humans regard life as worth living for the sake of the good and the beauty that can be accomplished in it, rather than for the sake of mere biological survival.[85]

Santayana, both in his life and in his philosophy, pursued the ancient standard of moderation, which meant blending the natural with the disciplined, and commencing in what is harmonious and *unforced*. A graceful life relates to the previously mentioned margin of redundancy, the "side effect" of a constant transmutation of the surplus vital energy into the playful spirituality of a human being. I interpret Santayana's ideal of *graceful authenticity* as becoming oneself in an anticipating way, when existence is "acted out" with a degree of artful deliberation, and "becoming" means also "creating." Being what one is, in this context of playfulness, loses its fatalistic shade of meaning. The thinker reflects upon the art of living as follows:

> [W]hether the visage we assume be [a] joyful or sad one, in adopting and emphasizing it we define our sovereign temper. Henceforth so long as we continue under the spell of this self-knowledge, *we do not merely live but act; we compose and play our chosen character*, we wear the buskin of deliberation, we defend and idealize our passions, we encourage ourselves eloquently *to be what we are* . . . [we] wrap ourselves gracefully in the mantle of our inalienable part.[86]

The Greek concept of *haris* (χάρις) stood for grace, charm, gift, source of joy, as well as gratitude. In orphic hymns grace is praised as a supernatural power, which transforms natural qualities of gods and men, endowing them with an irresistible charm. Later, the supernatural connotation of the term was emphasized in the context of Christian *grace* and of *charismatic gifts*. Polysemic and ephemeral *haris*, as opposed to the more static and spatial concept of natural beauty, connotes movement and relationality. It becomes subject to theoretical study in the work of an influential eighteenth-century historian of art—Johann Winckelmann, with whose work Santayana was well acquainted. Grace is explained in this—somewhat idealizing—reading in terms of a phenomenon observable in nature, an effect of harmony between a man confident in his calling and his activities. The medium of grace is movement, comportment, and its source—"beauty and peace of soul."[87] The moderation and sensitivity of a Greek artist allowed him to convey an effect of a natural, and at the same time effortlessly controlled composure and movement of human body. The ancients, according to this interpretation, praised a noble propensity of the soul to temper the pain involved in—always too great in any case—suffering in this world.[88] Modernity, according to Winckelmann, had lost this kind of sensitivity in favor of the fascination with subjective experience and literalness.

In line with Winckelmann, Schopenhauer holds grace to be "the adequate manifestation of the will through its temporal phenomenon, . . . the perfectly correct and appropriate expression of each act of will through the movement and position that objectifies it."[89] Another English translation of this passage is perhaps worth quoting, as it articulates a slightly different aspect of the concept: "grace consists in fact that every movement and posture is executed in the easiest, the most appropriate and most comfortable manner and is thus the entirely fitting expression of its intention, or the act of will."[90] Probably the best known philosophical exposition of this concept is one by Friedrich Schiller, who draws on the Greek idea of magical powers, and translates it into a subtle, yet definite *domination of the spiritual aspect in man*, when "the mind expresses itself in sensuous nature which depends upon it in such a way that nature accomplishes the mind's will most faithfully and expresses its sentiments most speakingly." Moreover, "only the supra-sensuous cause . . . makes grace speak."[91] Here, grace is defined as *"beauty of frame under the influence of freedom."*[92] Grace, then, is an expression of a spiritual freedom, which grants a deliberate yet forceless control over one's own potential. The lightness, the apparent ease of being, implies a spirituality which has understood its finitude and treats it not like a burden, but like a playground. The effect of gracefulness, intriguing and captivating for the observer, suggests a surplus inherent within human *self*. An alternative to that is the tragic sublime, which also implies the supremacy of spirit, but one achieved by spirit in a struggle to assert its dignity. *These digressions on the neo-classicist and romantic understanding of grace bring to our attention the fact that a specific synthesis of Greek naturalism and romantic quest for authenticity is present in Santayana's vision.*

The spiritual realm enriches life by broadening the spectrum of the possibilities of its fulfillment. Spiritual refinement of life assumes an indispensable degree of spontaneous idealization. Graceful life, as understood by Santayana, will consist in sublimation of impulses and spiritual transcendence reinforced by the attitude of openness to the world. Gracefulness, just as—two recurrent ideas in Santayana—sanity and wisdom, rely, metaphorically speaking, on the art of keeping silent in order to hear the world speaking. This explains Santayana's insistence on constraining the "ego." Contemplative practice enhances awareness and by keeping obsessive desires at bay, it harbors discovering and learning. It is an ethical catalyst, allowing for a momentary purification, or—as Santayana phrased it—a momentary "disintoxication" from all values. Subsequently, it enforces a radical self-reflection, which relieves understanding from dead conventions, stereotypes and phantasmatic desires fed by imagery which is no longer one's own. This "holding still" influences the quality of spiritual—and therefore—of the whole life. Spiritual discipline, demanding as it may seem for modern humanity, addresses specifically the fragile margin of human freedom, elevating it to a more prominent position in the dynamics of life. Grace trespasses the aesthetic context into an existential-hermeneutic one, where it articulates spiritual freedom. Perhaps we may even speak here about *the realm of ars vivendi*, where "it is life to give expression to life."[93] By articulating the art of living, Santayana may refer both to the Aristotelian idea of perfection and to Seneca's understanding of the excellence into which mortals should model their short lifetime.

It is not accidental that Santayana, despite all his critique of German egotism with its bombastic misinterpretation of classicism, evokes Goethe as the one who was wearing a beautiful mask. Charles Taylor, tracing the evolution and sources of the self, lists Goethe among those German artists of the era, who paved the way to the so-called modern expressivist turn, by contributing to the creation of its ethos, based on the idea that the actualization of one's own nature translates itself into a certain form of expression.[94] Santayana's Goethe was a figure symbolic of graceful acting out his own biography. Being "everywhere at home" he deliberately cherished lived experience, holding the key to salvation when alive. The ambivalence of Santayana's approach to Goethe, in whom he notices the harbingers of modern egotism, is visible in this partly ironic passage:

> Goethe *loved* them all . . . He kept his old age genial and green by that perennial love. In order to hold his head above water and be at peace, he did not need to be a Christian, a pagan, or an epicurean. The sympathy Goethe felt with things was that of a lordly observer, a traveler . . . a connoisseur.[95]

Interestingly, Edmund Wilson, whose memories of the last conversation with Santayana in Rome are evoked by Anthony Woodward, spoke in a similar way of the philosopher himself—as somebody whose life and thought constituted an integral and harmonious whole, like a "work of art."[96] Another scholar speaks of "Santayana's unbearable lightness of being,"[97] while yet another claimed that the thinker's idea of the role

> of a philosophically inclined mind . . . is not to serve any institutional . . . social, or specific pedagogic purpose, but rather to function very much as an artist who gives form to thought . . . and communicates with other individuals who are in the process of *fashioning themselves* as embodiments of philosophical art, i.e., as self-contained, self-composed, self-disciplined . . . [and] achieve some semblance of "harmony" in their lives.[98]

Even though the above quoted words are far from exhausting, as I believe, the scope of Santayana's philosophical interest and the potential of his heritage, they do offer an illuminating insight into the nature of the thinker's individualism and at once shed some light on the "difficult" reception of his views in America of the early twentieth century, which was fascinated with constructivist ideals.[99]

On the opposite side to grace, homage for being a human is paid in the battle of the dogmatic, "the masked" against life. The dark side of excessive and fanatical idealization rests in that, like death, it "turns everything into marble."[100] Yet, idealization is inescapable form of human life, it is "the escutcheon of human nature, in which its experience is emblazoned . . . In so far as men are men at all . . . they militate under this standard and are true to their colors. Whatever refuses to be idealized in this way, they are obliged to disown and commit to instant oblivion."[101]

Santayana's idea of authenticity with its platonic, contemplative tinge on one hand, and a romantic, expressivist on another, sounds unlike anything Heidegger had to say about authenticity. Their understanding of authenticity is indeed different, but that should not prevent one from noticing that both employ the concept of authenticity out of care about the possibility of freedom. None of them ever spoke about freedom in the sense of the modern idea of unrestricted agency, an external intervention of *Cogito* into the material world. They rather conceived of freedom as resting in thinking, understanding, enacting. Metaphorically speaking—*that man, as factical, lives by grace*—was the deepest conviction of both thinkers. An authentic (and graceful life), then, may be understood as an attitude of exercising the freedom a human being has at his disposal, the practice of enacting one's existence instead of "dragging behind" it.[102]

The reinterpretation of the Nietzschean motto of becoming oneself, which originally seems to be burdened with the problem of Augustinian evil (the *self's* "closing upon oneself"), nevertheless paves the way—along with ancient inspirations—for the category of authenticity in the context of freedom and *ars vivendi*, where the *self*, as Tischner notices, "plays a part in the drama of the truth of life."[103]

Having said all this, let me evoke in more detail—as a very important *post scriptum* to these fragmentary remarks on grace, authenticity, and *ars vivendi*—the attitudes of the three participants of a dispute in Socratic *Dialogues in Limbo*. To preserve the vividness of the debate and convey it to the reader, in many cases I decided to quote rather than to paraphrase passages from this splendid book by Santayana.

"I bring hope of health and prescribe the cure," declares Democritus preoccupied with the most persistent illusion of the mind—"the illusion of its own importance."[104] To tell apart convention from nature, to assume that there *is* truth and to set one's heart on it is part of the "relative wisdom" attainable for a "student of error and false philosophies" a man inevitably is, even at the price of preliminary disillusionment.[105] "So let your ship have an anchor laid deep in nothingness," Democritus advises, for "the consciousness of vanity is a great disinfectant: it fills religion, as it fills life, with fortitude, dignity and kindness."[106]

At the other side of this philosophical argument *in limbo* there stands Socrates. The task of philosophy, argues Socrates, is not so much to emphasize the gap between things as they are and as they appear, in order to unveil the vanity of all convention (that is a means rather than an end), but rather to facilitate the attainment of self-knowledge. This is where the idea of *inauthenticity* is most explicitly exhibited:

> The gods that admit spirits to these regions [the limbo] strip them of all false trappings and restore to them all their natural gifts. Sometimes, when the trappings are off, nothing whatever

> appears under them, for in some people the circumstances of
> life have created everything and suppressed nothing . . . And
> they were only wickerwork dummies dressed in the borrowed
> finery of their day, and hollow echoes of other men's words,
> they at once dissolve into the elements out of which they were
> patched together, and nothing of them remains to enter these
> shades.[107]

The Stranger, who is the only one actually living among the interlocutors, and most probably is closest to Santayana's own standpoint, seeks a possibility of reconciliation between the two divergent, although not contradictory views. His part is crucial for understanding the fragile, subtle connection between the ethical and the aesthetic in Santayana's thought. The Stranger approves of the anthropological skepticism of Democritus and his respect for the intrinsic nature of things, but, at the same time, accepts Socrates's wisdom in that it gives priority to the good of man. Democritus's words "By sanity I understand assurance and peace in being what one is, and becoming what one must become,"[108] hold valid as long as one understands and has learnt to judge, for, as warns the Stranger, the "margin of free choice and initiative for a man of understanding is exceedingly narrow"[109] (!). Becoming "what one is," here advocated by the scientifically minded Democritus, requires a correction, which is provided by Socrates:

> Are all fashions equally good? Are all transitions equally happy?
> (. . .) *Have you learned how to live? Do you know how to die?*
> If you neglected these questions your self-government would
> not be an art, but a blind experiment. Art, which is action
> guided by knowledge, is the principle of benefit, and without
> art the freer a man is the more miserable he must become.[110]

Respectively, while human life always tends to "some specific attainment," claims the Stranger, its particular expression will remain as unpredictable as unstable human nature and personality are.[111] The recognition of this element of contingency attached to the idea of one's own life as an expression of something deeper results in the intuition of insecurity about the very identification "with that odd creature . . . I call myself."[112] With accident and freedom inscribed in the very passage from potentiality to actuality, becoming oneself is not only not a fatalistic idea, but actually one which is quite demanding and requires an art. The Stranger, one of those "scattered and exotic souls"[113] who are aware of it, is particularly sensitive to the significance of hermeneia, on which (the value of) authenticity depends. *To understand in this context is to be engaged in a dialectic between "true" and "good," so that the very idea of authenticity might be worth preserving.*

From a Dogma to a Language: The Self and the Trinity

Santayana once declared that his four realms of being may be viewed as "a reduction of Christian theology and spiritual discipline to their secret interior source." More specifically, he said, he translated the doctrine of Trinity into ontology and "moral dialectic."[114] Still, he added, the analogy between theology and his ontology remains loose—"the one is a dogma, the other a language."[115] These words suggest to us a possible association between the triadic dynamics of the *self* and the Holy Trinity. First, let us see how Santayana develops the analogy between the realms of being and the three Persons.

The fundamental realm of matter—the "groundless reality, breaking in upon nothingness with an overwhelming irrational force" corresponds to the Father. Existence, this "assault of reality," confronts us with "the unfathomable mystery of the actual." Our encounter with existence *through* the actual (which, in a sense, "covers" the Father for us) reveals our inertia—as we know from previous sections of this book, what is actual in intuition, existentially is past. This was recognized by Heraclitus who noted that "everything existent does itself justice by presently disappearing."[116]

Next, the thinker explains the mutual dependence of matter and essence in reference to the Nicene Creed, which claims the Son to be the warrant of all creation and yet be begotten by the Father. Only then can "the selective fiat of power limit actual form to the Logos or the truth," which means that the Son corresponds to Santayana's realm of essences, which, in the generative process, becomes restricted to that of truth. The Father and the Son, as matter and essence, represent "two incommensurable and equally original features of existence itself."[117] As long as the Trinity is a dynamics, we may speculate that the Son—as the moment of truth—embodies the "impossible" existence—essence relation, their being two dimensions of one reality. Interestingly, Santayana sometimes refers to the realm of truth as the "tragic realm," and it is not uncommon in philosophy to view Jesus as a tragic hero.

In reference to Schopenhauer, Santayana remarks that material force, like the Will, breeds not essences/"eternal forms" but "the intuition or illustration" of them.[118] He thus articulates both the transcendental function of the spirit and the fact that spirit, as the locus of the epiphany of material reality, originates in matter (and, as we will next see, in essence). The dimension of actuality, namely—the realm of spirit, corresponds to the third Person of the Trinity—the Holy Ghost. The Spirit, "life-giver," has been somewhat marginalized by church dogmatics, claims Santayana, due to the personification of Jehovah and Christ. Meanwhile, it

> *gives* life in the sense that life would never be morally worthy of the name if the spirit were not actual there; but *the source of spirit* itself lies in the Father and the Son, or in my language *in matter organized into the form of a psyche*. . . . So that it is in the Holy Ghost that the Father and the Son are first truly vivified and united and adore and glorify one another. We may therefore say that the spirit, for all its dependence, is no less divine . . . and integral to reality . . . By the least joy it can redeem [moments of time] . . . from futility and by the least pain it can wring the conscience of the Fates and challenge their selfish somnolence.[119]

This reading—loosely referred to the Catholic dogma—reveals a number of other inspirations, from Plato and Aristotle to Schopenhauer. The spirit introduces a vertical temporal perspective, the perspective of eternity, to the effect that when we read that "the Holy Ghost spoke by the prophets . . . this past tense is accidental,"[120] for the Holy Ghost is constantly giving life through *utterance*. The organic life (psyche), which sustains the spirit, is transmuted in it into a qualitatively different life, and it is this Life, to stress it once again, that "vivifies and unites" the Father/material reality and the Son/its message and truth. In the book *The Idea of Christ in the Gospels or God in Man*, we can see that Santayana reads the words "in the beginning" in the Gospel of John as "in principle." He discusses dropping the linear temporality in favor of the idea of Logos/Sophia (the Word) being a divine emanation, *through* which all forms of creation arise. Christ/the Son is identified here with the Word.[121]

But if we accept this reading, ponders the author, an unfortunate tension appears between the idea of Christ as a principle of creation and as a redeemer and savior. Isn't it Life/Psyche that Christ may stand metaphorically for rather than the Word? This, of course, brings us closer to the association of the threefold *self* with the Trinity. Leaving cosmology for an existential interpretation present in Santayana's philosophy of religion, let us note the essentiality of Passion to incarnation and of incarnation to the spirit. Spirit, as incarnated, is always in the state of Passion. Incarnation implies the need for salvation from "the plight of temporal . . . existence," which, in Santayana's vision, is achievable through the spirit.[122] From the viewpoint of Santayana's eclectic, quasi-secular (or post-secular), existential doctrine of spirituality, the perspective of spirit incarnate is one of an individual, *self-procured salvation*. *The spiritual potential to redeem the futility or the nothingness of physical time* is the response to "the original sin" of existence. Those who ignore the integrating potential of the Trinity, and simply *rebel* against the source of it all—the Father—like Lucifer did, are doomed to exile.

It is not my intention to get into the details of Santayana's philosophy of religion here. What is interesting is his interpretation of the dogma of the Holy Trinity as representing an imaginative and symbolic rendering of a certain universal truth of human experience, which is perhaps expressive of both human nature and condition, and which may be conveyed also via an ontological language.

The aforementioned perspective of self-procured salvation is crucial, in my view, for understanding Santayana's idea of spirit in the light of his conception of the *self*. The spirit "redeems" by introducing the possibility of expression through language, love, and deeds; it brings the light of novelty and freedom to the singularity of a concrete life. *The articulation of the spirit in Santayana's pluralistic individualism is justified by the existential task of tracing one's "narrow path" through the limitations of a finite life.* What is at stake is *the possibility of seeing finitude as (the only) chance for the liberation of life towards love*. Existence opens in front of an incarnate spirit "an infinite complex of orders. In tracing any of these orders, a certain fidelity of intention, a serious self-limitation and consistency are requisite: whereby the vital presuppositions and conditions of spiritual life are manifested."[123]

Spirit is a divine spark within conscious existence, capable of redeeming it from the meaningless flux of physical time, from merely adaptive mechanical repetition, the blind suffering of an animal life. Thus, "the burden of Will is clarified by the Word."[124] Interestingly, the redeeming aspect of the spirit relies on its passivity and revelatory potential, which Santayana compares to *kenosis*, "*disponibilité*," when spirit "claims nothing, posits nothing, and is nothing in its own eyes, but empties itself completely."[125]

What do these hermeneutic negotiations of Santayana's own system with the mystery of Trinity add to our knowledge about the self? They suggest a possibility of considering selfhood as such in the symbolic terms of Trinity, insofar as selfhood is related to the realms of being. The most obvious configuration is the one suggested by Santayana, namely the triad:

the living body (the Father)—psyche as the vital code (the Son)—spirit (the Holy Ghost), which in their dynamic unity account for both *ipse* and *idem* and make up for a *self*. The trope represented by psyche stands for the Word, being constantly interpreted in its actualization. In other words, psyche is the voice of Logos, an abstract message corresponding to the "living word," which may be interpreted hermeneutically via the lens of Paul Ricoeur's reformulation of the biblical notion of *kerygma* in terms of selfhood.[126] Psyche indeed does not "stand for" anything else but herself. She calls for interpretation and for the enactment of her code through a concrete life. And, if we follow Santayana carefully, we find him giving us clear clues as to the possibility of such an analogy between psyche and the living Word, which "must be uttered":

> The Word must be *uttered*; and such utterance cannot be either momentary or endlessly repeated; it must progress, vary, and complete itself in endless ways. As the potentiality of matter and life is probably indefinite, and the variety of essence certainly inexhaustible, so spirit has an infinity of its own, *the infinity of the renewable*. One cry of moral actuality breaking out of the heart *leaves the heart free to repeat or not to repeat it; and the repetition if it comes will vary it*. One pleasure cannot prescribe the quality of another pleasure, or cause or prevent its existence; nor can one thought annul the deliverance of another thought.[127]

The dynamics of the *self* consists in the interpretation of a unique utterance, possible only within the framework of a sustained, continuous revelation of the world, which is its condition and its outcome at once.

Moreover, as Ricoeur asserts, in any hermeneutic vision of human subjectivity, where its integrity is based on a confrontation with a broadly understood "text" (the world, the others, culture, etc.), "ego" must be suppressed for the sake of a *responsive self* (which is contrasted both with a merely "reactive self" and with a strong conception of ego/*Cogito*). Santayana, as we already know, also emphatically endorsed diminishing "ego" in favor of the attitude of understanding and spoke even of *salvation through understanding*. But in order to understand, the *self* obviously can be neither dissolved nor fragmented. If there is any suggestion of post-modern fragmentation of the *self* in Santayana, it pertains to the idea of multiple masks—identities, possible within a narrative unity, and the very idea of essences, offering deconstructive possibilities. It guarantees a necessary flexibility of the medium, in which the "living Word" of the psychic, dynamic trope is embedded. Psychic code may become meaningful exclusively in the world, via the intelligible, symbolic, imaginative medium of culture. *Kerygma*, unlike any word/sign in a conventional sense, points to itself. Hence, Ricoeur says, the prophets can only *testify* to it, and the scriptures cannot be understood literally in any sense conceivable in the modern, logical discourse, operating with proofs and arguments. This is what, Ricoeur notes, links the language of the Bible and poetry. Needless to say, Santayana repeatedly stressed the shared imaginative and symbolic value of religion and poetry.

The specificity of Santayana here is that by placing God in the realm of matter and his Word within psyche, he naturalizes the divine, and at the same time "protects" its *sacred place* by delineating the non-objectifiable realm of spirit. Matter/the Father is transcendent in its being recondite, unfathomable, impenetrable, unapproachable to consciousness. Thus, the divinity of the First and the Third person are protected, while for the Son is reserved the experience of incarnation and the task of constant interpretation of the Word in the context of the world. Spirit appears "because the Word must be *uttered* . . . and complete itself in endless ways."[128]

The exposure of the psychic code to the available world of symbols, through which the former is mediated and at the same time confronted with, has—as has the basic text of Christian tradition in Ricoeur's account—the power of a constant reconfiguration, or—to use Ricoeur's term—"*refiguration*" within the *self*.[129] While for Ricoeur the Scripture offers a principle of self-organization, for Santayana, the dialectical relations within the triadic *self* represent the model of self-creation dynamics. Besides, this reading is in line with his idea of the existential symbolism inherent in the projections present in religious doctrines. In the case of this particular essay of Ricoeur, the solidifying and summoning function in relation to the *self* is attributed to the vanishing/absent name of God, which is constantly sought for. In a secular or post-secular context this function of the Other may be performed by different ideals, spiritual, social, political. To diminish the danger of certain "substitutes" of this sort, Santayana insisted on the preservation and cultivation of the ideal of *disinterestedness* and sanity, and, at the same time, exorcising the egotism of Western culture. After all, he himself declared an atheist on a number of occasions, although he did so as a participant of a culture dominated by the language of proof and argument[130]—a paradigm, in which, he thought, no religious dogma was tenable. Meanwhile he never dismissed the value of the symbolism conveyed by the Judeo-Christian tradition, which—like a mirror and a "fountain of truth and self-knowledge"—could possibly tell humanity more about itself than any other text of culture.¹³¹ Likewise, Ricoeur argues for the power and depth of an always incomplete and polyphonic self-interpretation in the light of the Scriptures.

Perhaps a support of sorts for my intuitions comes from a sympathetic review of the aforementioned Santayana's book on Christ in the Gospels, by Paul Tillich. Tillich considers the book an example of "sublime esotericism," which tends to naturalize the divine and, at the same time, to elevate the natural into the spiritual, without losing the purity of spiritual element altogether. He notes Santayana's selectivity—like his lack of attention to St. Paul and his reluctance to the idea of sin. The theologian finally describes Santayana's work as a synthesis of "Catholic mysticism," "modern skeptical naturalism," and Protestant method, in an overall effort to "existentialize" theology.¹³²

4

Life as Insinuation

In a previous section, in the discussion of the role of the "empty now" in the inner dynamic of selfhood, I related, metaphorically, the activity of interpretation (considered as life's strategy of writing a scenario for its own material dynamics) to *insinuation*. At this point I would like to dwell on this metaphor, as well as to take the opportunity this metaphor creates for bringing together Santayana's and his contemporary Henri Bergson's philosophies of life.[1]

Latin verb *insinuare* literally stands for: "to penetrate," "to drill," "to infiltrate," "to get inside." Metaphorically, it means to present what is false as true, usually in order to reach hidden aims, to develop a secret plan. In Cicero's writings, the term assumes the meaning of shrewdness, keenness, reaching the bottom of things. It is also associated with raising suspicions in someone, provoking disquieting thoughts. Finally, *insinuare* may stand for, as it does in contemporary Italian, "to weasel one's way into" or "to find favor with someone." Let us note the common denominator for all these meanings, namely, the idea of introducing something alien into something else, of grafting something upon something else.[2]

The theme of a shrewd, strategic "infiltration," along with the convention of theatrical farce, where something is pretended, "acted out" for the sake of a hidden agenda, is implicit also in Bergson's metaphor comparing life as such with insinuation. Let us have a look, then, at the meanings of life with which Bergson's thought confronts us. Let us not lose sight of the theme which is of interest for both thinkers: freedom.

The first semantic thread is represented by the idea of penetration and grafting as *incarnation of the past*.

4.1 Insinuation as Incarnation of the Past

> Now, living matter seems to have no other means of turning circumstances to good account than by adapting itself to them passively at the outset. Where it has to direct a movement, it begins by adopting it. Life proceeds by insinuation.[3]

We are in the context of the *vital flux*, caught intuitively as a forward movement, an impetus, which is overcoming obstacles. The initial, empirical conception of life is "prolonged"—typically of Bergson's method and not unlike Santayana's—into an ontological borderline concept, which becomes bedrock of the whole vision. Some interpreters of Bergson—Gilles Deleuze and Barbara Skarga—call Bergson's philosophy transcendental empiricism, but one may, alternatively, frame it as a metaphysical naturalism where two drives or two modes of differentiation—*natura naturans* and *natura naturata*—coexist and confront one another within the whole, which is Nature. This distinction illustrates the dynamic nature of reality, which is constantly being "born" and replacing the vanishing reality. The former represents the creative aspect of the movement of life, the latter, the inertia of spatialized matter. In Deleuze's words, "life as movement alienates itself in the material form that it creates."[4] At a certain evolutionary stage, life assumed human form, so that it could question the power of material, mechanical inertia as if from "within" via the *insinuation of incarnation*. Along with life incarnate, an active interiority is introduced, mere movement is replaced by intelligent action, and the automatism of reactions suspended. In the human being the vital flux becomes self-conscious. In this game, which echoes the ancient struggle between spirit and matter, and where freedom is at stake, life moves ahead victoriously while *insinuating* that it is merely adapting itself. Without entering into the details of Bergson's account of this evolutionary situation, let us note that each human life is a potential transgression of *conditio humana*, and—by the same token—it potentially enlarges the meaning of humanity.

For a better understanding of Bergson's conception of life and for the sake of its juxtaposition with Santayana's vision, let me recapitulate—in a nutshell and highly selectively—the premises of the original metaphysics designed by the author of *Matter and Memory*. The vision as a whole tells the story of life's errand toward liberation from material necessity. The movement of life, anchored in its own primordial, perfect unity, the first spark of the vital impetus, acquires at a certain stage a new weapon: spirit. Spirit is defined as the past deposited in the virtual register of memory, proper to each conscious life—hence the capital importance of the notions of "pastness," "anteriority," and "continuity within change" in this vision. Man is in touch with his memory daily, but he can most fully take advantage of its deepest resources by arriving at an intuitive synchronicity with his own endurance—*durèe*—which is the modality of being proper to man's *deeper self*. The opposite temporal modality is a material one—the system of images along with the so-called *pure perception* which each time gets limited to serve the needs of a concrete, conscious human being in action, by revealing, in representations, the actual possibilities of action. The axis of this process is the crossing of two lines occurring in an individual consciousness—the line of spirit (memory) and the line of matter (the actual state of the body), or, in other words, the crossing of the past and the present moment. It should be noted that it is through the current attitude of our bodies that we are in the closest proximity to the present moment.[5] Through our consciousness we are predominantly in the past but with a strong inclination toward the future. The gap between these two registers can be neutralized in the process of the actualization of memories, which takes place for an individual, embodied *self*, making it capable of recognizing and acting. Bergson calls this attitude *attention to life*, which roughly corresponds to Santayana's idea of intelligent action based on animal faith and transitive knowledge. Ontologically, within a human *self* the moment of monism is achieved, being the trace of the original unity of the primordial vital impulse.

If we ask, then, how Bergson conceives of a human being, one possible answer is that he conceives of man in metaphysical terms of incarnation as a means of spiritual/vital striving for freedom. And even though a human being, as a through-and-through dynamic being, is never fully identical with himself, this does not make him—as in the case of some existentialist accounts—essentially threatened by nothingness and rooted in *Angst* (although his action is threatened by the possibility of being superficial and merely adaptive). The prerogatives of man's integral continuity are memory of the past and endurance, which constantly inspire his life with meaning and direction. It is a unique dimension, according to Leszek Kołakowski, where "nothing is lost and nothing is reversible."[6]

By way of digression, the above concerns not only individuals but also, to some extent, human communities, even though here the danger of oblivion and ignorance is more realistic. One of the reasons for that is the fact that a community does not have a physical body and its access to *durèe* is always mediated by all kinds of common representations. Bergson's nominalism along with his conceptions of intuition, endurance, and the twofold, deep-superficial *self*, conspire to give birth to a deep distrust toward the whole symbolic sphere, particularly in its social and political dimension. This downplaying of the symbolic as the shared couples with the individualism of Bergson, for which he was criticized. Meanwhile, Bergson's individualism was—like that of James and, to a limited extent, Santayana—rooted in the organic unity of experience and action, the unity of inner time consciousness, of time lived, and the memory of it. It seems to me that the significance of this kind of individualism rests in the chance it offers for an unprecedented sense of authenticity and integrity inherent in the vision of the return to the original source of inspiration contained in the primordial vital impulse. This sort of individualism is not meant to squander *ex definitione* any vision of a meaningful community. What it does is grant an individual, conscious life the chance to evolve also in less favorable external circumstances by means of reference to the ultimate tribune that is situated beyond any local—be it social, political, or simply discursive—context. This is also a vision in which Augustinian individualism and the idea of introspection resonate. We may recognize a strategy aimed at similar ends in Santayana's realm of essences with their cathartic and liberating impact on conscious life. Last but not least, let us note that the individualism of Bergson is rooted in the already mentioned ontological *nominalism*, which is metaphorically conveyed in the shortest and simplest possible philosophical credo of the French thinker, as superbly formulated by Kołakowski: "time is real" (!).[7] By way of clarification, time being real means that the endurance of a concrete *self* is irreversible and efficacious in its creative power, it is irrevocably stored in memory in a form which abides of no fixed narrative, and, finally, nothing here is repeated, each memory is unique. We can see that Bergson's ontology of the concrete implies—and here I encourage the reader to go back to the section on individuation for an interesting comparison with Santayana's ontology—an *individualism of incarnation and of the experience of durée*.

In the creative power of a genius and the intuitive one of a mystic Bergson sees a contagious spark able to inspire a new quality, to raise a new emotion able to vivify old languages, and to define novel horizons as reference points for a community. As against his critics, who, like Horace Kallen, noticed in the drama sketched by the French thinker an anti-human, cosmic scale, where a concrete "I" is merely a puppet, one may look at this vision from the perspective of the aforementioned individualism and its moral stakes. To conclude, the transcendence of here-and-now contained in the vital impetus liberates the living consciousness and action from all unwanted entanglements. The conception of *durée*, as noticed by Skarga, may be used to support the interpretation of Bergson in terms of a specific (hermeneutic) formula of the *self*/the subject as capable of spontaneous generation of meaning.[8]

Still, the subject of life and creativity—despite the individualism and incommunicability implied by *durée*—cannot be abstracted from a sociocultural context. Historical and cultural consciousness is of major importance insofar as, according to Bergson, the whole difference between the so-called primitive man and the modern man rests in the continuity of memory ("we have remained, at bottom, what they were"),[9] which is conveyed as collective memory via symbolic forms. In this light, the role of an outstanding individual is to provide an impulse to transgress and actualize, every once in a while, all the adaptive, symbolic formations, so that they may serve what they were called for—cultivating life as freedom. However, before man can transgress, reminds Bergson, and before "man can philosophize, man must live."[10] Life also "insinuates" itself, then, into adaptive institutions which serve self-preservation, such as law and religion. Doesn't the very idea of religion as *fabulation function*—an instinctive, defensive mechanism, meant to prevent the transgressions of another function of life, intelligence—inscribe itself into the imagery of "insinuation"? This strategy, however, may turn against life, as it happens whenever adaptive forms of life loop around themselves in a vicious circle. In this case, while insinuation loses its impact, adaptation and securing the needs come to the fore and human morality is shaped by pressure and fear rather than by a calling and inspiration.

To sum up, in the language of ontology, a living, conscious, and enduring incarnated *self* takes over the present (moment) by carving in it its own path of freedom, which is simultaneously being contracted and accumulated in the virtual repository of memory. Memory, in turn, continually strives to "insinuate itself into the perception of the present."[11] To reformulate it slightly, the spirit grafts itself upon matter in order to use matter to win over matter itself. Each human *self* "steals" moments from matter to weave them, irrevocably, into the living fabric of its own trajectory. We are presented here with a theatrical scene, where "insinuation" acquires the meaning of an improvised screenplay or simply, of acting out. What is acted out is human life, out of which a character emerges.

4.2 Acting Out: A Hermeneutic Insinuation

We already know that recognition, which in Bergson's vision stands for the peculiar "recollection" of the present moment, is synonymous with the moment of fusion of spirit and matter. When something by nature always occurs as if "again," or simply occurs by reoccurring, it may be said to exhibit a sort of immanent anteriority. "In fact, there is for us nothing that is instantaneous."[12] In our conscious experience we indeed come across an anteriority of twofold nature. First, there is the essential anteriority of memory, related to the nature of the past deposited in it. As noticed by Deleuze, in Bergson's conception we proceed from the past toward the present and not the other way around, because if the past were not past immediately, from the beginning, it would never be able to become what it *essentially* is, the past. The difference between the past and the present is radical. While the past, as the condition of possibility of the present, is transcendental, the present always reemerges, resurfaces.

Second, there is a bodily, kinesthetic kind of anteriority, namely, the fact that our recognition is acted out by our body—via affect, reaction—before it becomes conscious, or, in other words, prior to the actualization of a memory image. The body *as* the present moment, with its attitude, which expresses the imitating movements, selects a proper memory from the crowd of memories and provides the framework within which the memory is projected onto the actual perception. The strategy of insinuation in this case consists in that memory, itself "powerless, borrows life and strength from the present sensation in which it is materialized" as a representation.[13] Thus, *the past*, which "tends to reconquer, by actualizing itself, the influence it had lost," *resurrects in the costume of the present moment*.[14] By the same token, however, memories liberate the present from a hollow materiality, oblivion, and mechanical blindness.

By the way, a sort disquieting radicalism may be intuited in the idea that man, insofar as he is a free being, is constantly re-living the past. The future, notices Kołakowski, does not exist for Bergson, while the present in itself—as I would suggest, against some other interpreters—is never truly experienced. The most "real" is the past, and the degree of its vitality oscillates along the continuum in-between two extremes—powerlessness and vital freedom. In the modality of duration, the present translates itself into the actuality of the past. That is one of the reasons Bergson famously says "but we endure and therefore are free" (!).[15] To endure means to be oneself, to be one's own past. Entering into a relation with the inner flow of *durèe* is for Bergson an act of freedom, which is ultimately expressed in the authentic "I." There is yet another reason for which endurance implies freedom—I will return to it later.

Coming back to the question of acting out one's own *durèe*, one may notice here a quasi-hermeneutic understanding of freedom as the authorship of life. As I have already mentioned, the very idea of fabulation function may evoke similar associations. What supports this interpretation is Bergson's understanding of free action in terms of intention and recognition. Life may be compared to writing a screenplay in which natural causality is not so much suspended but rather bracketed, and the so-called "causes" are of narrative nature. Like in the case of Santayana's dramatic and narrative strategies of retaining self-integrity, we take intention for the cause. "We begin by doing what depends on ourselves . . . we act and live the belief that we have" in the power of our agency, this is where we find "at least an encouragement and an incentive" for action.[16] This is yet another example of a subtle, hermeneutic insinuation, which involves inscribing a living screenplay onto existence. Bergson may represent a peculiar hermeneutics of temporal depths, distinct from the classical, symbol-based hermeneutics due to the assumed amorphousness of the original vital impulse. But this amorphousness, just like the "nothingness" of Santayana's realm of essence, is liberating. What is more, we may even see in the author of *The Two Sources of Morality and Religion* a forerunner of the hermeneutics of suspicion. His distrust toward the realm of symbols, even though partly corrected by late Bergson, manifests itself first, in the tendency to reduce culture and social life to an instrument of taming and dominating others, and second, in the disavowal of the traditional opposition nature—culture, and placing the latter within the natural realm in its crudest, "environmental" meaning.

The idea of the intervention of the past in the present or the "infiltration" of the present by the past as essential to human agency, is a response to the alternative freedom—determinism, inherited from Cartesianism and the persistent linguistic illusion contained in the phrase "things might have been otherwise," of which Bergson was a staunch critic. In his vision freedom starts with the very fact that we endure, have a history, and accumulate memories like a snowball, to re-live them creatively myriads of times when thinking and acting. Moreover, Bergson notes that a conscious being endowed with memory can never be identical with itself, because, as a result of temporal synthesis, it undergoes a constant transmutation. Human *self* is utterly unpredictable because one can never establish a reliable point of departure, a point "zero" definable by some definite conditions. In other words, we can never "catch" and freeze a free *self* in its endurance; there is no possible formal "now" moment for the *self*. Neither can we repeat experimentally a conscious experience since for a concrete, living consciousness nothing returns; everything is moving *for real* and irrevocably.

At this point I suggest we take a somewhat provocative turn in our reading of Bergson and note that in case we ask *the* proper question—"proper" along the lines of what Santayana thought about philosophy in general—namely, the question about human finitude, our considerations may lead us to a surprising and illuminating conclusion. *The conclusion is that Bergson translates finitude into the irrevocability of the past, while making it both the condition and the instrument of freedom (!). If it is so, then, not unlike for Santayana, caring about our finitude rests in our best interest!* In other words, we owe our freedom not only to the modality of our inner *self*, to endurance, and to creative action, but also, or maybe, first of all, to the "vertical," irreducible, metaphysical realm of spirit, which is the realm of memory. The *durèe* of a human *self* could never be what it is without memory. Notwithstanding the fact that both thinkers define "spirit" differently, its ontological status makes it in both cases one of the main anthropological prerogatives.

Conceiving of freedom in terms of the integration with one's own inner evolution is—besides being an obvious departure from the substantial understanding of the *self*—a departure from the idea of freedom as unconditioned deliberation and mind's *fiat*. Just like Santayana, Bergson considers a free choice between a few "neutral" options as a retrospective illusion. And just like Santayana, he will distinguish between logical possibility and potentiality or virtuality, i.e., a certain "propensity" of the present toward this or that direction. Let us not forget that behind the "now" of a human *self* there stands the whole accumulated past. And again, not unlike Santayana, he will note that to choose freely is to recognize the vector of the evolution proper to the deeper "I." As for recognition—the core of what Bergson considers "attention to life" and one of the key concepts in his philosophy–it belongs to the realm of the author, who—when writing the screenplay for the lived stream of time—is insinuating that nothing other than his own intention is the "cause" of the course of things. Acting out as expressing *durèe* in the human world is a strategy of life—a single life and life in general—which proceeds by way of insinuation.

Now, "acting out" cannot be utterly independent of the symbolic realm. Even though Bergson—according to what he declared and what is usually ascribed to him—designed a philosophy of directedness, he was aware of the decisive power of symbols. He evoked the power of words like "freedom" and "love," words which grant definition and mobility to certain unique, ineffable qualities of endurance and let them appear among people in the guise of new emotions and new ideas. The universality of these concepts helps memory actualize itself and preserve a meaningful continuity within the heterogeneous *durèe*. Another example of such an emancipatory concept may be the concept of "human being"—a vehicle for the idea of an open and indeterminate life, life capable of love and freedom, life transgressing all definitions and its own boundaries in an unpredictable direction.

4.3 An "Epitomized Form"

Let us for a moment devote our attention to a technical aspect of Bergson's thought and note that what prompts him to assume the imagery of the play, which—by the way—puts into doubt his declaration about getting rid of all mediation, are the pairs of opposites: matter-spirit, perception-memory. Philosophers, let me quote Santayana again, who do not understand the need to introduce "a medium of knowledge, if they have any speculative competence at all, have to introduce a medium of ignorance instead."[17] Let us once again lead this inquiry into a provocative direction and ask whether it is possible that the French thinker apparently rejects the traditional Greek formal medium to introduce another medium instead, namely, the past. I would risk such an interpretation. Moreover, this would explain why the tension between the opposite registers is revealed within the conscious *self* in the guise of the paradoxical "anteriority" (which, by the way, may be encountered in other configurations and contexts also in Husserl, Heidegger, Sartre, Merleau-Ponty, Santayana, or even James, as discussed in the first chapter).

Let us have a look at the imagery employed by Bergson to convey the anteriority in question. The "I" open to *durèe*, experiences life as "a continual treading on a future which recoils without ceasing."[18] Like in front of an approaching sea wave, "I am unceasingly, towards what is on the point of happening, in the attitude of a person who will recognize and who consequently knows."[19] The duplicating of each moment into perception and memory places me in a position "of an actor playing his part automatically, listening to himself and beholding himself play." I may even seem to "split into two personages, one of which moves about on the stage, while the other sits and looks." Two *selves* may be said to exist: one "conscious of its liberty, erects itself into an independent spectator of a scene which the other seems to be playing in a mechanical way."[20] It is so because perception sees itself in the mirror of recollection.[21] Our actual existence then, "whilst it is unrolled in time duplicates itself all along with a virtual existence, a mirror image." "The entirety of our present

[then] . . . is a recollection of the present moment in that actual moment itself. It is of the past in its form and of the present in its matter. It is a memory of the present."[22] This "oscillation," "a going and coming of the mind between perception and recollection" "transports us into a stage world or a world of dream."[23]

The past, we are told "should be acted by matter and imagined by mind."[24] Imagination, via recognition, endows acting out with meaning, and the past not only uses the present, but insinuates (pretends) that it is the present. Memory in action, inclined toward the future "no longer *represents* our past to us, it *acts* it."[25] Acting is not a repetition in a strict sense, it is a paradoxical new repetition (or: the repetition of the new). It cannot be otherwise, because, let us repeat, time is absolute, the endurance of the *self*—real and concrete. On the basis of memory and endurance, the history which constitutes personality of a concrete human being grows by accumulation, and the role played shapes a person. Our character is "the actual synthesis of all our past states," the "epitomized form" of all our "previous psychical life,"[26] or, the summary of our own history.

Isn't this unceasing, creative reenactment of one's own past a worthy alternative to both the Nietzschean "eternal return" and the Heideggerian horizon of death? The present is merely a scene, where the past wins its stakes by "deceiving" necessity. It is unlikely to understand or even to notice Bergsonian strategy of "separating" consciousness from the present, unless we realize that in his vision "to be in the present and in a present which is always beginning again—this is the fundamental law of matter: herein consists *necessity*."[27] This is to say that freedom "is" beyond the present moment. Ingraining past into the present empowers a conscious, free *self*. Every act of recognition and every deed is a symptom of freedom, an act of breathing spirit into matter. The above quoted statement is the final argument for Bergson's being legitimate—within the boundaries of his vision of course—when he says that to endure is to be free. *The acting out of the past within conscious life is the proper drama of resolutions, which is staged within the medium of necessity (because of incarnation) and against it at the same time.*

4.4 Domesticating Matter: Forms of Finitude

Having sketched a certain fragmentary image, or maybe having uncovered a certain hermeneutic dimension of the difficult thought of Bergson by means of such a non-philosophical notion as "insinuation"—let us simulate a dialogue between him and Santayana, who also imagined the freedom of conscious life in terms of playing a part in a drama, and who also—against the fads of his era—chose the path of ontology, saving (by reformulation) the traditional pairs of opposites, matter and spirit, existence and essence. And not unlike Bergson, besides these pairs of opposites, he offered a theatrical imagery, or maybe even a philosophy of drama, which opened for these pairs a synergistic perspective.[28]

No matter how different their philosophical visions may be, both represent an untypical kind of naturalism. In the case of the nonreductive naturalism of Santayana (which we have referred to in some contexts as *contemplative vitalism*) we are presented with the realms of being, "uncovered" within the human experience of the world by way of a specific existential-hermeneutic phenomenology. Both thinkers are particularly interested in the perspective of conscious life, which they conceptualize around the axis of the relation between matter and spirit, save for the fact that they define these concepts differently. In Santayana's vision spirit is a perfection of psychic life, and its emergence is in the perspective of Santayana's materialism merely an accident and not a manifestation of a cosmic evolution. The conception of life of the author of *Realms of Being* is pluralist and relies on a naturalized version of Aristotelian psyche.

The conception of the author of *Matter and Memory*, in turn, is referred to as vitalism, or metaphysical naturalism, in which life—as the realm of *natura naturans*—is a central and metaphysical category. Both thinkers, anti-dogmatic as they are, are nevertheless among the few of the twentieth-century philosophers who chose the language of ontology. Both are bold critics of Cartesianism, transcendentalism, and traditional empiricism, as well as the reductive tendencies of the era, positivism, and scientism in particular. Both may be associated with the attitude of critical realism, which assumes a limited faith in the evidence provided by the basic experience of the relative unity of the world of life and action as continuous with the thinking human agent. Conscious experience of a concrete *self* is rooted in the needs and limitations of an incarnated life, and is subordinated to the requirement of intelligent action. A certain disciplined approach, however, accompanied by a proper conceptual apparatus, allows for going beyond "the curve of experience," as Bergson thought of it. This is the "beyond" sought by philosopher's intuition.

What seems to dissociate the two thinkers most radically is Bergson's postulate of the directedness of experience (there is no medium of consciousness and knowledge) and the related therewith devaluation of the symbolic sphere.[29] Santayana, in turn, claimed that "conscious" stands for "mediated," and that the phenomenal reality is a sort of drama staged upon the surface of the generative, material reality. We may detect here an echo of Kantian "thing-in-itself" and the Greek worship of form, which we may be rightly tempted to contrast with Bergson's dynamism (*sub specie durationis*). But the power of this contrast seems less obvious once we realize that Bergson's concept of the virtual past plays the role of a medium. In the light of Santayana's skepticism as to the philosophy without a "medium," we are tempted now to note that the declaration of the immediacy and directedness of experience may be treated as—and there is no better word for that in the context of this book—an *insinuation* of sort, behind which there is the proper strategy not only of replacing formal medium with a temporal one, but also making the latter into a metaphysical and transcendental category (!).

Both thinkers agree that human consciousness projects a kind of sentimental time, which is adequate for the needs and faculties of the acting and perceiving body. They both speak about the "deeper self," hiding beneath everyday cover-ups. While Santayana emphasizes that masks are the only chance for the actualization of the abstract vital code and humanity is "contained" in imagination and the spiritual epiphany of the world, along with the epiphany of the *self*, Bergson downplays the phenomenal and symbolic "surface," focusing on the depth of *durèe* and the survival of the past.

Even though Santayana is attached to a more classical understanding of the opposition matter-spirit, not unlike Bergson, he decisively rejects the Cartesian model of the subject and freedom. Thinking and intelligent action belong to the material sphere of existence, while pure and impotent spirit (like pure and impotent memory of Bergson) is responsible for the actualization of existence and representing it in a certain perspective. *It is true for both visions that with the support of scenic imagery, on the canvas of opposite ontological registers a certain dramatic reality is presented. Human consciousness in this reality serves as a stage, where these registers encounter and cross one another, and, like a dancing couple, act out the freedom of a concrete life.* Unlike in the case of the French thinker, within the thought of the thinker from Avila we move in the world of the imagined theater without fear of space and without reluctance toward the free play of imagination and *vita contemplativa*. This, however, should by no means make us turn a blind eye to *the common denominator of both philosophies, of grave importance in my view, namely that acting out replaces the immediacy of the relation between conscious life and matter.* Acting out, staging, is an obvious strategy of introducing a mediation in disguise. While the past, stored in memory, plays in *Matter and Memory* the role of a medium, the absolute "now" seems to resemble a classical nothingness, or, at least, a vector opposite to the vector of life. It is precisely the "nothing" of the absolute present, the choking, overwhelming, paradoxical, material presence that requires mediation. Let me remind you that for Bergson to be in the present is to be overwhelmed by necessity. Hence, the acting *self*, insofar as it aspires to freedom, is *never in the present* (!). As mentioned in the chapter devoted to the issue of individuation, in Santayana's vision only twice is a human being confronted directly with matter, to the effect of being "identical" with what he calls a material event—at the moments of birth and death—and that is why both moments remain covered by darkness. *Conscious life means transcending or overcoming materiality.*

Nevertheless, the obscure secret of matter, covered so diligently by life, is responsible for the embarrassing dissonance between me as myself and me as a "bygone" *self*, which Heidegger described in terms of the scandal of the facticity of *Dasein* and Bergson in terms of actor-spectator duplication. Let us not lose sight of how close Santayana is to Bergson's duplication of the *self* into the observer and the observed, when he says that "*to experience" for a human being always means "to bear true witness to oneself.*"[30] The kernel of his conception of selfhood is bridging the gap between both figures, so that the first seems less distant, the other less mechanical. What may possibly happen in this respect is the transformation of the witness into the author, or an *insinuation* that the witness is in fact the author, and this is the *credo* of the vital liberty to become oneself. The insinuation here is possible thanks to the fact that qualitative differences within the lived flux of existence are revealed and placed in the temporal perspective of memory, reflection, and projection. In other words, spiritual transcendence cuts into the thrust of time, allowing for the recognition and choice of the forms of finitude, and, consequently, drawing the trajectory of life and the shape of an integrate character.

Every scene, every new metaphor reconfigures in a fraction of a second the whole past from the viewpoint of the biographical unity we are inevitably approaching. In the contemplative vitalism of Santayana, finitude is to become voluntary—then we are free, we are the co-authors of our "fate." The primary source of our finitude is our living principle, psyche, the dynamics of which was called by Heidegger—the self-reproducing "circle of one's own constitution."[31]

Finally, having said all this, let us shed some light on Bergson's idea of freedom as the past acting through the present. Santayana sees freedom in the adequacy with which we play our vital potential when "writing" our biography, remaining careful not to forget about the margin of disinterestedness. In temporal terms we may describe psyche as a constantly self-actualizing synthesis of the history of its own dynamics, which more or less adequately expresses itself in the phenomenal, symbolic reality, or, in other words, translates itself into a living autobiography. If psyche is, to use Bergson's metaphor, a snowball of our history, our momentary potential does not originate *ex nihilo*, but is a child of an unceasing transmutation of a certain beginning, which signifies a certain end and completion. *The integrity of the self emerging from this translation of psychic trope into a meaningful reality can by all means be said to be the measure of freedom.* This is something I have been trying to show throughout this book. Now, if psyche is a synthesis of her own history, it will not be a mistake to say, after Bergson, that freedom involves creative acting out of the past in the present, the "new" repetition of sorts, in the course of which some freedom is won. *Why freedom?*—you may ask. Because as "past" you are in a sense definite (finite) and by your very finitude you shape the future, you carve it out in a meaningless, "empty" now. In other words, *you become in possession of the future, and since you are part and parcel of a universal change, you influence the whole picture of reality.* Yet, in the case of Santayana—and this is where an important difference rests—one wins freedom to finitude, freedom to form, to Gestalt, and finally, the choice of fate instead fatality imposed. Mind you that freedom here is also related to *autoteleia*. Whereas, in the case of Bergson, the stakes oscillate in-between individual freedom of creative expression and the evolutionary progress of life via humanity. An individual wins a liberating immediacy of experience by entering into an intimate relationship with the primordial impulse contained in *durèe*, an impulse which prompts humanity (through individuals) to a greater openness and greater independence from necessity. Form, end, completion, horizon of death—these are not in the focus of Bergson because for him the horizon and the completion have already been contained within the beginning (!). It is about liberation of creativity, about progress and expansion of the meaning of humanity. *Finitude we already have (in the guise of irreversibility), Bergson might say, what we need is an infinite perspective, a new birth of sorts.*

Finally, let me evoke the Bergsonian intuitive category of the "dynamic schema"—a certain premonition, an imaginary projection of the completion of a work of art or another kind of a creative project in the making. The dynamic schema is an abstract idea of the future whole of something. This category may be considered a substitute for form and wholeness—ideas which are problematic in the context of Bergson's dynamic, anti-spatial ontology. How is the dynamic schema possible at all? I don't intend to get into the details of the formation of the schema in imagination, but rather to ask about its ontological status. It is virtual, structured like memories, and its unity reflects the primordial unity of the vital impulse, the inspiration or the trace of which (and consequently a tendency) remains present in all manifestations of life. In Santayana's vision, in turn, we miss the first vital impulse, the redeeming source, universal and personal at once. But isn't an individual human life an example of arriving at such a dynamic schema? Isn't psyche herself playing here the part of the primary impulse on a micro-scale? Every single conscious life seems to be a microcosm, realization of an idiosyncratic temporality organized around the axis of a psychic trope, the mission of which is decoding the message it carries and thereby winning its own temporality as against all the chaos around. Metaphorically speaking, the struggle between material inertia and spiritual inspiration occurs within every single life. Santayana's philosophy is a kind of naturalistic hermeneutics enriched with an ontology that allows for introducing—as if with the back door—an irreducible spiritual realm into human reality. It is more modest and decisively less openly metaphysical (if at all) in comparison with the bold vision of Bergson.

In both cases, however, we are presented with a sort of individualistic humanism, which—without being (excessively and openly) anthropocentric—conceives of humanity via the lens of a spiritual challenge. Moreover, what connects both thinkers is their endeavor to secure to an individual a margin of independence from society (and any local context), and—both happen to achieve it through a rich ontology. Interestingly, they are both acutely aware of the significance of the past for human life and autonomy. Santayana speaks of historical memory as an indispensable part of the conscious formation of the common world, of any reasonable projection of future; Bergson secures to a human individual participation in the metaphysically defined virtual register of memory. To be sure, they understand memory in a very different way, but nevertheless, they *both root autonomy in continuity*. They are both radical—each in his own way. Santayana's radicalism rests in the cathartic and deconstructive potential of essences and spirit, Bergson's radicalism lies in making each individual human being a carrier of a virtual, indestructible "cone" of his own past, which may also play a cathartic and deconstructive function in relation to any fiction. In a sense, they are both engaged in the project of designing a philosophy meant to *prevent humans from turning into lunatics*, as Daniel Moreno once humorously expressed Santayana's concerns about the elusive life of human mind. The most intimate synchronicity with one's own *durèe* is equally radical a disinfectant as contemplation of pure essences.

5

Coping with Finitude

Santayana Reading Heidegger

I have referred repeatedly throughout this book to Heidegger as I find elements of his thought extremely helpful in shedding light on certain aspects of Santayana's conception of the *self* and his philosophy of life in relation to contemporary non-analytical thought. I also believe that—despite all the obvious differences—one may speak about affinities here, as suggested by Santayana himself in a couple of enthusiastic remarks concerning Heidegger's philosophy, which may be found in his correspondence dating from 1933 to 1948.[1] They may be particularly worth attention in light of the evidence of his encounter with Heidegger's thought, which are now available in the form of marginalia. My interest in establishing a dialogue between both thinkers, supported by the marginalia from Santayana's original copy of Heidegger's *Sein und Zeit*, first commenced in an article published in 2015.[2] I approach Santayana's notes not as an evidence of similarities or of his ultimate views on Heidegger but rather as suggestions of possible affinities, which happen to confirm my previously existing ideas. This chapter is a modification of the aforementioned article, which in its original form is richer in technical details but lacks the part devoted to the early Heidegger's philosophy of life and his interpretation of Aristotle that prove illuminating in the context of this imaginary debate between Santayana and the thinker from Freiburg.

In the following sections, I will go beyond the attention given by the author of *Realms of Being* to *Sein und Zeit* and look at other texts while raising the question of differences and possible similarities between both thinkers. Obviously, the chapter is not meant to be a comprehensive and conclusive comparison of two respective philosophies. Attention will be given to the transformation undergone by the idea of the *self* in both philosophies—from the abandonment of the Cartesian formula of a free conscious agent to the reinterpretation of Aristotle and partial dissolution of the "vigorous" Western subjectivity in favor of a hermeneutic *self*, marked by an aspect of passivity. Finally, the analysis is meant to reveal a common effort in providing a novel understanding of fulfillment for the newly defined human *self* within a specific philosophy of life. To achieve this aim, I will guide the reader through a few thematic contexts that are central to this book, such as transcendence and time, authenticity and spiritual liberation, the recognition of finitude, and the theater of life.

5.1 Concepts and Strategies. From a Phenomenology of Daily Life to a Hermeneutic Ontology

"Note how entirely dramatic this psychology is," Santayana noted, for "it is not science but pedantic, minute literature."[3] This *post-rational* approach, to use Santayana's own term, was akin to his understanding of philosophy as self-conscious in terms of limitations and the questions it could ask. Deprived of the illusion that philosophy should compete with science, both thinkers bracketed the Cartesian *caesura* defining the standards and objectives of modern philosophy, and took a step back to reclaim and reinterpret ancient thought with its stress on the preoccupation with life and the existential status of human thinking and self-understanding. Heidegger's skeptical comments as to the scientific aspirations of philosophy, and even more so as to the totalitarian aspiration of the sciences, are accompanied by Santayana's highly approving comments.[4] Richard Rorty took notice that Santayana and Heidegger both belonged to a community of "disillusioned" thinkers, reluctant to embrace large, optimistic projects, and yet engaged in a sort of "edifying" existential discourse.[5] Santayana viewed "the task of philosophy largely negative," as Michael Hodges and John Lachs have claimed, and believed that "whatever has existential primacy should enjoy epistemic prerogatives as well."[6]

Santayana entertained an intuition of this kind of community with Heidegger, even though he might have been of two minds about existentialism being "a sort of religious revival without any dogma or leader."[7] His marginal notes in the text of *Sein und Zeit* show that initial attempts of translation often turn into those of paraphrasing, setting off a pattern of negotiating meanings and digressions, with relatively few critical remarks for an otherwise critical reader of other thinkers. Despite difficulties in translation and points of disagreement, Santayana seems to approve of the "big picture" and the "spirit" of the book, which he recognized as sharing in the effort of redefining the position of the thinking *self* in the world after the so-called epistemological crisis. This is reflected in a major and undeniable similarity between both thinkers, which was a penchant to ontologize epistemology, inscribed in a broader context of reclaiming Aristotle. While an existential and relativistic turn was a major trend on both sides of the Atlantic, the ontological turn, present in Bergson, Heidegger, and Santayana, exemplified a rather unique radicalization of this trend, bringing back philosophical discourse to its initial dignity consisting of basic questions but within new, "realistically" outlined scopes and interests. This concerns human existence and flourishing as dependent on sanity, clear-sightedness, and understanding, as well as a need for a new, timely definition of philosophy as human activity.

Having given up on the idea of any quest for certainty based on the distinction subject/object and interest in the objective validity of claims, they pose more fundamental questions instead, for example: *What do the facts of the centrality of awareness and thinking to this particular form of life tell us about its being/nature?* As a result, the interest in the first-person perspective is not reduced to the question of subjectivity, but assumes a broader idea of the *self*. While a *human self* is implied here, ontological language and phenomenological lens allow for stripping the discourse of anthropocentric and solipsistic projections so alien to both the Santayanan and Heideggerian ideals of philosophy. What is more, in both cases the tendencies of some philosophical anthropologies to consider human being in terms of a "thing" are avoided, and the ontological concepts are allowed to—not unlike in the case of Bergson—grant to the experience of the thinking *self* a distinct temporal mode whereby a status of irreducible uniqueness and a margin of ineligibility to scientific inquiry might be secured for it.[8]

Having mentioned that the turn to Aristotle signaled the shift of interest from human being *qua* subject toward human being *qua* being, it is worth emphasizing that even though Santayana may have remained within a more traditional philosophical language, his doctrine of *realms of being*, set in a wider context of existential concern, to some extent matched Heidegger's direction of inquiry in terms of interest and strategy. Both, in an Aristotelian manner, hold the conviction that "the good of the human being . . . is an end for the sake of itself,"[9] and systematic reflection may and should bring us closer to "the relation of man and his spirit to the universe."[10] Both take the level of everyday life as their point of departure and use a modified phenomenological-hermeneutic approach to reflect in ontological terms on the deeper reality standing behind conscious experience in the world. Whereas Glenn Tiller calls the philosophy of Santayana "ordinary reflection systematized,"[11] Krzysztof Michalski has summarized Heidegger's ontological reflection as "a self-knowledge of human existence, nothing more than mere radicalization of the themes of life itself."[12] In the preface to *Realm of Spirit*, Santayana writes that "a study of the realm of spirit is therefore an exercise in self-knowledge, an effort to clarify and to discipline itself."[13] Thematically, both are interested in the reformulation of ancient *logos* (λόγος) and move within the "realm of thinking" as a spectrum ranging from a basic responsiveness to environment to philosophical sophistication, with a measure of phenomenological interest in thinking as experience and interpretation as a form of being.

Nevertheless, we should be aware that at the point of departure we have two technically different philosophies. However, as Santayana–Bergson encounter in the previous chapter proves, it is in the light of differences that any discussion of affinities may be challenging and meaningful, particularly if it encourages one to go beyond mere definitions of concepts to conceptual strategies and their consequences. Let me address briefly the major differences, paying the price of inescapable simplifications.

Santayana's declared materialism and his objectification of the planes of reality into autonomous realms of being start the list of differences between him and the German thinker, who did not subscribe explicitly to any specific philosophical tradition and, despite his indebtedness to ancient masters, was more radical in his departure from classical categories, not to mention his idiosyncratic vocabulary. This was paralleled by his dismissal of the distinction between subject and object, expressive of his being extremely cautious not to bind *Dasein* to anything that might render it an objectifiable entity or a ghostly *Cogito*.

While Santayana, in a gesture of opposition to empirical reductionism, recognizes realms of matter, essences, spirit, and truth, Heidegger gave up the idea of pure consciousness as artificial and unworldly, and substituted it with a dynamic and temporal "field of consciousness"—*the world*. Consequently, he did not consider any existentially uncontaminated planes of reality and this fact accounts for some technically unbridgeable differences between the two philosophies. Apparently, Heidegger (like Bergson) did not—in contrast to Santayana—assume any mediation within the relation of *Dasein* with the world, at least not in the sense of a distinct realm. An immediate awareness characterizes *Dasein* and the world "structurally" is a part of it. There is no place for pure essences in the context of being-in-the-world. It may seem, then, that—at least nominally and at the face value of it—Santayanan opposition between existence and essence and the very idea of essences as the only immediate objects of consciousness find no possible equivalent in Heidegger's conceptual framework. Consequently, neither Santayana's "psyche" nor "spirit," which correlate with this distinction, opens a possibility of a direct translation into *Dasein*.

The very concepts such as "ontology," "essence," or "existence" are used differently by both philosophers. Focused on an inquiry into the nature of *being* (*Sein*), the German thinker rejected the static notion of "categories," which he replaced with *existentials*, explicitly equating his unorthodox "fundamental ontology," as he called it, with the analytic of *Dasein*.[14] Consequently, all his concepts seem relative to the central idea of *Dasein*. This relativity may be partly true also for Santayana—particularly if we consider his ontology as "ironic"—but still the doctrine of realms is more objectivist and dependent on tradition. Heidegger's assumption of the direct relation between appearance and the *being* of beings may have inspired in Santayana an association with subjectivist idealism he was so critical of.

Dasein or "being-there," is essentially existential, the term "essence" understood by Heidegger—and in a sharp contrast to Santayana—dynamically, in terms of a mode of being proper to a given being. While for Santayana "existence" denoted mainly remaining in the external relations of material flux, Heidegger reserved this concept exclusively for *Dasein* and meant by it its specific, interpretive way of being, or—ontologically speaking—a way of "temporalizing" the world by means of a *finite transcendence* of sorts. To simplify the matter, Santayana is somewhat closer to Heidegger in his use of this notion whenever he speaks of the specificity of "human existence," but more so—of "spiritual existence"—a phrase appearing in the marginalia, which suggests that he was aware of the difference in question.

These conceptual intricacies are important insofar as they draw our attention to the already mentioned existence-essence distinction, which is apparently absent in Heidegger, who speaks of one dynamic, temporal reality, which is considered at first as the experiential reality of *Dasein* or the reality of existence. At this point, however, there is no disagreement between both philosophers and Santayana explicitly says that "my own existence, is the only key to existence that is supplied to me."[15] The most fundamental belief that we, as humans, have *always already* assumed, claims Heidegger, concerns the *being* of beings and this reflection requires the recognition of the so-called ontological difference. The difference—between beings and their *being*—calls for two levels of interpretation and description to meet the criteria of Heidegger's fundamental ontology. The most fundamental belief that we, as humans, have *always already* assumed, claims Santayana in turn, concerns the *existence* of ourselves and the world, being an evidence of our life-sustaining *animal faith*. The difference between what is given in intuition and what is believed and known calls for an ontological distinction. This distinction—between *is* and *exists*—is reflected in the *essence-existence* opposition.[16] For Heidegger and Santayana, *being* and (material) *existence*, respectively, mark the boundary of rational investigation and reveal a sort of tacit, "instinctive" assumption determining the nature of human way of being. Heidegger's ontology, like that of Santayana, is—to use Glenn Tiller's words—grounded "in our pre-reflective thoughts and actions."[17]

This context provides an opportunity to look at an example of Santayana's hermeneutic negotiations with Heidegger—a major conceptual analogy he was trying to establish between the classical dichotomy existence/essence reinterpreted within his own realms of being and the Heideggerian *ontisch/ontologisch* distinction. He considered it even prior to reading *Sein und Zeit*, on the basis of an essay of Heidegger in Spanish, as we can read in one of his letters to Daniel Cory.[18] Marginal notes confirm the continuity of associations and Santayana describes spontaneous belief in the world of action based on animal faith as *ontisch*.[19] Consequently, he would link *verstanden* (understood) with "intended," and *ontologisch begriffen* (conceived of ontologically, or from the viewpoint of *being*) with "intuited."[20] Technically, this identification, because of the aforementioned differences in ontologies, cannot be correct. However, Heidegger's *verstanden* can indeed be compared to Santayana's "intended" in case intent leads to an adequate knowledge of, or acquaintance with some part of existence. The second part of this comparison is more problematic because an intuition of an essence, if taken *in abstracto*, has as its object just the given essence, which may as well be a meaningless object of contemplation, while Heideggerian *ontologisch begriffen* suggests a sort of in-depth insight into *being*, while keeping in mind that *being* rests at the heart of the reality of existence.[21]

Yet, strategically and pragmatically, Santayana's general association is telling, save for the fact that it seems to have proved valid in terms of providing a working hypothesis adequate for his reading of the difficult text of *Sein und Zeit*. *Dasein's* mode of being in the world is hermeneutic. On the ontic level, it encounters other beings always contextually, always *as something* in the shared world. These beings are, Heidegger would say, *understood* by *Dasein*, and it is in the context of these beings and of this world that *Dasein* understands itself. A comparison between this intentional and interpretive "comportment" and Santayana's idea of psychic activity based on intent, supported by *animal faith* and anchored in a uniform field of action seems meaningful. Knowledge, let us recall the first sections of the study, is an "urgent and perilous adventure,"[22] measured contextually, in terms of relevance to action. Giving existential priority to this kind of awareness, which responds to psychic intent rather than to intuition of essences, Santayana wrote that a "man might experience the whole realm of essence and know nothing of this world."[23] This contextuality and precariousness describing the human *self*'s cognitive situation in the world make it to some degree comparable with *Dasein*. For both thinkers *understanding stands for the ability to contextualize in a meaningful way.*

The existential articulation of conscious experience provokes a question about the idea of human *self* held by the thinkers. This will be addressed throughout this chapter. Let me start by reminding the reader that Santayana speaks of a "*deeper self*, which is a living part of that world, existing only in contact with the rest . . . immersed in the current of . . . events."[24] To its spiritual aspect the *self* owes a naturalized transcendental vantage point and phenomenal consciousness allowing for positing an "ego."[25] The emphasis on relationality, intent, and animal faith, provokes a parallel with *Dasein* described as being-in-the-world or a being that cares about itself.

The "world" in both cases has a "subjective" undertone. The *self* has its world, delineated by the horizon of familiarity it can afford. A metaphor, which seems most adequate in expressing the nature of the affinity in question, is that for both thinkers human *self* is *a piece of self-interpreting reality, struggling with existential obscurity and a degree of non-transparency this interpretation confronts.* This involves a constant risk of misinterpretation and misrecognition, which is more pronounced in Heidegger, for whom *anxiety*, being an ontological foundation of *fear*, next to *care* and *being-unto-death*, is one of the main existentials. "Dasein, *ontologically* understood, is care,"[26] which on the ontic level manifests itself in concern and preoccupation. Santayana also speaks of psyche in terms of expectation and care, and mentions psychic experience to be anxiety-ridden in front of the reality which is to some extent threatening because unfamiliar. Likewise, for Santayana primordial, psychic experience is one of "the horrid sense of something alien and undiscoverable."[27] Existential care, perhaps less articulated than in the case of Heidegger, stands behind *sentimental temporality*. The imaginative vistas of the spiritual vantage point, sometimes ironically called "normal human pathology," actually can and often do dominate the landscape of experience. Heidegger, in turn, spoke of *ordinary/vulgar time* in reference to a commonsensical experience of time, covering the fear of misrecognition and of encountering oneself without a mask. Interestingly, Heidegger notices in *Dasein's* everyday hermeneutics an *immobilizing fallacy* of sort, similar to that ascribed by Santayana to sentimental projection. For both thinkers *care is an inherently human attitude expressive of a tension involved in the "perplexing" experience of time and the insecurity of self-interpretation.* On the level of everyday day life it may point to a gap between expectation and fact, between projection and fate.

Now let me return to the possibility of the identification of *ontologish begriffen* with "intuited," which I have previously questioned. There seems to emerge a chance for a sympathetic take on this comparison by Santayana, provided that the question we ask is what both notions *do or achieve* rather than what they literally mean. For Heidegger ontological inquiry stands for uncovering the deep or a priori constitution of some phenomenon that on the ontic level usually is overlooked due to existential obscurity. As such, it aims directly at the *being* of beings. For Santayana, essences constitute an intelligible dimension of reality, insofar as existence embodies some forms. Psyche's becoming conscious is mediated by the intuitive actualization of essences. Intuitions, then, are treated as "clues to the physical world,"[28] and as such are translated into knowledge symbolic of the world.

In correspondence to Bergson, who, according to my interpretation, replaced a formal medium with a temporal one, Heidegger, having dismissed the idea of pure consciousness, assumed another medium of phenomenality and intelligibility—the so-called *being* (of beings). The nature of the medium is obviously different than Santayanan abstract and timeless essences. For Heidegger, however—as one might argue—reality in its fundamental dimension *is* this medium. This is true, but we must remember that only theoretically is *being* directly approachable to *Dasein*. As a matter of fact, access to the *being* of beings is as problematic as the possibility of intuiting *the* essences embodied in the flux for Santayana. *Dasein*, due to its temporal constitution and existential tendencies, normally functions in such a way that *being* remains to a great extent veiled by what appears. What is important is that in praxis both essences and *being* play a function of hermeneutic environment for a human *self*. Moreover, both philosophies, by different means, *make the right interpretation a problematic and challenging task*. In this respect they are both hermeneutically oriented thinkers, whose doctrines address the ancient distinction between being and appearance.

Looking at the same problem from a slightly different angle, *ontologisch* plane has for Heidegger transcendental connotations insofar as it pertains to the constitutive condition of *Dasein's* disclosing and hermeneutic mode of being in correlation with phenomenal reality. Santayana noticed that Heideggerian *being*, especially when evoked by the German philosopher as "transcendens pure and simple" in *Sein und Zeit*,[29] plays a function similar to that of his realm of essence. Although not an autonomous realm, it is that dimension of reality which can be revealed to and understood only *by Dasein* and *via* it. Correspondingly, the realm of essences for Santayana correlates with his idea of spirit as a transcendental vantage point, a naturalized reformulation of Kantian unity of apperception.[30] Ontologically, the *self*, via the actualizing function of spirit, may rely on intuition, which makes the world accessible for thinking and intelligent action. Likewise, Heidegger says that *being* conditions "every possible existent determination" while the *being* of *Dasein* "implies the possibility and the necessity of . . . individuation"[31] just as Santayanan essences do, being on one hand the object of spiritual actualization and on the other, the ultimate "theme" of truth.[32]

Being disclosed for and through *Dasein* is called by Heidegger "veritas transcendentalis,"[33] and the being to which and via which it is revealed (*Dasein*) is a being transcending itself, standing outside itself and "making place" for something to be revealed. Realistically, Santayana finds himself in agreement[34] with Heideggerian claims that "we *must* presuppose truth [independent of judgment] . . . just as *Dasein* itself *must* always be as my own."[35] An attempt at a comparison between the *realm of truth* and Heideggerian *aletheia*/"disclosedness"[36] seems meaningful to me only in terms of their common significance for human existence, resting in a somewhat Platonic function of establishing an ultimate, not fully achievable, standard for clear-sightedness in understanding and interpretation—key for sane existence. Besides, Santayana's essences and truth as well as Heideggerian *being* and *aletheia* are ontological concepts of hermeneutic function, devoid of any intrinsic moral value, but not without importance for the overall moral outlook of their philosophies.[37]

Heidegger's peculiar, existential appropriation of transcendentalism into the mode of being-in-the-world was not at odds with Santayana's assumption of the uniformity of the field of action as the context for *animal faith*, which arises out of psychic care and "turns essences into things for the spirit."[38] The holistic environment of understanding designed by Heidegger represented a chance for bridging the discontinuity between intent and intuition, material flux and consciousness in Santayana's thought. In other words, it offered a unifying light to his own philosophy "torn" in-between his divergent idealistic and naturalistic sympathies. The idea of the "naturalized" a priori quality of spiritual openness attached to psychic intent is reflected in marginal digressions, like the ones about "transcendental apology for naturalism" being possible since "the world must be discoverable to the mind."[39] Some other notes mention matter as transcendentally posited object of intent and substantiality being "a transcendental category,"[40] which "turns phenomena into knowledge."[41] The most striking expression of this existentialist "transcendentalism" is contained in a paraphrase from Heidegger: "We believe in people because we care for them" (!),[42] generalized elsewhere as a "prior assumption of existence in care."[43] The emphasis on the priority of care, the equivalent of which has been said to rest in Santayana's conception of psychic *deeper self*, suggests an implicit context of a finite life, even if the word "life" itself remains literally unuttered by the Heidegger of *Sein und Zeit* due to his choice of a less empirical concept of "death" as a horizon.

While reading the German philosopher, Santayana confronted some of his own philosophical antipathies, like the one toward instrumentalism of any sort. He criticized Heidegger's emphasis on the utility of things, calling it "a philosophy of acquisition," the danger of which rests in that it reduces things to their functions.[44] Yet, finally he seems to grant the possibility of a "tolerable interpretation" to this "utility criterion of reality," provided that "for utility we substitute *relevance to action*," meaning "a discovery of them [things] in their own dynamic locus which [at the same time] is the locus of the *self* though not of the spirit."[45] Heideggerian rejection to approach things via formal identity *in abstracto* was part of his overall project of understanding the world contextually, via *being* as a sort of dynamic reformulation of *logos*.[46] This was in line with Santayana's earlier position on "understanding" as meant to reveal not an abstract piece of reality but rather *a situation*.

Let us note that Santayana at this point uses the term *self* to refer to *Dasein* and to distinguish it from his notion of *spirit*. His marginal notes show his growing awareness of the fact that Heidegger replaced "consciousness" with an indefinite immediate awareness attuned to dynamic reality.[47] Clearly, due to the differences between their ontologies his reading would not benefit by an attachment to clear-cut technical distinctions and oppositions. Instead, he focused on certain strategic affinities among large concepts and ideas. His associations seem meaningful due to the fact that both were drawing on categories inherited from ancient metaphysics, which they reinterpreted in the light of what was at stake in their philosophical enterprises. We are presented with ontologies serving as a means of rendering and making philosophically operative the experience of conscious life in the world. In other words, conceptual framework captures the complexity and precariousness of human existence seen as an interpretative attitude toward the world *and* from within it. Correspondingly, Santayana made an insightful remark in one of his letters, calling Heidegger's philosophy a "conceptual idealism."[48] Once the contrasts between ontological tenets and meanings are acknowledged, the contextual, strategic affinities between their philosophies may still be appreciated, in particular in the resulting similarities between their visions of the *self* in the light of man's insecure existential status or—if you will—*conditio humana*.

5.2 The *Self*, *Dasein*, and Incarnate Spirit

In the marginalia, having noticed that *Dasein* cannot be identified with either of his own concepts—*spirit* or *psyche*—Santayana comes to refer to it synthetically as "spirit incarnate," "embodied mind,"[49] or "the self." These comments reveal his ambiguity toward the concept of *Dasein*, which was neither in line with his preferred Platonic vision of spirit "encaged" in matter and transcending existence, nor with his underlying naturalism. Dissatisfied with Heidegger's emphasis on in-worldliness and his unorthodox conception of transcendence within immanence, Santayana notices that "to see only the earthly predicament is lack of spiritual freedom."[50] On the other hand, however, "all this is most carefully imagined but would be clearer and less arbitrary if it were attached to animal instincts and organs."[51]

As we have seen in the preceding chapters, Santayana's psycho-spiritual *self* can neither be called immanent *in toto*, nor can it be reduced to an entity and fully objectified. "The self" or "spirit incarnate" seem closer to Heideggerian *Dasein* than "sprit" or "psyche" alone. The "embodied mind" appearing in the marginalia, a more "modern" version of "spirit incarnate," is interesting as it happens to anticipate future Heidegger's attention to embodiment. None of them may be treated as an equivalent of *Dasein*, but what Santayana hoped for was a possible approximation at best. Heidegger speaks of *Dasein* in terms of the *self* (*Selbst*) as follows:

> The ontological structure that I *myself* in each instance am is centered in the self-constancy of existence . . . the *self* cannot be conceived of either as substance or as subject, but is rather grounded in existence, . . . care and . . . temporality.[52]

The rootedness of the *self* in existence and care makes it structurally temporal, dynamic, and always "being-ahead-of-oneself."[53] Zahavi notes that in Heidegger's conception "the co-disclosure of the *self* belongs to intentionality as such." Every experience of the world implies that "I am always somehow acquainted with myself."[54] The existential intentionality of *Dasein* in some measure matches the idea of the *deeper self*. With the flux of existence defined as a "passage from potentiality to act,"[55] we may view psyche as a distinguished part of this flux, representing its own principle of change, with self-awareness (and self-consciousness) being part of—in Aristotelian terms—psychic *entelechia*.

Furthermore, *Dasein* exhibits an aspect of a "clearing"[56] (*Lichtung*), an opening of a revelatory potential, where the world can come to light and be understood. Marginalia suggest that Santayana was aware of the presence of this aspect in Heidegger and associated the quality of epiphanic "transparency" and the luminousness of *Dasein's* temporal stretching (*lumen naturale*) with his notion of impotent spirit. This negotiation of meaning can also be traced in some marginal digressions on spirit, inspired by *Dasein*: "Essentially open to truth and a witness of reality . . . rooted in the world revealed to him."[57] Interestingly, Heidegger explicitly claims that *Dasein* is ""spiritual"[58] but not in the sense of spirit as distinguished from matter but rather in an integral sense of a living, embodied, interpretive temporality. The finite transcendence of being-in-the-world and at the same time of being-ahead-of-oneself makes *Dasein* a spiritual being, namely, a self-transcending one, which cannot be reduced to a "thing" precisely because it is never "here." Such a conception of selfhood justifies Santayana's choice of the notion "spirit incarnate" as distinguished from a "pure spirit."

To sum up, Heidegger's existential position on selfhood might have inspired a sense of affinity in Santayana in as much as they share in an effort of exorcising the "phantoms" of a disembodied subject, a fixed "ego"/*cogito*, and a magical *fiat* of a powerful subject of will. They were moderately and not uncritically inspired by Kant. Heidegger considered transcendental subject as too "isolated" and unworldly. While saying "I," *Dasein* is expressive of itself as a worldly and caring being.[59] "Ego"/"I" for both thinkers is but an aspect of selfhood and the latter is unthinkable without a temporal, dynamic context of existence and care. For Santayana the continuity of selfhood is psychic; for Heidegger, "the only 'constancy' of the *self* rests in care." In other words, care cherishes primacy in relation to selfhood, "the structure of care . . . includes the phenomenon of selfhood" and makes it existential.[60] As existential and temporal, the *self* is potential, pregnant with futurity and sustained in the anticipation of itself.

Hermeneutic approximations suggested by Santayana in the marginalia show him moving in the right direction and possibly finding some inspiration for his ongoing work on *Realms of Being*, even if it be only a modest one. As for affinities, I would suggest that a common denominator should be sought in the idea of a caring, relational life that is the genesis of selfhood and of all meaningful contexts within an otherwise unfamiliar and threatening reality. This originated from Aristotle—a major source of inspiration for both thinkers.[61]

5.3 Lived Experience and Passivity

Santayana's account of the nature of psychic activity at the threshold of conscious life finds an equivalent of sorts in the early Heidegger's phenomenological analysis of life's movement described in terms of relationality, facticity, care, and meaningfulness.[62] Life in its basic dimension may be described as "unrest" and anticipation, with the *self*, still pre-reflective, encountering itself engaged in the world of action.[63] There is an aspect of passivity ascribed to life and reflected in lived experience, which is manifested in that "life abandons itself to a certain pressure exerted by its world"[64] and "in caring, life experiences its world."[65] This recognition of passivity, of being (an involuntary) subject to something, inevitably related to the condition of incarnation, brings to the surface—key in Santayana's philosophical investigations—the question of finitude. As we may remember from another section, Ricoeur, to highlight the aspect of finitude and helplessness, spoke of a *suffering subject*. In Heidegger's lectures on the basic concepts of Aristotle, *pathoi* (affects) determine and at the same time are symptoms of passivity in that they mean that "something may happen . . . something occurs to me . . . [and] my attunement to this occurring affects me."[66] Affects are related to *energeia*, and beings thus characterized "carry in themselves the possibility of something occurring to them in the circle of their constitution."[67] This, as we shall later see, would contribute to the idea of the so-called *ruinance*, but for the present moment it is important for us in terms of passivity.

The passivity of being affected, in *Being and Time* introduced under the label of *attunement*, is part of the integral experience of the *self*. In the case of Santayana's psycho-spiritual unity, psyche seems to be an active part, in the sense of agency, and the spirit is impotent or passive, but psyche as a principle of definiteness, determines organic responsiveness and vulnerability to the influence of the environment, and—as such—*is responsible for the experience of being affected*. At the ontic level, ordinary bodily experience contains an element of *inertia*. While my own physical well-being is the most immediate object of my care, things happen to my body, or I find it in pain beyond my control. Bodily states may enforce, despite my conscious will, different moods on me. I find my body as a fact having a powerful influence on my wellbeing. It is not uncommon for the experience of the *self* that psychic will proves a burden and counts as part of my *sphere of helplessness*. As long as "psyche is an object of experience to herself,"[68] notes Santayana, she is a "burden to herself, a terrible inner compulsion to care, to watch, to pursue and to possess."[69] No wonder that Santayana, in a sensible marginal note quoted previously, identifies care (*Sorge*) as "concern or care: the primary connection of spirit with flesh."[70] The element of material *inertia* and compulsion contribute to an experience of passivity or, at least, of dependence. Ontologically, these intricacies of lived experience are accounted for by the impotence of spirit or, in other words, its status of the "witness" of existence.

David Wood defines experience in Heidegger as an "appropriative recognition of our 'passivity.'"[71] "Response, dependence, essential relationality," notices the author, are ascribed to the subject by Heidegger and subjective experience is defined in terms of a fundamental openness.[72] "Recognition . . . of this structure of receptivity" belongs to the very idea of experience.[73] For the German thinker, of whom it might be said was engaged in a lifelong attempt of reinterpreting *animal rationale*, even the activity of speaking "is conditioned by something else—something more 'middle voice' than a passivity," as Wood has pointed out.[74] Interestingly, Santayana also considered speech as a psychic activity, to which spirit is a witness rather than the source of origin.[75]

Santayana's double-edged strategy of saving the idea of consciousness from empiricist reduction while depriving it of excessive ambitions resonates in the following passage: "when this exclusively spiritual autonomy of spirit is thoroughly understood," we read, "the existential dependence of spirit becomes inoffensive."[76] The condition of dependence "allows spirit to exist, since it exists precisely by feeling potentiality, momentum, interaction and tension."[77] The "intellectual dominion" of spirit is valid exclusively in its own perspective, for spirit as such "belongs here below, not yonder, *ekei*, in the Platonic heaven."[78] The sense of helplessness, spiritual dependence on existence, and impotence maintained in the actualization of essences leading to the "epiphany" of the world are those parts of Santayana's ontology of the *self* that justify his sense of affinity with the emphasis Heidegger placed on the receptivity and the epiphanic aspect of *Dasein*. This affinity alone between the two thinkers, inscribed in a broader context of ontologizing epistemology, is enough, despite all differences, to make any comparative effort justified and of value.

Undeniably, both thinkers defined themselves partly by opposition both to the idealistic solipsism and the imperialism of the subject of will. Santayana could not have been more clear about it and more akin to Heidegger than in his declaration from *Dialogues in Limbo*: "subjectivity is a normal madness in living animals. It should be discounted, not idolized, in the philosophy of the West."[79] Willing to preserve the dignity of consciousness as such, Santayana did not go as far as to get rid of the subject/object relationship in his own language, but the doctrine of impotent spirit does express an endeavor to diminish the ultimate power of this "grammatical" structure in shaping philosophical discourse.[80]

Accordingly, in both philosophies the meaning of the *self* is largely modified in relation to the aforementioned traditions. It is approached as a dynamic, open, relational, and caring being, usually described in terms of a movement, which ontologically exhibits an inner difference or a split on the account of the previously discussed distinctions between existence and essence or between beings and the *being* of these beings. The nature of its agency is more humble and no longer unquestionably associated with the idea of free will translated into the power of *cogito* over the world. The aspect of receptivity and dependence, far from signifying "uselessness" in the context of life, belongs to the redefinition of the concept of the *self* shared by both thinkers.

A look back at Heidegger's lectures on Aristotle reveals the emphasis placed by him on the idea of passivity in the writings of the Greek thinker, both in respect to psychic affects as well as *nous*, which, like *light*—is "the condition of possibility for something in general to be encountered by living things."[81] Santayana's spiritual epiphany may be associated with Heideggerian understanding of transcendence as described in the following passage:

> Dasein "transcends" means: in the essence of its being it is world-forming, "forming" [*bildend*] in the multiple sense that it lets world occur, and through the world gives itself an original view [*Bild*] that is not explicitly grasped, yet functions precisely as a paradigmatic form [*Vor-bild*] for all manifest beings, among which each respective Dasein itself belongs.[82]

Having said this, one attempting an honest comparison between both thinkers cannot fail to observe how far more radical Heidegger is in depriving *Dasein* of any trace of essentiality or definiteness, except for throwness and the horizon of death. Its ground is non-essence or "the abyss of ground." Some interpreters articulate Heidegger's transcendentalism more than others do. Paradoxically, *Dasein* is meant to be a condition of possibility for itself, making its own constitution resemble an "endless iteration."[83] "An empirical history of a human being," notices Jagiełło, is possible only on the ground of its a-priori basis.[84]

Meanwhile, we have Santayana claiming that "the process [of life] that is to be expressed in consciousness . . . must first have a particular character and scope of its own."[85] There is a limited determinateness resting in the idea of psyche, which might be contrasted with the transcendental, formal structure of *Dasein*. The question to ask is: *to what an extent throwness and death in their relation to the finite spectrum of one's own possibilities determine a "character and scope of its [Dasein's] own"?* Might it perhaps turn out that Dasein's freedom is ultimately narrower than that of Santayana's self? Let us now recall and rephrase the formula of the twofold individualization of human being discussed previously: *any particular human being "becomes" in a twofold sense: as a fact and as freedom.* The *self*, correspondingly, experiences itself in a double way and *strives to be the "cause" of its own fate (facticity), be it in the sense of co-authorship.* What is at stake here is to make use of the freedom the *self* has at its disposal in the light of the awareness of its own finitude. Now, psychic basis of human life may be compared to Heideggerian *throwness*, which was later associated by the thinker with embodiment.

5.4 Transcendence, Freedom, and the Non-Transparency of the *Self*

As we have concluded in the second chapter, Santayana seems to be drawing in front of the reader two *vistas*—that of a dynamic psycho-spiritual unity and that of an *abyss* underlying conscious experience, which is reinforced by his ontological distinctions. Hermeneutically speaking, both perspectives are complementary and may perhaps evoke associations with Heidegger's distinction between ontic and ontological plane. This fragile, aporetic unity of the *self* in Santayana's account places him close to the traditions of existentialism, phenomenology, and hermeneutics, which often draw on *aporias* and tensions, if not directly on nothingness, in their visions of selfhood. As evoked in the first chapter, Zahavi notices the presence of a "blank point" in some phenomenological theories of the *self*[86] while Heidegger's *credo* in this respect could not be more explicit: "*without the original manifestness of the nothing, no selfhood and no freedom*" (!).[87] Lionel Trilling, sensitive to the existentialist tinge in Santayana, recognized that "the knowledge of the abyss, the awareness of the discontinuity between man and the world . . . [was] the forming perception of Santayana's thought."[88] Daniel Moreno, as the readers already know, claims a dissolution of the *self* is implied in Santayana's philosophy.[89] I rather disagree with this idea, even though Santayana's poetics does evoke associations of this kind. Let us shed some light on the *abyss* in question in the context of time and transcendence.

Dasein, "being-there," is already from the get-go and by the very nature of its name self-transcending, which Santayana, in a brief but insightful remark, interpreted as "to be out of sorts is the beginning of self-consciousness."[90] It is crucial to note that in Heidegger's language "transcendence" replaced traditional epistemological concepts such as consciousness and subject-object relation. Human mode of being is that of going beyond, projecting, encountering, and understanding. These are not "activities" one may refrain from but something essential for *Dasein*. Human existence essentially *is* transcendence for Heidegger. The concept, loaded with the whole history of metaphysical and theological meanings, here is inscribed into a temporal and finite framework. The nature of transcendence is most clearly exposed here:

> Transcendence means surpassing [*Uberstieg*]. . . . Transcendence belongs to human . . . as the fundamental constitution of this being . . . [It] makes possible such a thing as existence in general . . . If one chooses the title of "subject" for that being that we ourselves in each case are . . . then we may say that transcendence designates the essence of the subject, that is the fundamental structure of subjectivity . . . to be a subject means to be a being in and as transcendence.[91]

Transcendence, as (self-) awareness of *Dasein*, acquires a transcendental connotation, as it conditions the possibility of any project of the world and of the *self*. Transcendence, we read, "means projection of world."[92] Projection is possible on the ground of an originary "being held out into the nothing,"[93] which is yet another description of *Dasein* as a transcending being, a description which articulates the task of establishing a relation between existence and meaning. This relation is what Heidegger calls *understanding*.[94] To translate understanding into the language of freedom—it involves a constant constructing and maintaining a meaningful relation of the *self* within the projected world of possibilities. Since the perspective Heidegger proposes is a finite one, the freedom he means is "freedom for ground," where "free selves . . . [are] obliged to themselves,"[95] or, in other words, *Dasein* is placed by freedom "before its finite choice, i.e., within its destiny."[96] If we are to preserve a traditional association of subjective freedom with spontaneity, we must understand that *"the selfhood of that self that already lies at the grounds of all spontaneity, however, lies in transcendence."*[97] The above quoted words are absolutely crucial for grasping the sophistication of this understanding of freedom. To be free is to be placed "within" and "before" one's own fate. To be free is to be ahead of time, a requirement which *Dasein* fulfills by way of its transcending, a priori status. Could it lead us to a conclusion similar to that reached in the analysis of freedom in Bergson's philosophy, namely that freedom is inalienable? I think such a conclusion would be legitimate. It seems that the strategy of Heidegger is to fortify the *self* in autonomy. But freedom is incomplete and fragile unless *Dasein* is ready to *decide*. Freedom, then—and this may be a Kantian heritage—implies both *obligation* (in relation to one's own fate) and *responsibility*. This conclusion, I would suggest, uncovers a certain *ethos* inherent in this vision.

Santayana was also sensitive to the idea of transcendence, which is in fact "imposed" by his ontological distinctions resulting in the lack of direct continuity between spirit and matter. Spiritual life and contemplation seem to be a quite common context for this concept in interpretations of his thought. Indeed, a promise of liberation is contained in that spirit should "disengage itself from . . . [material] process," and "transcend that remorseless flux . . . , look away from it to an eternal world."[98] This Platonic sympathy for eternity is probably an element that most sharply distinguishes the *tone* of Santayana's thought from that of Heidegger. His playing on the superiority, and at least partial autonomy of the spirit reflected in that "the contraposition of detachment/attachment, ever-present in Santayana's writings,"[99] is hardly reconcilable with Heidegger, even though mature Heidegger grew increasingly contemplative.

But in a number of Santayana's texts transcendence is mentioned as something more basic, implicit in the relation of spirit to time and inherent in the *structure* of the *self*. Conscious, embodied experience involves a temporal stretching in two directions, one longitudinal, "keeping pace with the changes of the body," and one vertical, which provides for a "synthetic survey" and involves going beyond the here-and-now.[100] The spirit, by its share in the eternal realm of essences, may be said to transcend the flux of existence by nature. If we probe deeper, transcendence begins already with psychic intent, which triggers the acts of spirit. Psyche transcends the flux in which it is anchored. Humans, as spiritual, imaginative beings, always to some extent transcend their own finitude in the process of thinking, which is manifest in the ability to manipulate absent objects. Finally, Santayana places "the root of self-transcendence" in the very "essence of existence" (!).[101]

Transcendence is intrinsically related to the blank point in conscious experience, as discussed previously. The transcending *self* always and inevitably "misses" something of its own temporal depth. In Santayana's words, as a result of the "very perplexing" relation to time, mind can be but "the voice of the passing moment."[102] Elsewhere we read about an "assault" of a groundless reality in the guise of the world revealed to the spirit, followed by its lapsing into non-being.[103] Heidegger locates the blank spot in a variety of *Dasein's* moments and modalities, for example underneath the already mentioned *vulgar experience of time*—when *Dasein* misses itself.

The infinity of the realm of essences apparently places no limits on spiritual transcendence, but a finite life, to which spirit is tied does. Otherwise there is no footing either for transcendence or for "finding oneself in the world." Not "by quitting it" but "by understanding the world" can spirit be liberated, for it "lives by finding itself in the world."[104] This idea is expressive of a "holistic" tendency in Santayana, where transcendence is curbed by life itself. Nevertheless, the "perplexing" experience of time provokes a question: *What impact on the self has this "ghostly" effect of the self's problematic relation to time, or, stated otherwise, its situatedness at the crossing of the longitudinal and vertical stretch?* A marginal note seems to provide an interesting hint. Santayana draws an association between the negative revelation of his own known as "nothing given exists" and the Heideggerian notion of "attunement" (*Stimmung*). Here I would like to ask the reader for some patience when following me through some more technicalities in the paragraphs to come, where I will try to account for this association with an interesting conclusion in view.

The temporal "perplexity" of the spirit diagnosed by Santayana, makes the *self aporetic*, and in some respect akin to *Dasein's* being always not-at-home. As discussed in the second chapter, an ontological discontinuity rests "underneath" the living process of interpretation and explains the fact that knowledge of the world is founded on faith. Let me also remind the reader of John Lachs's remark that the lack of continuity between perception and material reality may be the key to the sustaining of subjective autonomy in Santayana's vision.[105] Simultaneously, the setting of the *self* on the borderline between two registers makes human experience of existence a *liminal* one, as proposed by Levinson.[106] There is an aspect of illusion to it, experience, "as it comes, is illusion . . . the source of illusion [being] . . . my animal nature, blindly laboring in a blind world."[107]

As already mentioned, the gap between existence and essence is bridged in everyday life by animal faith, which, supported by memories and prediction, renders the world recognizable and relevant to action. A life-sustaining, moral, narrative unity of life is established by the price of the so-called "normal madness," as Santayana used to refer to the fictional and hypostatic nature of mental life. About the peculiarity of the transcendental temporality originating in consciousness and making possible world-formation, Santayana wrote:

> Consciousness has the privilege of actuality, in a sense not applicable to the other realms of being. . . . Consciousness does not share the temporal structure of the specious flux which it spans nor the material flux . . . in which the organ of consciousness, the psyche, participates. Should we say, then, that consciousness is out of time? . . . Consciousness is so truly in time that of all existences it is the most ephemeral; . . . a corollary to materialism: all nature lives, cares, and is conscious, in as much as it is all concerned in the process which culminates at times in life, consciousness and preference.[108]

Intuitions, as mentioned previously, miss the temporality of the flux and are only loosely connected to the dynamic reality and always late in relation to it. In the process of interpretation they become masks—meanings contingently attached to natural occasions yet adequate for a concrete life context. *This temporal "strategy" of conscious life, if analyzed in abstracto and in the context of the distinction between essence and existence maintained by Santayana, is a way of making a detour around the burdensome fact that "nothing given [meaning: no essence given in intuition] exists."* The necessity of this hermeneutic *detour* might be additionally illustrated in association with the experiment in radical skepticism (*SOPM*), where, after giving up all existential claims, the skeptic is left with a bare essence. Daniel Moreno draws an analogy between *solipsism of the present moment* and a mystical insight, which, once experienced, continually "haunts" one's perception of reality.[109]

Now, implicit in the idea of the *self* is some sort of self-givenness, required as the condition of subjective experience and any further self-referentiality. Santayana speaks of an "I," which he refers to in his phenomenological descriptions as *travelling now* or *migrating ego*. Considering this conceptually hypostatized object of self-reference in the light of the distinction essence-existence, a question arises: *How is the self given to itself?* This is where the aspect of ontological difference comes to the fore.

There is a bodily, "nagging" non-transparency aspect of self-experience which intrudes upon the field of consciousness. "Nothing could be more obscure" than "a direct experience of psyche," a "knot . . . of latent impulses," in "a certain sense of personal momentum."[110] This primordial background of conscious experience, a symptom of the relatedness and responsiveness of the psyche to the environment, is the condition and the very core of the *self*, a controlling factor of mental life, which itself is "verbal, heated, histrionic," and "superficial."[111] Psyche is the *self* insofar as "she is object of experience to herself," says Santayana; and the understanding of the *self* which psyche can achieve *via* the spirit is vague because it involves confrontation with "a foreign language" of existential flux.[112] *The uncanny intrusion of the foreign language into the conscious realm is referred to as "incarnation."* As mentioned earlier, human body belongs to the matter-of-factness of existence and as such is "given" *post-factum*. There is also an idea held by the *self* of itself as continuous, drawing on memory, preference, aspirations, and projections. This idea belongs to the fictive dimension of *sentimental time* and is always attached to the "I" posited. It may be true of Santayana that the *self*, as a psycho-spiritual unity supported by animal faith, confirms itself via effective and intelligent action and interaction with the world. This level corresponds to Heidegger's ontic dimension. It tells us only that the *self* believes in itself existing and action attests to this belief. But this is not what Santayana, considering his ontology, means by "givenness." There is no full immediate givenness of the *self*, for if there were, its object by definition would be nonexisting. If there is material existence involved, the *self* cannot be directly given in intuition, save by proxy, as an idea or a mask. Neither can the spirit, as an aspect of life, be given; first, because it consists in acts of actualization, and second, because Santayana holds that it cannot be fully objectified, even though it is said that there is a vague experience of an openness or light.[113]

The intrinsic non-transparency, the blank point within *self* and the fact of a hypostatic "ego" put forward or "risked" by the psychic *deeper self*, or by a life calling for identity, reinforce the enigmatic and elusive aspect of the nature of selfhood. The *self* seems to be constantly in the making, like a living costume assumed by the psyche in her dealings with the world, or, in other words—a Pascalian wager in her venture for fulfillment.

An association between the non-transparency of Santayana's *self* and *Dasein's attunement* enforces itself, and seems to appear in the marginalia too.[114] The fact that *Dasein* is always in such-and-such a mood, or, in ontological terms, is always somehow *attuned*, is, as Heidegger explains, evidence of its finding itself as already having been "disclosed."[115] *Dasein* is literally missing itself, it is always too late for itself. Heidegger explicitly says that normally *Dasein "fails to see itself"* in its *being*, it "overlooks" itself and it is a kind of fundamental overlooking.[116] This is because *Dasein* tends to see itself either as one of the things/masks it encounters in the world or as a fixed, disembodied "I." Its ignorance or "turning" away from this "burdensome fact" of *attunement* and *throwness* is but a reconfirmation of its factical way of being, just like Santayana's spiritual rebellion against the facts of existence. No declaration of "rational" justification for finding oneself thus-and-so can eliminate this uncanny aspect of *Dasein*, which is always already there and "stares at it with the inexorability of an enigma."[117] The paradox and "the scandal" of this matter-of-factness for the *self* lies in that "existentially and ontologically there is not the slightest justification for minimizing the evidence of attunement by measuring it against the apodictic certainty of the theoretical cognition of something merely objectively present."[118] Another aspect of this "thus-finding-oneself-again-and-again" is that one is placed in "the circle of their constitution" and a repetitive pattern of the *self* is established, upon which something new can occur and one can become affected anew by one's own "attunement to this occurring."[119]

In his reading of Aristotle, Heidegger notes that *soma* (usually translated as "body") for the Greeks connoted an *obtrusiveness* and "self-evidence" of a sort.[120] In case of a living being, it was the first psychic *entelechy*— "the ontologically basic determination of living" and its *ousia* (substance) at once.[121] As a seat of certain potentiality, human psyche is the source of preferences and subject to sensations, feelings, and moods.[122] Consequently, affects are psychic expressions and an evidence of some initial determination.[123] The future orientation of this being, rooted in potentiality, finds its expression in *hexis*—sometimes translated as a "state," "condition," or (in Heidegger's texts) as "disposition." This disposition, worked out on the ground of affects and attunement, and conceived of as *areti* (excellence), defines the relation a human being establishes with his own being in the world. According to my reading, *this is the way Heidegger endows becoming with a dimension of a self-imposed salvation* (!). It intrudes the psyche through affects, revealing the passivity of its finitude, and pushes it into regaining composure. "By way of something encountering me, occurring to me, I am not annihilated, but instead I myself first come into the genuine state, namely the possibility that was in me now becomes genuinely real."[124]

Attunement, as one of *Dasein's* existentials, finds an equivalent in what is called by Santayana the experience of "spirit incarnate." It involves an element of irrational *inertia*, which from the perspective of the spirit "imposes" on the *self* a certain non-transparent, persisting *status quo*, which by no means can be fully explored or rationally explained. A certain *mask* through which the *self* perceives itself does not reveal the dynamic, existing psyche because, as something given in intuition, it cannot do so. The object of self-reference, then, apparently in each case *is* but does not *exist*, even though it is fully dependent on existence.[125] Ultimately, the genesis of the problem may be said to begin along with the emergence of the psyche, which is alive, existing, and which displays a certain trope, and by being a pattern announces an essence. Self-consciousness then, conceived of in the language of the distinction between essence and existence, literally reveals the difference between *is* and *exists*. There is an explicit passage that accounts for the paradox of the unbridgeable difference between planes of experience within "one fact," and consequently, for the impossibility of givenness:

> A man habitually identifies himself as much with his body as with his spirit: and since both are called "I," it is no wonder if what happens in each is felt to be also the work of the other. And the connection is radical and intimate in reality; the problem not being how the two happen to be united but in what respect we may justly distinguish them. The difference between myself as a transcendental centre or spirit and myself as a fact in the world is, in one sense, unbridgeable; but not because they are two facts incongruously or miraculously juxtaposed in the same field, but because they are realizations of the same fact in two incomparable realms of being. *There is only one fact*, more or less complex and extended, an incident in the flux of existence; and this fact lying in the realm of matter by virtue of its origin, place, time, and consequences, contains a transcendental apprehension of all things, in moral terms and in violent perspective, taken from itself as centre.[126]

This dualism, or difference within a unity shares some implications of a Heideggerian ontological difference manifested by *Dasein* in that it opens the way to speaking of the *self* in terms of a problematic and fragile unity of life on its way to fulfillment. This explains why next to Heidegger's account of *attunement* Santayana concludes in the marginalia, that "nothing given exists."[127] The whole sense of this juxtaposition becomes more telling when this negative "revelation" is rephrased as "the existing is beyond givenness," or conscious existence is non-transparent to itself save as a mere fact or an idea. This context of *missing oneself* or *overlooking oneself* leads us directly to Santayana's *spiritual distraction* and Heidegger's *inauthentic being* as phenomena calling for the revision of man's relation to his own finitude.

5.5 Modalities of Life: Strategies of Missing Oneself and the Recognition of Finitude

Looking again at Heidegger's *Phenomenological Interpretations of Aristotle* helps us understand the basis for Santayana's sense of affinity with Heidegger, in particular the association of *distraction*, "impeding the proper movement of life,"[128] to which Santayana devoted a chapter in *Realms of Being*, and early Heidegger's *ruinance* or the *inauthentic being* of *Being and Time*. The principal focus of the preoccupation of the thinker from Freiburg is life as a movement of *factical* structure and of fundamental relational character identified as *care*. The interpreting *self* encounters itself in the world in a meaningful way whereby some possibilities of living are actualized and life can be defined as a "nexus of actualization."[129] In its maturation, life has a direction and there is always a distance in view to be covered and anticipation involved. When an element of inertia intervenes and prevails, direction turns into *proclivity*, which fossilizes life, which "abandons itself to a certain pressure exerted by its world."[130] Possibilities are lost from sight and expectation turns into *presence*. In other words, *Dasein* instead of initiating situations occupies the position of a spectator.

As a result of this "flight away from the life of encounter"[131] the *self* finds itself as "already there," as reflected. This is possible because life's nature is to be "outside itself" in the sense of "before itself," but "before" easily changes into "away" and "against itself"[132] and life engages into the "strategies of missing itself."[133] Nevertheless, just as Santayana noted that the fact of distraction implies something better or deeper, Heidegger says that the "against," which in *Sein und Zeit* appears as *inauthenticity* and *falling prey*, suggests immediately that there is "something else" against which this "against" mode can in the first place occur. What is meant here as endangered by the loss of proper direction is the movement of a particular life towards its good or the perfection, in the Aristotelian sense. To quote Scott Campbell once again, for the early Heidegger "the good of the human being is an end for the sake of itself."[134] Heidegger's concern about authenticity in the sense of *truth to the self* expresses his emphasis on the intrinsic dignity of fulfilled existence. In the other of his books on Aristotle mentioned here, Heidegger notes that "*telos* is what one quite generally designates as *eudaimonia*, and this is generally translated as happiness."[135] He warns emphatically against understanding Aristotle's general outlook as teleological in the modern sense of utility and interest—this ultimate *telos* is for its own sake. Aristotle's teleology is rather concerned with "the end" understood as completion, a limit that endows life with a proper meaning, where "proper" refers to the outmost possibilities of being hidden in this very life.[136] Santayana, by giving priority to "the hidden nature and real opportunities" in terms of an ultimate meaning of the good of human life, seems to be making a similar claim.[137] In this light, according to Heidegger, "even the end of life, death, is called consummation."[138] *Telos* or *eschaton* is an individualizing factor for a life, and along with the perspective of the good, it makes this life properly human. "The good" then is not only the horizon and the limit, but the criterion for "cultivating dispositions" with completeness in view.[139] Completeness pertains to *bios*, which implies a "life-account"—a "history of a life."[140]

In *Being and Time* the vocabulary is different but the idea is partly sustained and *Dasein*, being always on its way, must *understand* its own finitude and endow it with meaning. This *hermeneia* of existence involves risk of deception and misunderstanding, which is an Aristotelian and originally Platonic idea.[141]

Basic Concepts of Aristotelian Philosophy illuminates the origins of Heidegger's hermeneia of existence. Interpretation starts as immersed in everyday *logos*, a "prevailing intelligibility" aiming at "definite familiarity" in the realm of *doxa*. But it is not *any* interpretation that a human being is meant to develop. A human being is concerned with the truth and, therefore, with genuine interpretation. A disposition for the truth is addressed towards "a possibility of existing truthfully, implicit in which truthfulness is the interpretedness and transparency of being-there [*Dasein*] itself."[142] The attainment of this truthfulness requires a conceptuality clarified of deceptive meanings and stereotypes. In a certain sense, a human being, as a "carrier" of the potential which is to be actualized in the human world permeated by *logos*, "must *be* conceptuality . . . inexplicitly."[143] Doesn't it remind us of Santayana's idea of psychic "message" which must be *uttered*? "Insofar as this *logos* is that in which all that is conceptual occurs, it is also that which constitutes the possibility of error."[144] Conceptuality, then, needs to be retrieved and "therein, a general hermeneutical principle appears, that every interpretation is only genuine in retrieval."[145] A human being in Aristotle's vision, emphasizes Heidegger, is radically particular and so must be his interpretation of himself in the world. To fulfill this requirement of meeting one's own particularity, a human being should be able to articulate the temporality of the moment. In a clear-cut summary of the problem,

> We have a distinctive basic structure: being there [*Dasein*] insofar as it is living, is always being there *at the moment*; there is no being-there *in general*. Being there is always: *I am* not a being that *is*, but rather one that *I am*, and which at the same time has the possibility of being of the sort of being that *one is*. Corresponding to the particularity of being there, every disposition is always a *definite* one, for there is no finding oneself *in general*; every finding-oneself is thus and so. Every ἡδονή [pleasure] is a definite one as is every λύπη [pain, sorrow].[146]

To make this summary complete, let us quote yet another passage:

> For our being, characterized by particularity, no unique and absolute norm can be given. It depends on cultivating the being of human beings, so that it is transposed into the aptitude for maintaining the mean. But that means nothing other than *seizing the moment*.[147]

Importantly, implicit here is that the time of human being has an intrinsic quality and this quality of time is at stakes in this "game." This is why in *Being and Time* the thinker can still say that *Dasein* is spiritual. *Dasein* is neither substantial nor psychic but it is constituted in such a way that it is "given already in an entirely peculiar character, namely, as what has its most genuine being-possibility at its disposal."[148] This is where the "possibility of being of the sort of being that one is" stems from—*to the effect not really different from that implicit in being psychic* (!). For this possibility to be actualized *Dasein* must "have an interpretation of itself."[149] Interpretation constitutes the canvas where *bios*, the course of life, may be realized. Thus, the psychic aspect of substantiality and "thinghood" which bothered Heidegger in Aristotelian anthropology gets somehow neutralized via the idea of *bios*, which the German thinker translates as a life history with an integral sense of existential possibilities actualized.

Now, coming back to Santayana's reading of *Sein und Zeit*, *distraction* and the *inauthentic being* of *Dasein* are phenomena connected to the already mentioned specific type of temporality introduced along with the rise of subjectivity—the *sentimental time* of Santayana and the *vulgar time* of Heidegger. Without going into more detail, it suffices to say that these temporal modes, related with James's and Husserl's *specious present*, are hermeneutic ways of addressing existential *care* by rendering the world along with the *self* in this world as present and familiar. Interestingly, both Santayana and Heidegger point to the ambiguity of the term "present" to explain how *presence*, under an illusionary mask of intelligibility, replaces the truth and covers the actuality of the moment. On the one hand it is a survival strategy and on the other—a self-deception strategy.[150] Ontologically, both *spiritual distraction* and *inauthentic mode of being* are phenomena occurring in response to the *undeniable necessity of the acknowledgement of finitude* enforced by the non-transparency of selfhood.

What is the link between *"vulgar time"* and attunement? The original temporality of *Dasein* is that of the unity of an ontological stretching between what has already been and the future possibilities emerging from the fact of its *throwness*. Essentially existential, *Dasein* is *occurring* in its forward movement as its own projection in time, which may become meaningful only against a non-empirical horizon of finitude, which is identified by Heidegger as one's own death. Conceived of in a "vulgar" manner, time is a succession of "nows," which belong either to the past or to the future and as such, cover up both the horizon of death and the calling for a resolute actualization of one's own existential possibilities. On an everyday plane, the immersion in daily tasks, the dependence on irrelevant news, opinions, and standard public truths, all conceal the urgency of its own being before *Dasein*, creating an ambience of safe familiarity. This has been referred to as *strategies of missing oneself*. Interpretation becomes superficial, *Dasein* is entangled, loses its own overview, and loses track of death itself, the vital individualizing factor in Heiddegger's conception of *Dasein*, an idea deeply appreciated by Santayana.[151] *Vulgar time*, then, is *Dasein's* way of temporal appropriation of its own finitude. Likewise, *sentimental time* is the way a finite life projects itself along with the world it is immersed in.

Now, one of the main arguments of Heidegger seems to hang on the idea that there is only one "proper" mode of acknowledging finitude and a number of "derailed" or distracted ones, which he places under a common definition of *ruinance* or *inauthentic being*. The first draws on the original temporal stretching of *Dasein* and the actuality of the moment, resulting in a "proper" actualization of life, while the latter are modes of falling apart from oneself, typical of the vulgar conception of time. I would suggest that Heidegger's warning against a normative interpretation of this distinction in *Sein und Zeit* cannot dismiss the self-evidence of a normative claim underneath. The alternative is: a dynamic and resolute participation in one's own facticity as opposed to the factuality of a *factum brutum* passively accepted. Another way of expressing this difference is to draw an opposition between them: (a) denying oneself a choice in the face of contingency and dependence; and (b) "utilizing" the fact of contingence and dependence to create for oneself a space for meaningful choice. Either way, finitude not only must be acknowledged, but also granted a prominent position. The primary difference consists in the way it is acknowledged, as Heidegger might have insisted. Either the *self* leaves itself to be impressed on by its own finitude as a blunt matter-of-factness, or it "chooses" its own finitude as a chance for liberty.[152] As noticed by Jagiełło, for Heidegger, "finitude rests in man's most vital interest."[153] This aspect of Heidegger does bring to mind the urge to become the "cause" of one's own "fate" in Santayana, which I mentioned previously.

As for Santayana, his ontology makes the relevance of mental life to actual events precarious, whereby the so-called *narrative unity* or *the play of life* centered around psychic interest and preference seems to be a sort of second reality, a hypostatic fiction conveyable by his favorite metaphor of theater and actors acting out contingent roles. It is at the same time necessary, as expressive of psychic needs and interests, and dangerous as well, as inviting all sorts of projections and degrees of madness. Provided that the good and the fulfillment of human life are at stake, what is required from the *self* established on such precarious ground is a psycho-spiritual equilibrium, capable of developing and sustaining a mental fiction adequately expressive of the given life. Whatever derails the spirit from this equilibrium is for Santayana *distraction*. This seems to be the answer to the question posited by the thinker:

> From what does distraction distract the spirit? If the flesh, the world, and the devil impede the proper movement of life, they must impinge upon something deeper than themselves or degrade something better. But what is the deeper or better thing?[154]

The deeper thing, let me suggest, is the reality of the *self* as expressive of a concrete life in the light of its spiritual perfection.

The term "distraction" appears in Santayana's marginal notes twice and the context confirms these associations.[155] First, it appears right next to Heidegger's analysis of the *inauthentic*, everyday way of being, which is a *flight* from the "evasion of death"[156] revealing at the same time an alternative to authenticity. Second, next to the description of *inauthenticity* in terms of falling prey to "idle talk, curiosity and ambiguity" expressive of the "publicness of the they," whereby *Dasein* has initially always "already fallen away from itself."[157] Correspondingly, Santayana noted that "social malice, propaganda"[158] in "the world of fable" and "convention" constitutes "another life"—one, which "expressly refuses the control of fact."[159] Strikingly similar intuitions, captured by Pauline metaphors of the world, the flesh, and the devil, are to be found in the "Distraction" chapter of *Realm of Spirit*.[160]

The previously quoted longer passage from *Realms of Being* about there being only "one fact" informs us that what preoccupied Santayana at that stage of his thinking was the problematic psycho-spiritual unity within the context of the *self*. The marginalia and the letters suggest that he might have been influenced by Heidegger in this respect. In a letter to Daniel Cory, of February 24, 1936, Santayana called Heidegger's work "a great stimulus" to his thinking about spirit.[161] A number of passages in *Realms of Being* seem to confirm Santayana's maturing preference for the idea of life as a psycho-spiritual unity. As suggested by another of his letters, this might have been a direct influence of *Sein und Zeit*.[162] Santayana's sympathy for eternity is constantly challenged and verified by the other of his perspectives, from which it is "by a complete illusion, though an excusable one that the spirit denies its material basis and calls its body a prison or a tomb."[163] The escapist illusion of the spirit belongs to the experience of existence.

In one of his notes Santayana writes that spirit is necessarily "lodged in time and place. Incarnation begins the life of spirit."[164] Let me return to the conceptual equivalents of *Dasein* "tried out" by the philosopher in the marginalia—*spirit*, the *self*, and *incarnate spirit*. The last seems interesting and subtle since it conveys a transcendental viewpoint of sorts, "loaded" with an experience of being affected existentially in a way that is non-transparent and beyond control (*attunement*), with the psyche assumed in the background. "The *self*," in turn, is more dynamic and calls one's attention rather to Heidegger's earlier use of the concept of "life" and the common sources in Aristotle. In other words, in "the *self*" it is psychic aspect that is more pronounced as a source of self-reference, while "spirit incarnate" promotes spiritual vantage point. Neither of them being an accurate translation, both convey some of *Dasein's* aspects and meanings and both take into account the fact of finitude.

To end this part of my reflections, there is a ground on which a sympathetic reader of Santayana and his marginalia may contend that Santayana's intuition of some affinities with Heidegger is valid. Looking at the early Heidegger's *Phenomenological Interpretations of Aristotle* as well as his lectures published under the title *Basic Concepts of Aristotelian Philosophy* helps us understand the origin of these affinities and Santayana's taking account of them. At the same time, the comparison throws a new light on Santayana's philosophy as a whole. Being-in-the-world could be associated by Santayana with his idea of a relational psycho-spiritual unity, a concrete conscious life. Within this unity, psyche is uncovered as a life striving for realization, a nagging source of anxiety for the spirit, for which "to evade this predestined career would be a worse fate . . . Original sin must be purged, the burden discharged, the message delivered."[165] Heideggerian concepts of *attunement* and *falling prey* reassured Santayana in his sense of the experience of human existence as a condition of "entanglement" in an "inexplicable and fatal world."[166] There is a shared idea that "the [dramatic sense of] world involves my plight in it,"[167] and that an unavoidable, everyday way of being of the *self* involves an attempt at concealing this truth. The life-sustaining hermeneutics of a conscious *self* has its escapist side and is busy constructing a provisional "cover-up" or a "mask" which tends to overgrow its initial function and turn into a false replacement for life—a *presence* instead of living/being. Santayana was appreciative of Heidegger's hermeneutic understanding of nothingness[168] and could associate it with his "discovery" that "nothing given exists" in the light of the metaphorical contention that "literalness is impossible in any utterance of spirit, and if it were possible it would be deadly."[169]

5.6 The Drama of Life and Spiritual Liberation

The lack of "literalness" implicit in a hermeneutic outlook on life goes hand in hand with Santayana's dramatic imagery and vocabulary. Essences are "costumes" that existence "wears," and introduce a "plurality of descriptions"[170] granting a margin of freedom to the *personae dramatis*. Yet there is "one fact" and one corresponding, ultimate, final truth about this fact: the actor is a part of it. For Heidegger, in the human world conceived of as a cover-up for the truth of being, the "sparks" of truth may be revealed to and *via* human *selves*, and humans eventually come to be seen as "guardians" of truth. Truth is not a relation of correspondence but rather that which "shines through" existence. *Dasein* is "a stage" for the truth of *being* and *Dasein's* relation to it may be that of disclosing, unveiling, or of covering up. *Dasein* is *authentic* in its freedom to "act out its facticity."[171] Needless to say, the dramatic sense of existence was one of the characteristic themes of Santayana's philosophy. The setting of an ultimate, independent, "incorruptible" yet abstract truth is a background for the theater, which offers a variety of interpretive strategies, masks, requisites, and gestures for the performance of life to be staged. Interestingly, one finds among his marginal notes a number of references to the drama of life uncovered by him in *Sein und Zeit*.

The metaphor of a theater fits into the Heideggerian understanding of "the world" as a totality of intelligible reference points, vaguely threatened by the uncanny feeling of a possible unfamiliarity of something. For Santayana the world of experience is a stage I am familiar with, a setting of a specific, *pictorial space* and specious, *sentimental time*. That this human theater must be moral is inherent in the very idea of "a moral centre [which] is now active. Here is bodily life, the psyche: but the spirit is involved since there is a *centre*."[172] Places are viewed as "local points of view for others," "persons vaguely imagined" are "others [that] I constantly dramatize in my own play."[173] Sometimes those others are "hunting in my preserves."[174] Heidegger usually pictures others as always being there, next to me, encountered at work and confirming the phenomenon of intersubjectivity by common reference to publicly accessible tools.[175] This kind of physical presence of others, relevant to the field of action and taken for granted, must have, notes Santayana, "undoubtedly . . . inspired dramatic impersonations of one another."[176] The initial workplace is enlarged and trespassed, turning into a common playground or a scene where others and I are engaged in a "dramatic substitution of oneself for another." This "acting parts" involves idealization and expectancy directed at a possible "multiform enemy and the unexpected friend."[177] "We live dramatically, acting the parts of all interlocutors."[178] These notes show Santayana's dramatic interpretation of being-in-the-world. The sense that the world, as a result of human interpretation, conceals something more fundamental is emphasized, and not eradicated by this choice of philosophical metaphor.

A shared, modest hope implicit in Santayana and Heidegger is that existence, despite being a source of distraction, carries with it a hint of liberation. Distraction furnishes the ambience of plight but at the same time justifies visions of perfection, of the good possible, the attainment of which is occurring in each and every moment in the horizon of understanding.

"Emancipation by understanding"—noted Santayana in a margin.[179] An analogous formula of liberation "by understanding the world, not by quitting it" is to be found in *Realms of Being*, where "spirit, in the measure in which, by attentive study and sympathy, it may have understood the world, will be liberated . . . from distraction."[180]

Notwithstanding all the technical differences and different vocabulary, I hope to have convinced the reader that Heidegger's ancient inspirations and his general strategy may be recognized as having similar consequences on *Dasein* to those stemming from the existence/essence distinction and the *aporetic* psycho-spiritual unity in Santayana. The idea of *ruinance*, despite its alleged value-free tone, performs a similar function to that of *spiritual distraction*—it signifies the inhibition of the self-realization of life and points to a possible alternative. And that is of an authentic being, and an openness to one's own truth. Insofar as *Dasein* is self-transcending and is never "present"—not until death—it cannot be reduced to a fact or objectified, and it is free. Spirit, as an aspect of life, is similar to this concept in that it outlines a sphere where essence has a priority over existence, and in that it renders imagination operative, preventing life from automatism. Also, their technically different doctrines of truth converge in their function, introducing a certain independent "tribune," an ultimate plane ontologically challenging to thinking as well as a promise of sanity and authenticity. By the same token, this conceptual strategy—which is in fact Platonic in its function—allows for introducing degrees of "fallenness," "madness," or "distraction" to signify, except for existential vagueness, the urgency of the issue of truthfulness to oneself. The latter, as repeatedly emphasized in this essay, was inspired by the Aristotelian ideal of the fulfillment of life up to the standard of its own perfection. Interpreted as it was in the case of both Heidegger and Santayana, it implies a guiding ethical standard for measuring a life in its own terms. Adding to it their anti-dogmatism, both thinkers earned a history of accusations of moral relativism. But this *manoeuvre*, confirming the intuition of Rorty, gave rise to a perspective of liberation within the very scope of existence—one which must have been of importance for a thinker who, like Santayana, had claimed to be "considering the possible victory of spirit over distraction."[181]

The sympathy for spiritual detachment offered by *vita contemplativa* never ceased to determine the nature of possible spiritual freedom for Santayana and add to his philosophy a deconstructive, liberating, and somewhat escapist dimension—different in tone from Heidegger's "overwhelming" vision of existence as a spectrum of *real* possibilities. The other perspective, though, the more holistic one, brings him closer not only to Heidegger but to the existentialist-hermeneutic understanding of human life in general. There is a realistic possibility that under the influence of reading *Sein und Zeit*, where Santayana was confronted with a different understanding of existence, he started considering a synthesis of both. Heidegger utilized a spiritually loaded meaning of a medieval Latin term "ek-sistere" or "sistere ek"—"to stand outside"—to denote the particular, *finite transcendence* manifest in *Dasein's* mode of being. In other words, he retrieved the metaphysical idea of transcendence and inscribed it into that of existence. Santayana tried to capture the specificity of this hybrid meaning translating it in the marginalia into "spiritual existence." While his original understanding of existence was heavily freighted with the idea of materiality, in his *magnum opus* he could still reach for the unifying notion of life which provided a productive context for the essence-existence distinction and the doctrine of impotent spirit. While death, as a non-empirical horizon, frames finite human life, a constant interplay between facts and possibilities/ideals is being exercised. As long as a given life, counting as "one fact," is not yet framed by death, the scenario of the play of life remains undetermined. The evidence of Santayana's appropriation of the idea is explicitly mentioned in one of his letters, commenting on his "adventure" with Heidegger:

> With this insight on the one hand [that of death as a "totality of life"], and the insight that life is movement, on the other hand, I think a rather new and profound analysis might be made of the notion of immortality . . . souls in heaven are mythical impersonations of the truth or totality of these persons' earthly life. At the same time, this life, and anything truly living, is something dramatic, groping, planning, exciting . . . Nietzsche needn't have told us to live perilously: it would have been enough to tell us to live.[182]

An orthodox reader of Heidegger might conclude that it is Santayana's own appropriated version of the German thinker, but Santayana was not so naïve as one might conclude from his somewhat "old-fashioned" idiom. He was insightful in grasping the conceptual strategy in Heidegger, who by means of borderline concepts, such as "being" and "death," endowed the idea of existence with a dimension of a project and a promise, the fulfillment of which hangs on another idea—that of the world as a context in which the *self* can encounter itself in some of the spectra of existential possibilities. In one of his letters he commented briefly on Heidegger's use of the notions of "Nothing" and "Death":

> He sees perfectly that the intrinsic vacancy of these notions lends them the function of repeating or framing-in positive objects, as death, by terminating a life, makes a biographical unit and moral finality of it. This seems to me much more enlightening than leaps or shipwrecks of the Soul in the Infinite Unknown.[183]

To quote Heidegger, "authentic *Dasein* accepts the finitude of its own transcendence and, thus, the limitation of those possibilities for which it can be free."[184] It is worth noting that this position on freedom is at a great remove from that emblematic of existentialism as represented by Sartre's idea of absolute freedom of deliberation, "the scary power to create the world," which was foreign and absurd also to Santayana.[185]

Even if Santayana would never have fully approved of this wholly worldly ontology, as he sometimes spoke of it,[186] and would never embrace Heidegger's rhetoric of *decisionism*—the function of which in his thought was more subtly performed by the Socratic principle of *knowing oneself*—he understood and appreciated the potential of viewing existence via the interpretive possibilities it offers to a given life. Appropriating this idea into his own concepts, he defined Heideggerian "Möglichkeiten" as:

> regions of essence approachable to sensibility. Spirit has a grammar (imposed by the psyche) that opens possible paths to perception and thought . . . The scope of spirit is immensely greater than its punctiform actual spark. The spark lights (theoretically) the whole sky.[187]

By this inscription of spirit into the texture of life and therefore, of finitude, life acquires a dimension of a promise. Bringing what he called "the conceptual idealism" of Heidegger into a an interesting *liaison* with his own ontology, Santayana could notice the "new light," which he mentioned in the previously quoted letter, in a holistic perspective unifying psyche's dynamic locus and spirit's opening onto the eternal realm within a finite human life. Spirit, characteristic of Santayana's thought, retains its liberating function, but its escapist shade is undermined as merely ironic, though it may be preferable to think of it rather as noble and "bohemian." He is able to draw on spiritual "totality" as expressive of the "direction of life toward unaccomplished (transcendence)," yet at the same time to emphasize the fact that care or the psyche is not more of a burden than a life buoy. "Incompleteness of experience," one of the marginal notes says, "is essential to the attitude of life, not merely a failure of knowledge. (Full knowledge would arrest life, or eternalize it.)"[188]

The *vita contemplativa* in its escapist version as panacea for the plight of existence found a serious philosophical alternative in the Heideggerian *sein-zum-Tode*. The conception of death, as it stems from numerous remarks in the letters and marginalia was most appreciated by Santayana since "a spiritual vision of a total life must see it terminating in death."[189] Santayana notices that death, being absolutely beyond first-person experience, marks the borderline of all experience and all verbal expression and proves to be a fruitful concept in making the ineffable, "fugitive" notion of life philosophically operative. The tension between the psyche and spirit is justified within a broader idea of life, where "death modifies life as an eventuality"[190] and harnesses the *normal human pathology*. Spiritual longing for perfection and psychic finitude are aspects and the necessary co-partners in the venture of human life, inescapably idealistic, projecting, and inescapably finite. Without a finite perspective nothing could be understood or valued, as there would be no questions, no meanings, no philosophy, and no sense in the sense of meaningfulness of life, since only a finite, caring life identifies problems and asks questions. It is worth reminding at this point that for Heidegger the possibility of asking why-questions was a striking evidence of what he called *finite freedom* of *Dasein*.[191] Spirit as an aspect of life reveals its dimension of possibility and from the perspective of a dynamic life, "plausibility [is] more precious to the psyche than truth."[192] The idea of spiritual liberation commences in "emancipation by understanding" with the world revealing itself as "a panorama" of possibilities.[193] In this light, in the marginalia Santayana defines life as a promise *"that its vitality may prime its fulfillment."*[194] That there is a fulfillment in view may be proposed exclusively on condition that there is a horizon of finitude and the distinction between a *status quo* and the possibility of a good or a perfection desired.

6

The Tragic Aspect of Existence

> Fact-worship . . . [is] a fault in taste and in morals.
>
> —Preface to *Realms of Being*, xii–xiii

An insight into what Santayana understood by the tragic aspect of existence allows for a better understanding of his critique of egotism in culture and philosophy and a fuller grasp of the stakes behind his conception of the *aporetic self*. A brief presentation of selected, classical approaches to tragedy and the tragic will be followed by a discussion of Santayana's polemic with Nietzsche and a look at his reading of Shakespeare's tragedies with references to some contemporary critics.[1] To keep the discussion manageable, I operate mainly within the area of modern philosophy and focus on the idea of "the tragic" in existential, ontological, and cultural context,[2] without engaging in aesthetic considerations of tragedy as a work of art.

Modern understanding of the tragic articulates subjectivity. Kierkegaard was the first to note explicitly that along with the growing individualization of consciousness and stress on individual moral responsibility, the so-called "tragic" loses its ancient, fatal dimension in favor of an internal, perhaps more merciless one.[3] The path from tragedy as a work of art to the abstraction of the tragic quality or phenomenon, its attribution to the ethical realm and—finally—to human existence as such, is complex and unclear. A breakthrough in this development, according to Santayana, can be noticed as early as in Shakespeare, whose dramas anticipate modern, internalized tragic in an irreligious, utterly contingent reality.[4]

Pascal's meditations on man as torn in-between infinity and finitude were followed by other Christianity-inspired existential readings of the tragic as expressive of *conditio humana* by thinkers such as Kierkegaard or

Unamuno. Hegel inscribed his interpretation of tragedy into the scheme of spiritual movement toward universal reconciliation, highlighting the victorious ethical powers and approaching the tragic hero's fate as a means rather than as an end. Schopenhauer and Nietzsche were inspired by antiquity, which they read via the lens of German Romanticism. Their metaphysics of will engenders rather morbid visions of human existence conveyable by the drama of a tragic hero—"man heightened and intensified."[5] Tragedy here is attributed with a revelatory potential—through the effect of tragic sublimity it brings to light some fundamental truths about human being. Heidegger became a critical continuator of this path of interpretation. He evoked the uncanniness of human being recognized by Sophocles and reinterpreted it in terms of his ontology of the *self* based on the idea of fundamental uprootedness and constant coming to oneself.[6] Thus, he pointed to the very structure of existence as the genesis of Greek preoccupation with the inescapable inadequacy between the human and the divine (which for the Greeks was also natural) order. Max Scheler stands out among the thinkers mentioned as a proponent of an alternative reading of the tragic through the lens of an idealistic axiology.

An unceasing inspiration for all these nineteenth- and twentieth-century readings of the tragic comes from Aristotle, who in his discussion of tragedy as work of art in *Poetics* pointed to its "mechanics" and the logic of the tragic plot, by highlighting the circumstances of intentional human action. Among others, he mentioned its two key factors: error—*hamartia*, and recognition—*anagnorisis*. The interplay of ignorance with knowledge, attested to in the most indirect way probably by Sophocles's *Oedipus Rex*, comes back in modern philosophical readings, playing with the variety of meanings associated with Greek *hamartia*—from inescapable ignorance informing the matrix of human reality, to "unguilty" or "guiltless" guilt, sin, and moral responsibility. Aristotle was interested in the essence of tragedy in view of the powerful cathartic impact it exerted on the audience and, even though he treated tragedy first and foremost as a work of art, still, the very understanding he held of its *mimetic nature in respect to human action* clearly suggests that he acknowledged a "truth" aspect in the tragic drama. The plot formally reflects the conditions of human action, hence an easy identification with the hero on the part of a spectator, even if the tragic hero himself embodies a certain "unlikely" transgression. The primacy of the themes of human action and awareness has been sustained in the discussion of tragedy since Aristotle. To quote Paul Ricoeur, "to be sure, tragedy does have action as its theme, as Hegel will later be heard to stress. It is therefore the work of those who act and of their individuality."[7]

In the work of Ricoeur, ancient tragedy, as exemplified by *Antigone*, receives its contemporary, ethically oriented reading, the canvas of which is not an idealistic axiology like that of Max Scheler, but horizontally developed hermeneutics of action. What Ricoeur is interested in are human motivations and attitudes behind tragic moral conflicts. The thinker points to the incompatibility between practical and tragic wisdom, the latter being a moral mode of acting assumed by a certain type of hero in certain circumstances. The corresponding conflict between contextual, historicist ethics and universal moral norms, the origins of which are lost in the dark depths of myth, illustrate what George Steiner called the "agonistic ground of human experience."[8] Ricoeur claims that only a mediation on the ground of a mutual recognition and acknowledgment of one's own limits by each party—namely *the wisdom of judgment in situation*—might solve the conflict. This is what the Chorus is voicing when it speaks of *phronesis*. Yet, this is precisely what the tragic plot refuses to offer. The "instruction" carried by tragedy rests in that by refusing to bring a solution it provokes cathartic experience, which triggers a conversion of perspective toward understanding that *hubris* brings doom. Thus, tragedy is set in—but not reduced to—the context of the dialectic of ethics and morality central to the "making" of the narrative unity of the *self*, where virtues are arising in *praxis*, in the process of working out *the mean*.

Santayana, particularly sensitive to cultural patterns of constructing reality and their reflection in philosophical doctrines, recognized certain worldviews and philosophies to be conducive to tragic outlook and attitudes. There is a certain assumption of the tragic human predicament in his thought, which, as I suggest, may be associated with the tension between subjectivity and factuality.[9] The very concern with such fundamental questions may be viewed as challenging the discursive vacuum, the positivistic impoverishment of language and attempting to retrieve the possibility of speaking about humans in a holistic way, which *de facto* means speaking about humans *at all*. Santayana was standing in front of a major philosophical preoccupation of his time—how, after the world had lost its integrity, to address questions which require such integrity. William James had explicitly voiced this problem and tackled the issue of the tragic inherent in human experience by confronting it with human capacity for religious experience unrelated to any specific doctrine or denomination.[10] Santayana, who declared obliged by his intellectual honesty to avoid supernatural consolation, would handle it rather with the support of his apparently secular ontology, which, however, is indebted to both ancient Greek and Judeo-Christian tradition.

6.1 Some Philosophical Perspectives on the Tragic

A Macrocosm of Moral Possibilities

In his classical theory, Max Scheler[11] abstracted the notion of the tragic from the aesthetic context and transferred it onto ontological, ethical, and, finally, existential plane. By way of phenomenological reduction he arrived at the basic components of the tragic phenomenon—the conflict of values, significant inescapability, tragic knot, "unguilty guilt," and a certain objective grief or sorrow of this world. The tragic is inherent in the human world, where each man "carries" an individual vision of this world along with a set of objectively existing values that define his being in this world. The tragic occurs only in an ethical context, where intentional actions and conflicting values come into question. Whenever there is a purposeful act that represents a significant value and leads to the destruction of another significant value—we are confronted with a tragic phenomenon. The tragic itself lies in the inescapability of the destructive tendency of human action rather than in a concrete agent (hence, some modern heroes characterized by psychological flaws that produce actions leading to the conflict of values, do not meet the Schelerian criteria of a tragic hero).

The genesis of the tragic is related to the existence of the macrocosm of all possible values. Yet, the tragic conflict could not have occurred unless values were at play in the human world. The tragic knot, Scheler tells us, results from the crossing of two causal chains encountered in a dynamic unity of action—one which generates values and the other which destroys them. The heroic deeds of Jesus and Prometheus are particularly prominent exponents of the incompatibility of two different planes and orders. Both heroes have their share in the historical order, where they are judged, and the transcendent order, which represents the whole spectrum of values they choose from. Their insight into the realm of values exceeds any human ability in this respect. They are the focal points where the contingency and moral neutrality of the historical world meet the eternal realm of values. Thus, being "unguilty," they fall into a guilt which cannot be confessed.

While Santayana claimed that the tragic emerges out of the projection of human, sentimental perspective onto the physical time, Scheler held that only an agent of spiritual integrity may become both the subject to and witness of the tragic conflict. The tragic is revealed to him when he is aware of two distinct, autonomous aspects of action: causal and moral.[12] The so-called tragic necessity transcends both the nature of things and free will, and leaves room for the unpredictability factor and the effect of a "unique constellation." A conflict is tragic when it involves a premonition of the possible destruction of a value and an attempt at preventing it even in the face of its suspected inescapability. What is at stake here, except for the hero's high moral standards, is sustaining the agent's free will and introducing the "despite" factor. Thus, the tragic phenomenon is growing exceedingly complex and close to a paradox in that it combines unpredictability with inescapability. The mystery of it, as Scheler admits, arises out of the convergence of two radically different realms.

This idealistic theory of the tragic, based on the distinction of an autonomous realm of moral possibilities, stands in opposition to the theories of Nietzsche and Schopenhauer. It is sometimes emphasized that Scheler was one of the first thinkers who placed the tragic in the moral realm of human action. At the same time, there is something inhuman in his vision, where noble individuals are doomed in their effort because of an unearthly predicament. One of the most inspiring elements of his analysis seems to me to be his idea of "unguilty guilt." Whenever someone may be recognized as responsible for a wrongdoing, there is no tragic guilt. It is *the innocence of the hero that renders him guilty*, his guilt being beyond any earthly moral judgment. Thus, Scheler presents a distinguished tragic hero, one necessarily marked by a certain "noblesse oblige." On the crossroad of immanent history and ideal possibilities a noble individual becomes a tragic hero.

Acting as "Guilt"

At the time Scheler was writing his essay on the tragic phenomenon, for nearly a century there had been available the different, more modern and dynamic approach of Kierkegaard. Kierkegaardian perspective was inspired by Hegel's theory of tragedy. In *Phenomenology of Spirit* Hegel considers tragedy in terms of a spiritual work of art remaining in the religious context of Spirit's odyssey toward unity. Leaving aside this large picture into which tragedy is inscribed, it is of interest for us to recapitulate briefly Hegel's interpretation of the essence of tragedy, particularly in reference to the Aristotelian idea of the interplay between knowledge and the lack of knowledge. In a Greek epic the universal element dissolves all individual powers and the whole narrative represents, in a descriptive sense, deeds of equal powers—gods and heroes, who together make up the "irrational void of necessity."[13] Tragedy, as noted also by Lesky in a previously quoted passage, marks a major shift in consciousness, which is visible in the role of the medium. Not a narrative anymore but *enacting* conveys the story of a tragic hero, who speaks his own voice. An actor becomes tragic *persona*, he *represents* the hero *via* masks and makes the first-person perspective open and available to the spectators, each of whom can *feel* himself at the hero's place. Representation, moved onto another level (that of acting out), reveals "self conscious human beings who know their rights and purposes, the power and the will of their specific nature and know how to assert them."[14] In this adventure of individualization two worlds are set against one another: "the inner essential world and the world of action."[15] Through action, the heroes

> give utterance to the inner essence, they prove the rightness of their action, and the 'pathos' which moves them is soberly asserted and definitely expressed, . . . free from the accidents of circumstance and personal idiosyncrasies. Lastly, these characters exist as actual human beings who impersonate the heroes and portray them.[16]

A double split emerges out of this performance: (1) one between the two worlds, which may be called—for the sake of clarity—the world of necessity and that of subjective individuality, and (2) an internal one between the hero representing an essence or an ethical principle and the actor who himself represents the hero. No matter how closely the actor fits his *persona*, the distinction between his *self* and the *persona* of the mask is preserved, which is important for the specificity of Hegel's stake, which is always the unity or reconciliation in view. But what is important for our analysis is not so much the big picture of Hegel, but the type of consciousness involved and the nature of the conflict which happens to be portrayed by the tragic drama. Hegel followed Aristotle's insights in articulating the interplay between knowledge and ignorance involved in conscious action. For a definite individuality—like that of a tragic hero—knowledge can be but ambiguous. The distinction between truth and delusion is tragic because what is revealed is truth only as long as it doesn't become the object of hero's consciousness. Once subjectively conscious, it may well be treated as a warning against deception rather than simple truth. The truth is ultimately hidden from the hero in the realm of necessity, meaning his action is blind, like any action is for Hegel, who says, "the doer [always] finds himself thereby in *the antithesis of knowing and not-knowing*."[17] Action "*itself is this inversion of the known into its opposite, into being*,"[18] *and from this perspective acting translates itself into becoming guilty.*

The inescapability of the conflict is due to the "antithesis of the certainty of itself and objective essence," which is in fact grounded conceptually. Where Notion reigns, true individuality can be only ideal,[19] essential, and if it is to be saved, a substantial, accidental individuality must be sacrificed. Hence the death of the hero (but not of the actor). But even if the life of the hero is saved, his deeds are subject to oblivion, even though his *guilt* is not thereby erased. Hegel's conception emphasizes individualization and a clash, an inadequacy involved therein as essential for tragedy. *An element of blindness is the herald of any conscious action and every action takes its toll.* Even though the remaining thinkers evoked here have different stakes and are not interested in the idea of absolute knowledge, Hegelian conceptualization of some problems, earlier touched upon by Aristotle, has been inspiring, as it is evident in Kierkegaard's discussion of tragedy.

But prior to turning our attention to Kierkegaard, let us complete this brief discussion of Hegel with some of his insights from *The Philosophy of Fine Arts*. Tragic heroes are but means to an end held by the "forces which carry in themselves their own justification, and are realized substantively in the volitional activity of mankind."[20] The ethical substance, as a totality, must "transplant itself in the real actuality of phenomenal world."[21] When individualized, it is attached to particular human beings, who are distinguished or "elevated" by their unshakable resolution onto their aims. These ethical forces and aims may be contradictory and thus engender tragic conflicts in human reality, while their resolution on the objective plane is always a reconciliation.

> That which is abrogated in the tragic issue is merely the one-sided particularity which was unable to accommodate itself to this harmony, and consequently in the tragic course of its action, through inability to disengage itself from itself and its designs, either is committed in its entire totality to destruction or at least finds itself compelled to fall back upon a stage of resignation in the execution of its aim.[22]

The whole tragic action is developed on the basis of two aspects of the dramatic world: the "substantial and more enlightened intelligence"[23] shining through the simple consciousness of the passive *chorus*, and the individual pathos of human action, namely the *heroic figures*. Interestingly, as Hegel notes, the heroes in their full identification with their aim are not what "in the modern use of the term we describe as characters, nor are they mere abstractions."[24] That is why, as Alenka Zupančič emphasized, there always remains a suggestion of a distance between the actor and his mask. Meanwhile, the Aristotelian idea of the cathartic effect via emotional reaction of spectators is translated by Hegel, in accordance with his vision, into "a feeling of reconciliation" with the supremacy of "eternal justice" over any particularity.[25]

Anticipating Kierkegaard's discussion, Hegel notices that the modern tragedy is enacted by personalities of certain psychological traits and representing certain passions against the background of contingent circumstances. The greatness of the ancient "ethical right to a definite course of action" gives way to passions, evil, crime, stupidity or mere accident.[26] The trend toward personalization is visible already in Sophocles, who drew on the conflict between state law and the natural morality of family—one extensively used by future dramatists. Sophocles was also the one to expose the interplay of knowledge and ignorance inherent in human action as a key aspect for tragic action, endowing tragedy with a universal meaning. The tragic conflict here entails the contrast between "volition fully aware of its acts" and what has factually been done, apparently "without active participation either in will or in knowledge."[27] This is where Hegel is perhaps in the closest proximity to the difference between the modern tragedy interested in consciousness and responsibility, and the ancient one, which adheres to facts. The division between intention and fact is symptomatic of the modern tragic, and, as Santayana would later note, culminates in *Hamlet*, where the mind is an achievement for its own sake. This distinction triggers the whole discussion about the dialectic of guilt and innocence and precedes the idea of *unguilty guilt*. Ancient heroes simply *are* "just that what they will and achieve" and they fully accept the blame for the consequences of their actions. Chorus for Hegel expresses not a blind fate but a perfect spiritual reconciliation within which all conflicts find their justification. In contrast to that, modern heroes are self-reflective, "wavering," and dependent in decision on their psychological state and "caprice."[28] Moreover, they often operate on the territory where the good and the evil are active.

Reconciliation is at stake even in those ancient tragedies that anticipate modern tragedy by emphasizing *the personal*, as it is in the case of *Oedipus at Colonus*. This does not annul the suffering, but by no means are "suffering and misfortune the final issue" in Hegel's interpretation.[29] This last conclusion makes Hegel's interpretation different from that of Kierkegaard and radically opposed to that of Schopenhauer.

The issue of individualization is present also in Kierkegaard's reflections on the internalization of tragedy. Starting from the distinction between the ancient and the modern meaning of the concept of guilt, this Lutheran thinker managed to show the transformation both in the meaning and the experience of the tragic. The epic model of antiquity assumes a substantial hero who is subject to an objective fate or, in other words, he is determined insofar as he may be described in terms of a series of situations. His default mode of ignorance is interrupted by brief illuminations (*anagnorisis*), which are never sufficient to deliver a clear view of the whole entanglement, but are always enough to give rise to the sense of guilt and helplessness. Guilt is always already as if "out there," it causes grief and uplifts the hero to tragic sublimity making him statuesque and beautiful. The aesthetic sublimates suffering into sorrow and neutralizes the guilt. The exteriority of guilt plays a redemptory function.

On the other side, there is the tragedy of a modern, responsible subject, who is emblazed by the fire of his evidently own and "guilty" guilt. Unless religious faith endows this suffering with meaning and a horizon of salvation, it is bound to become comic in its gratuity. None of the two models autonomously conveys the essence of tragedy—neither Greek aesthetics nor individual moral responsibility, where "guilt becomes sin, suffering atonement and the tragic vanishes."[30] Only the dialectic of subjective suffering and objective sorrow, the movement between the ethical and the aesthetic, renders adequately the logic of the tragic, which entails both the ancient and the modern moment.

Unlike elitist, heroic requirement put forward by Scheler, in Kierkegaard's existential perspective any agent is a potential subject of interiorized tragicness. Thus, locating the problem within an individual, Kierkegaard paves a new path for the reflection on the tragic, without losing sight of its ancient meaning.

Existence as Original Sin

Among the important theories of the tragic that encountered a vivid reception in America and became a source of polemical inspirations for Santayana are those by Schopenhauer and Nietzsche.

In *Will and Representation*, with Platonic opposition between being and appearance in the background, Schopenhauer sets his dual metaphysics, where Will—a thing in itself and the principle of reality—has its intelligible correspondent called Idea or Representation. While both belong to the side of being, the world of phenomena—which is our world—belongs to the side of illusion. On the ground of Schopenhauer's ontology, man is a scene of the conflict between the principle of reality, which is Will, and its own

(Will's) self, or more specifically, between its objective universality and its individual, self-conscious representation (man). It is possible to interpret this conflict as the source of the tragic condition of man, who is determined by Will but deluded by faith in free will and the power of reason.

Thus, the roots of what is revealed in tragedy as a work of art—for the aesthetic is, to be precise, the only context in which the concept of the tragic is used by the thinker—may be found in the ontological status of man. Will as a whole (an irresistible, single principle of reality) is represented by Idea, which determines forms on which single phenomena (grounded by the principle of sufficient reason) are dependent. Within the form of man something peculiar, irregular occurs. In Man, considered here as the fullest embodiment of Idea (hence capital "M" Man), a double reflection occurs. Will sees its reflection in man (small "m" man), and man, as a particular act of will in which consciousness arose, is able to see *his own* reflection too, and sometimes—if his sight is clear enough—he can see the illusion of his own free will. This double reflection marks a contradiction and a conflict within Will itself—a conflict between its general aspect and the particular, individual, self-conscious act. Schopenhauer assumes radical domination of the objective over the subjective to the extent that the latter is a mere illusion or—an error (*hamartia*). Consequently, the human condition involves being deluded by the impression of free will, which arises on the ground of the multitude of motives and choices made. A conscious decision is indeed made by man, but, as an act, it is determined by Will. It cannot be otherwise because man's "knowledge . . . of the whole world as representation, is nevertheless given entirely through the medium of a body."[31] Bodily man, who is at the service of Will, may be metaphorically said to represent Will's "desire" for time and space. Life is a desire and a struggle *ad infinitum*, experienced subjectively as pain and suffering.

The conflict mentioned previously is not what Schopenhauer understands by the tragic, yet it is important because it explains the genesis of the art of tragedy, which aims at the revelation of the human condition by means of the effect of sublimity achieved by contrasting this general predicament with particular instances of heroism. Human attitude in the face of the truth of determinism may assume a few forms worthy consideration according to Schopenhauer: that of (1) a tragic hero, (2) a genius artist, (3) a stoic sage, and (4) the freedom of self-resignation. All these attitudes draw on the narrow margin of freedom man has by being self-conscious and endowed with imagination, but only the last two represent possibilities of liberation, of which only one is real. The first of the two assumes liberation through reason and was advocated by the Stoics. Illuminating deliberation sets a distance between mind and world, and commences in a closure in an inner citadel, where wanting and pain give way to the peace of soul. This attitude of control and inner discipline is meant to lead to happiness—the aim of stoic ethics. This peak achievement of practical reason was inspiring but not satisfactory for Schopenhauer, who doubted in the capacity of reason to control will. His solution is more radical, it calls for self-resignation and a definite departure from thinking in terms of happiness. It is important to note that *for Schopenhauer the aim is salvation from life and from the world*. It involves the rejection of *principio individuationis* by giving up the will. It is a particular ontological situation—one of a contradiction between phenomenon and its ground, which is possible due to the appearance of an individual will that may be willing to deny itself. Such an individual is a cognizing subject devoid of will.

The function of tragedy, being "the summit of poetic art,"[32] is to illuminate and encourage resignation. It shows the predicament of man as an inescapable entanglement in misfortunes—not necessarily of catastrophic dimensions, as it is in some ancient dramas, but also those of more common sort which still prevent man from achieving his ideals and happiness. *Fate as dependence on contingency* is essentially inscribed into human existence.[33] The determinism here is not meant as a sort of predestination or any "specific" fate but rather as *fate as such*, or—in other words—as being always in situation provided that situation implies a number of unknown factors beyond subjective control and hence, evolves in a direction unpredictable and unwanted. Thus, *to be a man in the empirical sense is to be fatal or to be one's own fate*.

Someone who despite the awareness of his condition asserts the will to live, chooses a particular kind of freedom which informs tragic heroism. The drama of freedom is radical on the grounds of Schopenhauer's overwhelming determinism, where subjectivity is but an illusion. Schopenhauer's hero is, in a way, closer to the comic than that of Kierkegaard. The former is but a momentary flashlight within the whole (Will), for the latter everything but himself seems an illusion. To restate—for Schopenhauer the aim of tragedy is to uncover:

> the wretchedness and misery of mankind, the scornful mastery of chance . . . It is the antagonism of the will with itself which is here most completely unfolded . . . It becomes visible in the suffering of mankind which is produced partly by chance, partly by error.[34]

What is revealed is the truth about humans being puppets animated by Will. The essence of tragedy rests in showing the structure of human action in the world. The essence of humanity, as presented in tragic art, is being always in situation, which means—dependent on accident and forces alien to consciousness.

Every great artist, claims Schopenhauer, aims at the essence and drops relations which belong to subjective perspective. Yet the essence of *being a man* rests precisely in relationality and dependence. Schopenhauer's vision, according to my interpretation, may lead to the conclusion that the so-called tragic fate consists in repetition: an individual, empirical man can be reduced to the reenactment of his fate, and mankind as such—to a kind of "eternal return"! Also, the world may be covered by this metaphor insofar as it is the Will's "self-knowledge" and hence, its Idea is one and eternal.[35] The world represents Will's desire, life represents "this willing for the representation."[36] *The Idea of mankind produces a history of repetitive dramas and suffering*. It is the share of the eternal Idea in human life that endows it with an aspect of repetition, which I call here "eternal return" in an anticipating reference to Nietzsche. The ideas of return and repetition, key in modern philosophy, are relevant whenever the eternal/timeless converges with the temporal and finite. The temporal, we may say, is lashed to the timeless.

Tragedy reveals man in the truth of his condition. But this is not the end. What is called by tradition "original sin" is revealed to be existence itself. "For man's greatest offence is that he has been born," Schopenhauer quotes Calderon de la Barca.[37] This conclusion is a landmark in thinking about existence and permanently links it with the category of the tragic, even though Schopenhauer does not say it *expressis verbis*. Greek *hamartia*, later translated as "sin," for Aristotle meant error caused by the ignorance of mortals and was one of the basic concepts in his analysis of the tragic plot. The idea, as noted by Jaspers, appearing already in Indian and pre-Socratic philosophy, suggests something about humanity's *complicity in guilt* and renders the so-called "tragic guilt" polysemic. It might mean that *existence is guilt*, "*a particular character is guilty because of what he is*," or that "*action is guilt*" in the sense that *any act has its "price."*[38] This meaning of the tragic appears in Schopenhauer's, Nietzsche's, and Heidegger's interpretations. It is also tackled in a brief essay "Fate and Character" by Walter Benjamin, where he exposes the *hubris* of Greek tragedy as a response to the challenge of fate and makes it an argument for preventing the final marriage of fate and character (the Nietzschean "becoming what one is").

The reality of fate, claims the thinker, cannot be denied, yet it concerns only the "parasitical," "inauthentic" temporality of "bare life" in man (!).[39]

Nevertheless, it is often admitted that individual fates, when considered collectively, call for the recognition of the so-called human condition. All mortals have a share in a non-transparent, existential entanglement, which makes human efforts co-dependent on chance. Tragedy has been said to offer a poetic exposition of this simple fact. Now, it would count as hypocrisy to turn a blind eye to the fact of our finitude and its consequences, Santayana claims, but wisdom rests in replacing the "involuntary finitude," referred to often as "fatality," with a voluntary one. Judeo-Christian tradition, in its dogmas of original sin, grace, and salvation, took account of both the human condition and nature. Santayana is skeptical about the modern attempts at exorcising these problematic concepts (human condition and nature), coming—in his era—from the side of scientists and pantheists alike. Rationality in action along with the idealization involved in the aspiration to some good seem to him the invariant within otherwise fluid and flexible human nature. It outlines "a definite scope by virtue of which alone he [man] can have a reliable memory, a recognizable character, a faculty of connected thought and speech, a social unity and a moral ideal."[40] It is

> the transcendental foundation of all science and morals . . . a functional unity in each man; it is no general or abstract essence . . . [but] the entelechy of the living individual, be he typical or singular. . . . If he can know himself by expressing the entelechy of his own nature in the form of a consistent ideal, he is a rational creature.[41]

To this invariant in man respond the core ideals transmitted within great religious traditions, which, historically, constituted fundamental sources of morality, without which all value would become "external and arbitrary." Such a "core of stability" secures inheritance and memory, while memory as "retentiveness is the condition of progress."[42] *Forgetting*, according to Santayana, is the greatest enemy of humanity; it leads to "perpetual infancy" and mechanical "self-repeating," which "degenerates into an instinctive reaction."[43]

"The variation human nature is open to is not . . . variation in any direction . . . even if [it] survives amid a continual fluctuation of its embodiment."[44] It is a manifestation of a most complex, natural, functional formation of man, who strives for fulfillment as against the background of what we have called the human condition. Mind you that the emphasis on individual entelechy promotes a vision of life as a chance for fulfillment rather than that of existence as sin. The flexible, aspiring human nature may be compared to an ineradicable "footnote" to the human condition. The latter may be exhibited, exposed, depicted (as in Greek tragedy), remarks Bielik-Robson, while the former, referred to sometimes as hypostatical in relation to *conditio humana*, renders itself for studying and explaining.[45] It belongs to human nature that man develops an individual character and follows certain ideals—a human response to the challenge of fate, as Walter Benjamin suggests.

6.2 Nietzsche, Santayana, and the Tragic

Sources: The Tragedy of Individuation

Nietzsche, polemically inspired by Schopenhauer's metaphysics, in response to the idea of self-resignation came up with an alternative one—that of Superman. Santayana undoubtedly was inspired by both thinkers, but at the same time remained critical of the philosophy of will in general, on the account of the morbid and "barbaric" visions of human existence it engendered. Let me evoke—very briefly and selectively—certain Nietzschean themes that are central for our discussion of Santayana's critique of Nietzsche and for grasping the essence of the unavoidable clash between both visions of human reality.

Nietzschean idea of the tragic originates in his early dichotomy between Apollonian and Dionysian—two "competing," yet mutually dependent principles of being, echoing Heraclitean struggle of elements. Both conspire to sustain the neverending flux of the suffering, striving for survival and, finally, dying individual lives. The Dionysian stands for the metaphysical will of Life to be preserved as a whole. The Apollonian is Maya's veil—the world of illusion, appearance and dream, necessary in the process of individuation as long as it instigates and sustains any particular will to survive. The pair serves as a mental matrix for viewing reality in terms of a spectrum of conflicting qualities, such as the raw force of naked life against the feebleness of the Apollonian, the affirmative aspect of vital powers against the reactive one, the general against the individual. The rationale for these dualisms rests in the idea—echoing some Buddhist, neoplatonic, and Schopenhauerian inspirations—of a primordial "One" giving birth to individual lives, by the annihilation of which it may achieve salvation. Human becoming, then, as an example of individuation, seems suspect, for "we should regard the state of individuation as the source and original cause of suffering, as something objectable in itself."[46]

The Dionysian–Apollonian dualism influences Nietzsche's paradigmatic thinking about the history of Western culture, including the genesis and the essence of tragedy, which he traces back to the Dionysian mysteries. In Dionysus we recognize a suffering god, subject to "the agonies of individuation."[47] His way to salvation is through regaining integrity—*apokatastasis*—occurring by means of the annihilation of the individual. In this light it would be preferable for a human being not to be born at all. Greek tragedy as a form of art, particularly in its early, orgiastic version, approximates this truth. Dionysian rituals are a collective expression of a longing for the return to oneness. Tragic effect is achieved through

> individual examples of . . . annihilation . . . the hero, the greatest phenomenon of the will, is negated for our pleasure, because he remains only phenomenon and the eternal life of the will remains untouched by his annihilation.[48]

Thus, Dionysian art is expressive of "the will in its omnipotence . . . , the eternal life beyond all phenomena and in spite of all annihilation."[49] The dramas of Aeschylus, closest to the sources of tragedy, display the Dionysian type of heroism, the titanic courage of his heroes affirms suffering and the necessity of death so that "joy [may be] experienced in the annihilation of the individual."[50] Even though the fusion of the two principles begins already with Aeschylus, the Dionysian element is still dominant in the figure of Prometheus. Later, in the context of his cultural critique, Nietzsche's vision of the tragic hero would evolve toward a different type of heroism, as represented by Zarathustra, who acts deliberately against nothingness.

Individuation and appearance, central for the Apollonian element, dilute the naked truth of the early tragedy, marking the beginning of a new culture which devaluates suffering and promotes pursuit of happiness. Representation prevails over will, words over action, image over music. The era of the hegemony of intellect marks the final stage of the collapse of tragedy. Socrates's *Daimonion*, a new modality of being, a human caricature exhibiting the exchange of roles between instincts (which now perform a function of warning and refraining from action) and reflection (which is now meant to trigger action), is a harbinger of *homo theoreticus*, an antimystic, whose "logical nature has through uncontrolled growth developed itself to excess in the same way as instinctive wisdom has in the mystic."[51]

Thus, the Apollonian assumes the mask of speculation, and the Dionysian, deprived of its wildness, of conventional feelings.[52] In a half-ironic way, Nietzsche admits that Socrates was a genius in developing the idea of salvation through illusion.

The theoretical attitude led to scientific optimism—the belief that progress in scientific knowledge may lead us to the very depths of being. Only Kant and Schopenhauer seriously questioned this optimism and placed man back in an uncertain position, while the status of religion, practical ethics, and art was at least partly restored. This recognition, in a sense tragic in itself, represented a ray hope for some of original Greek wisdom to be retrieved.

In response to nihilism, which, according to the Nietzschean diagnosis, was a dominant attitude of his contemporaries called by him famously the "blinking community of the last men," the thinker invented a tragic hero and a prophet: Zarathustra. The sage is fully aware of the impossibility of rendering his own mission of bringing the good message of eternal return legitimate, yet he decides to come down and pass the message. The "Yes" uttered by the hero in the face of the absurdity of individual life, his Promethean self-assertion in front of nothingness, introduce an element of tragic sublimity. Within the metaphysical vista of Schopenhauer, where an individual, both in his suffering and in his heroism, is but an illusion, self-resignation seems to be the most rational attitude. Here we are presented with a different sort of rebellion. Not a spectator, but a real, empirical man may coin himself into a hero by withholding the chaotic thrust he is part of. Zarathustra's prophecy is a chance for elevating the fading humanity in human animals to a dignified, tragic level by confronting it with the truth and providing with a vision of a new salvation, a way of transcending the absurdity of an accidental, individual being. Nietzsche, then, who initially understood tragedy in terms of an orgiastic, ritualistic expression of human condition, ultimately sided with an individual human being. The individual, ennobled by his titanic effort of becoming, replaced the collective hero.

Nietzsche *as* Zarathustra, as I tend to read him, *torn in-between contempt and love towards the fragile creature called man, relieved him even from the burden of his own history in the experiment of eternal return.*[53] Thus, at the turn of the twentieth century, Nietzsche, in the guise of a new Prometheus, articulated the tragic again in his attempt to overcome nihilism and to offer an alternative to Christian salvation. It is most explicitly audible in his mature writings, where he once again attested to the ineradicable dualism of his thinking and the existential primacy of suffering assumed by him. We read that the problem is that of the meaning of suffering: whether a Christian meaning or a tragic meaning. In the former case, it is supposed to be the path to a holy existence; in the latter case, being is counted as *holy enough* to justify even a monstrous amount of suffering.[54]

While Heidegger saw in Nietzsche's thought a turning point in Western consciousness as reflected in the development of metaphysics, Santayana considered it a culmination of German idealism and egotism, a moment when it turns against its own heritage. Hence, in a somewhat paternalistic tone, he notes that what counted more than *what* Nietzsche had to say, was "the fact *that* he said it. . . . We should forgive Nietzsche his boyish blasphemies. He hated with clearness, if he did not know what to love."[55] Now, leaving aside the fact that Santayana's critique of Nietzsche abounds in hasty simplifications and generalizations, the above quoted words are pregnant with meaning insofar as we consider them in their broader context, namely—Santayana's critique of egotism in philosophy and culture. An anthropological heritage of egotism, as Santayana viewed it, is one of a chronic immaturity, it signifies a *self* incapable of transcendence and, hence, of establishing harmonious relations with the world beyond. This disability is passed on to the heir of egotism, Nietzschean philosophy of will, where it turns into a vengeful will of power and expansion.

This theoretical evolution is said to be paralleled by the idiosyncratic German reception of classicism and the pathos of its attempt at the revival of antiquity within the womb of modern culture. The result of it was something artificial, turning classical studies into *Kulturgeschichte*.[56] In what we would call today a culturally biased way, Santayana wrote:

> In the attempt to be Greek the truly classical was missed even by Goethe, since the truly classical is not foreign to anybody. It is precisely that part of tradition and art which does not alienate us from our own life and nature, but reveals them in all their depth and nakedness, freed from the fashions and hypocrisies of time and place.[57]

Interestingly, both Heidegger and Nietzsche (in the *Birth of Tragedy*) express a similar criticism concerning the artificiality of *Kulturgeschichte*. Quite obviously, Nietzsche regarded his own analysis of the tragic pessimism in terms of the Dionysian element as a breakthrough in this fossilized academic approach. Nevertheless, Santayana disagreed with the Nietzschean dichotomy

Dionysian–Apollonian. He was rather inclined to see both sides as shades belonging to a single continuum, even if he would accept the existence of an ongoing polemic or maybe a dialogue between the tragic and the rational outlook. Santayana was decidedly against the anthropomorphic tendency of Nietzsche, who attributed nature with culturally distinguished qualities, in particular in the light of his declaration against anthropomorphism.[58] Nietzsche's metaphysical dualism, an idiosyncratic reversion of the Platonic dichotomy between being and appearance, became a matrix for his philosophy, even if he would later abandon it openly. In *Twilight of the Idols* he returns to the theme of the tragic, reconfirming literally his standpoint from years before. It is the sanctification of suffering and the sacrifice of individuality that remained for him the highly admirable essence of Greek tragedy. After the disappearance of the Dionysian drama, a Greek for Nietzsche is synonymous with someone, whose "apollonian consciousness . . . casts[s] a veil over this Dionysian world."[59] Without denying viability to this view, as a theory of everything it may seem one-sidedly dogmatic, if not, paradoxically, extremely Apollonian. Santayana wrote,

> He thinks he alone has discovered the divinity of Dionysus . . . which Plato took as a matter of course . . . Inspiration, like will, is a force without which reason can do nothing. Inspiration must be presupposed . . . this two-edged wisdom that makes impulse the stuff of life and reason its criterion, is, of course, lost on Nietzsche, and with it the whole marvel of Greek genius.[60]

Santayana, then, regarded the so-called Greek genius as protecting the Dionysian power under the control of reason. Nietzsche in his reading understood the classical always in terms of power and a sort of grandeur of style, which commences in control over happiness and despair. If there is peacefulness, it is underpinned by forcefulness. Heidegger, who himself spoke of the Greeks in terms of "taming" a great surplus into a simplicity, and did so in an idiom inclining toward the imagery of power, noticed a trace of genius in what he believed to be Nietzsche's rediscovery of the fact that "natural" should be conceived of in terms of *the uncanny*, "*deinon*," while he dismissed the positivistic and naturalistic aspect of Nietzschean thought. Santayana ascribed to such interpretations a tendency to mythologize antiquity.

While all of the three thinkers often refer to antiquity and to some extent they do so on the same ground—namely to neutralize the subjectivist *ressentiment* they recognize in Romanticism—their ways of appropriating antiquity differs. This difference in the approach to antiquity is telling in respect to their different approaches to the tragic. Santayana by "taking the side" of the classical simply means to express his distance to all fashions of the day. His outlook, being also expressive of his Mediterranean taste for harmony and humanistic sympathies, is naturalistic, critically realistic and moderately rationalistic, informed by the search for measure. This, by way of digression, should not overshadow the fact that he had his own "transcendental" (and romantic) side. Heidegger and Nietzsche in turn, dismiss rationalism altogether and get close, perhaps, to a sort of new mythology centered around "hidden powers" and the "*deinon*," which they try to legitimize by evoking the alleged uncanniness of pre-Socratic Greeks.

Being Never Too Late for Oneself: The Tragic and the Eternal Return

Nietzschean "most difficult" of all thoughts—the idea of eternal return, which dawned on Zarathustra—has triggered a great variety of readings, from cosmological to religious, and was often considered ambiguous and vague, let alone the fact that Nietzsche himself did not understand it and finally got rid of it. Some interpreters, though, assume it to be the key to Nietzsche's thought. In the interpretation of the thinker from Freiburg, this indeed abyssal idea has nothing to do with cosmological or scientific inquiry whatsoever.[61] It is impossible here to discuss all the spectrum of the shades of meaning listed in his detailed reading, so let us have a look at those that throw some light on the issue of the tragic.

Starting from what Heidegger considered a final conclusion of his analysis—the mystery of eternal recurrence rests in the idea of the constancy of the *being of a moment*. It has nothing to do with a cyclical concept of time or the idea that the past must be repeated. Instead, it is about keeping open the temporal gate of the moment in front of him who is standing at this gate. Eternity seems to be a source of constant beginning, as if the moment were a point of radiation or an unceasing micro-explosion, which is potentially giving birth to something new. A temporal metaphor of time giving itself or succumbing itself to being might also convey the idea. This reading, then, offers a sort of *metaphysics of the moment*. Let us recall Santayana's sentimental time, the subjective vision of time, where the phrases like "too late" and "not yet" express human dependence on the sense of pastness and the projects of the future alike. *The "eternity" of new beginning, which illuminated Zarathustra, is targeted precisely against this "sentimental" perspective.*

Zarathustra comes down to share his revelation with anyone ready to listen. This is where the tragic aspect appears, this is where it can appear as long as for Nietzsche there is no tragic without heroism. Zarathustra is conscious of the fact that there is no transcendent justification for his vision, neither is there any ethical grounding for his decision save his own will. With a full clarity that will and deeds speak only for themselves, and that there is no any ultimate fulfillment of his or anyone else's effort, Zarathustra says "yes" to the individual being. His tragicness hangs upon the juxtaposition between his action and his awareness of the ethical void underneath. His self-assertion expresses his freedom. This is why Heidegger said Nietzsche's reaching the bottom of nihilism is accompanied by his titanic effort to overcome it. There is a sense of courage and liberation in the consciousness of nothingness and the heroism of the affirmative choice. Yet, as Santayana believed, Nietzsche's alternative salvation offered no hope and no relief from despair, only the "despite."

Nevertheless, if read from a slightly different angle, the idea carries something "refreshing." In her interpretation Hanna Buczyńska-Garewicz also associates the idea of eternal recurrence with an everlasting moment giving rise to new beginnings.[62] As against those readings which explain Nietzsche's idea in terms of repetitions of worlds, biographies, and sequences of events, the author articulates something usually overlooked by interpreters—namely, the essentially *hypothetical* nature of the whole idea. If so, eternal recurrence is a *metaphysical experiment in thinking* and embarking upon its path—a conscious risk, a wager. The existential and psychological meaning of this experiment is the liberation of will, the affirmative movement of which is now to be directed precisely at what it is paralyzed by—the past, and the past as a whole. The affirmation saves from guilt, pity and vengeance—it saves from the masks of *ressentiment* and makes room for the desire of the future. The key to this earthly salvation rests in the choice of temporal perspective. At this point let me evoke one of Santayana's remarks on the tragic, which happens to bear semblance to Nietzschean perspectivism in this specific context:

> We are caught in the meshes of time, place and care; and the things we have set our heart on, whatever they may be, must pass away in the end . . . we cannot take a long view without finding life sad, and all things tragic. This aspect of vanity and self-annihilation, which existence wears when we consider its destiny, is not to be denied or explained away . . . [by] phi-

> losophies. It is a true aspect of existence in one relation and on a certain view; but to take this long view of existence, and look down the avenues of time from the station and with the emotions of some particular moment, is by no means inevitable . . . Things when they are actual do not lie in that sort of sentimental perspective, but each is centered in itself; . . . Life is free play fundamentally.[63]

There is a suggestion that the tragic is an *effect* of a certain subjective, linear perspective determined by interests, values, projects, aims, dependencies, and all the emotions related to the sense of guilt, hope, unfulfilled promises, and dreams proper to a given life. Some cultures, as Santayana would elsewhere say, produce such visions of man and such ways of shaping the *self* that are particularly conducive to tragic attitudes (in this context by "tragic" I mean simply fatalistic and pessimistic). But this passage says also something about the inevitable tension proper to human existence—the tension between the ideal and the factual. This tension cannot be fully removed by any experiment in disabling the sentimental perspective, although there is a degree of liberating consciousness in some such experiments, which may diminish the "human shade," to use the Nietzschean metaphor. It is interesting to note the semantic similarity between Nietzschean *"ressentiment"* and the "sentimental time" of Santayana, and the fact that each is but *a* perspective, although the most burdensome one. Saying that this burdensome perspective may be replaced by a different, emancipating one, makes it to some extent relative. But, by the very same token, as noted by Santayana, it can be made absolute, as it happens in the case of the early Nietzsche's thought. *The idea of eternal recurrence may be interpreted as an evidence of Nietzsche's effort to overcome the hopelessness of his own vision of a through-and-through immanent reality opened before human eyes.* This is what Santayana means by the arbitrariness of the tragic as a worldview established by a philosopher's doctrine. Another example of it provided by Santayana was the monistic system of Spinoza, who

> found a cruel pleasure in asserting that every part of it [essence] existed, thereby putting to shame the conceit of mankind . . . This tragic contradiction—tragic because so many instincts and passions meet and destroy themselves there—comes of hypostatizing essence and attempting to rationalize substance.[64]

Spinoza's system, notwithstanding the fact that Spinoza was among Santayana's favorite thinkers, may be counted as another theoretical epitome of the *vengeance* of time on human life—in that *everything* is *already there* and *it is there ideally and eternally*. Some philosophies seem to stage worlds particularly fit for tragedy. Santayana's diversified ontology, as I would suggest, may be counted as a counterexample, a system of thought where contingency in matter and freedom in spirit prepared a favorable ground for a pluralistic individualism and vital liberty.

Santayana's Critique of Nietzsche

To systematize and develop Santayana's main points in his discussion with Nietzsche, one may speak of two polemical perspectives: internal, which undermines the effectiveness of the strategy where the specific Nietzschean rationality turns against its own principle of serving individual life, and external, which is inscribed in a broader context of the critique of culture and in particular—of instrumental reason.

In the first context the argument against Nietzsche is that his metaphysics of will, being a return to pre-rational categories, makes man a *locus* of the conflict between the will to power and conscious self-creation, where the latter is bound to be defeated. As a result man's existential choice is reduced to an alternative between self-resignation and subordinating oneself to the will to power, which is blind willing of oneself. In fact, the alternative is illusory because both sides are reformulations of the same thing. Heidegger offered a solution by expanding the meaning of will to power and translating it into a synthesis of being, thinking, and the idea of eternal return. A sort of "rational will" is said to emerge, a thinking-as-acting, which aims at withholding the omnipresent chaos and strengthening the individual, or, in other words, preserving the individual being in its becoming. The will to power is not, as emphasized by Deleuze, a mere will to dominate, it rather stands for the principle of creative affirmation as opposed to reactive forms of life.[65] Deleuze also noticed a principle of selection contained in both the will to power and eternal return.[66] Heidegger's analysis brought to light the inversion or the turn which is present in Nietzsche—from the negation of becoming to its affirmation. As against these readings, Santayana believed that within Nietzsche's "flat" ontology and his hermeneutics of embodiment and power, the issue of conscious becoming can hardly be accounted for. In other words, he considered Nietzschean project an anthropological failure.

Heidegger's reading reveals a project of an overall mobilization of life forces on behalf of a becoming individual. But this idea seems more plausible within his own fundamental ontology with all its transcendental and temporal intricacies. In the light of Nietzschean thought, as Santayana saw it, what is left at man's disposal is ultimately his will translated into passions, and when these "see themselves in the mirror of reflection, what they behold is a tragic mask."[67] Nietzsche, out of his contempt for a certain style of spirituality, got rid of the whole margin of human transcendence at once, removing the possibility of projection, idealization, and any corrective tribunal of self-reflection and memory. It was symptomatic of both egotism and the metaphysics of will, as Santayana thought of it.

> By this rejection of harmony as the perfection and inner principle of life, egotism passes from the metaphysical sphere, where it is a delusion of self-consciousness, to the field of politics and morals, where it represents a reversion from rational to pre-rational morality. Vitality and integrity are again to assert themselves absolutely, in defiance of their natural source and natural limits, and of the trammels that might be imposed upon them by wisdom. This is the primary tragic courage.[68]

Santayana saw an aggravation of the tragic in the Nietzschean strategy of subordinating human being to the spontaneity of will and transgressing the boundaries of humanity, which replaced transcendence. *What logic stands behind Santayana's judgment?* Let me try to reconstruct his way of thinking.

An abstract and, in fact, anthropomorphic notion of self-redeeming chaos is projected by the early Nietzsche onto the being as a whole and set against human being. Man—an unfortunate, minute, bodily accident striving for individuation and survival—from the start is threatened by the annihilating power of chaos. In the light of the fact that everything, including reason, may ultimately be reduced to power or universal will, which is the sole principle of being, human becoming and self-preservation involve a struggle against an overwhelming, violent pressure located both beyond and within the body a human being is. "Living body is a passage. Through the body flows the flux of life, which we may sense always only in a fragmentary and ineffable way."[69] It is a struggle against everything, then, including oneself.

It is doubtful that Santayana might have missed the fact that Nietzsche's project was first and foremost a diagnosis and a prophecy concerning the status quo of modern humanity, accompanied by an attempt at tracing those cultural threads which conspired to the degradation of a certain vital and dignified ethos. Santayana's own critique of culture simply stood in stark contrast to Nietzschean and so did his anthropological project. The author of *Realm of Spirit* did not appreciate the novelty and cathartic nature of Nietzsche's idea of eternal recurrence, especially when supported by the conception of *amor fati* in the broader context of the idea of regaining *this* world for the humans too deeply immersed in otherworldliness. Buczyńska-Garewicz notes the wisdom and the liberating force of the Nietzschean idea to accept the past and, through it, one's own becoming. The attitude of *amor fati* throws a different, affirmative light on the so-called "fate," which often was thought of—simplistically—in terms of fatality. The author highlights, as against the common emphasis on Nietzsche's will to power, the gentle and positive aspect of his mature thought, which constitutes an inspiring response to the idea of otherworldly salvation.[70] But to accept the past as a whole and to affirm everything one has become may amount to ignoring a simple human assumption that one can learn from experience and grow mature. Any self-creation involves reflection, assessment, selection, rejection, acceptation, development.[71] It must entail a "no" except for "yes," otherwise there is no projecting. This selective rejection based on ideals and values, unless caricaturized, has not much in common with *ressentiment*. On the contrary—it requires courage to confront one's image. But this reflecting and selective attitude seems to have been neglected by Nietzsche. Was it an overlooking? No, it couldn't have been otherwise because Nietzsche approaches human being "as a fact" (!).[72] Facts may be either accepted or imaginatively transgressed. In Santayana's ontology the idea of man as projecting himself is legitimate due to the distinction of the non-volitional realm of spirit, where tensions maybe released and transmuted meaningfully, with respect to self-knowledge and circumstances. It is supported by the deconstructive power of the realm of essences, which carry a creative and liberating potential. Finally—to articulate it once again—an utterly new quality is introduced into nature, namely disinterestedness, which is priceless from the point of view of personal, intellectual, and spiritual freedom. While Nietzsche ridiculed the life of speculation and contemplative ideals, Santayana was concerned with their unfortunate collapse.

Nietzschean reduction of man to the empirical and sensual reality, even if ennobled by the tragic sublime, seems to leave to man not enough chance to neutralize the terror of the flux around not to mention self-creation. And it is probably not enough to say, as Deleuze did, that eternal return involves selectivity, as long as a radically affirmative attitude is a condition of it and makes of the *self* an accidental aggregate of powers. The proclaimed by Nietzsche *death of God* is synonymous with a dissolved *self*, as Deleuze elsewhere notes.[73] Respectively, since such a *self* can no longer commit itself to faith, neither is willing to model itself according to an ideal of perfection, it is offered the possibility of eternal return instead. The latter is a "clinical" version of faith, it employs its mechanics, it is "not a faith, but the truth of it," a "simulacrum of every doctrine (the highest irony)," and finally, "the parody of every belief."[74] Metaphorically speaking, the Deleuzian eternal return amounts to—according to my reading—*an intensification by constant repetition of the rite of passage aspect present in any religious belief but in a purely intensive or transcendental form. This kind of the experience of temporality is valid for the vision of reality held by Nietzsche—that of a field of pure powers*. Needless to say, it was incompatible not only with Santayana's philosophy but also with his sensitivity and taste for the refinement of life occurring in the ideal realm. To Nietzsche's credit though, we might recognize *amor fati* as a humble way of acknowledging finitude—something that Santayana overlooked in his criticism.

At this point we are already touching upon the second context of Santayana's critique, which refers to Nietzsche's thought as an embodiment of instrumental reason. Bodily, local life represented by the factuality of a concrete man is a point of reference for some basic concepts of this philosophy. As noticed by Heidegger, an experiment in thought becomes the ground for existence since man acts within an imagined freedom.[75] The will to power commences in the desire to sustain the becoming of a human being in its attempt at overcoming himself as chaos. Cognition and knowledge are mere means of survival and adaptation, a sort of mental *violence* and a form of sanity in action.[76] Thinking is a tool, and truth is equated with what is valuable for a concrete life, embracing the whole world of illusion. By "true" is meant "expedient."[77]

Human response to chaos is *praxis* as "reason, the essence of which is to receive and confront chaos."[78] Ridiculing the theoretical man did not stop Nietzsche from considering logic as the essence of reason as long "as man must think logically in order to survive."[79] Chaos and reason are well coupled since "where the world is ridden by irrationalism, rationalism triumphs. Technocracy and superstition go hand in hand."[80] According to Santayana, this vision is a continuation of German idealism in its pursuit to overcome the fluidity of life. The idea of existence as an attempt to gain control over chaos is an expression of the continuity of Western metaphysics, which is "logic in the sense that the essence of being is being shaped in the horizon of thinking."[81] The principle of constructing reality remains the same while the meaning of "thinking," "truth," "man," and other concepts is modified. Heidegger's analysis shows that this shift in meaning is symptomatic of Nietzsche's horror in front of change and unintelligibility, and places him within the tradition of German idealism, but at the point when this tradition turns against itself. Santayana would not disagree. In a vision like this, he says, "ego" "returns to haunt us in broad daylight and to persuade us with its ghostly eloquence that not that ego but this world is the ghost."[82] *Nietzsche tried to overcome the nihilism of his time but his strategy had at its disposal only the dispossessed new language.*

Santayana undoubtedly shared with Nietzsche some naturalist and pragmatic ideas. The target of his critique was the idea of will to power and the reductive, positivist anthropology. The depreciation of reflection and idealization gives rise to the problem of the thinking *self* which cannot be properly formed. As previously discussed, Heidegger attempted to account for this deficit and spoke of a "rational will to power." So does Hanna Buczyńska-Garewicz by calling Nietzsche a rationalist thinker. It is true in terms of a pragmatic conception of rationality and perhaps in the sense of an attempt to rationalize the power of the unconscious undertaken by him. Nietzsche assumed a limited rationality serving as an instrument in survival. Santayana pointed out that in Nietzsche's ontology there is no weapon at man's disposal which would substantially differ from the flux of nature, neither is there any realm of experience where tensions might be relieved. In other words, there is no room for transcendence in any of the meanings of this term. Man governed by the will to power seems doomed to blindness and suffering. Being a human does not offer any inspiring prospects other than immersion in the opium of the Apollonian, an obscure experiment with eternal return, or tragic heroism. In his revolt against the dogmas of Western tradition, Nietzsche caricaturized and excluded all the ways of neutralizing the iron cage of factual existence and domesticating the horror of death. In all his critical undertaking, Santayana notes, Nietzsche failed to recognize the absolutism of his philosophy of will and the dead-end of the strategy of will to power. This is why Santayana conceived of Nietzsche's project as desperate and hopeless from the point of view of what Nietzsche himself was after all concerned about—the possibility of salvation.[83] To bring to light the whole paradox of Nietzsche—finally he was unwilling to reject the idea of self-transcendence (see Superman as an example of peculiar transcendence) as the last attribute of dignity, but—in the face of the lack of any dimension of reality where self-transcendence might really occur—Nietzsche invented eternal return, which sanctioned the eternal now, a "now," which, as "now" in a sense has always . . . already been. *An interesting theoretical association which may support the rationale of Santayana's critique of Nietzsche is the brilliant idea of the revenge of factuality coined by Adorno and Horkheimer to describe the mechanism of enlightenment turning into positivism, which in the case of Nietzsche appears as the hegemony of will after spirituality has been done away with.*[84]

It is possible that Santayana, shaped by a different cultural tradition, could hardly understand Nietzsche's total rejection of both Greek style of liberation by reason and Christian salvation. One may speculate that Nietzsche, making Zarathustra reach the idea of eternal recurrence out of a titanic effort and inhuman suffering, was aware that his philosophy hardly opened other *vistas*. He presented the being called "man," like Schopenhauer did, in a self-destructive, perhaps even self-contradictory light, as a being confronted with the alternative: either self-transgression or a collapse. According to Santayana, this vision echoed Nietzsche's rejection of the mature art of tragedy, which was a victory of spirit over despair.[85]

Nietzsche, concludes Santayana, decapitated the Western man without offering a worthy alternative. Deprived of the ancient heritage of spirituality, man may at his best become a tragic hero instead of being merely an animal. Santayana believed in the benefits of wisdom gained by learning from experience in confrontation with tradition. He was inclined to see the emancipatory potential resting in rethinking tradition and drawing on the "transcendence-friendly" structures of multidimensional reality offered by a rich conceptuality. Nietzsche, in contrast, decided to start everything anew. Half a century later a similar judgment will be passed on by Karl Jaspers, who would claim that Nietzsche literally ruined the conception of salvation that he was concerned about.[86]

The polemic of Santayana with Nietzsche, then, was first and foremost an argument about the possibility and the necessity of spirituality. Santayana proposed an ontology that granted autonomy to spirit, without references to the supernatural. In this respect he belongs to the tradition of cultural reflection and critique targeted against positivism, scientism, and the principle of instrumental reason. Certain of his views are close to those of Husserl, Heidegger, Frankfurt School, or Charles Taylor. Interestingly, Eric Voegelin regarded his analysis of egotism understood in terms of spiritual disintegration to be a good diagnostic tool for a critique of cultural crisis, one comparable to and, to some extent, in line with Nietzsche's criterion of nihilism.[87]

6.3 *Nemesis* and Time

An attempt to organize Santayana's haphazard references to the tragic reveals a few contexts or, maybe, levels of description which may be covered by an overarching metaphor of spirit encaged in matter. The tragic aspect of existence may be traced in the discontinuities within the *self*, reflected in its *aporetic* status and fully revealed in the ontology of realms, where the *self* finds itself in a Pascalian suspension in-between "two abysses of infinity and nothingness."[88] In the presence of the impenetrable realm of matter, the infinite realm of essence, and the objective and incorruptible realm of truth, human life may be called metaphorically a wager, a trial, or an "insinuation." Ontologies of this kind happen to place man in a precarious situation, where—to use an irreproachably clear and persuasive description by a contemporary thinker—*"everything depends on recognizing under what description of the action the agent was unaware of what he was doing."*[89] In the face of this insecurity as to one's existential status, the tragic consists in "the compulsion to honor the facts . . . imposed on man by the destiny of his body."[90]

No matter how far these facts can be reformulated and reappropriated by the *self*, there is no ultimate *Aufhebung*. Guided by Santayana, we discover that the "tragic segment" is nested already in the realm of essence in the form of "absolute truth."[91] In the realm of truth the material and the essential realm achieve an ideal, extra-temporal unity, beyond the grasp of finite thinking. One way of explaining the tragic aspect of this objective and eternal truth in human terms is to say that we have our share in this truth without having an insight into this divine perspective. More emphatically, one of the sources of the tragic is the irrevocability of events reflected in eternity. Factuality, to which Santayana throughout all his philosophy keeps denying primacy on ethical and aesthetic grounds, nevertheless cannot be erased and takes its toll unless respected. That is why, Santayana claimed, *if philosophy is to illuminate the premises of human condition and action, it has to be concerned with the strategies of reconciliation between facts and ideals.* This is the voice of respect for the principle of reality, which is tragically transgressed by ancient heroes. The realm of spirit, which Nietzsche had rejected and of which Santayana was an advocate, facilitates such negotiations.

The *self*, then, seems to be at once the source and the recipient of the tragic clash. Jesus is an exemplary tragic hero, an illumination, a sort of a holographic display of tragicness, which brings to a completion the unfinished revelation of the ancient tragedy. Jesus has two perspectives at his disposal—human and divine—the latter being one of absolute truth and love. It is the difference between both that reveals all "the sadness of the world,"[92] which, as part of tragic sublimity, conveys the aesthetics of any tragic landscape, as evoked earlier by Scheler and Kierkegaard. In another book, representing—according to Paul Tillich's words—a "sublime esotericism,"[93] Santayana depicts Christ as the very "substance" of the tragic, containing its own solution already in itself. Christ personifies the drama of spirit incarnate, or, in other words, spirituality entangled in factuality.[94]

Between Spiritual Dissolution and the Invention of the Human[95]

> Tragic hero is more 'deinon' than any man.
> —Paul Ricoeur, *Oneself as Another*, 246

Santayana viewed the ancient tragedy—in the vein of Aristotle and Bruno Snell—as a child of reflection, which sublimated the non-discursive tensions of old cults into something, in a broad sense, intelligible.[96] As Albin Lesky, in a Hegelian spirit, comments on the language of mature tragedy, it does not describe things but rather originates from them and spontaneously expresses the spirit's synthetic inquiry into the world of human affairs. Through tragedy, Greek poets managed to "overcome what was barbaric and undisciplined."[97]

Likewise, for Santayana tragic art exemplifies "passion transmuted into discipline."[98] Mythology, tragedy, and the spirituality of mature religions belong to the same continuum of "disenchanting and re-enchanting" the world with an ultimate aim of "seeing this world in its simple truth."[99] Both art (poetry in particular) and religion idealize experience imaginatively and as such are an expression of human, spiritual freedom. Their subject matter is "all time and all experience . . . , and all the possibilities of being . . . [are their] ultimate theme."[100] While myth and tragedy draw predominantly on the repetitiveness in nature which sustains and legitimizes a certain *human condition*, mature religions offer a meaningful ethical language of negotiations between freedom and necessity. Already tragedy overcomes the mundane repetitiveness of myth, for it embodies an act of *understanding*. It is an expression of growing self-awareness of humans in respect to their own finitude experienced as confrontation with fate. The latter, along with the suggestion of a cosmic background, dramatized and poeticized, convey a "fine sense of the dignity and pathos of life."[101]

What is more, tragedy exhibits an early insight into the singleness and eccentricity of human being in nature. *Inasmuch man, being part of nature and subordinated to its irresistible laws, rebelliously strives to transcend it, he is "vengefully" transcended by it*. The hero's death provokes reflection on the fragility and destructibility of all values as against the durability of the laws of nature. Tragedy is

> dominated by the idea of fate. . . . [There is] the deep conviction of the limits and conditions of human happiness. . . . The fates guide the willing and drag the unwilling. . . . Life is seen as whole, although in miniature. Its boundaries and its principles are studied more than its incidents. The human, therefore, everywhere merges with the divine. Our mortality, being sharply defined and much insisted upon, draws the attention all the more to that *eternity of nature and of law*.[102]

And yet, as an evidence of illumination and transmutation of lived experience into an intelligible form,

> the blackest tragedy is festive; the most pessimistic philosophy is an enthusiastic triumph of thought. . . . It is no interruption to experience to master experience as tragedy aspires to do. . . . Tragedy, the knowledge of death, raises us to that height.[103]

As a result of the sublimating power of spirit, in Greek tragedy human condition could be synthetically conveyed as a dramatic matrix of all action. Aeschylus, for example, focusing on the circumstances and the process of decision-making strove to uncover "the archetype," "the hard core" of human action.[104] This sort of revelation was possible, Santayana claimed, due to the wholeness of Greek outlook, the condition of any wholeness always being "not this or that system but some system. Its value is not the value of truth, but that of victorious imagination."[105] Within an integral worldview man's "imaginative power" may give birth to "sublimity, as it gives sublimity to many passages in the Bible."[106]

Santayana, engaged in a cultural dispute of the time, enjoyed declaring sympathy to antiquity, the genius of which he saw resting in the unity of experience and art, and juxtaposed it with the tendency toward an unfortunate separation of both, exhibited, in his view, by Western culture ever since. Similar voices appear in contemporary interpretations of tragedy. Alenka Zupančič, combining elements of psychoanalytical and philosophical approach, writes of tragedy as "essentially the work of sublimation, in the precise sense of elevating a singular subjective destiny to that place of the symbolic structure that constitutes its blind spot, its inherent impasse."[107] Modernity is marked by a crisis (including the loss of the "tragic sense") manifesting itself in the experience "worse than tragedy"—the experience of *bare life*, beyond any sense of wholeness that might "inscribe death in the dimension of, for example, honor and dignity."[108]

Modern representations of the tragic often show man as a contextual being, always entangled in a situation which, inevitably, exceeds the limits of both his awareness and his action. The overwhelming complexity and moral ambiguity of reality stand in stark contrast to the hero's heightened subjectivity and the sense of personal responsibility. In fact, only if we assume the tragic hero to be *a spiritual* or *an inspired creature*, can something like a tragic conflict be experienced, imagined, woven into the plot, and recognized. "For what is tragedy but the conflict between inspiration and truth?"[109] On one hand, the fact that tragedy (ancient and modern) often ends in death establishes the paradigmatic triumph of truth over inspiration. On the other hand, though, it definitely belongs to a spiritual perspective to equate the death of the hero with the annihilation of the values he represented. Whatever might happen in future "makes no difference to the drama in this soul,"[110] because *the hero represents a principle contrary to that of the truth of tragedy*. The hero, then, is a rebel against the realm of facts. Interestingly, Walter Benjamin shared some of Santayana's reflections on tragedy. Tragedy is the work of genius, says Benjamin, since for the first time something *superior* to "demonic fate" is given artistic expression—namely a "pagan man becomes aware that he is better than his god, but this realization robs him of speech, remains unspoken."[111] There is no peaceful consent on the hero's part for the logic of guilt and atonement. Benjamin's (agonistic) *genius* of the tragic hero maybe translated into Santayana's language as the discovery of the hero's spirituality that inspires in him the pursuit of ideals.

According to Paul Ricoeur, tragedy is "the voice of nonphilosophy . . . untimely irruption" from which "we await the shock capable of awakening our mistrust with respect not only to the illusions of the heart but also to the illusions born of the *hubris* of practical reason itself."[112] Shakespeare, as noted by Santayana, assumed a disillusioned and nonreligious perspective on the tragic. Let us consider briefly Santayana's interpretation of Hamlet with reference to the most "old-fashioned humanist"[113] contemporary literary critic, Harold Bloom. The choice of Bloom as an imaginary interlocutor for Santayana is justified precisely by the "ancient" sort of humanism they both represent, an outlook which—no matter how untimely or anachronistic it may seem—is never dead and once in a while makes a brilliant come back as epitomized by *Shakespeare: The Invention of the Human*.[114] Bloom and Santayana, anti-dogmatic as they are, are of an opinion that much of literature remains in a strong bond with human existence, viewing the author as a particular individual, an (unconscious) voice of his times, and his work—to some extent—as representative of humanity at large. Interestingly, while some of the conclusions in their cultural-existential interpretations of *Hamlet* converge, they finally reveal two divergent *sympathies*. Besides being of interest for its own sake, the juxtaposition enhances our understanding of Santayana as a critic of culture.

Santayana reads Shakespeare's tragedies with reference to secularization. Within the worldview symptomatic of the progressing dissolution of faith in the playwright's era, Shakespeare reintroduced the non-discursive and inhuman in the form of a mere fact, an accident, an absurd. His detailed and rich depiction of human life conveys no larger cosmic structure and no hope for transcendent source of meaning, or—as a matter of fact—no integral meaning at all. Wholeness is replaced by fullness. The undeniable genius of the poet's use of language allowed him to render "human experience no longer through symbols, but by direct imaginative representation,"[115] by an almost literal "embodiment" of reality.

As previously discussed, Kierkegaard pondered over the shift of tragedy from the ancient objectivity to the psychology of a moral subject. He articulated the need for a religion of salvation as a response to the inhumanity of guilt interiorized (which replaced fate). Santayana, as we have just seen, articulated the function of imagination, as exemplified by religion and art, in providing a language on the ground of which the *self* may enter into a creative relation with the finite instead of subjugating itself to the mask of factuality—a fatal mask assumed by finitude in a culture that speaks a "lifeless," positivistic language.

In the light of Santayana's dialectical understanding of the relation between the *self* and culture, the character of Hamlet seems to embody a triple loss accompanying the change in the representation of the tragic: the world losing unity, man interiorizing and then "losing" the world, and, finally, man losing integrity, which manifests itself in the crisis of agency. It is not accidental that Santayana sees in *Hamlet* the "most psychological of tragedies"[116] and a full-blown anticipation of a modern tragic hero, if not a caricature of modern man, one of the participants of the "blinking community." I would suggest that "most psychological" here stands for something like: representing a turning point in the errand of human psyche toward its modern guise. Likewise, Bloom says,

> The internalization of the *self* is one of Shakespeare's greatest inventions, particularly because it came before anyone else was ready for it. There is a growing inner *self* in Protestantism, but nothing in Luther prepares us for Hamlet's mystery.[117]

The internalization of the tragic conflict results in Hamlet's balancing in-between the tragic and the comic. Santayana makes the prince exemplary of his own criticism of what he calls, alternatively, *spiritual discord* or *dislocation of reason*. Hamlet's romantic solipsism, his continuous introspection, hide "a mind inwardly rent asunder, a delicate genius disordered . . . a mind that with infinite sensibility possessed no mastery over itself nor over things."[118] At the same time, in a manner proper for a tragic hero, Hamlet is noble, sophisticated, philosophically oriented, yet doomed to a "moral dissolution," which starts with seeing the ghost.[119]

> The ghost scenes in Hamlet . . . are excellent examples of profound, ill-digested emotions breaking out fiercely against circumstances which are not well in hand . . . This ghost is not like the deities that often appear in Greek tragedies, a *deus ex machina* . . . this ghost is a party to the conflict, an instigator of sinister thoughts, a thing hatched in a nest of sorrow. Its scope is exclusively personal . . . at once a spectre and a suspicion, a physical marvel and an inward authoritative voice. . . . We feel that not Hamlet the Dane but the human soul in its inmost depths is moonstruck and haunted.[120]

There is some similarity between these remarks and Bloom's noting that "hesitation and consciousness are synonyms in this vast play . . . Hamlet inaugurates the drama of heightened identity. . . . His world is the growing inner self . . . [that] he celebrates almost continuously."[121] At the reverse side of the *drama of heightened identity* there is the crisis of agency. The logic of Hamlet, Santayana says, is that "he acts without reflection, as he reflects without acting."[122] In a similar vein, Zupančič called *Hamlet* a tragedy "entirely constructed around the hero's not being equal to his act."[123] Hamlet's "morbid indirection" and the "brilliant futility" of his mind, notes Santayana, render the tragic guilt resting not in an action but in refraining from action! Correspondingly, Bloom claims that "for Hamlet revisioning the *self* replaces the project of revenge,"[124] he is never "wholly committed to any stance or attitude, any mission or indeed to anything at all" (!).[125]

The world of Hamlet seems to resist any coherent meaning, it is even hard to speak of fatality on this ground of broken bonds between man and world. His heroes are left "in the presence of life and death with no other philosophy than that which the profane world can suggest and understand."[126] They are either immersed in their own interiority verging on madness, or they act motivated by needs, drives, and superstition. Their thoughts are sometimes inhabited by the remnants of virtue and saintliness, but these are no more operative in the world. Santayana sees in *Hamlet* (as he does in *Macbeth*) a critical moment for the shape of humanity. The quality of *uncanniness*, attributed to humans since antiquity, in the time of the devaluation of the idea of human being becomes a metaphor for the amazing independence of subjectivity and factuality, each standing in its own right. "Spirituality," historically related to the so-called inner man in relation *of* and *to* transcendence, in Shakespeare stands dangerously close to its own caricature: an immature and mad mind hovering around in a world full of pagan phantoms and ghost concepts inherited from Christianity. Shakespeare's theme is "a historical junk-shop [which] has become the temple of a new spirit,"[127] where reason is an "accomplishment rather than a vital function."[128]

In a striking correspondence to what Santayana says, Bloom notes that the secular nature of the world in the play makes Hamlet bear the possible Blessing of his brilliant mind "as though it were a curse."[129] His spirituality in the world, which is no longer *his* world, turns into a form of death.[130] Santayana comments on it: "here is immense endowment and strange incompetence, constant perspicacity and general confusion, entire virtue in the intention, and complete disaster in the result."[131] Shakespeare achieves an effect of suspension between horror and grotesque, leaving his spectators waiting "to see the spectacle of things dissolved and exorcised . . . and the rest, as says Hamlet, is silence."[132]

Bloom considers the ending phrase "the rest is silence" as a "secular triumph" sealing the tragedy of Hamlet's spirituality.[133] The immaturity of Hamlet evoked by Santayana is phrased by Bloom as Hamlet's being simultaneously "the youngest and the oldest . . . [due to] the catastrophic consciousness of the spiritual disease of his world, which he has internalized."[134]

Both interpreters articulate the spiritual crisis in the dramatic world. But in an apparently neverending debate between the moderns and the classics, they finally turn out to stand on the opposite sides. The author of *The Western Canon* sees in Hamlet a new beginning, a critical point triggering *the invention of the human* capable of preserving spirituality in a secular world, and in Shakespeare himself—as Agata Bielik-Robson notes—"a genius of instruction."¹³⁵ Without getting into the details of Bloom's complex interpretive strategy, what he admires in Shakespeare is the subjective, agonistic, and revisionist potential in relation to the overwhelming power of time embodied in tradition.¹³⁶ He seems to believe in the power of self-revision and the idea of self-cure. So does Santayana but the path of self-revision for him can be defended as long as there is a world, a "beyond" of some objectivity. The phase of solipsism, if a phase it be, Santayana might have argued with Bloom, is not conducive to a cure other than a *cure of oneself of oneself*, meaning it is a self-annihilating strategy. Santayana, like Bloom, was fascinated by the idea of secular transcendence, but did not trust so much the romantic genius.

Much as both thinkers associate spirituality with a specific temporal modality, they might rather disagree on Hamlet's relation to time. "Hamlet will not do anything prematurely; something in him is determined not to be overdetermined. His freedom partly consists in not being too soon, not being early," notes Bloom.¹³⁷ The key to his reading seems to rest in the quest for freedom from a fatal temporality. Hamlet, by means of deliberation, is *ahead of time* but also out of it, beyond its grasp—hence, he is *not too soon* so that he cannot be predetermined. Meanwhile, for Santayana Hamlet has neither himself nor the world ever "well in hand." He misses both. He cannot have it otherwise because his is the time of disowning first of *that* and then, logically, of *this* world. The inner man, if this "inner" is to have any meaning at all, must function in relation to something out there, something valid, and as Bloom admits, "Hamlet has usurped the Western literary consciousness, at its most self-aware thresholds, gateways no longer crossable by us into transcendental beyonds."¹³⁸ Bloom sounds uncertain as to his own optimism when asking questions such as "How much freedom can be afforded Hamlet by a tragic play?" or "What project can be large enough for him?"¹³⁹ Bloom suggests imagining Hamlet in a context different than tragic, but that would require another world, not this one. If Bloom hopes that Hamlet, by self-revision and a change by "self-overhearing," can change the world, Santayana would object because the world is lost for Hamlet, as he is for the world. By way of digression, Bloom mentions Nietzsche as amongst those saying "it is we who are Hamlet."¹⁴⁰ Santayana shared this intuition about the continuity of the process of subjectivization of human experience in his cultural diagnosis and polemic with egotism.

Santayana's interpretation, however, suffers from generalizations which come from a certain cultural bias. In his brief and panoramic essays, Santayana often chooses to *use Hamlet* to support his larger project rather than offering an in-depth analysis. Thus, no matter how insightful his conclusions may be, he loses something of its merit and undeniable intrinsic power. Bloom seems to have a point in emphasizing that

> Hamlet's freedom can be defined as *the freedom to infer*, and we learn this intellectual liberty by attending to Hamlet. Inference in Hamlet's praxis is a sublime mode of surmise, metaphoric because it leaps ahead with every change in circumstance, and inference becomes the audience's way to Hamlet's consciousness.[141]

The famous "to be" question for Santayana is rather futile because it simply has been already resolved; for Bloom it is absolutely vital, "a fullness and an emptiness playing off against each other."[142] The question might actually be paraphrased into the question Santayana let Oliver, the hero of his novel *The Last Puritan*, ask himself: once one believes in nothing, is life worth living? Likewise, it could be asked whether to live actively in and for this world or to turn into madness, i.e., to become dead for this world. But then again, another question arises: how to live with "a growing inner self"[143] synchronic with "a total lack of faith in language" and in oneself?[144] Wystan H. Auden has an insightful remark concerning the crisis of agency that preoccupies us here. Hamlet, he says, having lost faith in everything, cannot *act* "for he can only '*act*'"![145] Hence Hamlet's perverse theatricality, his hopeless desire of becoming "what Greek tragic hero is, a creature of situation,"[146] and his abdication expressed by "readiness is all." Worldly context, Santayana would say, is inadequate for the prince, the world can only kill him. Hamlet's consciousness had outgrown itself and debilitated even his ability to defend virtue until he understood in the final act, that when no ideals can be pursued everything vanishes.

There is no definite reconciliation and probably no last word in this imaginary dispute between both thinkers. Much as they agree upon some points in their reading, they differ in sympathies and, while Santayana sees not much hope for self-creation without limits and definition, Bloom sees a sort of unfathomable, abyssal hope in the protagonist of "character unlimited," even though he does not know what "to do with a new kind of human being, one as authentically unsponsored as Hamlet is."[147] The ground for their possible discussion is that both were convinced of an immense importance of Shakespeare's dramas as pre-defining the guidelines of what will be the key anthropological and existential issues Western culture would face in the coming centuries.

Let me complete the discussion of Santayana's reading of Shakespeare with a couple of relevant remarks concerning Macbeth, an antithesis of sort of "the hero of Western intellectual consciousness."[148] The loss of unity is equally visible in *Macbeth*, where we are confronted with a series of events, mere facts, crimes committed out of passions and yet without a genuine involvement or vision. The events in the corrupt and crime-ridden dramatic world seem to be happening by the force of some morbid inertia of matter animating the agent, and, at the same time, as if unfolding in front of this surprised actor-spectator in one. Unlike Hamlet, Macbeth does engage in action but with time his deeds are growing exceedingly irrelevant to anything one might call conscious action until he becomes a mere spectator rather than an agent, to his own surprise, horror, and the growing awareness of the futility of it all.

> Intellectually—and this is the tragedy of it—Macbeth is divinely human, rational enough to pause and survey his own agony, and see no escape, no alternative; he cannot rise morally above himself; his philosophy is that there is no philosophy, because, in fact, he is incapable of any.[149]

As Northrop Frye has phrased it, time in tragedy, as "the devourer of life," turns against the hero. A sort of "temporal hostility" surrounds Macbeth, for whom time is not only "out of joint," it is merely "one clock-tick after another."[150] While Hamlet was an actor for himself and a self-conscious creator of the inner *self*, Macbeth is being dragged along by the logic of events. The experience of disjointed time parallels the impossibility of any coherent worldview; the relation of subjectivity to the world of facts becomes unbearable in the situation of a "mimetic crisis," typical of spiritual dissolution.

To conclude my discussion of Santayana's understanding of the tragic, which is far from exhausting the whole spectrum of contexts present in his *oeuvre*,[151] let me invite the reader to the following, final section of this chapter, where I will try to clarify the connection between the tragic and the *self* with support from Northrop's Frye criticism of tragedy and the tragic.

Against Fatalistic Reduction

By reading *Hamlet* through the lens of the absence of religion in the dramatic world, Santayana illustrated his conviction about the decisive influence that different models of constructing unity of meaning have on the experience and representations of the tragic. The changing epistemic paradigms, in his view, reflect shifts in the dynamics of human *selves*. This idea is in line with Santayana's conception of the *self* as a psycho-spiritual, hermeneutic unity, the integrity of which may be metaphorically reduced to taking a position toward one's own "tragic moment." By the tragic moment I mean the critical "juncture" responsible for the phenomenologically acknowledged fact that one's own existence is, to some extent, always missed. We may well be tempted to play with this metaphor further and—in reference to the Heideggerian "strategies of missing oneself"—say that w*hat is at stake is the style of missing ourselves.*

The understanding of both the tragic and the *self*, which I propose in my reading, is in itself utterly modern and shows Santayana as the most modern critics of modernity. Still, I wished to bring to the fore his sort of distinctive, "ancient" distance, if not reluctance, toward inescapably tragic visions of man. Shakespeare's dramas, after all, exhibit that "the tragic" is not to be understood as a definite *predicament* coming from above. There is no fate in any strong sense of this term, just a more or less reflective, more or less passionate psychological hero and a challenging world of accidents and facts. The question is: What kind of mimetic/narrative tools of appropriating the reality are at the hero's disposal? Bloom may be right that there is a whole spectrum of possibilities open to Hamlet. The drama is that he is incapable of exercising his freedom in a world which he experiences as an *alien* medium because he is incapable of—to evoke Ricoeur's term—a successful *emplotment*.

Respectively, behind Santayana's critique of the tyranny of subjectivity is his concern about what happens *after* the world is internalized and dominated by it. One possible scenario is that the spiritual aspect of the *self* ceases to perform its reconciliatory function between "I" and the world, debilitating the ability to act, since there seems to be nothing real *outside there*. When accompanied by the will to power, reason may become instrumental and cognition may turn into violence that can be directed both at the other and at the *self*. In any case, the *outside there* tends to enforce itself back again, this time in a merciless form of matter-of-factness. At this point the tragic stands for "fate" again, but it is now deprived of the dignifying, divine aspect that it received in Greek tragedy. The fate is no longer of mimetic nature (it is not enacted or narrated), but rather of factual one (it simply "assaults"). This means—to come back to our metaphor of missing oneself—that what Santayana used to call "victorious imagination" is lost and the mode of the hero's missing himself is that of Nietzschean "t'was" (or, in other words, being too late for oneself).

Even if one remains mindful of what Frye calls existential projection of the tragic, it is hard to deny that there is an aspect of experience that had given rise to the very reflection on the conditions and specificity of human action, and found its sublime expression in the art of tragedy. The incompatibility between the world as imagined and the world as found or, as Santayana puts it, between inspiration and truth, seems to be the axis of the thinker's understanding of the tragic. Contingency, ignorance, and the irrevocability of the past cross and permeate the course of conscious action and conspire to "corrupt" the world of human affairs. In the context of the *self*, this "corrupting" irruption of fatality—we call it the order of nature, *dike*, or *ananke*—comes to be associated with the share of necessity in human life, and with the burden of coping with one's own finitude. This idea—as we shall see later—will ripen and reappear in Santayana's political reflections in *Dominations and Powers*.

In his discussion of tragedy, Northrop Frye credits tragedy with "the sense of the authentic natural basis of human character come into literature."[152] The tragic is actualized in action and revealed in critical moments of tragic recognition followed by suffering—for example, as an experience of helplessness and despair in confrontation with the unforeseen consequences of one's own action, which was conveyed by the Greeks in terms of *revenge* (*nemesis*). The tragic plot, *mythos*, recognized by Aristotle as the "what" of tragic art, conveys a sense of inscrutability resting in the "externality" of fate and "revenge," which may assume the mask of the order of nature ratified by gods.[153] The hero is the "outcome" of his/her action, which remains in an antithetic relation with fate. The tragic aspect in a modern guise, in its turn, is interiorized, as prefigured by Shakespeare. As for the tragic binary *mythos*,[154] it is represented by the doubling or the rift within the *self* and the vengeance exercised by finitude on ideals. The agent of *nemesis*—the principle of restoring order—is shifted from an impersonal force of nature toward one's own mortal body, sin, irresponsibility, or mistake, which, by the way, may also be experienced by the subject as impersonal and alienating. A response to this tragic dualism may be delivered, for example, by a religion of salvation and God, who is no more ratifying the order of nature, but is the addressee of what is most innately human. Therefore, the collapse of integral worldview is a critical moment in culture, posing the danger of spiritual dissolution but, at the same time, creating a chance for a sort of new "invention of the human," as Harold Bloom phrased it.

This is where Santayana's ontology seems meaningful. Its rich language legitimizes the redemptive function of the spiritual aspect of the *self*. It allows for preserving the idea and the experience of the *inner man* ("invented" by Christianity) and that of "victorious imagination," while avoiding excessive topologies of inwardness and the dangers of subjectivism. The spirit, referred to by Santayana in terms of coming out, transcending, making space for, allowing for epiphany, remains an "inner" source of synthetic harmony, spelling its cast on life as a whole. This is what Santayana has to say on the liberating dynamics of the spirit:

> To understand is pre-eminently to live, moving not by stimulation and external compulsion, but by inner direction and control. . . . Ideals . . . are possible forms of being and he who finds them divine and congenial and is able to embody them at least in part and for a season, has to that extent transfigured life, turning it from a fatal process into a liberal art.[155]

As the reader may have noticed, we are constantly oscillating here between Santayana's ontology and his cultural critique. As we have established in his polemic with Nietzsche, Santayana argues that the German thinker isolated the very tragic aspect of existence and then hypostatized it through the category of will to power. Moreover, by dropping the spiritual realm and getting rid of the idea of objective truth, Nietzsche undermined the major strategies of constructing unity of meaning delivered by tradition. As we already know, Santayana sees this aspect of Nietzsche's thought as *nemesis* in the modern guise, or, more specifically, as an unintended result of the evolution of transcendental idealism. Another example of cultural promotion of the tragic discussed by Santayana is secular positivism, prophetically permeating the world of some of Shakespeare's dramas, where the tension between subjective and factual dimensions escalates and finally turns into a grotesque independence of both.

Spiritual experience of incarnation reveals—to use Karl Jasper's words—"the terrifying aspect of existence . . . its entanglement with the uncharted background of man's humanity."[156] *Santayana acknowledges the tragic aspect of existence but is against philosophical modes of its absolutization.*[157] His ontology—aiming at the reconciliation between the truth of Democritus and the humanism of Socrates—might offer an antidote to "tragic readiness." The *self*, based on the canvas of the four realms of being, carries in itself the potential to neutralize the tragic knot, or, in other words, to compensate for it. *Spiritual existence* involves the cathartic, creative, hermeneutic movement of self-positioning in relation to one's own tragic aspect, the fatal juncture of missing oneself. There is a potential of overcoming the eternal recurrence of being in a stalemate of a definite situation and elevating oneself from mere factuality to the sphere of creativity, where "existence [is] the test of possibility. *Ab esse ad posse valet illatio.*"[158]

An objection to this spiritual "solution" may be formulated with the help of Jasper's insightful remark that "man's mind fails and breaks down in the very wealth of its potentialities."[159] However—Santayana might say—it is in the same "wealth" that it is constantly renewed. Northrop Frye says of the Greek tragic hero that he/she is "emancipated from dream, an emancipation which is at the same time a restriction, because the order of nature is present."[160] Yet—and this may be crucial for understanding Santayana's viewpoint—Frye points to a recurrent confusion in the interpretation of tragedy, a confusion visible in what he describes as two reductive formulas. One of them reduces the tragic conflict to moral terms, the other, more important from the perspective of our discussion, is *fatalistic reduction*, which, by insinuating that

> all tragedy exhibits the omnipotence of an external fate . . . confuses the tragic condition with the tragic process: fate in a tragedy, normally becomes external to the hero only *after* the tragic process has been set going. The Greek *ananke* or *moira* is in its normal, or pre-tragic, form the internal balancing condition of life. It appears as external or antithetical necessity only *after* it has been violated as a condition of life.[161]

Meanwhile, Rebecca Bushnell notes:

> The necessity implied in tragedy invokes the inevitability inherent in the recounting of the events that happened in real life. . . . When telling the truth about the past you cannot change it. Time cannot be reversed; therefore what happened appears in retrospect to be necessarily so.[162]

This supports Santayana's point about the arbitrariness of assuming a *tragic perspective*. The effort of saving this distinction and granting primacy to the perspective of the "internal balancing condition" was "understood" by Christian eschatology and specifically the conceptions of the soul and free will, which delineate the sphere of internal dynamics and freedom, and protect human life from reducing it to one-dimensional fate. I touched upon this question in the digression on the relation between the *self* and the idea of Trinity. Also, Paul Ricoeur shows that the position of fatality is one of *post-factum* translation of contingency into necessity or "fate." In a narrative, where a character's identity is shaped along the line of his/her story, "chance is transmuted into fate"[163] but this is not the actual reality of lived experience and the *self*. It seems to me that a similar logic prompted Walter Benjamin to notice the antidote to fatality resting in the very fact of *having a character* (!).

Frye's insight, probably most clearly of all other comparative contexts, provides a support for the validity of Santayana's insights and his argument about the relevance of temporal perspective and of cultural and religious patterns in the discussion of the tragic. "Tragic fate," Frye expands his point, is sometimes confused with "tragic irony," which is a post-factum or retrospective perspective.[164] Tragedy *en-acts*, it assumes a subject who is an agent and to whom freedom is not denied. There often is an initial promise of fulfillment. Yet the hero often chooses to destroy a balance, "which sooner or later must right itself" by the logic of *nemesis*, "the internal balancing condition of life."[165] Yet, as Auden reminds us, the hero's transgression rests in the flow of his "heroic" character, *hubris*, for which he is punished.[166] As for the second, moral type of reduction, Aristotelian *proairesis* is too often identified with ethical realm, while the very

> conception of catharsis, which is central to Aristotle's view of tragedy, is inconsistent with moral reductions of it. . . . [It is rather] the hero's act [which] has thrown a switch in a larger machine than his own life. . . . Tragedy, in short, seems to elude the antithesis of moral responsibility and arbitrary fate, just as it eludes the antithesis of good and evil.[167]

In Christian tradition, as epitomized by Milton's *Paradise Lost*, Adam was made by God as "sufficient to have stood, though free to fall."[168] The tragedy of existence

> seems to move up to an *Augenblick* or crucial moment from which point the road to what might have been and the road to what will be is simultaneously seen. . . . In Adam's situation there is a feeling, which in Christian tradition can be traced back at least to St. Augustine, that *time begins with the fall; that the fall from liberty into the natural cycle also started the movement of time as we know it*. In other tragedies too we can trace the feeling that *nemesis* is deeply involved with the movement of time, whether as the missing of a tide in the affairs of men, or as a recognition that the time is out of joint.[169]

In some secular tragedies man *makes a choice* to step onto the path of

> narrowing a comparatively free life into a process of causation. This happens to Macbeth when he accepts the logic of usurpation, to Hamlet when he accepts the logic of revenge. . . . [Tragic] recognition is the recognition of the determined shape of the life *he has created for himself,* with an implicit comparison with the uncreated potential life he has forsaken.[170]

Frye's discussion offers a precious insight into the problem of time in tragedy, and prompts one to go beyond the discussion of tragedy to the specific temporality of "t'was." The question arising here is: *How to switch time from the "devouring" mode, typical of the tragic "mimesis of sacrifice"*[171] *into the redeeming mode?* The problem has been tackled directly and indirectly in the context of Santayana reading Heidegger and Santayana's polemic with Nietzsche's attempt to liberate man from the temporal mode of "it was." Santayana's intuitions concerning the "promotion" of tragicness and placing Nietzsche's will to power on the same continuum with the romantic solipsism of Hamlet once again make for an interesting juxtaposition with what Harold Bloom says of Hamlet internalizing revenge:

> For Hamlet revisioning the *self* replaces the project of revenge. The only valid revenge in this play is what Nietzsche, theorist of revision, called the will's revenge against time, and against time's "It was."[172]

Let me repeat that Santayana insisted on preserving the notion of spiritual transcendence on the account of the fact that spirit is a realm of distance, negotiations and reconciliation, and, as such, it overarches the tragic modality of conflict. It makes possible entering into such a relation with one's own tragic aspect that its negativity may be transmuted into a potential, and life might become Life. To evoke Jaspers once again, "it is in acting out his own personality, in realizing his selfhood . . . that he [the tragic hero] finds redemption and deliverance."[173] Besides being a corollary to his materialism, the idea of spiritual life, and contemplative practice in particular, rather unpopular in the era of Santayana, served him to articulate the potential of the essential disinterestedness of spirit and oppose it to the paradigm of instrumental thinking. Dislocated reason is what remains after thinking abandons its spiritual potential; its manifestations oscillate between violent, conquering egotism, and a reactive, fact-registering tool of adaptation. In either case it dwells within the "realm of necessity." Santayana's diagnosis converges at some points with what the thinker probably unknown to him would later say of instrumental (i.e., strictly subjectivist) reason—that it is an "abstract functioning of the thinking mechanism."[174] Horkheimer noted that instrumental thinking is unable to constitute objectivity because it has discredited it as an illusion and has lost the ability to conceive of something as being an end in itself.[175] Point by point, the representative of Frankfurt School exposes the path leading from subjectivism to an extreme formalization of thinking.

The tragic for Santayana, then, involves a conflict or an inadequacy informing the relation between the world of facts and the human *self*, insofar as this *self* gives rise to some ideals and invests part of itself into future projections centered around these ideals. But to give up ideals in order to avoid the tragic clash is to intensify the latter by giving up Life before it naturally comes to an end. The art of life advocated by the thinker from Avila is the art of negotiation between both sides. Charles Padron proposes that "the *tragic* is a value for Santayana," just as finitude is. It

> allows for excellence of any human endeavor, activity, or achievement, for only by excluding other possibilities and options at any given moment . . . can one speak of theoretical or practical meaning at all.[176]

Santayana, however, was aware that to make a value of the tragic requires a systematic effort and a lifetime. It requires an art. The idea of the tragic becoming a value is only a possibility, never something simply given or to be taken for granted. The *self* is to acknowledge the objective validity of the external world so that it can make it a source of knowledge, of inspiration and, perhaps, of delight, while respecting spiritual reality and remaining in the process of negotiating with this world the boundaries of its own finitude and the shape of its "fate." Otherwise, without spiritual mediation, it remains for the *self* to enter into bare relations of power, where it will be, time after time, defeated by the rule of *nemesis* proper to the threatening "out there."

To let Santayana speak for himself, let me quote a brilliant (and particularly representative of Santayana) passage concerning the fate of imagination, which has suffered in the struggle of its too great aspirations—as it may happen to an "overall transcendentalist"—with the facts of existence.

> Imagination . . . seeks to reduce herself to conformity with existence, in the hope of vindicating her nominal authority at the price of some concessions. She begins to feign that she demanded nothing but what she finds. Thus she loses her honesty and freedom, becomes a *flatterer of things* instead of the principle of their ideal correction, and in the attempt to prove herself prophetic and literally valid . . . she forfeits that symbolic truth, that inner propriety, which gave her a moral value. Thus false steps of the imagination lead to a contorted science and to a servile ideal.[177]

No matter how often Santayana sounds skeptical about anthropomorphic or anthropocentric philosophies, the motivation of his own thought *is* anthropocentric; hence, he sometimes refers to himself as "a moralist." This Socratic and humanistic vein, definitely not the only one and perhaps even not the dominant one in the thought of Santayana, couples with the seriousness and honesty of his intellectual enterprise, targeted at the good of human being and the clarity of thinking. *This explains his concern with the fact that certain doctrines by their absolutism of the ego and some others by the absolutism of fact are bound to universalize the tragic in its most fatalistic guise.* The fatality of instrumental reason rests in that by itself incapable of addressing the tragic, it suppresses if not kills the spiritual potential (along with the idea of disinterestedness) which is the medium of all sublimation and of all earthly "redemption."

Another thing worth noting at this point is Santayana's idiom, rich in references to those areas which science habitually calls *myth and faith*. It reveals his skepticism toward any idea of revolutionary breaking with the past. Science is treated by Santayana sympathetically but clearly in its own measure—as a perspective and an attitude, one of many, demanding negotiations with other perspectives and their demands.[178] By the same token Santayana is far from absolutizing philosophy and engages in an attempt of finding a common language between the myths of science, religion, and those of philosophy.

To tackle the theme of the tragic is to respond to the so-called *metaphysical need* of human being, which, according to Kołakowski, is rooted in "the obscure and uncertain circumstances of the condition and status quo of human consciousness in the world."[179] Questions asked here concern an aspect of humanity which most probably cannot be clarified by scientific inquiry. It is about a unique experience of self-reflective human life, one which loves its "hopes and detest[s] the experience that seems to contradict them."[180] It can be reflected upon meaningfully with reference to its own *locus*—human *self*—with the possibility of appropriating and perhaps surpassing it in view. A philosophy that engages in the discussion of the tragic, does well to provide a language which respects spiritual reality and allows to catch the uniqueness of what Kołakowski calls the specifically "human issue." At the end of this chapter, let me quote once again Walter Benjamin, who juxtaposes the "genius" of a (personal) character with tragic fate:

> While fate brings to life the immense complexity of the guilty person, the complications and bonds of his guilt, character gives this mystical enslavement of the person to the guilt context the answer of genius. Complication becomes simplicity, fate freedom.[181]

7

Beyond the *Self* (into the Political Realm)

The Essential Negativity of Human Being and Rational (Self-)Government[1]

> Human life is hedged completely round with compulsory sacrifices. Yet they may be made gladly or as we say freely; for to be in harmony with necessity gives us a sense of freedom, which is the only freedom we have.
>
> —*Dominations and Powers*, 66

In the final chapter of the book let us consider the political realm, where an individual human *self* finds him/herself part of the common world. In the treatise *Dominations and Powers*, the idea of "the social" seems to be overshadowed by that of "the political." A possible explanation is that Santayana—not unlike, for example, Hannah Arendt—counts the former as belonging rather to the side of factuality, as something given, something always "already there," while he views the latter as a sphere of relative freedom of action, where the share of dependencies and that of initiative are constantly being negotiated. In other words, while man, as a contextual creature, is always embedded in a culture and a society, becoming political involves decision-making and action. Let me shed some preliminary light on Santayana's political hermeneutic or—alternatively—the ontology of political realm, while rethinking certain aspects of his understanding of government and self-government in terms of what I call *managing necessity*.[2]

More specifically, I will invite the reader to consider the following issues: (1) the vital bases of political life (governing life, the passage from *zoe* to *bios* as expressed in the translation of Primal Will into articulate forms, vital liberty); (2) politics as the interplay of powers and dominations;

(3) human negativity (*aporetic self, apophatic humanity*) and the idea of necessity in political context; (4) rationality as the main virtue in the context of (self-)government; and (5) Santayana's highly selective endorsement of liberal values and his preoccupation with what he calls the spiritual crisis in modern democracies.

In *Dominations and Powers*—the main exposition of Santayana's philosophy of politics—two perspectives intertwine. The first one, phenomenological-ontological, describes the dynamics hidden behind the political forms of modern Western culture in terms of power-domination dialectics. It introduces a distinction between the plane of material existence and the "imaginary" political realm grafted upon it. From this viewpoint any government may be described through the lens of its fundamental function of defining and imposing sacrifices on living beings, or—in other words—*managing necessity*. As such, any government, according to Santayana, hides an aspect of "a natural fatality."[3] It may be associated with a more rudimentary idea concerning the human condition, namely that others take advantage of the necessity we are confronted with and we, ourselves, tend to use other people's fatality against them.[4] The other perspective, which may be called moral or normative, consists in a critical reflection on the contemporary condition of cultural and political life in the Western world and its future prospects. It is motivated by the pluralist and individualistic ideal of creating favorable conditions for the fruition of diverse psychic potentialities represented by the participants of a given community, with *vital liberty* in view. These stakes are clearly inspired by the Aristotelian idea of the good life. As for Santayana's method, anticipating some future trends in philosophy, as exemplified by Foucault, Taylor, or Agamben, the thinker, instead of engaging in a technical discussion of the forms of government and the history of political doctrines, develops a kind of (critical) hermeneutics of government and self-government, which may also be approached as a political anthropology of sorts. I have proposed to call it *hermeneutics of managing necessity*. Let me note that a prominent contemporary theoretician of liberalism, John Gray, described this part of Santayana's philosophical reflection as "one of the most profound and incisive critiques of liberalism ever developed."[5]

7.1 Negativity

> The unfathomable non-ego dominates spirit in a man within and without, fitfully in the world and subterraneously in his hidden passions.
>
> —*Dominations and Powers*, 64

Conditio humana involves being confronted with facts (both external ones and those most intimately related to ourselves), and our finding ourselves thus-and-so, of which we are not the authors and which we often have neither foreseen nor wished for. Thus, the existence of each and every human being involves what we have been calling in this book *the sphere of helplessness*. Santayana takes this fact to be absolutely crucial for understanding politics. From the perspective of modern politics, which has been recognized as increasingly amounting to governing life, *the presence of the sphere of helplessness as an existential invariable* is indispensable and becomes the focal point of interest. For what, in the first place, does the governing address in the governed if not *that* which yields itself to governing? As if in contrast to that, the specificity of the least oppressive among the known political systems (at least in its ideal form)—democracy—is said to rest in the fact that it addresses freedom and appeals to freedom. Historically, as emphasized by Benjamin Constant, the freedom in question was of positive, participatory nature. Binding democracy with individualistic liberalism—with its concern for the protection of liberties—changed democratic ethos. But in both cases, democracy is a demanding political milieu and the most challenging one from the viewpoint of an individual. It is, perhaps, also the most risky one in the long run, as it tends to dilute the meaning of political responsibility and, as history has shown and a few thinkers have foretold, it is prone to totalitarian forms of degeneration.

Santayana, as discussed previously, was concerned with dangerous misconceptions about the notion of freedom and noted that the common opposition between necessity and freedom is, at best, unclear. Skeptical as to the ability of our language to grasp adequately existential reality, and aware of the fact that cultural and political factors may further inhibit our faculty of judgment, Santayana recommends particular caution with such abstract, yet key for our (liberal) culture, notions like "freedom." Leaving aside the specific kind of freedom which he called "spiritual," from the viewpoint of everyday experience, whatever concerns us but remains beyond the scope of our choice and decision is not freedom. Santayana refers to it sometimes as "necessity" or "necessities." Here, as in many other cases, he is more metaphorical than precise. Nevertheless, he uses the metaphor of "necessity" as an effective hermeneutic tool to convey his vision of political reality. The necessity in question is, as the reader has probably already intuitively grasped, not logical. Neither physical determinism nor the most liberal, moral kind of necessity (as presented in the eighteenth century by Anthony Collins, who viewed man as "determined by his [own] reason and his senses")[6] account for "necessity" in Santayanan sense, the roots of which may be traced back to Greek *ananke*. For Plato (in *Timaeus*) *ananke* stood for a universal, cosmological principle antithetic to reason. Reason, constantly challenged by necessity, was striving to "persuade" it. Another meaning of *ananke* may be associated with the so-called tragic fatality of human life manifesting itself in the unavoidable clash of ideals with an indifferent course of events. As discussed extensively in the chapter on the tragic, existential reading of the tragic fatality takes account of the fact that humans are inescapably confronted with unpredictable and unwanted circumstances, which challenge both their rationality and moral ideals. This may lead to the acknowledgement both of the finitude of human life and of contingency inherent therein. *Incarnation* and *care* are the two—to use Heidegger's language—"existentials" which are transcendental to our *vulnerability to necessity*. In Santayana's words there are two sources of necessity—the psyche and the world.[7] Freedom in Santayana's writings often stands for a harmonious *relation* between the *self* and necessity. Thus, it is closely related to the ideals of self-rule, vital liberty, and rationality, all of which contribute to "the art of satisfying our compatible inclinations in the midst of our inevitable circumstances."[8] This understanding seems to pertain to individual experience but it remains relevant in the political realm, which for Santayana is (or rather—ideally, should be) an extension of the individual.

Meanwhile, in the political realm our sphere of (personal and social) helplessness is both being co-determined and taken advantage of. In other words, necessity may be either "utilized" (at least partly) to our benefit (empowerment) or translated into domination. This is what Santayana is concerned with when he asks the question: "How far and in what direction may necessary servitude be sweetened and vital and spiritual liberty enjoyed, under any of these dominations?"[9] The stability and predictability of law, being part of what for Santayana counts as the life of reason, tends to facilitate arriving at vital liberty. And conversely, as Agamben notes, the suspension of law and resorting to the so-called state of exception, which is part of government's "militant scheme" (Santayana's phrase), creates a situation where a number of people is perceived as "bare life," i.e., potential subjects to unlimited domination. This danger appears not only during wars and revolutions—it may appear in a diluted and "peaceful" form—for example, through an increasing identification of politics with economy or, as it is currently happening, with medicine and healthcare. In the latter case it is precisely necessity in its crudest form that becomes the tool of governing (and manipulation). The greater the fear of death (which, as remarked by Santayana, has achieved its peak in the twentieth century), the more powerful the tool becomes.

Let me restate the point of departure in Santayana's political anthropology as follows: to exist for a human being means to bow to necessity either by imposing sacrifices on ourselves or by letting others do it.[10] Political action, being a more or less conscious and deliberate extension of it, may be referred to as the art of managing necessity, or, in other words, defining sacrifices, allocating them, and rendering them meaningful. Now, for the sake of his philosophical inquiry with rational (self-)government in view, Santayana chooses to express the dynamics of political reality reductively—in terms of the dialectic of powers and dominations. This reduction allows for showing politics as the play of interests. The moral *telos* assumed by Santayana, let us repeat, is creating a common world, where individual lives, which cherish primacy as the basic source of all meaningful dynamics, may thrive.

Let me direct the reader's attention to the fact that the distinction between powers and dominations is neither replaceable nor convertible into any other opposition, as we might be tempted to do, for example, by coupling power with freedom and domination with necessity. Despite minor conceptual inconsistencies, not untypical of Santayana, I propose to treat power-domination as *a pair of complementary borderline concepts exhausting the idea of political reality in its most rudimentary dimension*. Powers and dominations are active vectors in the field of forces experienced as empowering or inhibiting in respect to the possibility of the realization of individual vital potential. As political beings, we are either empowered or dominated, or—as usual—we share in both conditions simultaneously. The apparent relativity of the condition of empowerment/domination is a result of the primacy of the perspective of an individual life. This relativity is considerably limited by the standards of what Santayana calls the life of reason as well as by certain invariants proper to the human condition and nature, which Santayana—despite the widespread tendency at that time—is willing to preserve, be it in a minimalist version. There nevertheless remains the question: Is a force/a circumstance *experienced as a power really a power*? Or, might a domination turn out to be empowering? This relativity is not only hard to disavow (because of the involvement of subjective experience and cultural relativity) but—and this is perhaps more important—it sheds light on the precariousness of the very process of becoming political.

Let me ask, then: what it takes, according to Santayana, to be *zoon politkon*? First and foremost, I would suggest, it requires self-consciousness. By way of digression, from the contemporary perspective of *biopolitics*, it might be enough to be a living body to be "political;" paradoxically, as

Agamben would say, a non-agent or an unconscious body is more truly "political." But to come back to Santayana, from an existential perspective, leaving aside the question of citizenship and rights, to be self-conscious, in the sense of being able to articulate one's basic needs and preferences, as well as identify oneself as an agent, is a necessary and sufficient condition of becoming political. Every *self* may be described as "virtual self-transcendence of intelligent action."[11] But self-consciousness by no means amounts to self-knowledge and sanity, as Santayana repeatedly emphasizes. This very gap opens the scene on which a large part of the dynamics of governing in democratic systems (which in any case, like all governing, "distributes necessity") takes place.

The dynamic net of dependencies, including both the ones of which we are aware and those which remain hidden, at every moment co-shapes our life histories and our very *selves*. As living and acting creatures, we recognize some of the circumstances that occur to our consciousness as friendly or hostile, favorable or inconvenient. Our self-government depends to a large degree on our capacity to sustain equilibrium between dominations and powers. In other words, (self-)government is based on the faculty of judgment, which requires not only intelligence but also a degree of wisdom and maturity. Both are said to be aspects of *virtue*, the highest manifestation of which is *rationality*. In other words, rationality is a transcendental condition for *the art* of good (self-)government. Life of reason is rational in the Aristotelian sense of *phronesis*—it uses its "liberty to follow the golden rule."[12] Interestingly, Daniel Moreno sees *virtues* as entering into a tripartite relation with dominations and powers. And indeed, one may view virtues as constituting a principle of balancing and endowing with meaning the other two.[13]

Political realm, viewed as an evolving play of conflicting interests and ambitions, has existence in the background, defined by Santayana as a flux of incidents which displays certain forms and regularities. From this partly organic (naturalist), partly dramatic perspective, "conspiracies of physiological forces," psyches—"the willing connivance of a myriad fleeting . . . half-conscious human souls"[14] stand behind societies and groups. Human life (*bios*) involves sublimation of Primal Will by means of giving needs and potentialities articulate, individual, and collective forms. In other words, agency requires that life becomes increasingly symbolic, pregnant with meanings. This is where autonomy plays an important role and this is the space that ought to be protected in accordance with liberal ethos, which Santayana, despite all his skepticism, is willing to preserve. At the same time, the passage from the unconscious Will to articulate needs, preferences, and demands, then, with all its precariousness and contingency, is a potential battlefield for the competing political and economic forces. This is how Santayana explains, metaphorically, the relation between existence and politics in the context of the origin of ideologies:

> Thus two concomitant yet strangely different streams would seem to compose human life: one the vast cosmic flood of cyclic movements and sudden precipitations, in which man has his part like other animals; and the other, the private little rivulet of images, emotions, and words. . . . Political ideologies are attempts to collect these private murmurs into a chorus, so loud and imperative as to drown the concert of universal nature and turn it into an obedient accompaniment to the human voice.[15]

To sum up this part of our reflection, one may say that the contemporary, disenchanted, political-economic approach to human life seems to identify it with what Santayana thought it basically was prior to any symbolic entanglement or spiritual sublimation, namely a well of needs and potentialities. The more unsatisfied the former and the more unexpressed the latter, the more flexible and prone to manipulation the subject is. Such a conception of human being—let me call it *privative-potential*—the anticipations of which appeared already in antiquity, as exemplified by Aristotle's metaphysical conception of *psychic potentiality*,[16] resonates strongly in contemporary theories of biopolitics.

7.2 Realm of Politics

The following words of Santayana succinctly and explicitly reveal his naturalist view of the mechanism of the omnipresent and multifaceted competition and coercion underlying all political dynamics:

> To fight is a primitive necessity; life cannot take or keep any definite form without crowding out, crushing or devouring some other form of life. But there are gentle and violent methods of assimilation, and self-assertion may take the form of attraction as well as of suppression. The weaker life in any case perishes, but it may perish insensibly, by being transformed rather than annihilated. All depends on the mechanism that does

> the execution; and it is here that the great alternatives present themselves between the various forms of society, authority or political government. People long coerce one another of their private initiative or follow some tradition, before they begin to do so through special military or local agents. *Government concentrates domination in its own hands, and regulates it. It neither originates nor abolishes domination.*[17]

Having acknowledged the brutality and militancy latent in political life, Santayana, despite his own disenchantment, looks at the idealistic political design of Plato and the eschatological paradigm of Christianity not without reverence and nostalgia. To be able to rise—at least imaginatively—above the dimension of power is to endow culture with uniquely human dignity, the corruption of which became increasingly visible somewhere around the sixteenth century, when political power is openly recognized as an end in itself.[18] Not by accident was the reduction of human life to Will (i.e., force) paralleled by an anthropology of "plentiful lack."[19] Santayana is acutely aware of the fragility of human *self* and its deep codependence upon patterns of culture and hence, he associates the privative conception and experience of humanity with a type of disillusioned, instrumental political rationality. The shift of political horizon into the realm of pure forces, exemplified—as evoked by Santayana—by the political ideals of Trasymachus, Machiavelli, and Nietzsche, foretells a social order established on "the same old foundations of physical necessities and human accidents."[20]

What Santayana does mean, then, when talking about the spiritual crisis in his last *opus*? According to my reading, the thinker's main preoccupation is an unfortunate disunity of modern Western culture. We have already glanced at this split from the viewpoint of individual *selves*. From the political vantage point, the crisis in question stands for a situation when people have lost the virtues originally meant to co-shape and sustain the liberal ethos and hence, to make the best of their democratic privilege. *In other words, the freedom technically "provided" by democracy, misses a corresponding vital liberty in the selves of its participants.* As if paradoxically, the remnants of the old ideals of freedom and effective self-government coexist with a feeling of inertia and uprootedness. Thus, Santayana shares some of the concerns voiced by Alexis de Tocqueville almost a century earlier.[21] There seems to be continuity between de Tocqueville's thoughts about "democratic despotism" and its ability to "degrade people without tormenting them,"[22] and Santayana's warning about the "rebarbarization" of culture occurring within industrial, capitalist liberalism. Among the factors that conspire to the phenomenon of democracy losing its essential, empowering incentive of self-government, which is equal to the gradual deprivation of vital liberty, the author of *Dominations and Powers* lists historical ignorance, efficacy-oriented education, domination of means over ends, weakening of social and personal bonds, and the formalization (lifelessness) of language related to the dominance of mass media.

As we have said, politics, in a broad, anthropological sense attributed to this term by the author of *Dominations and Powers*, thrives precisely on the margin of the transformation of Primal Will into its expression in demands and decisions. Now, "the maxim that every man is the best judge of his own interests recommends itself by its simplicity and the air of honest and good sense"—says Santayana, adding, ironically, that "it can nevertheless be seriously questioned."[23] Meanwhile, the precariousness of the translation of what is latent and hidden into articulate voices and actions instigates the competition of forces, which may be willing to take advantage of the fact that it is

> not enough for us to know what we want; the crucial points are whether the present circumstances render it obtainable and whether we have the means of securing it. On both these points, in the political field, the ordinary man thinks little and gets that little wrong.[24]

We may imagine political reality as a theatrical stage where an ongoing, multileveled drama of competing interests, insinuations, wagers, hopes, ideals, and disillusions is performed. In the course of these transactions, as if behind the scenes, representatives of some ruling interests take over the authorship of the play and set new rules of bearing the costs of necessity. We may now have yet another intuition—that of *political reality as a double movement along two lines or two continua crossing one another: vertical, stretched in-between the real and the imaginative, and horizontal, where the vector points either to power or to domination*.[25] The growing complexity and "virtuality" of reality, along with the development of technology, affected the deeply human sense of finitude and increased both the value (and the price) of knowledge, and hence the level of ignorance, endowing the Hegelian words about the doer being always "in the antithesis of knowing and not knowing"[26] with a prophetic meaning. Individuals are entrapped within a continuous, non-transparent process of "emplotment," a multidimensional contextualization. Countless situations accompanied by correspondent visions of *things being thus-and-so* and *arbitrary versions of history* are being arranged, re-arranged, and transmitted by means of skillful symbolic persuasion. The players in what Santayana calls *wars of imagination* resort to all the more sophisticated means of colonizing people's consciousness. *Politics, one may say, increasingly relies on what we have called* aporetic *selves and what we should perhaps start calling apophatic humanity.* Needless to say, globalization, including *the globalization of imagination*, challenges the possibility of conscious self-government.

What Santayana calls *acquisitive vice* (and we call consumerism) is a milder face of *the militant scheme*, in which will tends to "monopolize the light of spirit."[27] The dominance of will over spirit and of means over ends, greed, fear, and poor memory easily become allies of totalitarian scenarios, warns the thinker. Naked forces, equipped with global tools of persuasion and modern technology, pose a threat of totalitarianism, perhaps a totalitarianism of a new, unknown type. To stress it once again, a vital message from Santayana seems to be that mid-twentieth-century Western world was at the threshold of the evolution of democratic system coming to a full circle, a moment when it became *unable to come up to the standards of its own liberal ideals*, tailored so as to suit a society of rational (in Santayana's understanding of the term) individuals. This moment opens, in his view, an era of a new barbarism, an era of the desire for *quantitative infinity*. Behind which there is the most perverse characteristic of liberal outlook, namely—the *belief* in progress, which Santayana consistently opposed, as expressed in the following passage:

> Progress is often a fact: granted a definite end to be achieved, we may sometimes observe a continuous approach towards achieving it . . . But belief in progress, like belief in fate or number three, is sheer superstition, a mad notion.[28]

Not only does the author of *Dominations and Powers* foretell, as pointed out by Gray, the transformation of liberalism "from a creed of liberty to a creed of progress through a new tyranny," but also considers it unavoidable.[29]

Santayana at some point provides us with a description of existence as "essentially blind and involuntary war."[30] Even peace may be described as "latent war."[31] Life finds itself in a condition of "universal passive war"[32] because it does not want to perish. When it passes from a passive to an intentional war, life becomes militant. Government, as follows from these definitions and as some theoreticians of politics have described it, is a restriction of war but also a potentiality of war, or—as Santayana phrased it—a "modification of war."[33] A manifestation of the new barbarism is remilitarization, a reinforcement of the most rudimentary and most brutal dimension of government as such. Meanwhile, the scale on the continuum of militancy and the use of violence to inflict necessity is ample. The actual political praxis depends—to put it in the simplest way possible—on one hand, on the aims and ideals under the *aegis* of which a given society organizes its political life, and on the other—on the criteria for the selection of means. The "evil" side of government may be limited and coined into a source of formative and supportive power by rational action. An enlightened and supportive government, in Santayana's view, is minimally oppressive; it seeks "to attain its purpose without making or inflicting unnecessary sacrifices."[34] It cares for delivering tools for the people to become better at self-governing, as long as governing in a democratic system is meant to be an extension of self-rule.

7.3 The Challenge of Integrity

One of the modalities of the omnipresent war or competition is "civil war" commonly taking place among contradictory impulses, tendencies, and ideas which bother human *selves*. Hence, the importance of rationality understood as a higher-order ability to recognize and harmonize the inner multitude of vital qualities which constitute experience. "The substance and joy of liberty begin—says the thinker—only when the well-integrated powers of the psyche *find and establish a world* in which they bear their specific and appropriate fruit."[35]

But for a life, which is multi-centered and to a large degree undetermined, integrity is a task and a challenge. Whereas Bergson had an intuition of a certain "derailment" occurring during the material realization of vital impulses, Santayana, to a similar effect, says that

> life has many centers and divergent developments, so that *natura naturans* or what it would be natural thing to become, is very far from being identical with what, under accidental circumstances, that thing actually grows into. Failure, at least partial failure, is therefore everywhere; and there is really no such thing as *natura naturata*, in the sense of native potentiality realized, but only *natura denaturata*, or a jumble of potentialities all more or less distorted and baffled.[36]

An ideal self-government, as we have noted, is based on self-knowledge and sanity, which, in their turn, rely on the faculty of judgment and wisdom. While some of the forces that count as necessity and/or dominations are definitely beyond our control, some others emerge from our primal Will, which—despite its invariant "hard core"—can be enlightened, disciplined, and "subject to internal variation,"[37] as discussed in the chapter on narrative and dramatic strategies of sustaining self-integrity. It involves some *deconstruction* and constant negotiations with the world. But the task goes far beyond individual, psychic endowment. Self-government is inseparable from culture insofar as culture is a medium that offers tools for the formation and articulation of the *self* among other *selves*, for the recognition of individual and common interests. This is the bedrock for rational action, be it personal or political. In the vein of Plato's idea of reason's capacity to persuade necessity, notwithstanding the fact that contingency continuously undermines visions of a better world, wisdom, which is unthinkable without reference to the past, allows to lodge rationality in specific ideals (without which rationality is but an empty procedure, a mere tool) and give action a proper direction. *Santayana, let me stress, casts off all illusions about the possibility of a livable world without memory and continuity. In other words, he casts off any utopia, any idea of a lasting, ideal order which is an ad-hoc construct.* This is justified by the assumption that man—as a historical and spiritual being of some nature and condition—can hardly flourish without the support of some sort of temporal synthesis, without learning from experience. Otherwise, we end up with what some critics of culture referred to as "momentary man." This, by the way, illuminates Santayana's criticism of the main dogma of liberalism, namely that human nature is "a fiction, a chaos or an unknowable thing."[38] Santayana, as Gray rightly notes, acknowledges of partial relativity and plasticity of human nature but not of its "unknowable openness to unheard-of novelty."[39]

On an individual level, the ultimate, ideal aim of a successful self-government is a situation when "your compulsion[s] have become your choices and your limitations your virtues."[40] This ideal, as Santayana admits, is fully achievable—if at all—only for someone who has learned to transcend worldly concerns and dwell in the realm of spirit. For a culture it means protecting the idea of *autotelic* values and preserving some areas of disinterested action, disinterested participation. These, along with the apparently abstract formula of *chosen finitude*, are ways of curbing the Primal Will and transcending the immediate, and hence, transcending the realm of powers. Expressive of "philosophy as a form of life," to evoke Daniel Moreno's phrase, Santayana's reflection is of practical relevance and responds to a specifically Santayanan question (definitely of Platonic inspiration), namely: how to *"redeem human life from vanity and barbarism."*[41] Concerned with a vision of *human life* and *modus viventi*, it constructs passages between the spiritual and the practical, the individual and the social. The main idea of *rationality* (as something essentially human) oscillating in-between self-government and governing others is perhaps the most emphatic expression of this reconciliatory attempt. The good and the beauty having its origin in the vital dynamics of an individual psyche can be actualized and flourish only in the common world, where it finds means of formal expression and other spirits capable of its epiphany, or, in other words, of spiritual "deliverance."

7.4 Threats

Finally, to end this brief, introductory reflection on Santayana's political philosophy, let us have a look at the threats pointed out by the thinker as most vital and pressing, while recapitulating, partly, what has already been said. The two World Wars and the emerging totalitarian regimes on one hand proved to Santayana the relevance of some elements of his critique of culture and, on another, made him revise some other convictions and abandon certain hopes. It definitely deepened his overall anthropological skepticism, although not to the point of pessimism, and made him even more sensitive to the threats latent in the ways of modern culture. This is what *Dominations and Powers* is expressive of. He was bothered, as we have seen, by what he interpreted as a growing disparity between the actual quality of liberal democracy and the ideal function of it. The spiritual crisis he would sometimes associate with a certain "dislocation of reason" consisted in, among others, forgetfulness and short-sightedness of the elites, negligence of virtue, misunderstanding of freedom, and failure in coping with finitude. Interestingly, it had a specific counterpart in the fear of death or expelling the idea of one's own death beyond the scope of everyday imagination, of which Heidegger famously spoke. Santayana comments on it as follows:

> a smiling and mystic neighborhood with death, as with one's own shadow, intensified life enormously in the dramatic direction . . . In contrast with that freedom and richness we can see to what a shocking degradation modern society has condemned the spirit . . . Our one preoccupation is to be safe.[42]

"How can tyranny be resisted and liberty preserved where each individual is weak?"[43] asked de Tocqueville, concerned with the atrophy of personal integrity and individual agency, which undermined self-government and cooperation among individuals. He noted, anticipating future critics of liberal democracy, the weaknesses of the atomistic freedom of the "private" type of individualism, concentrated solely on self-realization and self-expression (which were secured by liberties). A society of such individuals, in particular when it is a big society, characterized by complex and non-transparent relations of power, exhibits a considerable and dangerous *inertia*. In the 1920s a famous Polish sociologist, Florian Znaniecki, pondered over the decline of the Western civilization, saying: "we have worked centuries . . . to liberate man from the shackles of the old, *external discipline* inherited from the older forms of civilization, but *liberty requires inner discipline* and we were unable to achieve one."[44] Even though Santayana represented a more decisive kind of individualism, one which considered a retreat from the life of community as a tempting option, he was clearly aware of the problems related to the crisis in the formation of *selves* and interpersonal bonds.

The unprecedented violence of the twentieth century brought to light the tragic discrepancy between facts and the ideals on which Western culture was founded. "Europe" (and the Western world as a whole) as a phenomenon, an idea, a spiritual community of persons agreeing to live by certain standards, argued Edmund Husserl,[45] embodied an ethos. It implied that both the aims of human action and the means of achieving them should respect a certain model of being a human, which involves—Husserl claims—"a rational sense of life."[46] Different as Santayana's understanding of rationality may be from that of Husserl, he nevertheless shared the other philosopher's concern about the spiritual crisis of "Europe." Coming back to certain issues, which were previously mentioned in this book, namely—"the will to power," by which Santayana understood the dominance of will over reflection, lack of moderation, and the desire for unlimited expansion, went hand in hand with the negligence of the intrinsic connectedness between freedom and limitation, or—if you will—freedom and discipline. In the context which interests us at this point, these phenomena may be understood hermeneutically (or even psychoanalytically) as a kind of *nemesis*, or, in other words, as representing *a curse of negativity*, which Santayana used to oppose to "enlightened Will." Totalitarianism in the form known to Santayana, could be associated by him with masses of "unreconciled" individuals, a "conspiracy" of half-conscious, uprooted psyches led astray by skillful propagandists beyond the point of what is reversible. It is obvious that certain ideas and ideologies tend to become operative forces in the political realm. The problem with the ideologies disrespecting finite forms and forgetful of the past is that they tend to take their toll relatively quickly and in a merciless way, in accordance with the words of Henri Amiel, who said that "every fiction is self-expiating."[47]

The point to remember is, Santayana claims, that *directive imagination*—standing in the language of *Dominations and Powers* for the ideas guiding human action, political action in particular—must not be uprooted. Ideally, it should be an expression of vital maturity and wisdom. Furthermore, solely negative understanding of freedom, as freedom from excessive oppression, may be not enough to allow anybody to enjoy vital liberty, not to mention spiritual freedom. Likewise, government in its schemes should be mindful of the fact that it must not disregard and underestimate the individual; it must not "try to get on without reconciling the individual."[48] A crowd of individuals who have not been "reconciled" by society and culture forms a potential, collective subject of totalitarian or authoritarian, domestic or alien domination.

Finally, a word concerning Santayana's critique of technology. There is a deep ambiguity behind the scientific discoveries and the development of technology in the "mechanical melting pot"[49] of the twentieth century, he believed. On one hand they empower an individual and society in an unprecedented way, on the other, though, they may ricochet and become a means of achieving pernicious domination (if not the destruction and annihilation of lives), be it of economic, military, or cultural nature. Leaving the very possibility of the concentration of enormous material power aside, contemporary rapid technological progress seems to Santayana a "blind lead"[50] because he believes that the benefits humans may have from the (material) domination over the material aspects of life are "naturally" limited due to the anthropological forestallment and *conditio humana*. More specifically, the desired equilibrium within the powers-dominations dynamics, as well as the ideal of vital liberty, require a considerable share of the civil and the spiritual element in culture. Meanwhile, the threat posed by technology is that it may give "*brute humanity* . . . the power to destroy *polite humanity*. . . . Armed with this prodigious mechanism, any hand at headquarters can spread death and ruin over the earth."[51] Notwithstanding the fact of all the benefits it bestows on humans, technology has its dark side insofar as it represents militant ambitions and is the vehicle for unlimited material expansion. Thus, it contributes directly to the barbarization of culture. Let me note that Benjamin believed that "barbarism lurks in the very concept of culture"[52] as a tendency for abstraction and reification of the values surviving a culture from which they arose.

In his eclectic philosophy of politics and culture, which is predominantly a critical undertaking supported by an ontological frame, Santayana, while remaining idiosyncratic, presents a broad spectrum of inspirations and affinities, from Plato, Aristotle, and the Stoics, to Voegelin, Taylor, Agamben, and others. In *Dominations and Powers* we are led by the thinker along the mental paths of rational (self-)government, which are expressive of a certain ethos of civility, vital liberty, and spiritually controlled aims, as opposed to instrumental and power-oriented models, which are believed to represent a kind of retreat to unenlightened forms of Will, or, in other words, to barbarism. Despite the alleged moral relativism ascribed by some critics to Santayana, the overall outlook of his philosophy of politics is a voice of respect for capital "L" Life—an art and not merely a biological process. *Most importantly, Santayana—and this is despite the powers-dominations distinction—insists on refusing to reduce life—and consequently, politics, which is but an expression of life—to Will, or any other idea representative of power.* This, I would say, is one of the most distinct and persisting traits of his thought. He insists that culture preserves respect for disinterestedness and finite forms while saying a decisive "no" to utopian phantasms of unlimited power, growth, and progress. Perhaps the most explicit expression of his motivation may be found in the already quoted credo—"*to redeem human life from vanity and barbarism.*"[53] Despite the tragic fallibility of human reality in confrontation with the standards of reason and spiritual values, we must never "confuse the natural history of politics with rational government."[54]

Notes

Introduction

1. Chapters 1, 2, and 3, as well as parts of chapters 5 and 6 of this book originate from my PhD dissertation entitled "Mask and Thought: The Conception of the Aporetic Self in George Santayana's Philosophy," (Institute of Philosophy and Sociology, Polish Academy of Sciences, Warsaw, 2015).

2. Nathan A. Scott, Jr., *The Poetics of Belief* (Chapel Hill and London: The University of North Carolina Press, 1985), 91–92.

3. George Santayana, "Fifty Years of British Idealism," in: *Some Turns of Thought in Modern Philosophy. Five Essays* (Cambridge: CUP, 1933/2014), 63. I will refer to this source subsequently as *STTMP*.

4. This criticism, natural for pragmatism, which partly defined itself via opposition toward the "artificial" problems of continental philosophy, has been summarized and addressed by Henry S. Levinson in: Henry S. Levinson, *Santayana: Pragmatism, and the Spiritual Life* (Chapel Hill and London: University of North Carolina Press, 1992), 211–17.

5. See: Michael Brodrick, "Blessings of a Spiritual Life," *The Transactions of Charles S. Peirce Society* 49, no. 4 (2009): 546.

6. George Santayana, "Apologia Pro Mente Sua," in *The Philosophy of George Santayana*, ed. Paul A. Schilpp (Evanston and Chicago: Northwestern University, 1940), 503–04. My emphasis. Consequently I will refer to this source in text as *APS*.

7. Scott, *The Poetics of Belief*, 93.

8. As did Morris Grossman, who noted ironically that any orderly, analytical approach striving to uncover a definite and dominant doctrine in Santayana, is more than likely to come across a number of contradictory "arguments and claims that somehow got lodged in the texts in some insecure and potentially embarrassing way." See: Morris Grossman, "Interpreting Interpretations," *Overheard in Seville. Bulletin of the Santayana Society*, no. 8 (Fall 1990): 18.

9. Henry S. Levinson discussed Santayana's connections with the pragmatist tradition and the idiosyncrasy of his idea of spiritual life. See: Henry S. Levinson, *Santayana. Pragmatism and the Spiritual Life* (Chapel Hill and London: University of North Carolina Press, 1992).

10. Timothy Sprigge, *Santayana. An examination of his Philosophy* (London and Boston: Routlege and Kegan Paul, 1974), 85.

11. Michael Hodges and John Lachs, *Thinking in the Ruins: Wittgenstein and Santayana on Contingency* (Nashville, TN: Vanderbilt University Press, 2000), 90.

12. See: Edward W. Lovely, *George Santayana's Philosophy of Religion: His Roman Catholic Influences and Phenomenology* (Lanham, MD: Lexington Books, 2012).

13. Daniel Moreno, *Santayana the Philosopher. Philosophy as a Form of Life*, trans. Charles Padron (Lewisburg, PA: Bucknell University Press, 2015).

14. John McCormick, in his biography of Santayana, mentions his engagement with reading German and French existentialists. See: John McCormick, *George Santayana: A Biography* (New York: Alfred A. Knopf, 1987), 345, 349, 470–79.

15. William G. Holzberger, ed., *The Letters of George Santayana: Book Five, 1933–1936* (Cambridge, MA: The MIT Press, 2003), 302.

16. See: McCormick, *George Santayana: A Biography*, 319. Also in Richard Butler's memories of his friendship with Santayana, the old philosopher, who had once traveled to Paris to attend Bergson's lectures, called the French thinker "the only great philosopher I knew personally." See: Richard Butler, *The Mind of Santayana* (Chicago: H. Regnery, 1955), 37–38. See also: Richard Butler, "George Santayana: Catholic Atheist," *Spirituality Today* 38 (Winter 1968): 319–36.

17. George Santayana, preface to *Dialogues in Limbo* (Ann Arbor: University of Michigan Press, 1957). The source is hereafter cited as *DL*.

18. Martin Heidegger, *Basic Problems of Phenomenology*, Albert Hofstadter trans. (Indianapolis: Indiana University Press, 1988), 155. I will be referring to this source as *BPP*.

19. Kenneth Burke, *A Grammar of Motives* (Berkeley: University of California Press, 1969), 222.

20. Burke, *A Grammar of Motives*, 223.

21. Moreno, *Santayana the Philosopher. Philosophy as a Form of Life*, 87–88.

22. See: George Santayana, *Dominations and Powers* (New York: Scribner's, 1951), 52–54; George Santayana, *Skepticisms and Animal Faith: Introduction to a System of Philosophy*, in *The Works of George Santayana*, vol. 13, Triton edition (New York: Scribner's, 1936), 130–46 (hereinafter cited as *SAF*); George Santayana, "Locke and the Frontiers of Common Sense," and "Fifty Years of British Idealism," in *Some Turns of Thought in Modern Philosophy* (Cambridge, UK: Cambridge University Press, 2014), 33–41, 62–65 (hereinafter referred to as *STTMP*).

23. John Lachs, *George Santayana* (Boston: Twayne Publishers, 1988).

24. Irving Singer, *George Santayana, Literary Philosopher* (New Haven, CT, and London: Yale University Press, 2000), 28.

25. This issue has been subject to research by Charles L. Padron in: "Reflections on Santayana and Tragic Value," (PhD dissertation, Vanderbilt University, May 2000). Subsequently I will refer to this text as *RSTV*.

26. Jacques Derrida, *Of Spirit. Heidegger and the Question*, trans. Geoffrey Bennington and Rachel Bowlby (Chicago and London: University of Chicago Press, 1991).

Chapter 1

1. St. Augustine, *Soliloquies*, in *The Fathers of the Church*, trans. Ludwig Schopp (Washington DC: CUA Press, 1948), 5: 381.
2. Charles Taylor, *Sources of the Self, The Making of the Modern Identity* (Cambridge: Cambridge University Press, 1989), 119. Hereinafter I refer to this source as *SSMMI*.
3. *SSMMI*, 120.
4. *SSMMI*, 139. My emphasis.
5. Michel Foucault, *Hermeneutyka podmiotu* [Hermeneutics of the Subject], trans. Michał Herer (Warsaw: PWN, 2012), 266.
6. Foucault, *Hermeneutyka*, 301–02.
7. Following Aristotle, virtue is "a state of character concerned with choice, lying in a mean (. . .) relative to us, (. . .), determined by a rational principle." See: Aristotle, *Nicomachean Ethics*, bk. 12, chap. 6, 1106b 36ff.
8. Martin Heidegger, *Basic Concepts of Aristotelian Philosophy*, trans. Robert D. Metcalf and Mark. B. Tanzer (Bloomington: Indiana University Press, 2009), 57. Subsequently I am referring to this source as *BCAP*.
9. *SSMMI*, 76–77.
10. On *Cogito*'s corporeality see for example: Katarzyna Gurczyńska-Sady, *Człowiek jako słowo i ciało. W poszukiwaniu nowej koncepcji podmiotu* [Man as Word and Flesh. Searching for a New Conception of Subjectivity] (Cracow: Universitas, 2013), 121–31.
11. *SSMMI*, 146. See also: Max Weber, *Economy and Society: An outline of interpretive sociology*, 2 vols. (Berkeley and Los Angeles: University of California Press, 1978), 1: 541–43.
12. *SSMMI*, 147.
13. *SSMMI*, 157–58.
14. Martin Heidegger, *Being and Time*, trans. Joan Staumbaugh (New York: SUNY, 1996), 89 (hereafter cited as *BT*).
15. See: Joanna Trzópek, *Na tropach podmiotu* [Tracing the Subject] (Cracow: Wydawnictwa UJ, 2013), 23. My emphasis.
16. Agata Bielik-Robson, *Na drugim brzegu nihilizmu* [On the Other Side of Nihilism] (Warsaw: IFiS PAN, 1997), 71–73. The author notes that even Freudian "structural" ego echoes this powerful model.
17. *SSMMI*, 159.
18. *STTMP*, 35.
19. Charles Taylor, *A Secular Age* (Cambridge, MA: Belknap of Harvard University Press, 2007), 171.
20. Taylor, *A Secular Age*, 173.
21. *STTMP*, 45.
22. David Hume, *Treatise of Human Nature* (Oxford: Oxford University Press, 2000), 165. Santayana in his experiment with radical skepticism is probably making a reference to Hume's "bundle theory."

23. Gilles Deleuze, *Empiricism and Subjectivity. An essay on Hume's Theory of Human Nature*, trans. Constantin V. Boundas (New York: Columbia University Press, 1991).

24. Mind is for Hume quantitative, a mere collection of data. The smallest empirical unit may be referred to as "the mind's moment." Relations and human nature are for Hume—and for Deleuze himself—qualitative and *external* to ideas, which are quantitative. See: Deleuze, *Empiricism and Subjectivity*, 85.

25. Deleuze, *Empiricism and Subjectivity*, 93.

26. Deleuze, 26.

27. Deleuze, 85.

28. Deleuze, 80.

29. Deleuze, 49.

30. Immanuel Kant, *Critique of Pure Reason*, trans. Werner S. Pluhar (Indianapolis, IN: Hackett, 1996), A 105, A 124. Subsequently I cite this source as *CPR*.

31. *CPR*, B32.

32. *CPR*, A109. Manfred Frank calls Kant's "I think" an unceasing, self-reflexive "doubling." Manfred Frank, *Świadomość siebie i poznanie siebie* [Self-consciousness and Self-knowledge], trans. Zbigniew Zwoliński (Warsaw: Oficyna Naukowa, 2002), 25–30.

33. *CPR*, B136.

34. *CPR*, A125.

35. *CPR*, A119, A124–25.

36. *CPR*, A120.

37. *CPR*, B159.

38. *CPR*, B133.

39. *CPR*, B156.

40. These exact words appear in an older translation of Kant's *Critique of Pure Reason*—by J. M. D. Miklejohn (London: Henry G. Bohn, 1855), 94.

41. *CPR*, B157.

42. *BPP*, 125–29.

43. *BPP*, 131–36.

44. Marian Zdziechowski, *Pesymizm, romantyzm, a podstawy chrześcijaństwa* [Pessimism, Romanticism, and the Foundations of Christianity] (Warsaw: Hachette, 2011), 51–52.

45. *SSMMI*, 363–64.

46. For more on this issue see: George Santayana, *The German Mind: a Philosophical Diagnosis* (New York: Apollo Editions, 1968).

47. *BPP*, 152–53.

48. *BPP*, 153.

49. William James, *Principles of Psychology*, 2 vols. (New York: Cosimo, 2007), 1: 400.

50. Owen Flanagan, *Consciousness Reconsidered* (Cambridge, MA: MIT Press, 1992), 178.

51. Flanagan, *Consciousness*, 183.
52. Flanagan, 182.
53. Frank, *Świadomość siebie*, 350.
54. Edmund Husserl, *Medytacje Kartezjańskie* [Cartesian Meditations], trans. Andrzej Wajs (Warsaw: IFiS PAN, 2009) 165–69. Dan Zahavi calls early Husserl's vision a non-egological one, even though "Ego" does appear in *Meditations*. See: Dan Zahavi, *Subjectivity and Selfhood: Investigating the First-Person Perspective* (Cambridge, MA: MIT Press, 2005), 32. Hereafter this source will be referred to as *SSIFPP*.
55. *SSIFPP*, 32, 20, 61.
56. Zahavi, *Husserl's Phenomenology*, 82–85.
57. *SSIFPP*, 69–70. A reference is made here to Derrida's PhD dissertation (1953/54) published as: Jacques Derrida, *The Problem of Genesis in Husserl's Phenomenology*, trans. Marian Hobson (Chicago: Chicago University Press, 2003).
58. *SSIF*, 70. The idea of the temporal difference within the self in Husserl is also discussed by Jacques Derrida in: *Voice and Phenomenon. Introduction to the Problem of the Sign in Husserl's Phenomenology* (Evanston, IL: Northwestern University Press, 2011).
59. Edmund Husserl, *Ideas Pertaining to a Pure Phenomenology and to a Phenomenological Philosophy*, 2 vols., trans. Richard Rojcewicz and A. Schuwer (Dordrecht/Boston/London: Kluwer Academic Publishers, 1989), 2: 107.
60. Husserl, *Ideas*, 109–10.
61. Husserl, 107.
62. Husserl, 120.
63. *SSIFPP*, 92.
64. Husserl, *Ideas*, 101–02.
65. Husserl, 129.
66. Husserl, 140.
67. Husserl, 144–45.
68. Husserl, 145.
69. Husserl, 145.
70. Husserl, 146. My emphasis.
71. Husserl, 148.
72. What I mean by "the sphere of helplessness" is this part of "me-ness" that is experienced as being beyond subjective control. It involves the experience of both finitude and otherness within our own selves.
73. It was Jean Paul Sartre, Zahavi reminds, who was the first to articulate two different "modes of existence of consciousness"—pre-reflective and reflective. See: *SSIFPP*, 21.
74. *SSIFPP*, 176.
75. *SSIFPP*, 84.
76. *SSIFPP*, 85.
77. *SSIFPP*, 89.

78. *SSIFPP*, 97. The original source of this quotation is: Steven G. Crowell, *Husserl, Heidegger, and the Space of Meaning* (Evanston, IL: Northwestern University Press, 2001), 25–127.

79. *SSMMI*, 526.Charles Taylor, with his vision of self-interpreting animal, shares in the effort to reconstruct the shattered, post-modern subject by reestablishing its connection with some sort of meaningful, objective reality, which is vital as long as it is "essential to the Ego that it orients itself in a space of questions about the good, that it stands somewhere on these questions." See: *SSMMI*, 33.

80. As Manfred Frank reminds, Schleiermacher was also the one to articulate the distinction between individuality and personality. The qualitative idea of "personality" had been rather neglected by both German and Anglo-Saxon philosophy, which preferred the notion of "individuality" as rendering the meaning of being *one of many subjects* rather than *a unique one*. Thus, an individual subject could easily be recognized as a manifestation of something universal or referred to something universal.

81. Unlike for Kant, whose *personalitas moralis* has been said to reveal an a priori respect, according to Scheler it is experience that uncovers meanings and values and activates ideals. An assumed objective hierarchy of values (which exists a priori) becomes available to persons via their very experience of the world.

82. Frank, *Świadomość siebie*, 20–21.

83. See Paul Ricoeur's polemic with contemporary analytical takes on subjectivity in: Paul Ricoeur, *Oneself as Another* (Chicago: University of Chicago Press, 1992). Still, one must distinguish between "classical" hermeneutic conceptions and some others which draw on the general idea of interpretive and narrative identity. While the first ones usually defend an irreducible individual and personal perspective of narrative unity, the latter treat interpretation as a form of adaptive behavior (Dennett), an epiphenomenon (F. Nietzsche, R. Rorty) or an inherently deconstructive activity (J. Derrida).

84. *BT*, 229, my emphasis.

85. Rorty, however, with his fictive and ironic self, may be placed next to the previously mentioned post-modern thinkers endorsing some form of the "escape from the self."

86. Frank, *Świadomość siebie*, 17–19.

87. *SSIFPP*, 156.

88. *SSIFPP*, 115.

89. The experiential aspect individuates the subject formally, the narrative dimension adds a personalization to the self. See: Flanagan, *Consciousness*, 129.

90. Daniel Dennett, "The Self as a Center of Narrative Gravity," in *Self and Consciousness: Multiple Perspectives*, eds. Frank. S. Kessel, P. M. Cole, and D. L. Johnson (Hillsdale, NJ: Erlbaum, 1992).

91. Frank, *Świadomość siebie*, 53–54.

92. Frank, 69.

93. Frank, 73.

94. *SSIFPP*, 132. My emphasis.

95. Freedom is replaced by the experience of freedom, see for example: Daniel Wegner, *The Illusion of Conscious Will* (Cambridge, MA: MIT Press, 2002), 317.
96. Trzópek, *Na tropach podmiotu*, 83.
97. Trzópek, 201.
98. Trzópek, 199.
99. Trzópek, 195.
100. Trzópek, 195.
101. Yet, Joanna Trzópek makes an important remark concerning this reasoning. Not only is the very way we formulate the question about the power of our will and conscious decisions to influence our action burdened with a sort of dualism (material-mental) at the point of departure, but the very rhetoric of a "fiat" in which we speak about freedom suggests perhaps an excessive Cartesian residuum. See: Trzópek, *Na tropach podmiotu*.
102. John R. Searle, *Mind: a Brief Introduction* (Oxford: Oxford University Press, 2004), 124.
103. For more see: Trzópek, *Na tropach podmiotu*, 133–34.
104. *SSMMI*, 307.
105. *SSMMI*, 315.
106. *SSMMI*, 319.
107. *SSMMI*, 356–57.
108. *SSMMI*, 408.
109. *SSMMI*, 345–46. My emphasis.
110. *SSMMI*, 293.
111. *SSMMI*, 513.
112. *SSMMI*, 175.
113. Thomas Metzinger, *The Ego Tunnel* (New York: Basic Books, 2009). Metzinger's argument against the existence of ego/I seems to be targeted at a Cartesian "phantom."
114. Taylor, *A Secular Age*, 359.
115. *SSMMI*, 462–63.
116. *SSMMI*, 390.
117. *SSMMI*, 490.
118. *SSMMI*, 451–52. My emphasis.
119. *SSMMI*, 449.
120. *SSMMI*, 428.
121. *SSMMI*, 459–60.
122. Lucy Beckett, *Wallace Stevens* (Cambridge: Cambridge University Press, 1984), 29.
123. *SSMMI*, 467. My emphasis.
124. David Dilworth, "Mediterranean Aestheticims, Epicurean Materialism," in: *Santayana at 150. International Interpretations*, ed. Matthew.C. Flamm, Giuseppe Patella, and Jennifer Rea (Lanham, MD: Lexington Books, 2013): 53–87. See also my review of this book: Katarzyna Kremplewska, "Review: *Santayana at 150. International Interpretations,*" *Overheard in Seville. Bulletin of the George Santayana*

Society, no. 32 (Fall 2014): 71–76. Recently David Dilworth published a very interesting, thought-provoking text on Santayana–Stevens relations in the light of Santayana's anti-romanticism. See: David Dilworth, "Santayana's Anti-Romanticism versus Stevens' New Romanticism," *Overheard in Seville. Bulletin of the Santayana Society*, no. 35 (Fall 2017): 32–49.

125. Friedrich Nietzsche, preface to *The Gay Science*, trans. Walter Kaufman (New York: Vintage, 1974), 35. Charles Taylor also refers to this passage, see: *SSMMI*, 467.

126. *SSMMI*, 468.

127. *SSMMI*, 51.

128. *SSMMI*, 34.

129. Paul Ricoeur, *Oneself as Another* (Chicago: University of Chicago Press, 1992), 274–75. Subsequently I am referring to this source as *OAA*.

130. *SSMMI*, 50–51.

Chapter 2

1. Subchapter 2.2. of this chapter was first published in a modified form in Polish language as an article: Katarzyna Kremplewska, "Maska i myśl. Soboŝć a *ars vivendi* w myśli George'a Santayany" [Mask and Thought. Self and *Ars Vivendi* in the Thought of George Santayana], *Analiza i Egzystencja*, no. 26 (2014), 87–110.

2. *APS*, 586.

3. What is important is that in all these meanings *spirit* is considered as naturally grounded, so when Santayana sometimes identifies spirit as "mind," which may be particularly misleading, it is immediately implied that the "organ" of mind is psyche.

4. George Santayana, *Realms of Being*, one-volume ed. (New York: Cooper Square Publishers, 1972), 457. Subsequently I will use the abbreviation *RB* for this source.

5. John Lachs, "Santayana's Philosophy of Mind," in *Animal Faith and Spiritual Life* (New York: Appleton-Century-Crofts, 1967), 255.

6. George Santayana, *Obiter Scripta: Lectures, Essays and Reviews* (New York: Charles Scribner's Sons, 1936), 115. Consequently I will use the abbreviation *OS* for this source.

7. *OS*, 111.

8. *OS*, 148.

9. *OS*, 129. My emphasis.

10. In *APS*, in retrospect, Santayana mentions "empirical confidence" and "cognitive instinct" as possible equivalents of the term "animal faith." See: *APS*, 586. This sort of immediate awareness enabling intelligent action is juxtaposed with intuitions of essence, which, when considered *in abstracto*, stand only for appearances, which may but do not have to be an index to material reality.

11. Sprigge, *Santayana. An examination of his Philosophy*, 44.

12. Lachs, "Santayana's Philosophy of Mind," 261.
13. *APS*, 501. My emphasis.
14. Metzinger, *The Ego Tunnel*, 3–12. Metzinger proposes that as a result of our brain functions we hold a sustained simulation of the world as well as a transparent model of ourselves, an image of "our body and our psychological states but also our relationship to the past and future." See: Metzinger, 7. The fact that Santayana—understandably for his era—sketched only a very general direction for his naturalist philosophy of action allows me to associate loosely some of its major tenets to a contemporary philosophy, without making binding commitments.
15. *APS*, 501.
16. Sprigge, *Santayana. An examination of his Philosophy*, 35.
17. Sprigge, 35.
18. Sprigge, 35.
19. The transcendental illusion of an ungrounded "ego" is corrected by realism based on (animal) faith, which, indirectly, leads to the acknowledgment of one's own finitude. Santayana would declare as a moderate epistemological skeptic and a critical, ontological realist. Thus, Santayana claims, "with St. Augustine and with nature in me, I would retain faith to give breath to knowledge" (*APS*, 512). For more details in a clear-cut self-exposition see: *APS*, 510–18.
20. *APS*, 518.
21. Santayana's kinship with the latter, by the way, is far deeper, as persuasively presented by Michael Hodges and John Lachs in *Thinking in the Ruins*.
22. Agata Bielik-Robson, *Inna Nowoczesność. Pytania o Współczesną Formułę Duchowości* [The Other Modernity: Questions Concerning the Future Prospects of Our Spiritual Life] (Cracow: Universitas, 1998), 125–58. The author is critical of this position on account of its presumed contribution to nihilism.
23. Scott, *The Poetics of Belief*, 95.
24. This version appears in *Apologia Pro Mente Sua*.
25. Husserl, *Ideas*, 109–10.
26. See for example: *POML*, 142, 151.
27. *RB*, 47.
28. *RB*, 259.
29. *RB*, 557. Compare with Heidegger's remarks about Dasein and time in Western metaphysics in: M. Heidegger, *What is called thinking* (New York: Perennial 2004), 101.
30. Subjectivity, from its own spiritual perspective, tends to regard itself as ungrounded or grounded only in itself, which results in a sort of transcendental illusion of an absolute "I." A *here-and-now*, technically speaking, marks an intuition, and in ontological terms is a sort of a subjective and *a priori* correlate of an essence.
31. *RB*, 76.
32. Martin Heidegger, *Ontology. The Hermeneutics of Facticity*, trans. John van Buren (Indianapolis: Indiana University Press, 1999), 12.
33. *POML*, 65.
34. *POML*, 66.

35. *RB*, 259.
36. *RB*, 255, 259.
37. *OAA*, 45.
38. *OAA*, 48–49.
39. *OAA*, 48–49, 53.
40. *RB*, 256.
41. Ricoeur also calls "I" a "migrating" term but in a different sense—as one applicable to *anyone*, any speaking subject. See: *OAA*, 48. The meaning of "migration" involved is changed into temporal only outside linguistic context.
42. *RB*, 257.
43. *OAA*, 54–55.
44. *OAA*, 74.
45. Heidegger, *Ontology. The Hermeneutics of Facticity*, 78. See also: *BT*, 349.
46. Lachs, "Santayana's Philosophy of Mind," 256.
47. Santayana comments on Josiah Royce's remark on his separation of essence and existence: "I do not separate the two, I merely distinguish them . . . they may be simultaneous dimensions of the same world." See: *APS*, 525.
48. An event is "a sequence of natural moments," which themselves are "durations." An event as such exhibits a complex essence called "a trope." Santayana also speaks of "facts," but the term "fact" is generic and refers to the perspective of a speaker/observer. What is important, material flux for Santayana is primary in relation to physical time. Angus Kerr-Lawson notes that Santayana was skeptical about understanding time in terms of mathematical instants and the paradoxes it produced. He insisted that "time be reinstated as a derivative aspect of existence." See: Angus Kerr Lawson, "Natural Moments in Santayana's Philosophy of Nature," *Transactions of the Charles S. Peirce Society* 16, no. 4 (Fall 1980): 309–28.
49. Lachs, "Santayana's Philosophy of Mind," 260.
50. By way of digression, it is worth noting that Santayana seemed to anticipate contemporary, interdisciplinary issues developed by cognitive and neuroscience. Had psychology and other sciences, he writes, "completely mapped the machinery of the human automaton . . . there would still be something essential undiscovered . . . something on another plane of being altogether, which this automatic life and this mental discourse involve, but do not contain. It is the *principle of both and of their relation*; the system of repetitions, correspondences, developments, and ideal unities created by this march of human life in double column . . . I do not mean the ideas of these things in the mental discourse of this or that man; but the groups or cycles of facts designated by these ideas." In other words, a major scientific challenge to be faced, as predicted by Santayana, would be the question of the nature of the passage from the chain of material events constituting a life to the chain of mental events, and the establishment of something called human *self*. See: George Santayana, *Soliloquies in England and Later Soliloquies* (New York: Scribner's, 1922), 220. Consequently I refer to this source as *SiELS*.
51. Lachs, "Santayana's Philosophy of Mind," 262. My emphasis.

52. *Possibility* here should not be mistaken with material *potentiality*. Santayana's emphasis on the distinction of essences was part of his polemic with empiricism, positivism, and nominalism, which tended to reduce data to facts or the other way round. See: *APS*, 535–37.

53. *APS*, 528.

54. Save for the fact that it is not a power, but precisely by *not* being a power it introduces *disinterestedness* as a value and creates a space where human being stays out of the relations of power—something that Nietzsche had overlooked, as emphasized by Santayana.

55. Lachs, "Santayana's Philosophy of Mind," 265.

56. Its price may be higher—including the total annihilation of the subject and the dehumanization of human being. The psycho-spiritual unity present in Santayana's vision is meant to prevent such radical consequences.

57. *DL*, 154.

58. An interesting attempt to shed a new light on his thought is that proposed by Michael Hodges and John Lachs in *Thinking in the Ruins*, where Santayana's ontology is treated as "ironic" in a comparative context of Wittgenstein's thought. More recently, Edward Lovely in *George Santayana's Philosophy of Religion* discusses the affinity of Santayana's thought to Husserl's phenomenology.

59. Martin Coleman, "On Celebrating the Death of Another Person," in: *Santayana at 150. International Interpretations*, in: *Santayana at 150. International Interpretations*, ed. Matthew.C. Flamm, Giuseppe Patella, and Jennifer Rea (Lanham, MD: Lexington Books, 2013), 182.

60. Matthew. C. Flamm, "Free Will for a Materialist," in *Santayana at 150. International Interpretations*, ed. Matthew C. Flamm, Giuseppe Patella, and Jennifer Rea (Lanham, MD: Lexington, 2013), 25.

61. *APS*, 509. The term "exists" is used here loosely, if not metaphorically, and may be misleading. In this context "exists" stands for "has a (sort of) reality."

62. George Santayana, *Interpretations of Poetry and Religion*, in *The Works of George Santayana*, vol. 2, Triton edition (New York: Scribner's, 1936), 13. Subsequently this source is referred to as *IPR*.

63. *IPR*, 20.

64. *IPR*, 12.

65. While one has to accept that his philosophy lacks any specific theory of symbol or language, I would suggest that Santayana's broad and humanistic understanding of the term "symbol" might be considered in reference to Ernst Cassirer's comprehensive theory of *expressive* and *representative* symbolic meanings being a natural outcome of the activity of *animal symbolicum*. See: Ernst Cassirer, *An Essay on Man: An Introduction to a Philosophy of Human Culture* (New Haven, CT: Yale University Press, 1944): 26–27.

66. This remains open for discussion, as long as the reality of spiritual life is reflected in the realm of truth. The intuition of an invariant ego, and we surely do enjoy such an intuition, finds its reflection there.

67. Lachs, "Santayana's Philosophy of Mind," 258.
68. *RB*, 258.
69. *APS*, 586.
70. Lachs, "Santayana's Philosophy of Mind," 258.
71. Sprigge, *Santayana. An examination of his Philosophy*, 10.
72. Sprigge, 97.
73. Lachs, "Santayana's Philosophy of Mind," 270. See also: Lachs, *George Santayana*, 12–13.
74. Lachs, *George Santayana*, 13.
75. Lachs, 91.
76. This subchapter is a revised version of the following article written by me: Katarzyna Kremplewska, "The Authorship of Life: Narrative and Dramatic Strategies of Sustaining Self-Integrity in Santayana's Thought," *Overheard in Seville. Bulletin of the George Santayana Society*, no. 33 (Fall 2015): 56–67.
77. Lachs, *George Santayana*, 45.
78. Lachs, 48–49.
79. See: *RB*, 338.
80. Sprigge, *Santayana. An examination of his Philosophy*, 101.
81. See: *OAA*, 86–94.
82. Flamm, "Free Will for a Materialist," 17–42.
83. George Santayana, *Dominations and Powers* (New York: Scribner's, 1951), 46. Subsequently I refer to this source as *DP*.
84. *DP*, 53.
85. Flamm, "Free Will for a Materialist," 28–29.
86. Flamm, 25.
87. Flamm, 26.
88. Flamm, 32–33.
89. I assume a broad and liberal understanding of action as proposed by Max Weber (and after him by Paul Ricoeur). Action embraces the whole range of attitudes, including refraining from action, as long as the subject identifies them as his own ("attaches a subjective meaning to them"). See: Max Weber, *Economy and Society: An outline of interpretive sociology*, vol. 1 (Berkeley and Los Angeles: University of California Press, 1978), chap. 1.
90. *APS*, 542. My emphasis.
91. *RB*, 81.
92. *RB*, 102, 103.
93. *RB*, 296.
94. *RB*, 622.
95. *OAA*, 91.
96. In Ricoeur's account, of which I use here only very few, selected elements, action, as identity-shaping, is deeply embedded in the human, moral and ethical realm, where the ideas of otherness and seeking for recognition play a vital part. Santayana, in turn, articulates reflection and the margin of *redundancy* allowed for by one's spirituality. A greater emphasis is put on the contemplative mode of existence and the possibility of partial detachment.

97. *OAA*, 64.
98. *OAA*, 162.
99. I am using the terms "hermeneutic" and "dramatic" interchangeably, suggesting a quasi-equation which is legitimate in the light of the narrative theory proposed by Paul Ricoeur. See: Paul Ricoeur, *Time and Narrative*, vol. 1 (Chicago: University of Chicago Press, 1990). To be precise, "hermeneutic" is a broader term, "dramatic" denotes a variety of hermeneutic mode.
100. *SSMMI*, 50–51.
101. *RB*, 387, 388.
102. *RB*, 97.
103. *RB*, 98.
104. *RB*, xxx.
105. *RB*, xxxi.
106. RB, xxxi.
107. *RB*, xxxii.
108. *RB*, xxxii.
109. Michael Brodrick, "Transcending Means and Ends Near the End of Life," in *George Santayana at 150*, in: *Santayana at 150. International Interpretations*, ed. Matthew.C. Flamm, Giuseppe Patella, and Jennifer Rea (Lanham MD: Lexington Books, 2013), 241.
110. *RB*, 5.
111. *RB*, 335.
112. *RB*, 335.
113. *RB*, 335.
114. *RB*, 336–37.
115. *Encyclopedia Britannica*.
116. *LR*, 441.
117. *RB*, 296.
118. *OAA*, 105.
119. *OAA*, 106.
120. *OAA*, 128.
121. *OAA*, 122.
122. *OAA*, 150.
123. This issue is tackled extensively by Paul Ricoeur in vol. 1 of *Time and Narrative*.
124. *RB*, 387–88.
125. *RB*, 298.
126. *RB*, 389.
127. *RB*, 334.

Chapter 3

1. *RB*, 747. It is also interesting to compare it to a Nietzschean idea of a bodily transfiguration: "the most sensual functions are finally transfigured by a

symbol-intoxication of the highest spirituality: they experience a kind of deification of the body in themselves." See: F. Nietzsche, *The Will to Power*, ed. and trans. by Walter Kaufman (New York: Random House, 2011), bk. 4, 1051. Nietzsche speaks here of an alternative for the "saintly" *vita contemplativa*, which in his eyes always involved a contempt for the body. The distinction is, of course, relevant also to Husserl's distinction between *Leib* (Body) and *Körper* (body).

2. *APS*, 154.
3. *APS*, 504.
4. *APS*, 524.
5. *RB*, 555.
6. Scott, *The Poetics of Belief*, 95.
7. *APS*, 525–26.
8. It is a being cut off from real time by consciousness. It is symptomatic of Santayana, a reader of Freud, that he never accepted the idea of subconscious, he accepted only the alternative conscious–not conscious.
9. Mari Ruti, *The Singularity of Being: Lacan and the Immortal Within* (New York: Fordham University Press, 2012), 14.
10. *OS*, 143–44.
11. A great elucidation of this topic in terms of epiphenomenalism has been offered by Angus Kerr-Lawson in: "Santayana's Epiphenomenalism," *Transactions of the Charles S. Peirce Society* 22, no. 4 (Fall 1986): 217–432. "Does spirit not perhaps become efficacious just by enhancing the clarity and precision of our interactions with the environment?" Santayana, notes Kerr-Lawson, wouldn't exclude "the possibility of an evolutionary advantage to consciousness, which happens to arise in organisms that evolve spirit." See: Kerr-Lawson, "Santayana's Epiphenomenalism," 424.
12. This reduction, by the way, was Santayana's main point in his polemic with Nietzsche.
13. Flanagan, *Consciousness*, 45.
14. Persons deprived of normal p-consciousness of their visual field are asked to report what they see/are aware of and to initiate actions. Despite their lack of awareness (consciousness p), if pressed to initiate some action toward objects in the field (like grabbing a glass of water), they perform better than expected. Without an external pressure, however, even if thirsty, they do not initiate this action. See: Flanagan, *Consciousness*, 140–41.
15. Flanagan, *Consciousness*, 149.
16. See: Trzópek, *Na tropach*, 140–43. The idea of *authorship emotion* was put forth by Wegner in *The Illusion of Conscious Will* (Cambridge, MA: MIT Press, 2002).
17. Jessica Wahman, "Corpulent or a Train of Ideas? Santayana's critique of Hume," *Overheard in Seville. Bulletin of the Santayana Society*, no. 25 (Fall 2007): 1–10.
18. Jessica Wahman, "Santayana, Identity Theory, and the Mind-Body Problem," 34–45, in *Under any Sky: Contemporary Readings of George Santayana*, eds. Matthew.C. Flamm and Krzysztof P. Skowroński (Cambridge: Cambridge Scholars,

2007), 40. Let me note at this point that Santayana seems to have bracketed the classical body-mind dualism and the dualism implied by his ontology is of a different sort.

19. Wahman, "Santayana, Identity Theory, and the Mind-Body Problem," 40. Santayana's definition for "is" of identity is as follows: "*Is* applied to spirit or to any of its modes, accordingly means *is actual*; in other words, exists not by virtue of inclusion in the dynamic, incessant, and infinitely divisible flux of nature, but by its intrinsic incandescence, which brings essences to light and creates the world of appearance." See: OS, 209.

20. John Searle, *Mind. A Brief Introduction* (Oxford: Oxford University Press, 2004), 124. My emphasis.

21. *APS*, 512.

22. *RB*, 96.

23. *RB*, 96.

24. Lachs, *George Santayana*, 53.

25. *APS*, 506.

26. John Lachs, "Moral Philosophy of George Santayana," in: *Mind and Philosophers* (Nashville, TN: Vanderbilt University Press, 1987), 140.

27. *RSTV*, 68.

28. For "no analysis can threaten the reality of appearances *as appearances*." See: *APS*, 500.

29. Brodrick, "Transcending Means and Ends," 244.

30. Brodrick, 243.

31. It is difficult to resolve the question of whether Santayana may have defended some sort of epiphenomenal relation of acts of consciousness to organic life. The thinker used a couple of times the term "epiphenomenal" but its meaning is vague. Moreover, at some points his views seem contradictory to this doctrine. It can hardly be labeled as epiphenomenalism under the criteria of contemporary classification. A general direction of his philosophy of mind may well be compared to some contemporary doctrines of the embodied mind (like the one by Thomas Metzinger), combined with elements of nonreductive materialism like that of John Searle.

32. *BT*, 135.

33. Santayana's distinction of objective ideal realms contrasts him from Heidegger. However—if one sees Santayana's ontology as hypostatizing the planes of experience—this difference is minimized.

34. *POML*, 84. The significance of this difference between the two modes of thinking should not be overestimated, as emphasized by the thinker himself. Later, the "discovery" of the realm of essence will attest to the ontological unity of *all* conscious experience.

35. *POML*, 84.

36. Lachs, "Santayana's Philosophy of Mind," 262. My emphasis.

37. *OS*, 142.

38. *OS*, 143–44.

39. All quotations in this paragraph: *POML*, 65.
40. *POML*, 66.
41. *POML*, 65.
42. *POML*, 67.
43. Lachs, *George Santayana*, 81, 84.
44. *RB*, 166.
45. *RB*, 81.
46. *APS*, 505.
47. Thus, paradoxically, the ontological realms seem to justify the SOPM effect.
48. Krzysztof Michalski, *Zrozumieć przemijanie* [To Understand Passing Away] (Warsaw: Biblioteka kwartalnika Kronos, 2011), 113.
49. Michalski, 175.
50. *DL*, 154.
51. Ricoeur quotes from *Antigone*: "Many the wonders [deina] but nothing walks stranger [deinon] than man" and translates deinon as "formidable," and "oscillating between the admirable and the monstrous." See: *OAA*, 245.
52. *OS*, 140.
53. Santayana, in *Apologia Pro Mente Sua*, mentions two of his critics, Friess and Rosenthal, who, in his opinion, most rightly "hit the nail on the head," noticing that it is his materialism that best "serves his spiritual and intellectual emancipation (. . .) his freedom to confront the world." See: *APS*, 504.
54. *SiELS*, 127. My emphasis.
55. *SSMMI*, 357.
56. *SSMMI*, 374–75.
57. *SiELS*, 126–27. My emphasis.
58. Moreno, *Santayana the Philosopher. Philosophy as a Form of Life*, 5.
59. All quotes in this paragraph: Moreno, *Santayana the Philosopher. Philosophy as a Form of Life*, 3–5.
60. Heidegger, *Ontology. The Hermeneutics of Facticity*, 26. This passage refers specifically to the inauthenticity of self-interpretation mediated by public opinion, yet it uncovers the constitution and unsubstantiality of *Dasein*. The fear of nothingness resting in the gap between *Dasein* and its "realization" wasn't at all an existentialist novelty but was known, according to Heidegger, already to Sophocles.
61. *RB*, 253–54.
62. *BT*, 315.
63. *RB*, 307.
64. *DL*, 185.
65. *SiELS*, 139. As I mentioned previously, death means becoming equal to an event.
66. Hans Georg Gadamer, *Truth and Method* (London: Continuum, 2004), 350.
67. *OS*, 144.
68. *SiELS*, 263.
69. See for example: Heidegger, *Ontology. The Hermeneutics of Facticity*, 80.

70. *APS*, 514.
71. *SiELS*, 138.
72. *SiELS*, 139.
73. *SiELS*, 126–27. My emphasis.
74. On spiritual freedom see: Flamm, "Free Will for a Materialist," and Broderick, "Transcending Means and Ends."
75. *SiELS*, 134.
76. *SiELS*, 133. My emphasis.
77. *DL*, 40.
78. See for example: Theodor W. Adorno, *The Jargon of Authenticity* (Evanston, IL: Northwestern University Press, 1973). The idea of authenticity is criticized mostly as linked to hegemonic and essentialist discourses. But the way Santayana conceives of authenticity morally works towards opposite ends—toward a *self* free of fanaticism and egotism, and one not susceptible to manipulation. A great exposition of the ambiguity of the ideal of authenticity is to be found in Charles Taylor's *The Ethics of Authenticity* (Cambridge, MA: Harvard University Press, 1991). Taylor claims that the contemporary, subjectivist "culture of authenticity"—paradoxically—is responsible for the deconstruction of its original ideal.
79. *RB*, 389.
80. *SiELS*, 130.
81. The engagement in life manifests itself, among others, through the activity of valuating, establishing ideals, and making choices, notices Charles Padron. Values, then "are a rational-sentient expression of an individual trying to be authentically what s/he is." *RSTV*, 38. Once the notion of authenticity comes into question, another idea, the Socratic postulate of knowing oneself appears. Padron quotes from an early letter of Santayana (1886) to another Harvard student: "It isn't at all a question of what you can accomplish; it is only a question of what attitude you are going to take, what sort of things you are going to attend to." See: *RSTV*, 45.
82. "Wisdom lies in voluntary finitude" wrote Santayana in *RB*, 55.
83. *RB*, 747.
84. Heidegger, *Ontology. The Hermeneutics of Facticity*, 16.
85. This of course, has nothing in common with passing judgments on others people's lives and comparing which are more and which less worth living—a dangerous tendency which appeared, as noted by Giorgio Agamben, in the guise of biopolitical eugenic and "hygienic" tendencies in 1930s. Santayana's pluralism and defense of some liberal values would oppose totalitarian tendencies to govern "bare life."
86. *SiELS*, 133. My emphasis.
87. Johann Winckelmann, *Reflections on the painting and sculpture of the Greeks*, trans. Henry Fusseli (London: A. Millar, 1765), 273.
88. Winckelmann, *Reflections*, 278.
89. Arthur Schopenhauer, *The World as Will and Representation*, trans. E. F. J. Payne (New York: Dover, 1969), 224.

90. Arthur Schopenhauer, *The World as Will and Representation*, trans. Judith Norman, Alistair Welchman, and Christopher Janway (Cambridge: Cambridge University Press, 2010), 250.

91. Friedrich Schiller, *Letters upon the Aesthetic Education of Man*, trans. George Gregory, 360, <http://www.schillerinstitute.org/educ/aesthetics/Schiller_On_Grace_and_Dignity.pdf>

92. Schiller, *Letters*, 349. My emphasis.

93. *SiELS*, 128.

94. *SSMMI*, 374. Santayana otherwise was critical of Goethe as a forerunner of German romantic egotism with its tendency to misread antiquity by clothing in into an unnecessary pathos, or grandeur.

95. George Santayana, *The German Mind: A Philosophical Diagnosis* (New York: Scribner's 1915), 44–45.

96. Anthony Woodward, *Living in the Eternal. A Study of George Santayana* (Nashville, TN: Vanderbilt University Press, 1988), 20. It should not be mistaken for an endorsement of any easy slipping into *ars vivendi* in the post-modern sense of a "life-style." Santayana's idea of authenticity was also related to his uncompromised intellectual honesty, which was rather demanding in its individualizing if not socially alienating effect.

97. Thomas Alexander, "Santayana's Unbearable Lightness of being: Aesthetics as a Prelude to Ontology," *Overheard in Seville* (Fall, 1993): 1–10.

98. *RSTV*, 81. My emphasis.

99. They also explain the ground for the long-lasting misunderstanding accompanied by a certain aura of suspiciousness and scorn for the alleged "elitism" of Santayana, which in fact was an expression of his genuine attachment to classical philosophy but conveyed in a modern fashion—something hardly digestive, if not offensive, for a part of the intellectual Anglo-Saxon milieu of the time.

100. *SiELS*, 133–34.

101. *SiELS*, 133–34.

102. Heidegger wrote: "what, in which direction, to what extent and how it [Dasein] actually discovers and discloses is a matter of freedom but always in the limits of its thrownness." *BT*, 334.

103. Józef Tischner, *Spór o istnienie człowieka* [*An Argument About the Existence of Man*] (Cracow: Znak, 2011), 83.

104. *DL*, 44–45.

105. *DL*, 26–27, 37.

106. *DL*, 64.

107. *DL*, 176.

108. *DL*, 40.

109. *DL*, 123.

110. *DL*, 95. My emphasis.

111. *DL*, 152.

112. *DL*, 154. Philosophers had previously articulated the uncanniness of the very idea of an "I." Friedrich Schlegel for example called subject "Unding,"—"one nothing and anti-thing." See: Frank, *Świadomość siebie*, 147.

113. *DL*, 177.
114. *RB*, 845.
115. *RB*, 853.
116. All quotes in paragraph come from *RB*, 845–46.
117. *RB*, 847.
118. *RB*, 848.
119. *RB*, 848–49. My emphasis.
120. *RB*, 849.
121. George Santayana, *The Idea of Christ in the Gospels or God in Man* (New York: Charles Scribner's Sons, 1946), 30–31.
122. Santayana, 38.
123. *RB*, 852–53.
124. Santayana, *The Idea of Christ in the Gospels*, 65.
125. Scott, *The Poetics of Belief*, 100. Quoted after: George Santayana, *Platonism and the Spiritual Life* (New York: Charles Scribner's Sons, 1946), 81.
126. In particular I am referring here to the essay by Paul Ricoeur "Soboność w zwierciadle Pisma" ["The Self in the mirror of the Scriptures"], in *Miłość i sprawiedliwość* [*Love and Justice*] (Cracow: Universitas, 2010).
127. *RB*, 852–53. My emphasis.
128. *RB*, 853.
129. Ricoeur, "Soboność w zwierciadle Pisma," 69.
130. "Now in verbal sense, and in respect to popular religion that thinks of God as the creator of the world and the dispenser of fortunes, my philosophy is atheistic" (*RB*, 838).
131. *RB*, 854.
132. Paul Tillich, "Christianity without Paul," in: *The Nation*, October 12, 1946, 412–13.

Chapter 4

1. This chapter is based on the author's translation of her article in Polish: Katarzyna Kremplewska, "Życie jako insynuacja w ujęciu Henri Bergsona i George'a Santayany" [Life as insinuation according to Henri Bergson and George Santayana], *Diametros*, no. 52 (2017): 47–63.
2. J. B. G. Dusmenil, *Latin Synonyms with Their Different Significations and Examples Taken from the Best Latin Authors* (London: R. Taylor, 1809).
3. Henri Bergson, *Creative Evolution*, trans. Arthur Mitchell (Boston: University Press of America, 1911), 70–71.
4. Gilles Deleuze, *Bergsonism*, trans. Hugh Tomlinson and Barbara Habberjam (Cambridge, MA: MIT Press, 1988), 104.
5. Bergson is clear about it when he writes: "Our present is the very materiality of our existence, that is to say, a system of sensations and movements, and nothing else." In: Henry Bergson, *Matter and Memory*, trans. Nancy Margaret Paul

and W. Scott Palmer (London: George Allen and Unwin, 1911), 178. Subsequently I refer to this book as *MM*.

6. Leszek Kołakowski, introduction to *Ewolucja Twórcza* by Henri Bergson, trans. Piotr Kostyło and Krzysztof Skorulski (Cracow: Homini, 2007), 3.

7. Kołakowski, 6. My emphasis.

8. Barbara Skarga, *Czas i trwanie. Studia o Bergsonie* [Time and Endurance. A Study on Bergson] (Warsaw: PWN, 2014), 376–77.

9. Bergson, *The Two Sources of Morality and Religion*, trans. R. Ashley Audra and Claudesley Brereton (London: Macmillan, 1935), 146.

10. Bergson, *The Two Sources*, 149.

11. Henri Bergson, *Henri Bergson. Key Writings*, eds. Keith Ansell Pearson and John O. Maoilearca (London, New York: Bloomsbury Academic, 2014), 191.

12. *MM*, 76.
13. *MM*, 163.
14. *MM*, 169.

15. Henri Bergson, *Time and Free Will: An Essay on the Immediate Data of Consciousness*, trans. F. L. Pogson (London: George Allen and Unwin, 1910), 209. For more on the relation of time and human freedom in Bergson's philosophy see also my article: Katarzyna Kremplewska, "Time as the Source of Inalienable Freedom: Henri Bergson's 'Immunizing' the Self," *Eidos. Journal for Philosophy of Culture*, no. 1 (2017): 76–88, http://eidos.uw.edu.pl/time-as-the-source-of-inalienable-freedom-henri-bergsons-immunizing-the-self/

16. Bergson, *The Two Sources*, 118.
17. *OS*, 144.
18. Bergson, *Mind Energy*, in *Henri Bergson. Key writings*, 188.
19. Bergson, 182.
20. Bergson, 183.
21. Bergson, 182–83. My emphasis.
22. Bergson, 182. This is where mediation is visible. The present is mediated by memory and only in this way can we experience it consciously.
23. Bergson, *Mind Energy*, 183.
24. *MM*, 298.
25. *MM*, 29.
26. *MM*, 188.
27. *MM*, 279.

28. Interestingly, a historical link between the two thinkers not knowing each other personally (besides a possible exchange of glances during Bergson's lectures in Paris attended by Santayana) was their common friend and a source of inspiration—an American connection, so to say—William James.

29. But the major reason for the unfortunate "bankruptcy" of Bergson's doctrine at a certain point was his aspiration to compete with sciences. Santayana, instead, believed that the questions asked by philosophy belong to a different register, while philosophy, religion, and science should negotiate their positions as sources of knowledge.

30. *SiELS*, 138.
31. *BCAP*, 131.

Chapter 5

1. As exemplified by the following letters to Arthur Allen Cohen of February 9, 1948, and to Richard Colton Lyon of August 1, 1949. See: William G. Holzberger, ed., *The Letters of George Santayana: Book Eight, 1948–1952* (Cambridge, MA: MIT Press, 2003), 20–21, 185–86.

2. Katarzyna Kremplewska, "Coping with Finitude: Santayana reading Heidegger," *Transactions of the Charles Sanders Peirce Society* 51, no 2, 225–65. This chapter is an expanded and revised version of the article, reprinted with the permission of Indiana University Press.

3. Marginalia in Santayana's personal copy of Martin Heidegger, *Sein und Zeit* (Halle: Max Niemer Verlag, 1931), 137. Microfilm. Consequently I will use the abbreviation *SZ* for this source.

4. *SZ*, 96.

5. Henry S. Levinson, *Santayana: Pragmatism, and the Spiritual Life* (Chapel Hill, NC, and London: University of North Carolina Press, 1992), 180.

6. Hodges and Lachs, *Thinking in the Ruins*, 50, 65.

7. See: letter to Rosamund Sturgis of August 1, 1947 in: William G. Holzberger, ed., *The Letters of George Santayana: Book Seven, 1941–1947* (Cambridge, MA: The MIT Press, 2003), 357. In fact Heidegger never considered himself an existentialist thinker.

8. See for example: Scott M. Campbell, *The Early Heidegger's Philosophy of Life* (New York: Fordham University Press, 2012), 36–37. See also: Sprigge, *Santayana. An Examination of his Philosophy*, 102–03.

9. Campbell, *The Early Heidegger's Philosophy of Life*, 181.

10. Hodges and Lachs, *Thinking in the Ruins*, 33.

11. Glenn Tiller, "Commonsense Ontology," *Transcactions of the Charles S. Peirce Society*, no. 45 (2009), 506.

12. Krzysztof Michalski, *Zrozumieć przemijanie* [To Understand Passing Away] (Warsaw: Biblioteka kwartalnika Kronos, 2011), 18.

13. *RB*, 551.

14. Martin Heidegger, *Being and Time*, trans. Joan Stambaugh (New York: SUNY, 1996), 33. Subsequently I will use the abbreviation *BT* for this source.

15. *POML*, 60.

16. "Playing" with different modes of being in Heidegger's case is related to, as McGrath notices, his early interest in the discussion of different meanings of the verb "to be" by Aristotle. See: S. J. McGrath, "*The Interpretive Structure of Truth in Heidegger*" *Analecta Hermeneutica*, no. 1 (May, 2009). Web: May 30, 2017. <http://journals.library.mun.ca/ojs/index.php/analecta/article/view/5>. There is an interesting analogy with Santayana's analysis of the same issue in: George Santayana, "Some Meanings of the Word 'Is,'" in *OS*: 189–213.

17. Tiller, "Commonsense Ontology," 506.

18. See letter to Daniel Cory of September 25, 1934 in Holzberger, ed., *The Letters of George Santayana: Book Five, 1933–1936*, 136.

19. *SZ*, 164.

20. *SZ*, 147, 164.

21. One might be tempted, then, to think of Heideggerian *being* as corresponding rather to the material flux of existence, particularly if understood according to the definition sometimes used by Santayana, namely: "passage from potentiality to act" (*RB*, 285) and with respect to its reflection in the realm of truth. This option, however, from a hermeneutic and phenomenological viewpoint, makes decisively less sense than the one put forward by Santayana.

22. *OS*, 111.

23. *OS*, 129.

24. *APS*, 501.

25. According to my reading, Santayana, typically of phenomenologically oriented thinkers, assumes experience—be it pre-reflective, non-verbal and no matter how vague—to have *some* quality and hence to be always conscious, while he explicitly denies the possibility of "sub-consciousness." There is only the non-conscious. For a relevant discussion see: *SSIFPP*, 12–13.

26. *BT*, 53.

27. *RB*, 307.

28. Sprigge, *Santayana. An examination of his Philosophy*, 44.

29. *SZ*, 38.

30. See for example: *POML*, 142, 151.

31. *BT*, 33–34.

32. By way of digression, one may consider a possible comparison of the Heideggerian indeterminate and undisclosed implied in the notion of "nothingness" with Santayana's "matter" (whenever treated as distinct from "substance").

33. *BT*, 34.

34. *SZ*, 228.

35. *BT*, 209.

36. *SZ*, 38, 230. See also: John McCormick, ed., *George Santayana's Marginalia: A Critical Selection, Book One* (Cambridge, MA: MIT Press, 2011), 338, 349.

37. Otherwise, the two are different concepts. For Santayana, an eternal realm reflecting all the essences ever embodied in the flux; for the Heidegger of *Sein und Zeit*, *aletheia*, a disclosure of *being* which on the ontic level of daily life is usually covered and may be merely partially revealed to *Dasein*, under the condition of a proper, temporal "tuning" with the *actuality of the moment*, possible in the light of one's own death as a horizon.

38. *SZ*, 138. Santayana remarked in the marginalia something about an "interesting transcendental turn given to the intent of mind in following the direction of bodily action. Your thought is turned a priori upon a world because it is the notice that one part of the world takes of another part." See: *SZ*, 87. Heidegger, after *Sein und Zeit*, indeed dealt with the question of *Dasein*'s embodiment. See: David Wood, *Thinking after Heidegger* (Cambridge: Polity Press, 2002), 99.

39. *SZ*, 15.
40. *SZ*, 64.
41. *SZ*, 63–64, 124. The editor of the two volumes of the *Marginalia* (John McCormick, MIT Press) quotes here a passage in which Santayana explains his usage of the traditional term "matter" as meant to emphasize its ontological function. His choice of "matter' instead of a more 'fashionable' term as "the realm of event," "space-time," or simply "nature," is meant to "distinguish in this vast flood of existence the planes and qualities of reality which it contains." See: John McCormick, ed., op. cit., 339, and George Santayana, *Realms of Being*, vol. XIV, Triton Edition (1937), 183.
42. *SZ*, 124.
43. *SZ*, 76. In one of his marginal notes Santayana identifies "Sorge" as "Concern or care: the primary connection of spirit with flesh." (*SZ*, 57). Heidegger, who did not use the dualism also pointed to it as the origin of the idea of *care*, mentioning Seneca as the first who articulated it. (*BT*, 185) Moreover, the distinction of the realm of spirit leads Santayana to emphasize *care* as a result of bodily-spiritual way of experiencing the *self*. In Santayana this classical dualism is gone but still "matter" and "spirit" are its symbolical remnants. One could say they are hypostatical symbols of a certain inadequacy within conscious life, which is a source of tension. The fact that this tension is central to human experience opens the way to further discussion of semblance with Heideggerian "ontological difference." This discussion, however, cannot fail to confront the fact that Santayana operates with the concepts of "substance" and "matter"—both decisively rejected by Heidegger. One might speculate that Santayana's "matter"—as something radically alien to consciousness—corresponds to Heideggerian "nothingness," particularly in the context of embodiment and matter-of-factness pertaining to the *self*.
44. *SZ*, 69.
45. *SZ*, 71.
46. This association made by Santayana becomes particularly meaningful in the light of Heidegger's interpretation of Aristotle's psychology. Human being, potentially determined by the psyche, is actualized by means of hermeneutic activity, which occurs in the element of intelligibility, the two co-dependent aspects of which are *logos* and *eidos*. *Logos* addresses beings in an essential way. Any substance may become visible to a human being only under the aspect of *eidos*. There is a static aspect of thinghood in Aristotle's concept of *theorein*, but Heidegger in his interpretation emphasizes the dynamic aspect of basic human activity—namely, orienting oneself in the world. In *Being and Time*, Dasein is oriented toward beings and understands them via their *being*. Santayana, then, trying to equate his realm of essences with *being* is, perhaps unconsciously, addressing possible inspirations of Heidegger. See: *BCAP*, 24, 137, 153.
47. This kind of awareness had previously been characterized by Santayana as knowledge of fact or symbolic knowledge (which informs of the relations of the embodied *self* to its dynamic environment) and contrasted with literal knowledge or intuition of essences. Existential priority is ascribed to the former. See "Symbolic Knowledge," 108–150, in: *OS*, 129. In the same essay Santayana criticizes the classical

notion of "content of consciousness" for substituting "inclusion for pointing" (OS, 113). What differs his standpoint from that of Heidegger is his stronger realistic assumption of mind and things being "separate existences" and his understanding of phenomena mainly as signs of the outside world, the connection between both being conventional. Nevertheless, having said that, Santayana emphasizes that those existences, whatever their intrinsic nature may be, matter for us mainly "for what they do not for what they are." In this theory of transitive knowledge, man being *a creature of circumstance* (DL, 185) looks "in order to understand, not merely to see." And understanding "reveals to us . . . a possibility, a dramatic figment," which suggests some ways to act and behave (OS, 143–44). Otherwise important to Santayana, at this point of his considerations, contemplation of essences, is a redundant activity related to a "sensuous idolatry" proper to man.

48. See letter to Richard Colton Lyon of August 1, 1949 in Holzberger, ed., *The Letters of George Santayana: Book Eight, 1948–1952*, 186.

49. Interestingly, it was only in his lectures of the 1950s–'60s that Heidegger developed a phenomenology of the body and the idea of "incarnate life"—"das Leiben." See for example: Jarosław Jagiełło, *Niedokończony Spór o Antropologię Filozoficzną (Heidegger-Plessner)* [An Unfinished Argument About Philosophical Anthropology (Heidegger-Plessner)] (Warsaw: Wydawnictwo IFiS PAN, 2011), 297.

50. SZ, 98.

51. SZ, 111. Similar criticism was directed at Heidegger's doctrine of *Dasein* by some other thinkers, most notably by Helmuth Plessner. For an in-depth study of this polemic see: Jarosław Jagiełło, *Niedokończony Spór*.

52. BT, 305.

53. BT, 305.

54. SSIFPP, 11.

55. RB, 285.

56. BT, 133, 159.

57. SZ, 221.

58. BT, 336.

59. BT, 296.

60. All quotes in this paragraph: BT, 296–97.

61. Interestingly, both thinkers translate the so-called four grounds of Aristotle into transcendental categories of the mind. Heidegger reduces them to three principles of understanding and constituting beings, which occurs as part of the temporalizing transcendence of *Dasein*: possibility, basis, and account. These are the ways in which beings are *grounded* in the projected world and ontic truth is made possible. See: Heidegger, "On the Essence of Ground," 131–34. Santayana speaks of three transcendental principles—existence, essence, and harmony, as revealed by and originating from the three "rays" of human mind—senses, logic, and desire. There is yet another principle, which corresponds to the intrinsic nature of reality—material change or movement—and it is reflected in memory. See: DL, 239–41.

62. Martin Heidegger, *Phenomenological Interpretations of Aristotle: Initiation Into Phenonmenological Research*, trans. Richard Rojcewicz (Bloomington: Indiana University Press, 2001), 68.

63. Heidegger, 72.
64. Heidegger, 76.
65. Heidegger, 70.
66. *BCAP*, 131.
67. *BCAP*, 131.
68. *RB*, 338.
69. *RB*, 341.
70. *SZ*, 57.
71. Wood, *Thinking after Heidegger*, 32.
72. Wood, 22.
73. Wood, 32.
74. Wood, 21. According to Heidegger, *animal rationale*, being Latin translation of Aristotle's *zoon logon ehon*, wasn't simply false but began a reductive tendency to interpret human being in terms of thinghood.
75. See: *POML*, 162.
76. *RB*, 844.
77. *RB*, 844–45.
78. *RB*, 845.
79. Preface to *DL*, n.p.
80. By the way, this is something he shared with Nietzsche. See Friedrich Nietzsche, *Twilight of the Idols*, trans. Duncan Large (Oxford: Oxford University Press, 1998), 28.
81. *BCAP*, 135.
82. Martin Heidegger, "On the Essence of Ground," 96–129, in: William McNeill, ed., *Pathmarks* (Cambridge: Cambridge University Press, 1998), 123.
83. Heidegger, "On the Essence of Ground," 134.
84. Jagiełło, *Niedokończony spór*, 325.
85. *POML*, 155.
86. *SSIFPP*, 70.
87. Heidegger, "On the Essence of Ground," 91.
88. Lionel Trilling, "That Smile of Parmenides Made Me Think," in: *A Gathering of Fugitives* (Boston: Bacon Press, 1956), 160–61.
89. For an interesting discussion on the *self* in Santayana, see: Moreno, *Santayana the Philosopher. Philosophy as a Form of Life*, 87–88. Moreno seems to assume a somewhat different meaning of the *self* than I do—namely that of an "ego" assuming identities and that of "a person at all her/his stages of life," while I tend to articulate a hermeneutic perspective of self-interpreting life.
90. *SZ*, 134.
91. Heidegger, "On the Essence of Ground," 107–08.
92. Heidegger, 128.
93. Heidegger, 91.
94. Martin Heidegger, "Introduction to 'What is Metaphysics,'" 277–90, in *Pathmarks*, trans. Walter Kaufmann, ed. William McNeill (Cambridge: Cambridge University Press, 1998), 286. It should be noted that understanding is in its deepest sense temporal.

95. Heidegger, "On the Essence of Ground," 126.
96. Heidegger, 134.
97. Heidegger, 126–27. My emphasis. It is worth noting that the way Heidegger defines concepts here logically leads to the conclusion that *Dasein*, as transcendence, is itself freedom (of human being). Dasein is free to the world it has projected and *via* this world to itself. The world is not that of unlimited possibilities but that of *possibilities of itself* which are open in this world for *Dasein*, which is *thrown and factical*. A kind of finite transcendence or transcendence with immanence, tightly connected with temporality is implied here.
98. *RB*, 185.
99. Moreno, *Santayana the Philosopher. Philosophy as a Form of Life*, 30.
100. *POML*, 158.
101. *POML*, 201.
102. *POML*, 65.
103. *RB*, 844–46.
104. *RB*, 748.
105. Lachs, *George Santayana*, 81–84.
106. Levinson, *Pragmatism and the Spiritual Life*, 210–13.
107. *SAF*, 50.
108. *POML*, 156–57.
109. Moreno, *Santayana the Philosopher. Philosophy as a Form of Life*, 55–56.
110. *RB*, 337.
111. *RB*, 337–38.
112. *RB*, 338.
113. See for ex ample: *POML*, 152.
114. *BT*, 126–31.
115. *BT*, 127.
116. *BT*, 296.
117. *BT*, 128.
118. *BT*, 128.
119. *BCAP*, 131.
120. *BCAP*, 21.
121. *BCAP*, 69.
122. *BCAP*, 113.
123. *BCAP*, 120.
124. *BCAP*, 132.
125. The situation may be viewed as a reversal and naturalization of the Kantian problem of the inaccessibility of the "I think" discussed in the first chapter.
126. *RB*, 564. My emphasis. Compare with the results of Edmund Husserl's "phenomenological analysis of the body (. . .) [which reveals] its peculiar two-sidedness. My body is given to me as an interiority, a volitional structure, and as a dimension of sensing, but it is also given as a visually and tactually appearing exteriority" (*SSIFPP*, 156).

127. *SZ*, 135.
128. *RB*, 736.
129. Heidegger, *Phenomenological Interpretations of Aristotle: Initiation Into Phenonmenological Research*, 77.
130. Heidegger, 76.
131. Heidegger, 91.
132. Heidegger, 98.
133. Heidegger, 92.
134. Campbell, *The Early Heidegger's Philosophy of Life*, 160.
135. *BCAP*, 53.
136. *BCAP*, 57.
137. *DL*, 106.
138. *BCAP*, 57.
139. *BCAP*, 46.
140. *BCAP*, 51.
141. Campbell, *The Early Heidegger's Philosophy of Life*, 180. See also: *BCAP,* 75. Due to the fact that humanity is defined by Aristotle in terms of *logos*, it is constantly endangered by what logos involves: falseness, deception, sophistry, idle chatter. The idea is developed in *Being and Time* under the concept of *Gerede* and "the They."
142. *BCAP*, 192.
143. *BCAP*, 184.
144. *BCAP*, 187.
145. *BCAP*, 184.
146. *BCAP*, 165.
147. *BCAP*, 126.
148. *BCAP*, 58.
149. *BCAP*, 51–52.
150. For a remark about the double meaning of the term "present" see: *POML*, 142.
151. See letters to Corliss Lamont of March 5, 1935 and to August Wagner of January 17, 1937 in William G. Holzberger, ed., *The Letters of George Santayana: Book Five 1933–1936*, 178 and *Book Six 1937–1940*, 7.
152. See the motto for this chapter—Santayana's words: "Wisdom rests in voluntary finitude."
153. Jagiełło, *Niedokończony spór*, 162.
154. *RB*, 736.
155. *SZ*, 259, 175.
156. *BT*, 235–36.
157. *BT*, 164.
158. *SZ*, 174.
159. *SZ*, 169.
160. Both alternatives: distraction/union and inauthenticity/authenticity can be said to be examples of the influence of the Platonic and the Christian

tradition. Jagiełło traces the Heideggerian notion of *ruinance* and his emphasis on individualistic introspection back to St. Augustin and Luther. See: Jagiełło, *Niedokończony spór*, 173, 329.

161. See: *The Letters of George Santayana: Book Five, 1933–1936*, 301.
162. Letter to Corliss Lemont of March 5, 1935, in Holzberger, ed., *The Letters of George Santayana: Book Five 1933–1936*, 178.
163. *RB*, 339.
164. *SZ*, 125.
165. *RB*, 341.
166. *SZ*, 131.
167. *SZ*, 137.
168. Letter to Daniel Cory of October 13, 1933 in W. G. Holzberger, ed., *The Letters of George Santayana: Book Five 1933–1936*, 55.
169. *SiELS*, 139.
170. Hodges and Lachs, *Thinking in the Ruins*, 95.
171. Michalski, *Zrozumieć przemijanie*, 70–71. What is interesting here, is that the mood corresponding to an authentic being oneself is for Heidegger the "peace of the soul" (*BT*, 449).
172. *SZ*, 134.
173. *SZ*, 117–18.
174. *SZ*, 119.
175. *SSIFPP*, 160–61.
176. *SZ*, 125.
177. *SZ*, 129.
178. *SZ*, 223.
179. *SZ*, 172.
180. *RB*, 748.
181. *RB*, 702.
182. Letter to Corliss Lamont of March 5, 1935, in Holzberger, ed., *The Letters of George Santayana: Book Five 1933–1936*, 178.
183. Letter to Arthur Allen Cohen of February 9, 1948, Holzberger, ed., *The Letters of George Santayana: Book Eight, 1948–1952*, 20–21.
184. Campbell, *The Early Heidegger's Philosophy of Life*, 218.
185. Flamm, "Free Will for a Materialist," 28–29.
186. *SZ*, 84.
187. *SZ*, 145.
188. Both quotations in this paragraph come from: *SZ*, 311–12.
189. *SZ*, 234.
190. *SZ*, 261.
191. Heidegger, "On the Essence of Ground," 129–30.
192. *SZ*, 174–75.
193. *SZ*, 172.
194. *SZ*, 173.

Chapter 6

1. Some of the ideas developed in this chapter appeared for the first time in an article in Polish: Katarzyna Kremplewska, "Tragiczność a duch w ujęciu Santayany" [The tragic and the spirit in Santayana's thought] *Przegląd Religioznawczy*, 2/248 (2013): 63–75.

2. For a respective analysis in a more antiquity-oriented context see an insightful and meticulous study devoted exclusively to Santayana and the notion of the tragic by Charles L. Padron—*RSTV* ("Reflections on Santayana and Tragic Value").

3. Søren Kierkegaard, "Ancient Tragedy's Reflection in the Modern," in *Either/Or: A Fragment of Life*, trans. Alastair Hannay (London: Penguin Books, 1992).

4. George Santayana, "Hamlet," in: Norman Henfrey ed., *Selected Critical Writings of George Santayana* (Cambridge: Cambridge University Press, 1968). Consequently this source will be referred to as *HA*.

5. Jaspers means a man whose existence is "in each case (. . .) shipwrecked by the consistency with which he meets some unconditional demand." See: Karl Jaspers, "Basic Characteristics of the Tragic," in *Tragedy. Vision and Form*, ed. Robert W. Corrigan (San Francisco: Chandler, 1965), 51.

6. Martin Heidegger, *Introduction to Metaphysics*, trans. Gregory Fried and Richard Polt (New Haven, CT, and London: Yale University Press, 2014), 128–219.

7. *OAA*, 241.

8. *OAA*, 241.

9. This formula of my choice may to some extent overlap with Charles Padron's idea of the "tragic value." I agree with Padron that the tragic for Santayana is related to an individual *self* in the light of one's lifetime. As such, it assumes an element of self-reflection and of understanding, of taking a step back from "this unrehearsed (. . .) prizeless drama of biological enactment known to us as life." (*RSTV*, 3–4). In other words, to acknowledge the tragic requires a certain spiritual attitude, the source of which is the *self*, which, as I claim here, is inherently relational, dynamic, and temporally complex. On the other hand, if my reading of Padron is correct, I am not fully persuaded by his attribution of an "overarching tragic world view" to Santayana, particularly to the mature Santayana, who managed to synthesize two apparently divergent, dominant threads of his thinking—naturalism and idealism—nto one system of ontology. Padron, with the support of George Steiner's *Antigones*, rightly links "the tenacious, stubborn, lucid anthropocentrism" with the tragic worldview. Then, he equates the anthropocentrism with the refusal "of any and all casuistic (philosophical or religious) assuagements," and concludes that "individuals who have incorporated tragic value into their living orientation and attitude (. . .) accomplished nothing more than to adopt a brutal honesty vis-à-vis the facts." (*RSTV*, 24–25). Santayana at some occasions advocated an honest acceptance of facts but I find a reluctance toward what he called *fact-worship* to be a more prominent or representative *credo* of his philosophy. Precisely because of an

anthropocentrism of sorts, Santayana would often downplay *factum brutum* in favor of the faculty of imagination and a possible spiritual life. Positivistic recognition of brute facts, he says, is an "apathetic naturalism," in comparison with which "all the errors and follies of religion are worthy of indulgent sympathy." (*IPR*, 6) On the other hand, I couldn't agree more with Padron's remark that Santayana "always managed to discover within himself the spontaneous resolve to side with life and the living, against any cost" (p. 26). My claim is that the philosopher had overcome the tragic worldview both in his life and his philosophy by his high appreciation of the spiritual, clearly maintaining at the same time that there is a tragic *aspect* to existence. A difference in emphasis and vocabulary may be at play here, save for the fact that hardly a last word might be said in a discussion of such a vast topic. A thorough confrontation of my conclusions with those of Charles Padron is definitely beyond the scope of this dissertation, nevertheless, what I think to be the main difference in our interpretations will become clear in the discussion of Santayana's polemic with Nietzsche. Ultimately, I think Padron may be seeing in Santayana much more of the Nietzschean "human, all too human" tragicness than I do. Although I admit the presence of an important Nietzschean thread in his thinking, in the light of his opus magnum, *Realms of Being*, I am more inclined to highlight the thinker's debt to the Christian tradition, either in a secular or the so-called post-secular context.

10. William James, *The Varieties of Religious Experience* (New York: Routledge, 2004), 269.

11. Max Scheler, "O zjawisku tragiczności" [On the phenomenon of the tragic], trans. Roman Ingarden, in *O tragedii i tragiczności* [Of Tragedy and the Tragic].

12. Scheler, "O zjawisku tragiczności," 74.

13. Georg W. F. Hegel, *Phenomenology of Spirit*, trans. A.V. Miller (Delhi: Motilal Banarsidass, 1998), 443.

14. Hegel, *Phenomenology of Spirit*, 444.

15. Hegel, 443.

16. Hegel, 444.

17. Hegel, 446. My emphasis.

18. Hegel, 447. My emphasis.

19. Hegel, 468.

20. Georg W. F. Hegel, "From *The Philosophy of Fine Arts*," in *Tragedy. Vision and Form*, ed. Robert W. Corrigan, 428.

21. Hegel, "From *The Philosophy of Fine Arts*," 429.

22. Hegel, 430.

23. Hegel, 434.

24. Hegel, 433.

25. Hegel, 431–32.

26. Hegel, 434–35.

27. Hegel, 437.

28. Hegel, 439.

29. Hegel, 438.

30. Kierkegaard, "Ancient Tragedy's Reflection in the Modern," 168.
31. A. Schopenhauer, *The World as Will and Representation*, vol. 1 (New York: Dover Publications, 1969), 99.
32. Schopenhauer, *The World as Will and Representation*, 252.
33. Schopenhauer, 249–52.
34. Schopenhauer, 253.
35. Schopenhauer, 272.
36. Schopenhauer, 275.
37. Schopenhauer, 254.
38. Jaspers, "Basic Characteristics of the Tragic," 51.
39. See: Walter Benjamin, "Fate and Character," in: *Walter Benjamin: Selected Writings*, ed. Marcus Bullock and Michael W. Jennings (Cambridge, MA: Harvard University Press 1996), 1: 201–06.
40. George Santayana, *The Life of Reason* (New York: Scribner's, 1954), 78. Consequently this source is referred to as *LR*.
41. *LR*, 80.
42. *LR*, 83.
43. *LR*, 82–83.
44. *LR*, 83.
45. Bielik-Robson, *Na drugim brzegu nihilizmu*, 201.
46. Friedrich Nietzsche, *The Birth of Tragedy*, trans. D. Smith (Oxford: OUP, 2000), 59–60.
47. Nietzsche, *The Birth of Tragedy*, 59.
48. Nietzsche, 90.
49. Nietzsche, 90.
50. Nietzsche, 90.
51. Nietzsche, 75.
52. Nietzsche, 78.
53. In 1884 Nietzsche wrote: "I want to teach the idea that gives many the right to erase themselves—the great *cultivating* idea." See: Friedrich Nietzsche, *The Will to Power*, Walter Kaufman ed. and trans. (New York: Random House, 1968–2011), §1056, 544.
54. Nietzsche, *The Will to Power*, §1052, 543.
55. *GMPD*, 135. My emphasis.
56. *GMPD*, 47–48.
57. *GMPD*, 47–48.
58. Heidegger in *Nietzsche* explicitly identifies Nietzsche's thought as anthropomorphic metaphysics, although he also shows how mature Nietzsche tried to get rid of this tendency.
59. *TBT*, 26.
60. *GMPD*, 141.
61. See: Heidegger, *Nietzsche*, 373.
62. Buczyńska-Garewicz, *Człowiek wobec losu*, 124–30.
63. *SiELS*, 140.

64. *RB*, 161. Notwithstanding this opinion, Santayana was an admirer of Spinoza's philosophy and the author of the introduction to the first English translation of *Ethics*.

65. Gilles Deleuze, *Nietzsche*, trans. Bogdan Banasiak (Warsaw: Wydawnictwo KR, 2000), 29–30.

66. Deleuze, *Nietzsche*, 59–78.

67. *SiELS*, 134.

68. *GMPD*, 183.

69. Heidegger, *Nietzsche*, 562.

70. Buczyńska-Garewicz, *Człowiek wobec losu*, 145–52. Even though Hanna Buczyńska-Garewicz disagrees with Heidegger's reading, they seem to agree on this issue, the difference being that Heidegger made it a point of his critique addressed at Nietzsche's raising in fact an anthropomorphic and anthropocentric monument.

71. Deleuze claims that the idea of eternal return at some point in Nietzsche's work assumes the merit of selectivity, but hardly supports this idea with a concrete argument. See: Deleuze: *Nietzsche*, 42–44, 112. Even if Superman be an evidence of the selectivity of eternal return, the whole process of it is at least unclear. However, some clarification, I suppose, may be found in chapter 1 of *Beyond Good and Evil*. See: Friedrich Nietzsche, *Beyond Good and Evil*, trans. H. Zimmern (New York: Dover, 1997), I, §19, 13–14.

72. See: Buczyńska Garewicz, *Człowiek*, 110.

73. Deleuze, *Nietzsche*, 42, 70.

74. Deleuze, 95–96. Interestingly, Nietzsche, like Santayana, was a philosopher of *masks*. Deleuze calls his philosophy a "psychology" or "typology of masks." The will to power itself is "the power to create masks." But while in Santayana, masks are the existential expression of the psyche, the superficial *self* of Nietzsche is free to assume any mask in this parody of itself. See: Deleuze, *Nietzsche*, 61, 63.

75. See: Heidegger, *Nietzsche*, 604.

76. Heidegger, 65, 380.

77. Nietzsche rejected classical meanings of truth as more or less directly related to the Platonic idealism. The loss of faith in any sort of metaphysical reality and its replacement with the reality of becoming involved for him a radical redefinition of truth: "Truth is the kind of error without which a certain species of life could not live." See: Nietzsche, *The Will to Power*, §493, 272.

78. Heidegger, *Nietzsche*, 570.

79. Heidegger, 588.

80. Heidegger, 528.

81. Heidegger, 527.

82. *GMPD*, 155.

83. At this point a digression is needed in reference to Santayana's critique of Nietzschean philosophy as a whole. One must admit that Santayana was sometimes biased in his approach to other philosophers, especially when using selectively some aspects of their thought within a larger effort to advocate his own views. To some extent this is the case with Nietzsche. Santayana made generalizations which

allowed him to place Nietzsche within a larger context of German egotism. At the same time, though, his insights often do not miss the point, as I tried to show in confrontation with some other, more rigorous critics of the author of *Thus Spake Zarathustra*. Interestingly, some of Santayana's beliefs, particularly those related to his naturalism and atheism, make him more a partner than an adversary of Nietzsche. An example is the conviction about the illusionary nature of agency understood in terms of the Cartesian *Cogito*, and the intuition of the need to exorcise this kind of an over-blown "ego." Santayana would—at least to some extent—agree with Nietzsche saying in *Beyond Good and Evil* that we have grown accustomed to "deceive ourselves about the synthetic term "I" . . . to such an extent that he who wills believes firmly that willing *suffices* for action," and that making a decision implies "a necessity of effect." We are, then, deluded by a schematism based on a specific meaning of subjectivity and freedom of will, while ignoring the "affect" aspect of human will. See: Nietzsche, *Beyond Good and Evil*, chap. 1, §19, 13–14.

84. Theodor W. Adorno, Max Horkheimer, *Dialectic of Enlightenment: Philosophical Fragments*, trans. Edmund Jedphcott (Stanford, CA: Stanford University Press: 2002), 8.

85. Bruno Snell seems to share this opinion about Nietzschean interpretation of tragedy in: Bruno Snell, *The Discovery of the Mind*, trans. T. G. Rosenmeyer (New York: Dover Publications, 1982).

86. Karl Jaspers, *Rozum i egzystencja. Nietzsche a Chrześcijaństwo*, [Reason and Existence. Nietzsche and Christianity], trans. Czesława Piecuch (Warsaw: PWN, 1991), 222–23.

87. Eric Voegelin, "Nietzsche, Crisis and the War," in *Collected Works of Eric Voegelin, Vol. 10: Published Essays, 1940–1952*, ed. Ellis Sandoz (Columbia: University of Missouri Press, 2000), 138.

88. Pascal, *Pensees*, trans. Roger Ariew (Indianapolis, IN: Hackett, 2005), 59.

89. *OAA*, 69. My emphasis. Paul Ricoeur paraphrases Elizabeth Anscombe here.

90. All quotations in this paragraph: preface to *RB*, xii.

91. *RB*, 15.

92. *LR*, 477.

93. Tillich, "Christianity without Paul," 413.

94. George Santayana, *The Idea of Christ in the Gospels or God in Man* (New York: Scribner's, 1946), 266.

95. The subchapter "Between Spiritual Dissolution and the Invention of the Human" is a revised version of my text which appeared as: Katarzyna Kremplewska, "Between Spiritual Dissolution and the Invention of the Human: George Santayana and Harold Bloom on Hamlet and the Crisis of Agency," *Overheard in Seville. Bulletin of the George Santayana Society*, no. 35 (Fall 2017): 50–59.

96. For an extensive discussion of this topic, see: Bruno Snell, *The Discovery of the Mind* (New York: Dover Publications, 1982).

97. Albin Lesky, *Greek Tragedy*, trans. H. A. Frankfort (London: Ernest Benn, 1965), 30.

98. George Santayana, "The Absence of Religion in Shakespeare," in: *Selected Critical Writings of George Santayana*, 63. Consequently this source will be referred to as *ARS*.

99. George Santayana, *Platonism and the Spiritual Life* (New York: Scribner's; London: Constable, 1927), 42.

100. *IPR*, 3–4.

101. *ARS*, 71.

102. *ARS*, 66–67. My emphasis.

103. *SiELS*, 132.

104. Snell, 106–07.

105. *ARS*, 71. Santayana was a critic of modernity as expressive of the loss of unity and of discipline, which in his view was symptomatic of spiritual disintegration.

106. *ARS*, 71.

107. Alenka Zupančič, *The Odd One In. On Comedy* (Cambridge, MA: MIT, 2008), 176.

108. Zupančič, 175.

109. George Santayana, "Tragic Philosophy," in: *Selected Critical Writings of George Santayana*, op. cit., 219. Consequently this source will be referred to as: *TP*.

110. *TP*, 219.

111. Benjamin, "Fate and Character," 203.

112. *OAA*, 241.

113. This comes from a review by: Michiko Kakutani, " 'Shakespeare': The Vast Shakespearean Drama With All People as Players," *New York Times*, October 27, 1998.

114. Harold Bloom, *Shakespeare: The Invention of the Human* (New York: Riverhead Books, 1998).

115. *ARS*, 69.

116. George Santayana, "Hamlet," in: *Selected Critical Writings of George Santayana*, 128. Consequently this source will be referred to as *HA*.

117. Bloom, "Hamlet," in: *Shakespeare: the Invention of the Human*, 409.

118. *HA*, 130.

119. *HA*, 132.

120. *HA*, 143.

121. Bloom, "Hamlet," 405.

122. *HA*, 135.

123. Zupančič, *The Odd One In*, 160–61.

124. Bloom, "Hamlet," 400.

125. Bloom, 406.

126. *ARS*, 63.

127. *HA*, 131.

128. *HA*, 139, 136.

129. Bloom, "Hamlet," 406.

130. Bloom, 406.

131. *HA*, 142.

132. *HA*, 143.
133. Bloom, "Hamlet," 431.
134. Bloom, 430.
135. Agata Bielik-Robson, *Inna Nowoczesność. Pytania o Współczesną Formułę Duchowości*, 105.
136. Bielik-Robson, *Inna Nowoczesność*, 87–122. The author analyzes the connection between Bloom's conception of a strong subject/selfhood and his interpretation of Shakespeare.
137. Bloom, "Hamlet," 407.
138. Bloom, 412.
139. Bloom, 418.
140. Bloom, 412.
141. Bloom, 419. My emphasis.
142. Bloom, 409.
143. Bloom, 409.
144. Bloom, 410.
145. Bloom, 410.
146. Bloom, 410.
147. Bloom, 418.
148. Bloom, 429.
149. *TP*, 212.
150. Northrop Frye, "The Mythos of Autumn: Tragedy," in: *Tragedy. Vision and Form*, ed. Robert W. Corrigan, 105.
151. In particular Santayana's fiction—the novel *The Last Puritan: A Memoir in the Form of a Novel* (London: Constable 1935; New York: Scribner's, 1936), and his play: *Lucifer. A Theological Tragedy* (Chicago and New York: Herbert S. Stone, 1899), are of interest for the discussion of the tragic. Both have been analyzed in this context by Charles Padron.
152. Frye, "The Mythos of Autumn: Tragedy," 99.
153. Frye, 101.
154. Frye, 101.
155. *LR*, 441.
156. Jaspers, "Basic Characteristics of the Tragic," 43.
157. Jaspers evokes "tragic readiness" as a kind of awareness and passive attitude represented by Hamlet's "the readiness is all." See: Jaspers, "Basic Characteristics of the Tragic," 43.
158. *LR*, 81. By the way, Hugh W. Auden said that "Greek tragedy is the tragedy of necessity . . . , Christian tragedy is the tragedy of possibility." See: Hugh W. Auden, "The Christian Tragic Hero," in *The Complete Works of W. H. Auden: Prose* (Princeton, NJ: Princeton University Press: 2002), 2: 258.
159. Jaspers, "Basic Characteristics of the Tragic," 44.
160. Frye, "The Mythos of Autumn: Tragedy," 99.
161. Frye, 102. My emphasis. These intricacies involved in the issue of time and consciousness in tragedy and the tragic may probably be noticed already in the

semantic differences among the variety of Greek words standing for fate, justice, and necessity, such as *dike, tyche, ananke, moira, nemesis*.

162. Rebecca Bushnell, *Tragedy: A Short Introduction* (Malden, UK: Blackwell, 2008), 53.

163. *OAA*, 147.

164. A philosopher who clearly emphasized the mistake of fatalistic reduction, without naming it so, was Anthony Quinton. I am quoting here after Charles Padron, who evokes Quinton's views. Given an assumption about a radical contingency of human-made values set within and at the same time *against* an objective reality in itself (a sort of metaphysical realism), tragedy "asserts that value is contingent for its realization on the agency of men. The tragic view of life rules out both the kind of optimism represented by Hegel . . . and the kind of pessimism by Schopenhauer." See: *SNTV*, 27, after Anthony Quinton, "Tragedy," *Proceedings of the Aristotelian Society*, 34, suppl. vol. (1960), 162. In this value-oriented view of the tragic, human action may fall victim to contingency and its fulfillment is difficult due to the nature of finite knowledge, but it cannot be said to be doomed to failure from the outset. If the latter were the case, there would be no action or freedom in any proper sense and the whole concept of the tragic would assume a purely "mechanical" sense. Charles Padron, despite having attributed to Santayana a tragic worldview of sort, notes that the philosopher's early poetry, saturated with a certain premonition of the tragic, never "presages doom or misfortune." Santayana, and here my point is in accord with that of Padron, was not guilty of fatalistic reduction. "The individual as a spectator to his/her own tragic unfolding, and hence a participatory agent in tragic sensibility and consciousness, can recognize from a detached, vicarious perspective, in a self-referential manner, the unavoidability of the perishing of the finite." See: *RSTV*, 50. This type of tragic consciousness, though, does not imply an inevitable doom reigning over the realm of human action. What it does imply is that human life is informed by risk, uncertainty, limitations, fragility, and transitoriness.

165. Frye, "The Mythos of Autumn: Tragedy," 102.

166. Auden, "The Christian Tragic Hero," 259.

167. Frye, "The Mythos of Autumn: Tragedy," 102–03.

168. Frye, 103.

169. Frye, 104–05. My emphasis.

170. Frye, 104. My emphasis.

171. Frye, 106.

172. Bloom, "Hamlet," 400.

173. Jaspers, "Basic Characteristics of the Tragic," 44.

174. Max Horkheimer, *Eclipse of Reason* (London: Bloomsbury Academic, 2013), 1.

175. Horkheimer, *Eclipse of Reason*, 3.

176. *RSTV*, 40.

177. *IPR*, 13–14. My emphasis.

178. "Science is something human and its language should not be hypostatized." See: *APS*, 508.

179. All quotations in this paragraph come from: Leszek Kołakowski, *Obecność mitu* [The Presence of Myth] (Warsaw: Prószyński i Spółka, 1972), 14.
180. *IPR*, 13.
181. Benjamin, "Fate and Character," 205–06.

Chapter 7

1. This chapter is part of my research in the field of George Santayana's philosophy of culture and politics, project no. 2016/23/D/HS1/02274, sponsored by Narodowe Centrum Nauki (National Science Center, Poland).
2. I introduced the term "managing necessity" for the first time and discussed the idea in the context of contemporary terrorism in: Katarzyna Kremplewska, "Managing Necessity: Santayana on Forms of Power and the Human Condition," in *The Life of Reason in an Age of Terrorism*, ed. Charles Padrón and Krzysztof Piotr Skowroński (Leiden and Boston: Brill, 2018).
3. *DP*, 419.
4. Kremplewska, "Managing Necessity," 36.
5. John Gray, *Post-Liberalism* (New York and London: Routledge, 1993), 18.
6. Anthony Collins, preface to: *A Philosophical Inquiry Concerning Human Liberty*, London: 1717, iii. Web: Jan. 2, 2018, <https://archive.org/details/aphilosophicali00collgoog>
7. *DP*, 63.
8. *DP*, 159. "Reason" is described by Santayana as "not a new force in the physical world but a new harmony in vital forces."
9. *DP*, 69.
10. This is how I defined existence in: Kremplewska, "Managing Necessity," 32.
11. *DP*, 239.
12. *DP*, 238.
13. Moreno, *Santayana the Philosopher*, 104–05.
14. *DP*, 203.
15. *DP*, 15.
16. Aristotle influenced the ideas of Giorgio Agamben, see for example: Giorgio Agamben, *Homo Sacer: Sovereign Power and Bare Life*, trans. Daniel Heller-Roazen (Stanford, CA: Stanford University Press, 1998). The influence of Aristotle on Santayana and his conception of life has been tackled by John Lachs. See: John Lachs, *George Santayana*, 12–13.
17. *DP*, 82.
18. Foucault notes that somewhere around the sixteenth century the idea of *raison d'etat* is born and the government becomes interested in preserving itself rather than in facilitating salvation to the subjects. Michel Foucault, *The Birth of Biopolitics: Lectures at de Collége de France, 1978–1979*, trans. Graham Burhell (London: Palgrave Macmillan, 2008), 4–5.
19. This type of anthropology could be found, according to Santayana, in some of Shakespeare's works. See: *DP*, 40.

20. *DP*, 209.
21. See in particular Alexis de Tocqueville, chap. 6 "What sort of despotism democratic nations have to fear," in *Democracy in America*, vol. 2, trans. Henry Reeve, ed. Francis Bowen (Cambridge: Sever and Francis, 1863).
22. Tocqueville, 390.
23. *DP*, 184.
24. *DP*, 185.
25. See: Kremplewska, "Managing Necessity," 33.
26. Hegel, *Phenomenology of spirit*, 446.
27. *DP*, 53–54. By way of digression, the actual rule of militant scheme, as noted by Agamben in *Homo Sacer*, translates itself into the rule of militant law, where the "state of exception" tends to dominate life. This is where Santayana's contention about government being "potential war" is of importance.
28. *SiELS*, 207–08.
29. Gray, *Post-Liberalism*, 24.
30. *DP*, 178.
31. *DP*, 82.
32. *DP*, 179.
33. *DP*, 79. See also: Kremplewska, "Managing Necessity," 37.
34. *DP*, 120.
35. *DP*, 60. My emphasis.
36. *DP*, 181.
37. *DP*, 43.
38. Gray, *Post-Liberalism*, 21.
39. Gray, 22.
40. *DP*, 148.
41. *DP*, 209. My emphasis.
42. *DP*, 207.
43. Tocqueville, 97.
44. Florian Znaniecki, *Upadek Cywilizacji Zachodniej* [The Fall of Western Civilization] (Warsaw: WUW, 2013), 78–79. My emphasis.
45. Edmund Husserl, "Philosophy and the Crisis of European Man," in: *Phenomenology and the Crisis of Philosophy*, trans. Quentin Lauer (New York: Harper & Row, 1965), 149–92.
46. Husserl, "Philosophy and the Crisis of European Man," 192.
47. H. Amiel, *Amiel's Journal: The Journal Intime of Henri-Frederic Amiel*, trans. H. Ward (New York, 1890), 238.
48. *DP*, 72–73.
49. *DP*, 180.
50. *DP*, 180.
51. *DP*, 208. My emphasis.
52. Walter Benjamin, *The Arcades Project*, trans. Howard Eiland and Kevin McLaughlin (Cambridge, MA, and London: Harvard University Press, 1999), 467–68.

Benjamin understood barbarism differently than Santayana did—as part of the dialectics culture-barbarism—yet, the general idea of its latency in the very concept of culture and its tendency to reify and "utilize" the surviving fruits of a perishing culture are valid also for Santayana's understanding of the barbaric mode of being.

53. *DP*, 210. My emphasis.

54. *DP*, 208.

Bibliography

Primary Sources

Animal Faith and Spiritual Life: Previously Unpublished and Uncollected Writings by George Santayana with Critical Essays on His Thought. Edited by John Lachs and Shirley Lachs. Nashville, TN: Vanderbilt University Press, 1969.

Atoms of Thought: An Anthology of Thoughts from George Santayana. Edited by Ira D. Cardiff. New York: Philosophical Library, 1950.

Character and Opinion in the United States: With Reminiscences of William James and Josiah Royce and Academic Life in America. New York: Charles Scribner's Sons, 1920.

The Birth of Reason and Other Essays by George Santayana. Edited by Daniel Cory. New York: Columbia University Press, 1995.

Dialogues in Limbo. Ann Arbor: University of Michigan Press, 1957.

Dominations and Powers:Reflections on Liberty, Society, and Government. New York: Scribner's; London: Constable, 1951.

Egotism in German Philosophy. Volume 6 of *The Works of George Santayana.* Triton edition. New York: Scribner's, 1936.

The Essential Santayana. Edited by Santayana Edition. Bloomington: Indiana University Press, 2009.

The Genteel Tradition: Nine Essays by George Santayana. Edited by Douglas L. Wilson. Cambridge, MA: Harvard University Press, 1967.

George Santayana's Marginalia: A Critical Selection. Book One: Abell—Lucretius. Edited by John McCormick. Volume VI of *The Works of George Santayana.* Cambridge, MA, and London: MIT Press, 2011.

George Santayana's marginalia in his personal copy of *Sein und Zeit* by Martin Heidegger. Halle: Max Niemer Verlag, 1931. Microfilm.

The German Mind: A Philosophical Diagnosis. New York: Apollo Editions, 1968.

A Hermit of Carmel, and Other Poems. New York: Scribner's, 1901.

The Idea of Christ in the Gospels; or, God in Man: A Critical Essay. New York: Scribner's; Toronto: Saunders, 1946.

The Idler and His Works, and Other Essays. Edited by Daniel Cory. New York: Braziller, 1957.

Interpretations of Poetry and Religion. Volume 2 of *The Works of George Santayana*. Triton edition. New York: Scribner's, 1936.

The Last Puritan: A Memoir in the Form of a Novel. London: Constable, 1935; New York: Scribner's, 1936.

The Letters of George Santayana. Vol. 5 of *The Works of George Santayana*. Book One: *[1868]-1909* (2001), Book Two: *1910-1920* (2002), Book Three: *1921-1927* (2003), Book Four: *1928-1932* (2003), Book Five: *1933-1936* (2003), Book Six: *1937-1940* (2004), Book Seven: *1941-1947* (2006), Book Eight: *1948-1952* (2008). Edited by William. G. Holzberger, Herman, J. Saatkamp Jr., and Marianne S. Wokeck. Cambridge, MA: The MIT Press.

The Life of Reason: Or, The Phases of Human Progress. One-volume edition. New York: Scribner's, 1954.

Little Essays, Drawn From the Writings of George Santayana by Logan Pearsall Smith, With the Collaboration of the Author. New York: Scribner's; London: Constable, 1920.

The Letters of George Santayana. Edited by Daniel Cory. New York: Scribner's; London: Constable, 1955.

Lucifer: A Theological Tragedy. Chicago and New York: Herbert S. Stone, 1899.

The Middle Span. New York: Scribner's, 1945; London: Constable, 1947.

My Host the World. New York: Scribner's; London: Cresset Press, 1953.

Obiter Scripta: Lectures, Essays and Reviews. Edited by Justus Buchler and Benjamin Schwartz. New York: Scribner's; London: Constable, 1936.

Persons and Places: The Background of My Life. New York: Scribner's; London: Constable, 1944.

Philosophy of Santayana: Selections from the Works of George Santayana. Edited by Irwin Edman. New York: Scribner's, 1936.

Physical Order and Moral Liberty: Previously Unpublished Essays of George Santayana. Edited by John and Shirley Lachs. Nashville, TN: Vanderbilt University Press, 1969.

Platonism and the Spiritual Life. New York: Scribner's; London: Constable, 1927.

Realms of Being. One-volume edition. New York: Scribner's, 1942.

Scepticism and Animal Faith: Introduction to a System of Philosophy. Volume 13 of *The Works of George Santayana*. Triton edition. New York: Scribner's, 1936.

Selected Critical Writings of George Santayana. Edited by Norman Henfrey. 2 vols. Cambridge: Cambridge University Press, 1968.

The Sense of Beauty: Being the Outlines of Aesthetic Theory. New York: Scribner's; London: A. and C. Black, 1896.

Soliloquies in England and Later Soliloquies. New York: Scribner's; London: Constable, 1922.

Some Turns of Thought in Modern Philosophy: Five Essays. New York: Scribner's; Cambridge: Cambridge University Press, 2014.

Sonnets and Other Verses. Cambridge and Chicago: Stone and Kimball, 1894.

Three Philosophical Poets: Lucretius, Dante, and Goethe. Volume 6 of *The Works of George Santayana*. Triton edition. New York: Scribner's, 1936.

Winds of Doctrine: Studies in Contemporary Opinion. New York: Scribner's; London: Dent, 1913.

Secondary Sources

Adorno, Theodor, W. *The Jargon of Authenticity.* Evanston, IL: Northwestern University Press, 1973.
Adorno, Theodor, W., and Max Horkheimer. *Dialectic of Enlightenment. Philosophical Fragments.* Translated by Edmund Jedphcott. Stanford, CA: Stanford University Press, 2002.
Agamben, Giorgio. *Homo Sacer: Sovereign Power and Bare Life.* Translated by Daniel Heller-Roazen. Stanford, CA: Stanford University Press, 1998.
Agamben, Giorgio. *Homo Sacer: suwerenna władza i nagie życie.* Translated by Mateusz Salwa. Warsaw: Prószyński i S-ka, 2008.
Alexander, Thomas. "Santayana's Unbearable Lightness of being: Aesthetics as a Prelude to Ontology." *Overheard in Seville. Bulletin of the Santayana Society,* no. 11 (Fall 1993): 1–10.
Amiel, Henri. *Amiel's Journal: The Journal Intime of Henri-Frederic Amiel.* Translated by Humphry Ward. New York: A. L. Burt, 1890.
Aristotle. *Nicomachean Ethics.* Translated by M. Ostwald. Upper Saddle River, NJ: Prentice Hall, 1999.
Aristotle. *Metafizyka.* Translated by K. Leśniak. Warsaw: PWN, 2009.
Aristotle. *De Anima.* Translated by Mark Shiffman. Indianapolis, IN: Hackett, 2011.
Aristotle, *Poetics.* Translated by Samuel Hnery Butcher. London and New York: Macmillan, 1895.
Auden. Hugh, W. "The Christian Tragic Hero." In *Prose 1939–1948,* edited by Edward Mendelson, 258–61. Vol. 2 of *The Complete Works of W. H. Auden.* Princeton, NJ: Princeton University Press, 2002.
St. Augustine. "Soliloquies." In *The Happy Life; Answer to Sceptics; Divine Providence and the Problem of Evil; Soliloquies,* trans. Ludwig Schopp. Vol. 5 of *The Fathers of the Church.* Washington, DC: CUA Press, 1948.
Beckett, Lucy. *Wallace Stevens.* Cambridge, MA: Harvard University Press, 1984.
Benjamin, Walter. "Fate and Character." In *1913–1926,* edited by Marcus Bullock and Michael W. Jennings, 201–06. Vol. 1 of *Walter Benjamin: Selected Writings.* Cambridge, MA: Harvard University Press, 1996.
Benjamin, Walter. *The Arcades Project.* Translated by Howard Eiland and Kevin McLaughlin. Cambridge, MA, and London: Harvard University Press, 1999.
Bergson Henri. *Creative Evolution.* Translated by Arthur Mitchell. Boston: University Press of America, 1911.
Bergson, Henry. *Key Writings.* Translated by Keith Ansell Pearson and John Mullarcey. London and New York: Bloomsbury, 2014.
Bergson, Henry. *The Two Sources of Morality and Religion.* Translated by R. Ashley Audra and Claudesley Brereton. London: Macmillan, 1935.

Bergson, Henry. *Matter and Memory*. Translated by Nancy Margaret Paul and W. Scott Palmer. London: George Allen and Unwin, 1911.
Bergson, Henry. *Time and Free Will: An Essay on the Immediate Data of Consciousness*. Translated by F. L. Pogson. London: George Allen and Unwin, 1910.
Bielik-Robson, Agata. *Inna nowoczesność. Pytania o współczesną formułę duchowości*. [The Other Modernity: Questions Concerning the Future Prospects of Our Spiritual Life]. Cracow: Universitas, 2000.
Bielik-Robson, Agata. *Na drugim brzegu nihilizmu* [On the Other Side of Nihilism]. Warsaw: IFiS PAN, 1997.
Bloom, Harold. "Hamlet." In: *Shakespeare: the Invention of the Human*, 383–431. New York: Riverhead Books, 1998.
Boundas, Constantin F. "Translator's Introduction." In Deleuze, Gilles. *Empiricism and Subjectivity. An Essay on Hume's Theory of Human Nature*. New York: Columbia University Press, 1991.
Brodrick, Michael. "Transcending Means and Ends Near the End of Life." In *Santayana at 150. International Interpretations*. Edited by Matthew.C. Flamm, Giuseppe Patella, and Jennifer Rea, 241–48. Lanham, MD: Lexington Books, 2013.
Brodrick, Michael. "Blessings of a Spiritual Life." *The Transactions of Charles S. Peirce Society* 49, no. 4 (2009): 543–50.
Buczyńska-Garewicz, Hanna. *Człowiek wobec losu* [Man against Fate]. Cracow: Uniwersitas, 2010.
Buczyńska-Garewicz, Hanna. *Czytanie Nietzschego* [Reading Nietzsche]. Cracow: Universitas, 2013.
Burke, Kenneth. *A Grammar of Motives*. Berkeley: University of California Press, 1969.
Bushnell, Rebecca. *Tragedy: A Short Introduction*. Malden, UK: Blackwell, 2008.
Butler, Richard. *The Mind of Santayana*. Chicago: H. Regnery, 1955.
Butler, Richard. "George Santayana: Catholic Atheist." *Spirituality Today* 38 (Winter 1968): 319–36.
Campbell, Scott. M. *The Early Heidegger's Philosophy of Life*. New York: Fordham University Press, 2012.
Cassirer, Ernst. *An Essay on Man: An Introduction to a Philosophy of Human Culture*. New Haven, CT: Yale University Press, 1944.
Coleman, Martin. "On Celebrating the Death of Another Person." In *Santayana at 150. International Interpretations*, edited by Matthew C. Flamm, Giuseppe Patella, Jennifer Rea, 175–92. Lanham, MD: Lexington Books, 2013.
Collins, Anthony. *A Philosophical Inquiry Concerning Human Liberty*. London: 1717. Accessed July 10, 2017. https://archive.org/details/aphilosophicali00collgoog
Corrigan, Robert W., ed. *Tragedy. Vision and Form*. San Francisco: Chandler, 1965.
Cory, Daniel M. *Santayana: The Later Years, A Portrait with Letters*. New York: Braziller, 1963.
Crowell, Steven G. *Husserl, Heidegger, and the Space of Meaning*. Evanston, IL: Northwestern University Press, 2001.

Deleuze, Gilles. *Bergsonism*. Translated by Hugh Tomlinson and Barbara Habberjam. Cambridge, MA: MIT Press, 1988.
Deleuze, Gilles. *Empiricism and Subjectivity. An Essay on Hume's Theory of Human Nature*. Translated by Constantin V. Boundas. New York: Columbia University Press, 1991.
Deleuze, Gilles. *Nietzsche*. Translated by Bogdan Banasiak. Warsaw: Wydawnictwo KR, 2000.
Dennett, Daniel. "The *Self* as a Center of Narrative Gravity." In *Self and Consciousness: Multiple Perspectives*, edited by Frank S. Kessel, P. M. Cole, and D. L. Johnson, 257–88. Hillsdale, NJ: Erlbaum, 1992.
Derrida, Jacques. *The Problem of Genesis in Husserl's Phenomenology*. Translated by Marian Hobson. Chicago: University of Chicago Press, 2003.
Derrida, Jacques. *Voice and Phenomenon. Introduction to the Problem of the Sign in Husserl's Phenomenology*. Translated by Leonard Lawlord. Evanston: Northwestern University Press, 2011.
Derrida, Jacques. *Of Spirit. Heidegger and the Question*. Translated by Geoffrey. Bennington and Rachel Bowlby. Chicago and London: University of Chicago Press, 1991.
Dilworth, David. "Mediterranean Aestheticism, Epicurean Materialism." In *Santayana at 150. International Interpretations*. Edited by Matthew.C. Flamm, Giuseppe Patella, and Jennifer Rea, 53–87. Lanham, MD: Lexington Books, 2013.
Dilworth, David. "Santayana's Anti-Romanticism versus Stevens' New Romanticism." *Overheard in Seville. Bulletin of the Santayana Society*, no. 35 (Fall 2017): 32–49.
Dusmenil, J. B. G. *Latin Synonyms with Their Different Significations and Examples Taken from the Best Latin Authors*. London: R. Taylor, 1809.
Flamm, Matthew C., Giuseppe Patella, and Jennifer Rea, eds. *Santayana at 150. International Interpretations*. Lanham, MD: Lexington Books, 2013.
Flamm, Matthew C., Skowroński, Krzysztof, eds. *Under any Sky: Contemporary Readings of George Santayana*. Cambridge: Cambridge Scholars, 2007.
Flanagan, Owen. *Consciousness Reconsidered*. Cambridge, MA: MIT Press, 1992.
Foucault, Michel. *The Birth of Biopolitics: Lectures at de Collége de France, 1978–197*. Translated by Graham Burhell. London: Palgrave Macmillan, 2008.
Foucault, Michel. *Hermeneutyka podmiotu* [Hermeneutics of the Subject]. Translated by Michał Herer. Warsaw: PWN, 2012.
Frank, Manfred. *Świadomość siebie i poznanie siebie* [Self-consciousness and Self-knowledge]. Translated by Zbigniew Zwoliński. Warsaw: Oficyna Naukowa, 2002.
Frye Northrop. "The Mythos of Autumn: Tragedy." In *Tragedy. Vision and Form*, edited by Robert W. Corrigan, 99–113. San Francisco: Chandler, 1965.
Gadamer, Hans G. *Truth and Method*. London: Continuum, 2004.
Gray, John. *Post-Liberalism. Studies in political thought*. New York and London: Routledge, 1993.

Grossman, Morris. "Interpreting Interpretations." *Overheard in Seville. Bulletin of the Santayana Society*, no. 8 (Fall 1990): 18–28.
Gurczyńska-Sady, Katarzyna. *Człowiek jako słowo i ciało. W poszukiwaniu nowej koncepcji podmiotu* [Man as Word and Flesh. Searching for a New Conception of Subjectivity]. Cracow: Universitas, 2013.
Hegel, Georg W. F. *Phenomenology of Spirit*. Translated by A. V. Miller. Delhi: Motilal Banarsidass, 1998.
Heidegger, Martin. *Basic Problems of Phenomenology*. Translated by Albert Hofstadter. Indianapolis: Indiana University Press, 1988.
Heidegger, Martin. *Basic Concepts of Aristotelian Philosophy*. Translated by Robert D. Metcalf and Mark. B. Tanzer. Bloomington: Indiana University Press, 2009.
Heidegger, Martin. *Being and Time*. Translated by Joan Staumbaugh. New York: SUNY, 1996.
Heidegger, Martin. *Introduction to Metaphysics*. Translated by Gregory Fried and Richard Polt. New Haven, CT, and London: Yale University Press, 2014.
Heidegger, Martin. *Nietzsche*. 2 vols. Translated by Andrzej Gniazdowski, Piotr Graczyk, Wawrzyniec Rymkiewicz, Mateusz Werner, and Cezary Wodziński. Warsaw: PWN, 1999.
Heidegger, Martin. *Ontology. The Hermeneutics of Facticity*. Translated by John van Buren. Indianapolis: Indiana University Press, 1999.
Heidegger, Martin. *Pathmarks*. Edited by William McNeill. Translated by Walter Kaufmann. Cambridge: Cambridge University Press, 1998.
Heidegger, Martin. *Phenomenological Interpretations of Aristotle: Initiation Into Phenonmenological Research*. Translated by Richard Rojcewicz. Bloomington: Indiana University Press, 2001.
Heidegger, Martin. *Sein und Zeit*. Halle: Max Niemer Verlag, 1931.
Heidegger, Martin. *What is Called Thinking*. Translated by J. Glenn Gray. New York: Perennial, 2004.
Horkheimer, Max. *Eclipse of Reason*. London: Bloomsbury Academic, 2013.
Horkheimer, Max, and Theodor W. Adorno. *Dialectic of Enlightenment: Philosophical Fragments*. Translated by Edmund Jedphcott. Stanford, CA: Stanford University Press, 2002.
Hume, David. *Treatise on Human Nature*. Oxford: Oxford University Press, 2000.
Husain, Martha. *Ontology and the Art of Tragedy*. New York: State University of New York Press, 2002.
Husserl, Edmund. "Philosophy and the Crisis of European Man." In *Phenomenology and the Crisis of Philosophy*, translated by Quentin Lauer, 149–92. New York: Harper & Row, 1965.
Husserl, Edmund. *Medytacje Kartezjańskie* [Cartesian Meditations]. Translated by Andrzej Wajs. Warsaw: IFiS PAN, 2009.
Husserl, Edmund. *Ideas Pertaining to a Pure Phenomenology and to a Phenomenological Philosophy. Second Book*. Translated by Richard Rojcewicz, André Schuwer. Dordrecht/Boston/London: Kluwer Academic Publishers, 1989.

Jagiełło, Jarosław. *Niedokończony Spór o Antropologię Filozoficzną (Heidegger–Plessner)* [An Unfinished Argument About the Existence of Man (Heidegger-Plessner)]. Warsaw: Wydawnictwo IFiS PAN, 2011.

James, William. *Principles of Psychology.* 2 vols. New York: Cosimo, 1890/2007.

James, William. *The Varieties of Religious Experience: A Study in Human Nature.* New York: Modern Library, 1936.

Jaspers, Karl. *Rozum i Egzystencja. Nietzsche a Chrześcijaństwo* [Reason and Existence. Nietzsche and Christianity]. Translated by Czesława Piecuch. Warsaw: PWN, 1991.

Kakutani, Michiko. "'Shakespeare': The Vast Shakespearean Drama With All People as Players." *New York Times,* October 27, 1998.

Kallen, Horace. *William James and Henri Bergson; A Study in Contrasting Theories of Life.* Chicago: University of Chicago Press, 1914.

Kant, Immanuel. *Critique of Pure Reason.* Translated by Werner S. Pluhar. Indianapolis, IN: Hackett, 1996.

Kant, Immanuel. *Critique of Pure Reason.* Translated by J. M. D. Miklejohn. London: Henry G. Bohn, 1855.

Kerr-Lawson, Angus. "Natural Moments in Santayana's Philosophy of Nature." *Transactions of the Charles S. Peirce Society* 16, no. 4 (Fall 1980): 309–28.

Kerr-Lawson, Angus. "Essentialism and Santayana's Realm of Essence." *Transactions of the Charles S. Peirce Society* 21, no. 2 (Spring 1985): 201–22.

Kerr-Lawson, Angus. "Santayana's Epiphenomenalism." *Transactions of the Charles S. Peirce Society* 22, no. 4 (Fall 1986): 217–432.

Kierkegaard, Søren. "Ancient Tragedy's Reflection in the Modern." In *Either/Or: A Fragment of Life,* translated by Alastair Hannay, 137–62. London: Penguin Books, 1992.

Kołakowski, Leszek. Introduction to *Ewolucja twórcza* by Henri Bergson, translated by Piotr Kostyło and Krzysztof Skorulski. Cracow: Wydawnictwo Homini, 2007.

Kremplewska, Katarzyna. "The Authorship of Life: Narrative and Dramatic Strategies of Sustaining Self-Integrity in Santayana's Thought." *Overheard in Seville. Bulletin of the George Santayana Society,* no. 33 (Fall 2015): 56–67.

Kremplewska, Katarzyna. "Between Spiritual Dissolution and the Invention of the Human: George Santayana and Harold Bloom on Hamlet and the Crisis of Agency." *Overheard in Seville. Bulletin of the George Santayana Society,* no. 35 (Fall 2017): 50–59.

Kremplewska, Katarzyna. "Coping with Finitude: Santayana Reading Heidegger." *The Transactions of Charles S. Peirce Society* 51, no. 2 (2015): 225–65.

Kremplewska, Katarzyna. "Review: *Santayana at 150. International Interpretations.*" *Overheard in Seville. Bulletin of the George Santayana Society,* no. 32 (Fall 2014): 71–76.

Kremplewska, Katarzyna. "Maska i myśl. Sobość a *ars vivendi* w myśli George'a Santayany" [Mask and Thought. Self and Ars Vivendi in the Thought of George Santayana]. *Analiza i Egzystencja,* no. 26 (2014): 87–110.

Kremplewska, Katarzyna. "Life as Insinuation according to Henri Bergson and George Santayana." *Diametros*, no. 52 (June 2017): 47–63.

Kremplewska, Katarzyna. "Managing Necessity: Santayana on Forms of Power and the Human Condition." In *The Life of Reason in an Age of Terrorism*, edited by Charles Padrón and Krzysztof Piotr Skowronski, 28–42. Leiden and Boston: Brill, 2018.

Kremplewska, Katarzyna. "Time as the Source of Inalienable Freedom: Henri Bergson's 'Immunizing' the Self." *Eidos. Journal for Philosophy of Culture*, no. 1 (2017): 76–88. http://eidos.uw.edu.pl/time-as-the-source-of-inalienable-freedom-henri-bergsons-immunizing-the-self/

Kremplewska, Katarzyna. "Tragiczność a duch w ujęciu Santayany" [The Tragic and the Spirit in Santayana's Thought]. *Przegląd Religioznawczy* 248, no. 2 (2013): 63–75.

Lesky, Albin. *Greek Tragedy*. Translated by H. A. Frankfort. London: Ernest Benn, 1965.

Lachs, John. *George Santayana*. Boston: Twayne Publishers, 1988.

Lachs, John, ed. *Animal Faith and Spiritual Life: Previously Unpublished and Uncollected Writings by George Santayana with Critical Essays on his Thought*. New York: Appleton-Century-Crofts, 1967.

Lachs, John. *Mind and Philosophers*. Nashville, TN: Vanderbilt University Press, 1987.

Lachs, John, and Michael Hodges. *Thinking in the Ruins: Wittgenstein and Santayana on Contingency*. Nashville, TN: Vanderbilt University Press, 1999.

Levinson, Henry S. *Santayana, Pragmatism, and the Spiritual Life*. Chapel Hill: University of North Carolina Press, 1992.

Lind, Bruno. *Vagabond Scholar: A Venture into the Privacy of George Santayana*. New York: Bridgehead, 1962.

Lovely, Edward W. *George Santayana's Philosophy of Religion: His Roman Catholic Influences and Phenomenology*. Lanham, MD: Lexington Books, 2012.

McCormick, John. *George Santayana: A Biography*. New York: Alfred A. Knopf, 1987.

Metzinger, Thomas. *The Ego Tunnel*. New York: Basic Books, 2009.

Michalski, Krzysztof. *Zrozumieć przemijanie* [To Understand Passing Away]. Warsaw: Biblioteka Kwartalnika Kronos, 2011.

Moreno, Daniel. *Santayana the Philosopher. Philosophy as a Form of Life*. Translated by Charles Padron. Lewisburg, PA: Bucknell University Press, 2015.

McDowell, John. *Mind and World*. Harvard, MA: Harvard University Press, 1996.

McGrath, Sean. "The Interpretive Structure of Truth in Heidegger." *Analecta Hermeneutica*, no. 1 (May 2009), 46–55. Accessed July 1, 2017. <http://journals.library.mun.ca/ojs/index.php/analecta/article/view/5>

Nietzsche, Friedrich. *The Will to Power*. Translated and edited by Walter Kaufman. New York: Random House, 2011.

Nietzsche, Friedrich. *Twilight of the Idols*. Translated by Duncan Large. Oxford: Oxford University Press, 1998.

Nietzsche, Friedrich. *The Birth of Tragedy*. Translated by Douglas Smith. Oxford: Oxford University Press, 2000.

Nietzsche, Friedrich. *Beyond Good and Evil*. Translated by Helen Zimmern. New York: Dover, 1997.
Nietzsche, Friedrich. *The Gay Science*, 2nd edition. Translated by Walter Kaufman. New York: Vintage, 1974.
Padron, Charles L. "Reflections on Santayana and Tragic Value." Dissertation, Vanderbilt University, 2000.
Pascal, Blaise. *Pensees*. Translated by Roger Ariew. Indianapolis, IN: Hackett, 2005.
Quinton Anthony. "Tragedy." *Proceedings of the Aristotelian Society* 34, suppl. vol. (1960): 145–64.
Ricoeur, Paul. "Soboŝć w zwierciadle Pisma" [The *Self* in the mirror of the Scriptures]. In *Miłość i sprawiedliwość* [Love and Justice], translated by Marek Drwięga, 55–95. Cracow: Universitas, 2010.
Ricoeur, Paul. *Oneself as Another*. Chicago: University of Chicago Press, 1992.
Ricoeur, Paul. *Time and Narrative*. 3 vols. Chicago: University of Chicago Press, 1990.
Ruti, Mari. *The Singularity of Being: Lacan and the Immortal Within*. New York: Fordham University Press, 2012.
Scott, Nathan A., Jr. *The Poetics of Belief*. Chapel Hill, London: The University of North Carolina Press, 1985.
Scheler, Max. "O zjawisku tragiczności" [On the phenomenon of the tragic]. Translated by Roman Ingarden. In *O tragedii i tragiczności* [On Tragedy and the Tragic], edited by Władysław Tatarkiewicz, 49–95. Cracow: Wydawnictwo Literackie, 1976.
Schilpp, Paul Arthur, ed. *The Philosophy of George Santayana*. Evanston, IL: Northwestern University Press, 1940.
Schopenhauer, Arthur. *The World as Will and Representation*. 2 vols. Translated by E. F. J. Payne. New York: Dover, 1969.
Schopenhauer, Arthur. *The World as Will and Representation*. Translated by Judith Norman, Alistair Welchman, and Christopher Janway. Cambridge: Cambridge University Press, 2010.
Schiller, Friedrich. *Letters upon the Aesthetic Education of Man*. Translated by George Gregory. Schiller Institute. 1992. <http://www.schillerinstitute.org/educ/aesthetics/Schiller_On_Grace_and_Dignity.pdf>
Searle, John R. *Mind: a Brief Introduction*. Oxford: Oxford University Press, 2004.
Singer, Irving. *George Santayana, Literary Philosopher*. New Haven, CT: Yale University Press, 2000.
Snell, Bruno. *The Discovery of the Mind*. Translated by T. G. Rosenmeyer. 1953. Reprint, New York: Dover Publications, 1982.
Sprigge, Timothy. *Santayana: An Examination of his Philosophy*. London and Boston: Routledge & Kegan Paul, 1974/1995.
Stone, Jeremy A. *Religious Naturalism Today: The Rebirth of a Forgotten Alternative*. New York: State University of New York Press, 2008.
Taylor, Charles. *The Ethics of Authenticity*. Cambridge, MA: Harvard University Press, 1991.

Taylor, Charles. *The Sources of the Self: The Making of the Modern Identity.* Cambridge: Cambridge University Press, 1995.
Taylor, Charles. *The Secular Age.* Cambridge, MA, and London: Harvard University Press, 2007.
Taylor, Charles. *Varieties of Religion Today: William James Revisited.* Cambridge, MA: Harvard University Press, 2003.
Tiller, Glenn. "Commonsense Ontology." *Transactions of the Charles S. Peirce Society* 45, no. 4 (2009): 506–15.
Tillich, Paul. "Christianity without Paul." *The Nation*, October 12, 1946.
Tischner, Józef. *Spór o istnienie człowieka* [An Argument about the Existence of Man]. Cracow: Znak, 2011.
Tocqueville, Alexis de. *Democracy in America.* 2 vols. Translated by Henry Reeve. Edited by Francus Bowen. Cambridge, UK: Sever and Francis, 1863.
Trilling, Lionel. "That Smile of Parmenides Made Me Think." In *A Gathering of Fugitives*, 153–67. Boston: Bacon Press: 1956.
Trzópek, Joanna. *Na tropach podmiotu* [Tracing the Subject]. Cracow: Wydawnictwa UJ, 2013.
Voegelin, Eric. "Nietzsche, Crisis and the War." In *Published Essays 1940–1952*, edited by Ellis Sandoz, 126–56. Vol. 10 of *Collected Works of Eric Voegelin.* Columbia: University of Missouri Press, 2000.
Wahman Jessica. "Corpulent or a Train of Ideas? Santayana's Critique of Hume." *Overheard in Seville. Bulletin of the Santayana Society*, no. 25 (Fall 2007): 1–9.
Wahman, Jessica. "Santayana, Identity Theory, and the Mind-Body Problem." In *Under any Sky: Contemporary Readings of George Santayana*, 34–45, edited by Matthew C. Flamm, Krzysztof P. Skowroński. Cambridge: Cambridge Scholars, 2007.
Weber, Max. *Economy and Society: An Outline of Interpretive Sociology.* 2 vols. Berkeley, Los Angeles: University of California Press, 1978.
Wegner, Daniel. *The Illusion of Conscious Will.* Cambridge, MA: MIT Press, 2002.
Winckelmann, Johann. *Reflections on the Painting and Sculpture of the Greeks.* Translated by Henry Fusseli. London: A. Millar, 1765.
Woodward, Anthony. *Living in the Eternal.* Nashville, TN: Vanderbilt University Press, 1988.
Zahavi, Dan. *Husserl's Phenomenology.* Stanford, CA: Stanford University Press, 2003.
Zahavi, Dan. *Subjectivity and Selfhood: Investigating the First-Person Perspective.* Cambridge, MA: MIT Press, 2005.
Zdziechowski, Marian. *Pesymizm, romantyzm, a podstawy chrześcijaństwa.* [Pessimism, Romanticism, and the Foundations of Christianity]. Warsaw: Hachette, 2011.
Znaniecki, Florian. *Upadek cywilizacji zachodniej.* [The Fall of Western Civilization]. Warsaw: WUW, 2013.
Zupančič, Alenka. *The Odd One In. On Comedy.* Cambridge: MIT Press, 2008.

Index

actor (a human being as), 76, 77–78, 81, 105, 109, 154–156, 185. *See also* drama, *persona*, theater
Adam (of The Old Testament), 190
Adorno, Theodor, 25, 175, 227n78
Agamben, Giorgio, 46, 196, 198, 200, 210
agency, 21, 42, 43, 47–52, 103, 127, 200; crisis of, 180–181, 184, 208
Amiel, Henri, 209
ananke (necessity), xvi, 187, 189, 197–198, 245–246n171. *See also* necessity
animal faith, xv, 31–33, 39, 42, 47, 62, 67, 73, 118–119, 121, 132, 133
Antigone (Sophocles), 151, 226n51
Apollonian-Dionysian dualism, 162–166
Apologia Pro Mente Sua (Santayana), 45
aporetic self, 41–42, 81, 128, 131, 176, 204
apothatic humanity, 204
apperception (transcendental), 8, 34, 35, 74
Arendt, Hannah, 46, 195
Aristotle: Heidegger's interpretation of, 125, 127, 134, 136–138, 233n46, 234n61; on (human) life, 4, 69; on individuation, 60; as an inspiration for other thinkers, 45, 46, 47, 55, 115; on tragedy, 150, 160

atheism, 23; Santayana's, xv, 95, 229n130
attunement (Heidegger's category), 125, 126, 134–136, 142
Auden, Wystan, 184, 190, 245n158
Augustine, St., 1, 2–3
authenticity, 16, 38–39, 80, 83–91, 144. *See also* inauthenticity
authorship of life, xvii, 10, 21, 80. *See also* authenticity, freedom, vital liberty
autonomy, 4, 130; moral, 9–10; spiritual, 45, 61, 67, 126; subjective, 10, 28, 50, 74, 111, 131

barbarism, 204, 209–210
Barca, Pedro, Calderon de la, 160
Basic Concepts of Aristotelian Philosophy (Heidegger), 137, 142
Being and Time (Heidegger), 125, 136, 137, 138
Benjamin, Walter: on barbarism, 209; on character, fate, and the tragic hero, 160–161, 162, 179, 190, 194
Bergson, Henri, xi, 18, 120, 130; on dynamic schema, 111; on finitude and freedom, 104, 110; on human self and the past, 101–103; on incarnation of the past in the present and memory, 98–103; and individualism, 100; and Santayana (compared) 107–108, 110–111; on symbols, 100–101

Beyond Good and Evil (Nietzsche), 242–243n83
Bielik-Robson, Agata, 32, 162
biopolitics, 199, 201; and governing the living, xvi. *See also* politics
bios: and *zoe*, xvii, 46, 48, 51, 57, 61, 137, 138, 195, 200
blank point (within human self, technical term), 13, 14, 71, 74, 78, 128, 131, 134. *See also* empty "now"
Block, Ned: on a-consciousness and p-consciousness, 65–66
Bloom, Harold, 179–184, 186, 187, 191
Brodrick, Michael, 53, 69
Buczyńska-Garewicz, Hanna, 168, 172, 174
Burke, Kenneth, xv
Bushnell, Rebecca, 189
Butler, Richard, 212n16

Campbell, Scott M., 137
care (in existential context), 119–120, 122, 124–126
Cartesian Meditations (Husserl), 215n53
character: and authorship of life, 21; Bergson's conception of, 106, 109; *Dasein's*, 138; fatality and, 57; fate and, 160, 162, 190, 194; hermeneia of the self and, 55, 59, 77; human self and, 42, 56; as a personage or a character in the play, 81, 83–84, 85, 101, 154
Claudel, Paul, 77
Cogito (the Cartesian "ego"), 1, 4, 5–6, 32, 38
Coleman, Martin, ix
Collins, Anthony, 197
comic characters/personages, 81
consciousness, xiv, xv; Bergson's and Santayana's approach to (compared), 108; Bergson's vision of the relation between time and, 99–100, 103, 106; a blank point/a fissure in, 60–63, 73–75, 78; freedom and non-reductive take on, 20–22; Heidegger's and Santayana's approach to (compared), 116–121, 124, 126–127, 129, 132–133, 135; as human self-consciousness, 8–10, 12–15, 19–20; Santayana's conception of, 29–35, 39–43, 48, 70; Santayana's conception of in the light of contemporary theories, 65–68. *See also* essences, intuition, solipsism of the present moment/SOPM, spirit
Constant, Benjamin, 197
contemplative vitalism (author's term), xiv, xvii, 68–84, 107, 109
contingency, 21, 44, 56, 85, 90, 140, 159
Cory, Daniel, xiii, 118, 141
Crowell, Steven, 16
cultural critique, 25–26, 165, 170, 172–176, 186, 188, 207, 209

death, 15, 61, 63; *being-unto-death*, 119; fear of, 198, 207; as a horizon, 18, 106, 122, 127, 137, 139, 145–146, 147; tragedy and 178, 179
deconstruction: of the self and subject, xv, 16, 20; spiritual and hermeneutic, 44, 206
deeper self: Bergson on, 99; Santayana's conception of, 29, 31, 33, 48, 50, 63, 122. *See also* psyche
Deism, 22, 23
Deleuze, Gilles: on David Hume, 7–8; on Friedrich Nietzsche 170, 172, 173; on Henri Bergson, 98, 102
democracy, 197, 200; crisis of, 202–203, 204, 205, 207–208
Democritus, 89–90, 188
Dennett, Daniel, 19
Derrida, Jacques, xvii, 13–14, 72
Descartes, René, 1, 5, 10, 30, 114; the *Cogito* of, 1, 32, 38; dualism, 14, 16, 33; *fiat*, 11, 20, 22

determinism, 20–21, 103, 159
Dewey, John, xi
Dialogues in Limbo (Santayana), 89
Dickens, Charles, 24
Dilworth, David, 27, 217n124
Dionysus, 163, 166
discipline: self-/inner, 6, 159, 208; spiritual, 2, 69, 83, 87, 91
disinterestedness, 41, 44, 69, 70, 95, 172
domination, 198–199, 200, 209
Dominations and Powers (Santayana), xiii, 187, 195–196, 204, 207, 210
drama (of human life), 61, 77, 142–143. *See also* actor, play (of life), theater
durée (Bergson's term), 99, 100–105, 110

ego/"I," 9–14, 16–19, 20–21, 25–29, 34, 37–38, 42, 43, 44–48, 63, 75, 76, 78, 94, 124, 133, 174
egotism, 3, 25, 28, 75, 87, 95, 149, 165, 171, 175, 192
Eliot, T. S., 24
embodiment, 14, 19, 36, 123, 128, 233n43
emplotment, 55–56, 79, 84, 186, 203
empowerment, 198, 199
empty "now" (temporal failure/failed "now"), 71–75, 78, 97, 110. *See also* blank point, hermeneutic detour
Epicurus, 23
epiphany (in expressivist context), 24–26, 108, 127
epiphenomenalism, 20, 22, 224n11
essence(s), 27, 30–31, 33, 37, 39–41, 44–45, 61–62, 66, 72, 74, 78
eternal return (Nietzsche's idea), 160, 164, 167–170, 173–174, 175
Europe (as an idea), 208
event(s): material, 31, 42, 60, 63, 67, 109, 220n50; mental, 22, 33, 66, 220n50

existence, 30–31, 33–34, 39–41, 43, 46; acting out one's own, 85; Bergson's idea of, 105; contingency of, 56; domination of essence over, 84; the drama of, 143; gap between essence and, 132–133; Heidegger's idea of (compared to Santayana's), 117–119, 123–124, 129, 131, 145; hermeneia of, 137; individuation of a human being and, 60–63; language of, 55; as "original sin" (metaphorically), 160–162; and politics, 197, 200–201; as a source of possibilities, 146; spirit and, 92–93; spiritual, 188–189; the time of, 72; the tragic aspect of, 169, 176, 186, 188, 190; in relation to transcendence and interpretation, 73–74
existentialism, xiii, 114, 129, 146
expressivist turn (Charles Taylor's term), 22–28

fabulation function (Bergson's technical term), 101, 103
facticity (Heidegger's category), 109, 125, 140, 143
falling prey (Heidegger's category), 136, 141, 142
fatality, 57, 110, 161, 172, 187, 189–190, 193, 196, 198
fate, 56, 83, 84, 128, 130, 140, 159–162, 178, 179, 186–190, 192, 194
Fichte, Johann, 10, 19
finitude (of a human being), xviii, 2; Heidegger's and Santayana's approach to (compared), 113–147; as a philosophical problem, 10–11, 18, 23; the recognition of, 43, 44, 54–55, 63; subjective strategies of coping with, 73–74, 80, 84, 86, 93; time and freedom in relation to, 104, 106, 109, 110
Flamm, Matthew Caleb, 44, 49
Flanagan, Owen, 12–13, 19, 20, 21, 65

forgetting, 161, 207
Foucault, Michel, 3–4, 46
Frank, Manfred, 12, 19–20
Frankfurt School, the, 69, 175, 192. See also Adorno, Theodor, Horkheimer, Max
Frankfurt, Harry, 21
freedom, xvii, xviii, 10, 20–22, 47–57, 61, 68–69, 80–84, 89, 101, 102, 103–105, 106–107, 197–199; Bergson's and Santayana's idea of (compared), 108–110; in democracy, 202, 207, 208, 209; Heidegger's and Santayana's ideas of (compared), 128–130, 144–147; spiritual, 49, 86, 87, 144, 172; tragic, 158–159, 183–184, 190. See also autonomy, liberty, necessity
Frye, Northrop, 185, 187, 189–191

Gadamer, Hans Georg, 80
God, 1, 2, 5, 22–23; the Creator, 190; death of, 173; the Father in the Holy Trinity, 92–96
Goethe, Johann Wolfgang, 23, 24, 26, 87–88, 165
golden rule, 44, 200
grace (as an aesthetic and existential category), 84–89
Gray, John, 196, 204, 206
Greeks, the (ancient), 27, 134, 150, 165–167
Grossman, Morris, 211n8

Hamlet (of Shakespeare's *Hamlet*), 156, 176, 180–186, 191
happiness, 69, 70, 137, 159, 163
Hegel, Georg Wilhelm, 10, 150; on tragedy and the tragic hero, 153–156
Heidegger, Martin: on the ancient Greeks, 165, 167; on Kant's conception of the self, 9–10; on human self (*Dasein*), 16–18, 26–28, 70, 74, 78; on human self, finitude, freedom and transcendence in comparison to Santayana, 113–147; his interpretation of Nietzsche, 167–168, 170–171, 173, 174, 175; on the tragic, 150, 160; on "vulgar time" and inauthenticity, 38–39. See also Aristotle, attunement, authenticity, care, falling prey, inauthenticity, missing oneself, ruinance
Heraclitus, 91
hermeneia/hermeneutics: dramatic, 53–54, 75–79; of life, 59, 68, 74–75, 136–137; of the self, 17, 45, 47–57, 68–69
hermeneutic detour (author's technical term), 72, 132. See also blank point, empty "now"
Hermes, 80
Holy Ghost, the, 92, 94
Holy Trinity, the, 91–96
Horkheimer, Max, 25, 175, 227n78
hubris, 151, 160, 179, 190
human condition, 80, 158, 161–162, 164, 176, 177–178, 196–197, 199, 209
human nature, 7, 90, 93, 161–162, 206
humanism, 23, 111, 179, 188
Hume, David, 7–8, 19, 23
Husserl, Edmund, 12, 20, 21, 27, 33, 37–38, 42, 43; on Europe, 208; his conception of human self, 13–16, 72, 105, 139, 175. See also body, consciousness, incarnation, passivity, stream of consciousness
hypostatic: "I"/"ego," 45, 74, 75, 133; nature of mental life, 132

Idea of Christ in the Gospels or God in Man, The (Santayana), 92
idealism: conceptual, 123, 146; elements of in Santayana, xiv, xvii, 34, 63; transcendental, 10, 11, 18, 173, 174, 188

identity (self-, subjective, personal), 17, 21, 23, 24, 28, 64
ideologies, 80, 201, 208. *See also* propaganda
ignorance: historical, 203; medium of (ironically), 80, 105; tragic/fatal, 157, 160, 187, 203; within knowledge 32–33, 150, 154, 156
imagination, 35, 44–45, 50, 56, 57, 70, 180, 192–193; Bergson on, 106, 108; directive, 209; expressivist turn and, 23, 24, 26; globalization of, 204; human nature and, 7–8; pure, 8–9; wars of, 204
inauthenticity, 38–39, 89, 136, 141. *See also* ruinance
incarnation, 14, 15, 18, 38, 42, 92, 95, 99, 100, 125, 133, 188, 198. *See also* embodiment
individualism, xii, 6, 24, 63, 75, 88, 93, 100–101, 208
individuation (of a human being), 15, 59–63, 109, 162–163
inner time consciousness (phenomenological term), 13, 100
insinuation (metaphorically, as a strategy of living), xi, 50, 73–74, 97–111
instrumental reason, 69, 170, 173, 193
intent, 30, 31, 33–36, 41, 72–73. *See also* animal faith, intuition, psyche
interpretation: conventional interpretations, 83; *Dasein's* genuine self-, 137–139; and expressivism, 24; and faith, 131; freedom of, 60; of life, 57, 65, 68; and masks, 78–79; and nothingness, 74, 132; of psyche, 94; the risk of misinterpretation, 119–120; self-, 16, 21, 47, 70, 74; of time, 17; as transcendence, 71, 73–75; and truth, 121, 137–138; of the Word, 95; of the world of symbols, 43. *See also* hermeneia

intuition/intuitions (of essences), 30, 31, 33, 34–35, 37, 40, 72–73, 118, 119, 120, 121, 132, 133
ironic nihilism, 74
ironic ontology, xiii, 44, 117

James, William, 12–13, 100, 139, 151. *See also* stream of consciousness
Jaspers, Karl, 11, 160, 175, 191, 239n5
Jesus Christ, 91, 92, 152, 176, 177
Judeo-Christian tradition, 95, 151, 161

Kant, Immanuel, 8–10, 20, 51, 56, 124, 164
Kerr-Lawson, Angus, 40, 220n48, 224n11
kerygma (in Paul Ricoeur's interpretation), 94–96
Kierkegaard, Søren, 149, 153, 155, 156–157, 158, 180
knowledge: Cartesian standards of, 5, 30; symbolic, transitive (Santayana's views on), 30–31, 32–33, 40, 45
Kołakowski, Leszek, 99, 100, 102, 193, 194

Lachs, John, xii, xiii, xv, 31, 39, 40, 41, 42, 46, 68, 74
Lesky, Albin: on the art of tragedy, 153, 177
Levinson, Henry, 132, 211n4, 211n9
liberty: vital, 49, 69, 81, 83–84, 109, 196, 198, 203, 209, 210. *See also* freedom
Life of Reason: Or, The Phases in Human Progress, The (Santayana), 80
lifetime, 24, 61, 68–71
Locke, John, 6–7, 23
love, 84, 93, 104, 105
Lovely, Edward, 222n58
Lucifer, 93
Lucretius, 23
Luther, Martin, 181

Macbeth (of Shakespeare's *Macbeth*), 185, 191
mask(s), 75–79, 80–84, 85, 143, 154
materialism, 75, 76, 107, 116, 132, 217n124; nonreductive, xii, xvii, 22, 38, 41, 42, 44–45, 39, 61; reductive, 66
Matter and Memory (Bergson), 98, 107, 109
matter: 39, 43, 44, 60; in the context of the three divine Persons, 91–92, 95; the relation between conscious life and, 72, 74, 98, 99, 101, 106–109
McCormick, John, 233n41
Meditations on First Philosophy (Descartes), 1
memory: and Bergson's conception of human self, 98–107; and continuity, 161, 206; and the first-person perspective, 34–37, 73; historical, 111; Santayana and Bergson on, 110–111
Merleau-Ponty, Maurice, 14, 18, 105
Metzinger, Thomas, 25, 31
migrating "ego"/"I" (Paul Ricoeur's term), 34, 37, 133
Milton, John, 190
mimesis, 56, 191
mimetic capacity/activity (of a human being), 51, 54–55, 56–57, 82. *See also* emplotment, narrative unity
missing oneself (existential category): strategies of, 136, 139, 186
Montaigne, Michel de, 6, 23
Moreno, Daniel, 77, 111, 129, 200, 206

narrative events, 56
narrative identity, 19, 216n83
narrative unity (of life), 19, 20, 21, 94, 132, 140, 151. *See also* narrative identity, relatively first beginning
natural moments (Santayana's technical term), 40, 60, 220n48. *See also*: event(s), spirit: moments of spirit
naturalism: nonreductive, 19, 22, 26, 65–68, 107
nature, 5, 23, 24, 57, 69; and conscious life, 71; and culture, 8, 103; and masks, 75–77, 79; as *natura naturans* and *natura naturata*, 98. *See also* human nature
necessity, 9–10, 106, 152–153, 154, 187, 189, 245n158; managing necessity, 195–196, 197–200, 201, 203, 205, 206. *See also ananke*
negativity (of human beings), 196
nemesis (the inescapable, "revenge" of time), 176–177, 187–192, 208, 245n161
Nicene Creed, the, 91
Nietzsche, Friedrich, 11–12, 25, 27, 150, 160; Santayana's polemic with, 170–175; on the tragic, 162–169, 186, 188, 191. *See also* eternal return, spiritual crisis, Zarathustra
nihilism, xii, 27, 77, 164, 174, 175
nominalism, 99, 100
nothingness, 74, 78–79, 103, 109, 142, 176

Oedipus at Colonus (by Sophocles), 156
Oedipus Rex (by Sophocles), 150

Padron, Charles, 192, 227n81, 239n9, 246n164
Pascal, Blaise, 23, 149
passivity (within human self), 43, 68, 93, 125–127, 134
person (human), 12, 15, 17, 42, 59, 77, 83, 106
persona (as a character in the play of life), 81, 82, 142, 154. *See also* actor, mask(s), theater
personal narrative, 44, 51
personality, 15, 106, 191, 216n80

Persons and Places (Santayana), 24
Phenomenological Interpretations of Aristotle (Heidegger), 136
Phenomenology of Spirit (Hegel): on tragedy, 153–155
phenomenology: as an approach to human self, 19–20; of daily life, 114; everyday, 54, 56; Heidegger's, 16; of human self according to Husserl, 13–16; Santayana and, 128, 212n12. *See also* Husserl, inner time consciousness, Lovely, Edward, memory, Merleau-Ponty, time, Zahavi, Dan
Philosophy of Fine Arts, The (Hegel): on tragedy, 155–157
philosophy of mind, 20–22, 65–67
phronesis (practical wisdom), 4, 151, 200
pictorial space, 36–37, 57, 143
Plato, 2 3, 197–198
Platonism, 33; Santayana's Platonic sympathies, 130, 206
play (of life), 77, 80, 140, 145. *See also* actor, masks, *persona*, theater
poet(s), 27, 53, 60, 177. *See also* poetry
Poetics (Aristotle), 55–56, 150
poetry, 27, 57, 95, 177, 246n164
politics, 195, 197–199, 201, 203, 204; philosophy of, 196, 209–210
power: human self and, 5–6, 44, 47, 53, 192; in a political context and in relation to domination, 196, 199, 200, 210; will to power (Nietzsche's idea), 12, 25, 81, 170, 172–173, 174, 208. *See also* domination, empowerment, violence, will
process-activity (distinction, in reference to human life), 45, 46–47
progress, 204, 209, 210
Prometheus, 152, 163, 164
propaganda, 148, 201

psyche, 14, 29–32, 34–36, 38, 45–47, 48, 50, 52–53, 54–55, 60–61, 63–64, 76, 78, 93–94, 110–111, 125, 133, 134–135, 146, 147
psycho-spiritual unity, 39, 46, 126, 128, 133, 141, 142
punctual self, 6, 23
Pure Being (Santayana's term), 83
Putnam, Hilary, xiii

qualia, 65, 66

rationality, 20, 23, 50, 161, 170, 174, 198, 200, 205–206, 207, 208
Realms of Being (Santayana), xiii, 33, 74, 107, 124, 136, 141
reason, 247n8, 50; as antithetic to necessity, 197–198, 206; chaos and, 173; control of, 166; detached from the world, 182; dislocated (Santayana's term), 80, 81, 181, 191; liberation by, 175; practical, 159, 179; reduced to power, 171; as a unifying principle, 2, 5; universal, 10; violence and, 186. *See also* apperception, instrumental reason, Kant, Immanuel, thinking
relatively first beginning (Kant's and Ricoeur's term), 56
religion, 95, 101, 164, 177, 180, 185, 187
ressentiment (Nietzsche's idea), 36, 169
Ricoeur, Paul: on human self and authorship of life, 18, 21, 26, 28, 37, 38, 42, 50–51, 55–56, 58, 75; on human self and *kerygma*, 94–96; on tragedy, 150–151, 177, 179, 189–190. *See also* authorship of life, emplotment, *kerygma*, narrative identity
Rilke, Reiner M., 24
Romanticism, 23–24, 150, 167
Rorty, Richard, 18, 26, 114, 144
Rousseau, Jean J., 24

Rubin, Richard, ix
ruinance (Heidegger's category), 81, 125, 136, 139–140, 144. *See also* inauthenticity

Saatkamp, Herman, ix
salvation (metaphorically: as worldly or self-procured), xi, xviii, 28, 53, 93, 94, 134, 159, 161; Nietzsche's idea of, 163–164, 168, 172, 174–175
sanity, 44, 87, 90, 95, 115
Sartre, Jean Paul, 14, 49, 105, 146
Scheler, Max, 17, 150, 151
Schiller, Friedrich, 86
Schleiermacher, Friedrich, 17, 216n80
Schopenhauer, Arthur, 10, 11, 86, 91, 150, 157–161, 164
Scott, Nathan, 60
Searle, John, 21–22, 67
secularization, 23, 180
self-awareness, 13–14, 19
self-consciousness, 8–10, 19, 129, 135
self-givenness, 16, 132–133
self-government (self-rule), 195, 196, 198, 200, 202–203, 204–207, 208
self-integrity, 47–57, 79, 84, 85, 206
self-knowledge, 19, 50, 52–54, 64, 70, 83, 205
Seneca, 3–4, 87, 233n18
sentimental time (Santayana's term), 34–39, 79, 119. *See also* pictorial space
Shakespeare, William, 148, 179–188
Singer, Irving, xvi
Skepticism and Animal Faith (Santayana), 30, 32
skepticism, 23, 32–33, 73, 78
Skowroński, Krzysztof, ix
Snell, Bruno, 177, 243n85
Socrates, 89–90, 163, 164, 188
solipsism of the present moment (SOPM, Santayana's term), 32–33, 42, 62, 132
solipsism, 42, 75, 127; Hamlet's, 181, 183, 191

Sophocles, 75, 150, 156, 226n60
soul, 2–3, 5, 145–146; Christian conception of, 189; in Husserl's conception of human self, 15; therapy of the soul, 53
sphere of helplessness (author's technical term), 16, 38, 59, 126, 197, 215n72
Spinoza, Baruch, 169–170
spirit, 29–39, 45–47, 57, 70, 71, 74; Bergson's idea of, 98–99, 101, 107–108; distraction of, 38, 43, 81, 136, 139–141, 143–144; encaged in matter, 23, 141, 176, 177; finitude and, 146–147; impotent, 42, 64–66, 69, 126–127; incarnate, 123, 124, 135, 141; moments of, 40; as part of the Holy Trinity, 92–94; pure, 48; and time, 130–131. *See also* consciousness, contemplative vitalism, essences, imagination, intuition, spiritual life
spiritual crisis, 182, 185, 202–204, 207–208. *See also* spirit, spiritual life
spiritual life, 45, 63, 68–70, 87, 93. *See also* spirit
Sprigge, Timothy, 32, 40, 46, 48
Steiner, George, 151
Stevens, Wallace, 217n124, 27
Stoics, the, 5, 159. *See also* Seneca
stream of consciousness, 12–14. *See also* James, William, Husserl, Edmund, Flanagan, Owen
sublimation, 46, 50, 87, 178, 200

Taylor, Charles: on the expressivist turn, 22–28, 76, 83, 86–87; on the sources of human self, 2–3, 5–6, 17, 18
technology, 26, 203, 204, 209
telos (the end, completion in the context of human life), 4, 137, 199
theater (of life), 140, 143; the stage of, 77, 203. *See also* actor, drama, *persona*, play (of life)

thinking: and consciousness, 21–22; in the context of existence, 114, 116, 121, 144; and freedom, 44, 49; instrumental, 192; in Kant's interpretation, 8–9; materiality of, 65–67, 108; psyche and, 50, 64, 65; *res cogitans*, 5; and will to power, 170, 173; and wisdom, 43
throwness (Heidegger's category), 127, 128, 139
Tiller, Glenn, 116, 118
Tillich, Paul, 96, 177
time: Bergson's idea of past and present, 100–106, 109; *Dasein* and, 130, 138–140; hermeneutics of, 17; individuation of a human being and, 59, 62–63; selfhood and, 71–75; of subjective experience, 34–39; the tragic aspect of existence and, 176, 183, 185; in a tragic drama, 189–191; vulgar/ordinary time (Heidegger's term), 119, 131, 139. *See also* eternal return, empty "now," lifetime, memory, natural moments, *nemesis*, sentimental time
Tischner, Józef, 89
Tocqueville, Alexis de, 202, 207–208, 248n21
totalitarianism, 204, 208
tragic hero, 150, 152–154, 155, 163, 164, 179, 180–181
transcendence, 2, 63, 109, 171, 174, 191; hermeneutic, 71–72, 73, 117, 124, 127, 128–131, 145–147; within immanence, 49, 123
Trilling, Lionel, 128–129
truth, 30, 89, 121, 142; concealment of, 139, 142; Nietzsche's interpretation of, 173–174; realm of, 40, 41, 43, 45, 46, 91, 176; to the self, 137, 143–144; in the tragic drama, 150, 154, 160, 179
truthfulness, 137, 144

Two Sources of Morality and Religion, The (Bergson), 103

Unamuno, Miguel de, 150
unitary self, 11, 23
utopia, 206, 210

violence, 205, 208
virtue(s), 4, 151, 200
vita contemplativa, xiv, xv, 4, 49, 68–69, 108, 147. *See also* contemplative vitalism, spiritual life
Voegelin, Eric, 175, 210

Wahman, Jessica, 66
war, 198, 204, 205, 207
Weber, Max, 5, 222n89
Wegner, Daniel, 217n95
Whitehead, Alfred, xiii
will, 171, 204; Primal Will (Santayana's conception of), 195, 200–201, 203, 206, 208; Schopenhauer's idea of Will, 157–160. *See also* power, will to power
Wilson, Edmund, 88
Winckelmann, Johann, 85–86
wisdom, 3, 4, 43–44, 87, 89–90, 151, 161, 200, 206; practical (*phronesis*), 4
Wittgenstein, Ludwig, xiii, xv, 24, 32, 51, 222n58
Woodward, Anthony, 88
World as Will and Representation, The (Schopenhauer), 157

Zahavi, Dan, xix, 15–16, 19–20, 123–124, 128
Zarathustra (of F. Nietzsche's *Thus Spake Zarathustra*), 163, 164, 167–168, 175
Zdziechowski, Marian, 9, 10
Znaniecki, Florian, 208
Zupančič, Alenka, 156, 178, 181

www.ingramcontent.com/pod-product-compliance
Lightning Source LLC
Chambersburg PA
CBHW020641230426
43665CB00008B/268